The Personal Correspondence of Sam Houston

Volume I: 1839–1845

The Personal Correspondence of Sam Houston

Volume I: 1839–1845

edited by
Madge Thornall Roberts

University of North Texas Press ∞ Denton, Texas

Requests for permission to reproduce material from this work
should be sent to:

Permissions
University of North Texas Press
PO Box 13856
Denton TX 76203

The paper used in this book meets the minimum requirements of the
American National Standard for Permanence of Paper for Printed
Library Materials, Z39.48.1984.

Library of Congress Cataloging-in-Publication Data

Houston, Sam, 1793–1863.
The personal correspondence of Sam Houston / edited by
Madge Thornall Roberts.
p.   cm.
Includes bibliographical references and index.
Contents: v. 1. 1839–1845 —
ISBN 1-57441-000-8 (alk. paper)
1. Houston, Sam. 1793–1863—Correspondence. 2. Governors—
Texas—Correspondence. 3. Legislators—United States—Correspon-
dence. 4. Texas—Politics and government—To 1846. 5. Texas—Politics
and government—1846–1865. I. Roberts, Madge Thornall, 1929–   . II.
Title.

F390.H833   1994   95–36738
976.4'04'092—dc20   CIP

Cover art by Dana Adams
Cover design by Amy Layton

iv

To my cousin Charlotte Williams Darby, who together with her father, Franklin Weston Williams, was responsible for preserving the vast collection of Houston correspondence, this work is lovingly dedicated.

TABLE OF CONTENTS

Preface

In the mid-nineteen thirties Dr. Eugene C. Barker and Dr. Amelia Williams began the monumental undertaking of publishing a complete compilation of the available writings of Sam Houston. It would result in an eight-volume collection of mainly political letters which authors, archivists, and historians will continue to use for years to come. Sue Flanagan, author of *Sam Houston's Texas*, described the collection to me as the "backbone" of her book, and indeed it was the starting point for research on my first book, *Star of Destiny: The Private Life of Sam and Margaret Houston*. It proved invaluable as a calendar of Houston's activities.

But Houston was a prolific writer, and *The Writings of Sam Houston* was by no means a complete collection. In the preface to the first volume Dr. Barker stated that it was necessary to emphasize the word "available," for Houston's letters were widely scattered and by no means completely available. He pointed out that many were in the possession of descendants of the Houstons who chose to withhold them from publication or examination. While family members usually cooperated with historians and writers in releasing public documents, the personal correspondence was an entirely different matter, and family privacy was fiercely protected.

Interest in Houston did not wane, however. After reading my grandmother's collection of personal letters, noted historian Dr. Llerena Friend wrote in the April, 1971, issue of *Southwestern Historical Quarterly* that there was a "need for a new editing of Houston correspondence to include all known and available Houston writings," including the personal letters.

When I began research for *Star of Destiny*, I collected just such a file of Houston correspondence, which soon consisted of photocopies of nearly a thousand previously unpublished letters.[1] As I picked out passages from the letters to use for that book, I could not help but notice the wealth of historical information I was leaving out. When I went back later to carefully reread each letter, and to read some of the correspondence written *to* Houston, I knew that Dr. Friend had been right, and I resolved to start on the project myself.

The massive Franklin Williams Collection, which provided the framework for my first book, also provided the bulk of the letters for this multivolume work. Unless otherwise identified, the letters in this volume are from that collection, although there are numerous letters included here from other public and private collections.

It is amazing that the vast collections of personal correspondence have survived years of being stored in various barns, attics, and closets. While a few are too faded to read and had to be omitted, the majority are in surprisingly good condition. Some of the most difficult to read are those which are "cross-written"—that is, after filling up one page with writing, the writer would turn the paper sideways and write directly on top of the original words, giving a "cross-hatched" effect which makes some words impossible to read. Some other letters exist only in fragments, leaving the reader with a tantalizing puzzle as to what was in the missing part. The reader is left with further mysteries when events are alluded to that happened when the couple was together. Included in this group are the incomplete stories of Vernal Lea's first marriage, Nancy Lea's legal problems in Galveston, the unidentified man who slandered Margaret and her mother, and the problems the Houstons had with the emotionally disturbed Virginia Thorn.

One can only wonder about the contents of the missing letters and what happened to them. Margaret Houston is known to have destroyed a group of letters on at least one occasion. Others were lost in the late 1930s, when Madge Williams Hearne presented to Andrew Jackson Houston, the last surviving Houston child, a number of Margaret's letters and poems. A few years later there was a fire in his home and the letters were presumably destroyed. In the spring of 1995, I discovered that an Andrew Jackson Houston collection of Houston papers had been donated to the Catholic Archives in Austin, Texas. My hopes were raised that I would find the missing correspondence. What I found was a wonderful collection of letters written to Houston by various contemporaries, several of which I have mentioned in footnotes in this work,[2] but none of the personal correspondence was included. In the last box, however, I found a fragment of a document showing signs of having been through a fire. It was Andrew Houston's will. Enough of it was left for me to read the instructions concerning a chest of family papers. Andrew specified that, upon the deaths of his daughters, only the Catholic priest of the local parish would be allowed in the Houston home, and he was directed to burn the chest without examining its contents. Once more, personal items had been destroyed in order to protect family privacy.

Fortunately for the historian, the majority of Houston's personal correspondence has been preserved, and many family members have agreed that now is the time to make it available. No Houston descendant refused my request to have his or her collection included in this series. I have included all of the available letters which were previously unpublished, including those written to and from Margaret, additional family members, and some close friends.

This volume furnishes new information about Sam Houston and his family concerning many subjects that Houston scholars have long debated. The letters show clearly that he did, in fact, give up alcohol. New facts are presented about his law practice and finances. Insights into Houston's relationship with Margaret and other family members are revealed. Both Houston and Margaret are quite candid in their descriptions of persons and events during this time.

I have attempted to identify all the people mentioned in the letters. Although an amazing paper trail has been left dealing with the Republic of Texas, this task has not been easy. All too often, few clues have been left to identify the friend or foe, and sometimes there was more than one person who fit a certain description and even a name. Unfortunately a few still remain a mystery.

I began my research into the identities and events mentioned in the letters by consulting *The Writings of Sam Houston*, in which Amelia Williams and Eugene Barker provide marvelous biographies in their footnotes. From there I went to *The Handbook of Texas*, followed by tax rolls, census lists, marriage and cemetery records, and various books written about life in the Republic. I sifted through the correspondence of Houston's contemporaries looking for clues. I studied early maps which listed property owners, and sought advice from local historians throughout the state. If evidence was found that the person was the only one by that name who resided in the correct location at the proper time, I assumed he or she was correctly identified. The occupation, age, place of birth and date of death furnished other clues. Although I often list only one source for identification in a footnote, I usually found the person in several sources. When only one source existed, I used the phrases "possibly" or "probably."

Many of the letters in this volume were difficult to read due to the quality of the paper. Words from the opposite side bled through the thin paper. Some letters were water spotted; others were torn; and the ink on a few was so faded as to make them completely illegible. Fragments exist and are placed in an appropriate time frame. (Some of the fragments and illegible letters may be the ones identified as missing.) A few were not dated. Using clues presented in the content, I attempted to insert them in a logical place. During the time that Houston spent in Austin, he numbered the pages of his letters, making it easy for me to arrange those in the correct order.

In transcribing the letters, I used the following editorial procedures:

Missing words or phrases are identified as [torn] and illegible ones are identified as [blurred]. When the writer has omitted an obvious word, it is included in brackets. If words have been omitted and the meaning is not clear, the letter is reproduced exactly as in the original and "[sic]" is used.

Houston consistently used certain abbreviations, such as "yr" for "your" or "oclk" for "o'clock," and he left apostrophes out of possessive words and words that are contractions today—using "mothers" instead of "mother's," for instance, and "dont" instead of "don't"—but he did use apostrophes liberally in contracted words such as "wou'd," "Gen'l," "render'd." These words are printed in the book as they appear in the original letters, without labeling them as "[sic]." Several words are always misspelled. For instance, Margaret used "thier" for "their" and "realy" for "really," "simpathy" for "sympathy," and both spelled "separation" as "seperation." These consistent errors are printed as written, without comment, not noted, but the *occasional* misspellings are noted with "[sic]." Words which today are compounded, like "anything," "tonight," and "therefore," Sam and Margaret usually wrote as two separate words or used a hyphen to separate them. Thus we read "any thing," "to night," "where-ever" and "there fore," and I have not added a "[sic]" to those types of "errors." The couple both misspelled proper names at times, and I have reproduced them exactly as in the letters, although I have put the corrected spellings in the footnotes.

Both Sam and Margaret frequently used small letters to begin days of the week and other proper nouns. All of these inconsistencies and all underlined words are reproduced as in the original.

Most of the letters contain postscripts, some at the end of the main letter, others in the margin or on the outside of the envelope. In these printed versions, all postscripts appear at the end of the letter.

I greatly appreciate the help of the wonderful staffs of the Daughters of the Republic Library in San Antonio, the Sam Houston Library and Research Center in Liberty, the Woodson Research Center of Rice University in Houston, and the Sam Houston Memorial Museum in Huntsville. I am indebted to the wonderful historians who helped me: Paul Culp of Sam Houston State University, who found the Andrew Jackson Houston and Woods collections for me; Vera Wimberly, who introduced me to the wonders of the genealogical library in Conroe; Cathy Herpich of the Daughters of the Republic of Texas Library, who found research for materials for me; Dick Rice of the Sam Houston Memorial Museum, who helped me match the museum artifacts with the letters; Frances Condra Pryor, who let me use her personal library; Linda Hudson of the University of Texas, Arlington, who furnished me with information on Jane Cazneau; Gifford White, whose prolific research furnished me with many identities of the people of the Republic of Texas; my son-in-law Bryce Jacobson, who helped me prepare the maps; and many others who encouraged my efforts.

In organizing these letters for publication, I obviously chose a chronological arrangement. Beyond that, I also decided to separate them into chapters according to the Houstons' whereabouts at the time—Sam's congressional sessions in Austin or Washington-on-the-Brazos, for instance, or Margaret's trips back to Alabama to see her relatives. This has necessarily made some chapters much shorter than others.

This volume deals with the years of the Texas Republic, beginning in 1839 when Houston met Margaret Lea, and continues until the end of 1845. At this point, I plan to divide the future volumes by Houston's senate terms, as follows: Volume II will cover March 6, 1846–June 14, 1849; Volume III will cover November 24, 1849–April 11, 1853; and Volume IV will cover December 2, 1853–April 10, 1862. There is also a chance, however, that letters for the latter dates will have to be split into two volumes.

My efforts to find more of Houston's letters to family members such as Nancy Lea and both Sam's and Margaret's siblings, as well as Margaret's friends such as Ellen Reily and Catherine Flood, have been largely unsuccessful. Perhaps publication of this first volume will stimulate those who may have these letters in private collections to contact me.

It is my hope that publication of these letters will provide valuable information about other historical figures, as well as the government, medical practices, travel, farming, and daily life in the early days of Texas and our nation, in addition to giving new insights into the lives of Sam and Margaret Houston.

Madge Thornall Roberts
San Antonio, Texas

[1]Because my interest for that book was in the time period beginning when Sam Houston met Margaret Lea in 1839, I have only sought out letters from that year forward. Obviously, Houston kept up personal correspondences before that time, and much of that may remain in private collections also. One publication I am aware of which contains a collection of Houston's pre-1839 personal correspondence is *Ever Thine Truly, Love Letters from Sam Houston to Anna Raguet*, (Austin, Jenkins Garrett Press, 1975). Most of the correspondence in it is also contained in Barker and Williams's *The Writings of Sam Houston*, however.

[2]The letters are all political, rather than personal, and the copyright belongs to the Catholic Archives of Texas, so they were not included in this volume.

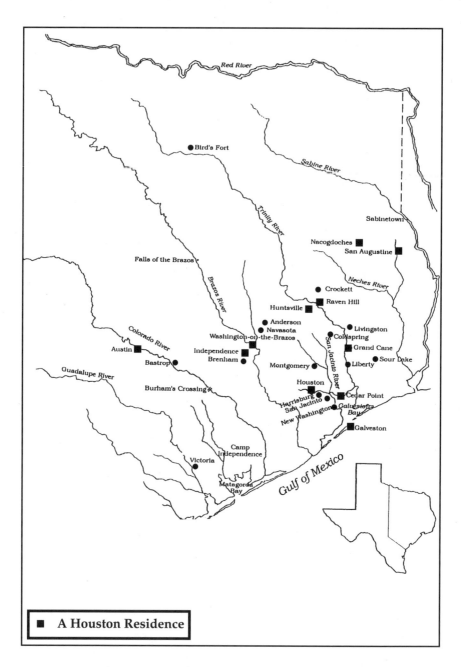

Texas locations referred to in Houston's personal correspondence.

Chapter I

July 17, [1839]–October 4, 1840

In the spring of 1839 Sam Houston visited Mobile, Alabama with the hopes of finding investors for the city of Sabine, Texas. There he met Martin Lea and William Bledsoe. He was invited to a social at the Lea home in Sommerville, Alabama, where he met and fell in love with Margaret Moffette Lea, Martin's sister. After a few weeks' courtship Houston left to visit Andrew Jackson in Tennessee and Margaret and her mother returned to the home of Margaret's brother, Henry Clinton Lea, in Marion, Perry County, Alabama. Two copies exist of the first letter written by Margaret to Sam Houston. One is a first draft on which she practiced her handwriting skills and made changes in wording. I have included in the footnotes any changes which were made to the final letter.

Marion, Perry Co., [Alabama] July 17 [1839]

Your letter from Nashville[1] was received on last night. Strange as it may seem, it is my first news of you since your departure from Mobile. The one written from Columbus was never received. I remained for several days in constant expectation of it, but at length I concluded that the mail had been miscarried. At last however, I have heard from you and the tidings are truly welcome I assure you. My answer may be taken as a strong evidence of that, for it is the first I have addressed to any gentleman.

We are once more in our native county, and Marion—our own Marion is still happy and flourishing. Surrounded by its green hills, groves, and bowers, it is like a sweet wood-nymph untarnished by the wiles and cold deception of the world. I am in the midst of my childhood's friends, and greeted on every hand with gentle words and soft endearing epithets and I am happy; quite happy? Ah no— there are those absent whose station within my heart remains unfilled. Alas it is ever thus through life! Happiness is a grand union of tender associations, ties, and friendships. Let but the smallest of these be removed, and the whole is incomplete.[2]

I have taken my seat in the library. For several reasons it is a favorite resort. Now in the early morning it looks out upon a[3] range of wild hills, still slightly obscured by the mist of the night, and in the evening, the sunset rays will beautifully gild their rich verdure. How solemn the place! Sacred to holy musings and communion with the genius of ages gone bye! I am in the midst of a band of heroes, both ideal and real, and sages with thier wisdom[4] are here and[5] yet though it may seem sacrilegious [sic], my heart is not with them today. It is like a caged bird whose weary pinions have been folded weeks and months—at length it wakes from its stupor, spreads its wings and longs to escape, but ah, my heavy words still weigh it down, it can not go forth.

Last night I gazed long upon our beauteous emblem the star of my destiny,[6] and my thoughts took the form of verse, but I will not inscribe them here, for then you might call me a romantic star-struck young lady, and you know I would be very unwilling to have myself put in that sublime class of individuals.

I regret that it will[7] be impossible for me to see you at the Blount-springs.[8] Mr. Bledsoe and my sister[9] will be there and will be delighted to meet you. Marion is but a trifling journey from that place and we will expect you to perform it. Mr. Bledsoe and my sister, mother[10] and a large portion of my relations will set off for Texas in Oct. Those of my family who remain are unwilling, under existing circumstances, that I should accompany the others until you have visited Marion. It is natural that [they] should wish to see you, and I agree with them in this course upon which they have resolved upon [sic]. Therefore if you do not take Marion in your homeward route, the probability is that you will not see your rustic Esperanza[11] for ages (months I mean) to come. My brother H.[12] met with Gen. Parsons[13] in Cahawba[14] 20 miles from this place. He is to make us a visit very soon. Dear good old man, he speaks so affectionately of you! I have become much attached to him, and will suffer no one to question his bravery in my presence. Well, I believe I have no more to tell you now except that you must write to me immediately and constantly until I see you. I fear if Dr. Sheperd does not return to Mobile shortly, the preference will be given to Meritt. I do not prefix Superior. That is for the young lady to decide.

Forever thine own
Esperanza[15]

---

[1]No copies of this letter have been located. Apparently none of Houston's letters written during the courtship have survived.
[2]Margaret would add to the final draft the following: "What being can ever be so blessed as to embrace all at once? And even if that were accomplished, would it not

be in constant dread of severing some link of the beautiful chain?"

³In this draft, the word "beautiful" is crossed out in front of "range of wild hills."

⁴The words "and philosophy" are added to the final draft at this point.

⁵At this point Margaret added to the final letter the words "and orators and poets with thier dusty laurels. A majestic host!"

⁶On the night they met, Houston pointed to a bright star in the sky and told Margaret Lea that this was their "star of destiny" in the western sky. For the poem she wrote that night see Madge Roberts, *Star of Destiny: The Private Life of Sam and Margaret Houston*, (Denton: University of North Texas Press, 1993), 26–27. Although this poem was written earlier, Margaret may be referring to it since no poem has been located with the date July 17, 1839.

⁷On this draft, "be out of my power" is crossed out after the words "it will."

⁸A community in southern Alabama known for its mineral springs. James T. Sulzby, Jr., *Historic Alabama Hotels and Resorts*, (Montgomery: University of Alabama Press, 1960), 59.

⁹William Bledsoe was married to Margaret's sister, Antoinette.

¹⁰Nancy Moffett Lea.

¹¹Spanish for "the one hoped for," a name given Margaret by Houston.

¹²Henry Clinton Lea.

¹³General Enoch Parsons. Thomas McAdory Owen, *History of Alabama and Dictionary of Alabama Biography*, v. 4, (Chicago: S. J. Clarke Publishing Company, 1921), 1323.

¹⁴A small town in Perry County, Alabama, located on the west side of the Cahaba River near the mouth of Old Town Creek. Ibid, v. 1, 188.

¹⁵The final draft contains a postscript in another handwriting, probably that of William Bledsoe, but it is water spotted and too badly blurred to be read.

Nancy Lea, along with Antoinette and William Bledsoe, planned a visit to Texas. Houston apparently had written Margaret that it was necessary for him to return home and that it was impossible for him to come to Marion. He begged her to come with her family and marry him in Texas. Her reply follows.

Marion Perry co. Aug. 1st [1839]

Dear Sir:

We learn from your letter¹ that it is impossible for you to return by Marion. Your reasons are good—yet we can not but regret [the] necessity of your declining the visit. I stated to you in my last, that it was the wish of myself and relations that you should visit Marion before our departure for Texas. With regard to that our opinions are unchanged. I have never yet taken sides in any affair of moment without being guided in a great measure by my relations and in this case alluded to, I shall rely entirely on thier discretion. Far be it from me to raise my voice against that [torn] country! No, if she requires your presence, go without delay! I would scorn to call him friend—who would desert his country at such a time. Go—and when her cries of oppression are hushed, we will welcome you again to my native state. Let the time of your return depend entirely on the state of your country. It is my wish that you should do so. You request me to reconsider the propriety of accompanying Mr. Bledsoe and my sister and Mother to Texas. I will not refuse to deliberate upon it, but I imagine that my second decision will not differ from the first. I will promise however to think of it.

Mr. [William] Bledsoe has suffered from a long protracted illness from which he is just now recovering. He will set off in a few days for the Blount springs. We were delighted with his accounts of Texas. He gave us many amusing stories of his travels.

I have been a great student since my return home, so that I am unable to give you any of the fashionable news of Marion, and at present have not time to philosophise. However politics is the engrossing theme and I prefer my books, music and needle-work. When I write again I will endeavor to interest you more, but the mail will set off immediately and I am anxious that this should meet you in Nas[hville]. I will expect an answer very soon.

Je suis tou jour la même.

Margaret

Direct to Marion as before.

¹The letter referred to has not been located.

After receiving this letter Houston changed his mind and made the trip to Marion. A wedding was planned, and Houston returned to Texas believing that Margaret would make the trip to Texas and marry him there. He was elected to serve in the Texas Congress and went to Austin. From

there he wrote of his plans to his friend Robert Irion of San Augustine. The following letter is in the Irion Collection of Original Documents in the Archives Division of Sam Houston State University Library.

Austin
29th Jany, 1840

PRIVATE

Dear Irion

I wrote to you, but have heard from you only by chance. What has become of you? Are you really so much in love that you forget your old friends? Or is it that I am about to marry, and that you cannot be at the wedding? I cannot say, my dear fellow, when the frolic will take place, but my notion is that it will be previous to the 15th February. I told you all about matters, and the only thing which has changed the news is the removal of the young lady and family to Texas. She is a "clever Gal" and I hope to show her to my friends as such in March at farthest.[1]

Today I am up and in the House after being three days in bed with a miserable cold owing to this accursed place in which villany has located the seat of Government. Ah my country! No one can fancy its afflictions, and every day adds to its calamities. The day is not distant when the veil of futurity will disclose scenes of extravagance and corruption that will awaken the most miserable sensations and strike the mind with horror. No patriot can anticipate the future of Texas without the most acute and heavy anguish. I have not since the revolution began entertained such gloomy hopes for my country. Heretofore God has saved us and can continue his kind favors, but without them we are gone. The nation cannot bear the burden of Taxation. The people are too poor to pay taxes on oxen, work horses, and in short everything and then obtain <u>no</u> protection for the little remnant left for their enjoyment.

But to other matters. When we meet I will have endless chat for you. I must pass by Houston, the Bay and City of Sabine. If it can come within your power see [to] my horses. Do pray say to Major Roberts[2] to have my house finished in neat order. He has not treated me fairly and I am disappointed by him. I wou'd not have done so! If you have any business at Houston or "fifth proof," I wou'd be happy to see you at either place! But do not let my wishes by any means influence your convenience. I wish you wou'd see if Roberts has anyone of my "Dor Place."[3] A Squire John G. Easly was to come and take the place. Shou'd he be in Texas and wish it, he is to have precedence of all persons, but should he not come—do see that some person shall be there who will take care of it. I want no rent, but the place to be taken care of—Henderson and his Lady[4] send you all Kind wishes with high regards. Gen'l Rusk[5] says he will see me well married, as he goes home, and will go by Houston and the Bay.

Salute Miss A[6]—& the family—indeed all my friends—I add my blessing to this.

Ever thine truly,
Sam Houston

[1] Houston was expecting Margaret to accompany her mother and the Bledsoes to Texas and marry him there.

[2] Elisha Roberts of San Augustine. For a biography see Amelia W. Williams and Eugene C. Barker, eds.,*The Writings of Sam Houston,* v. 2, (Austin: The University of Texas, 1938), 311–12n. Hereafter this eight-volume series will be referred to as *Writings*, and the volume number will be put in Roman numerals.

[3] John M. Dor was Houston's law partner in Nacogdoches. W. Eugene Hollon and Ruth Lapham Butler, eds., *William Bollaert's Texas*, (Norman: University of Oklahoma Press, 1956), 107. See also Walter Prescott Webb, et. al., *Handbook of Texas*, I, (Austin: The Texas State Historical Association, 1952), 514. Hereafter this will be referred to as *Handbook of Texas* and the volume number will be put in Roman numerals.

[4] James Pinckney Henderson and Frances Cox Henderson. For more information about this family see Annie Doom Pickrell, *Pioneer Women in Texas*, (Austin: State House Press, 1991), 172–79.

[5] Thomas Jefferson Rusk. Sam Houston Dixon and Louis Wiltz Kemp, *Heroes of San Jacinto*, (Houston: Anson Jones Press, 1932), 57.

[6] Anna Raguet, whom Houston had previous courted. She would marry Robert Irion, March 20, 1840, a few weeks before the wedding of Sam Houston and Margaret Lea. Norma Rutledge Grammer, compiler, *Marriage Records of Early Texas, 1824–1846*, (Fort Worth, Texas: Fort Worth Genealogical Society, 1971), 61.

Nancy Lea and William and Antoinette Bledsoe came to Texas early in 1840 to inspect land investments. Nancy refused to let Margaret accom-

pany them to be married in Texas, telling Houston, "My daughter goes forth to marry no man. He who receives her hand will receive it in my home, and not elsewhere." The wedding was postponed until Houston could make the trip to Alabama. Houston's letters during this period of the courtship did not survive. When Mrs. Lea was in Galveston, Texas, Margaret wrote her the news from Marion.

A copy of the following letter is in Sam Houston State University Library. The original is in the collection of Margaret Houston correspondence at the Barker History Center, University of Texas, Austin.

Marion, April 25th, 1840

Dearest Mother

I had hoped long before this to have been with you. I therefore deemed it unnecessary to write. This will account to you for my long silence, but I do not offer it as an excuse because I might have foreseen the probability of a disappointment. We have received several letters from you and bro. Martin, and each one had us to think that <u>our friends</u> would be here before we could finish reading it. We have been tantalized in this way for three weeks at least. I should not be so anxious about them, if bro. M[artin] had not mentioned that General Houston's health was bad. And yet I hope that this is not the cause of their detention.

Dear Mother I will not now attempt to reconcile my feelings during your voyage, nor the sweet thankfulness to Heaven that has enlivened my heart ever since I heard of your safe arrival. No, my pen would grow lame beneath the ardour of such feelings. I will reserve the delightful task of narrating them, until we meet again. Marion is much the same as when you left it. One or two marriages have varied the monotony a little. Miss Miller and Mr. Wytt [? name blurred] are married,[1] Mr. Crook and Miss Sanderson,[2] and Mr. Coggod and Miss Loveland.[3] It is said that Lucinda Tarrant will marry Dr. Yarborough, but I do not know the truth of it. Among the deaths in the county are Mr. Kent and old Mr. Locket, Mrs. Watson's father. A very melancholy thing happened a few days ago. Mrs. Vincent Sanders committed suicide by hanging herself. Her little son found her dead in a closet—suspended by a trunk.

Our relations here are generally well. Sister Serena's[4] health is delicate, but she manages so as not to be confined by it. Sumpter[5] has suffered intensively with a rising but it has been lanced and he is recovering rapidly. Sister Serena's only brother Jaquelin[6] is in Athens[7] with his wife and the children, and I expect he will be here in a few days. Br. Henry says, if it is his intention to remove to Texas, that he thinks he will go with him. Sister S[erena] seems to be perfectly willing to do so. She sends her love and says she expects to see you all before long in Texas. Brother Royston's[8] family are all well, and he thinks he will be off in the fall. He has planted his land in corn entirely, as he does not want to be detained by the trouble of gathering cotton. The children are grown very much. Sarah[9] is nearly as tall as I am and the others are grown in proportion. The schools are flourishing still, especially Mr. Wright's.[10] He has 116 scholars. I do not know Mr. Jewett's number.[11] General Thomas is to enclose a little note from me to Maria.[12] So I must bid you adieu and write her a line or two. I am delighted to hear that you have met with her. I will also enclose a letter to Mr. and Mrs. Bledsoe which I wish you to direct for me as I do not know where to send it. My health is very good. My cough disturbs me occasionally, but does not cause me any great inconvenience. We think the Gen. will certainly be here this evening. If he is you may be sure I will not detain him long. I have made me a white satin dress, a purple silk and a blue muslin. I have not gone to any exp[ense] which I thought you would object to.

Your affectionate Margaret

---

[1] An Eliza Ann Miller and a William Wyatt were married February 26, 1840. Altan Kartaltepe, *Early Alabama Marriages,* Vol. M, (San Antonio: Family Adventures, 1991), 311.

[2] A Cornelia Sanderson married a James Crook on February 24, 1840. Ibid., Vol. S, 22.

[3] An Ann Loveland married a Henry Gadden on March 11, 1840. Ibid., Vol. L, 182. Margaret may have made a mistake on the surname of the groom.

[4] Serena Lea, the wife of Henry Clinton Lea. Madge W. Hearne Collection of papers, in the possession of the author, San Antonio, Texas.

[5] Sumpter Lea, Margaret's nephew (the son of Serena and Henry Lea). Ibid.

[6] Jaquelin Rootes. Ibid.

[7] Probably Athens, Georgia.

[8] Robertus Royston, husband of Varilla (also spelled Virilla) Lea, Margaret's sister. Hearne Collection.

[9] Sarah Ann Royston, also called Sallie and "Tose," was Margaret's niece (the daughter of Robertus and Varilla Royston). Ibid.

[10] Rev. S. R. Wright was in charge of the Marion Female Seminary. Samuel A. Townes, "History of Marion and Sketches of Life 1844," reprinted in the *Alabama Historical Quarterly* 14 (1952): 222.

[11] Rev. Professor M. P. Jewett of Judson Institute had seventy students for his third term. Ibid.

[12] Margaret is probably referring to her friend Maria Blassengame.

Sam Houston and Margaret Lea were married at the home of her brother, Henry Lea, on May 9, 1840. Shortly after that they traveled to Texas, landing at Galveston. Here Margaret's mother, Nancy Lea, was renting a house. The couple visited with Mrs. Lea while they were building a home on property Houston owned across the bay at Cedar Point. Their first separation as husband and wife occurred when Houston traveled to Houston City on business. Here Houston wrote her his first letter after their marriage.

Mrs. M. M.[1] Houston
Galveston, Texas
by Tucker[2]

on the Dayton[3]
30th June 1840

Like one of your old Beaux I am at a loss how to address you when a Wife! So much for bashfulness! I was in time to day and will use my time well. I walked down in such haste that I can hardly write you an intelligible letter or note.

I pray that you may be as happy as I desire you should be. Have no bad dreams, as I intend to furnish <u>excuses for now</u>. I will attend to Joshua![4]

I beg you to be happy or as happy as you can on account of the musquitoes [sic]. I hear no news from above, and if matters are easy there, I will have the less detention from you, which will be a cause of much felicity to me. I write only for two reasons—one is that I have little else to do, and the other is that I love you "<u>verrie much</u>."

My kind regards to Mrs. Lea, and be assured of my devoted love and imperishable affection.

Thy Husband
Sam Houston

Mrs. M. M. Houston

My friend Dr. Tucker will hand this note to you.

Thine truly
Houston

[1] Margaret sometimes signed her letters Margaret Moffett Lea, and so her husband is addressing her as M. M. Houston rather than M. L. Houston.

[2] Dr. Edmund Tucker, a surgeon in the Texas army (*Writings,* II, 263n) and a member of the Medical & Surgical Society of Houston formed in 1840. Pat Ireland Nixon, *The Medical Story of Early Texas, 1528–1853,* (San Antonio: Mollie Bennett Lupe Memorial Fund, 1946), 461–62.

[3] The steamship Dayton ran from Houston to Galveston in a ten-hour trip. The charge was $5.00 for cabin and $2.50 for deck passengers. Marilyn McAdams Sibley, *The Port of Houston: A History,* (Austin: University of Texas Press, 1968), 40.

[4] Joshua was one of four Lea slaves willed to Margaret by her father, Temple Lea. See Temple Lea's will, *Alabama Will Book,* v. A, 57–58 (a copy of which is in the possession of the editor). See also Patricia Smith Prather and Jane Clements Monday, *From Slave to Statesman: The Legacy of Joshua Houston, Servant to Sam Houston,* (Denton: University of North Texas Press, 1993), 2.

July 1, 1840

To Mrs. M. M. Houston
Galveston, Texas
Capt. Cannan[1] will hand this in person—Houston

City of Houston
1st July, 1840

My Dearest Mag,

A thousand things I cou'd say, were I present. Yes present in person, for my heart and affections are always where my dear Mag is. This moment I have been tendered a fee of $1,000, but if it wou'd detain me from you, I might hesitate as to its acceptance.

I intend to see you, as I have proposed—ascribe it to business if I am delayed—but I cannot remain from one to whom I am so much devoted. I left Joshua well, and all well at Spillmans.[2] Yates[3] was defeated when he called at the Point [Cedar Point]. You charmed Mr. Fleming,[4] and I can only say, "So much for a wife." My affectionate regards to your Mother.

<u>Always</u>
thy Husband, Houston

[1]Probably William Travis Cannan, a San Jacinto veteran. For a biography see *Writings,* II, 194n and Dixon and Kemp, 227–28.

[2]James Spillman owned property at Spillman's Point and Spillman's Docks on Galveston Bay. See map of "Original Land Grants and Selected Landmarks" in Dorothy Knox Houghton, et. al., *Houston's Forgotten Heritage,* (Houston: Rice University Press, 1991), xv.

[3]Anthony Janeway Yates was involved in a dispute with Houston over ownership of Cedar Point. *Handbook of Texas,* II, 942. For a biography see *Writings,* I, 491n.

[4]Angus Fleming. Identified in Daughters of the Republic of Texas, *Defenders of the Republic of Texas,* (Austin: Laurel House Press, 1989), 271.

To Mrs. M. M. Houston
Galveston City, Texas
Mr. Sturdivant[1]

Houston
2nd July— 40

My dear Margaret,

 Yesterday I wrote to you. To day I write again by Mr. Sturdivant who will tell you, and our excellent Mother all about Anto[i]nette.[2] You will be happy, and I am so, only that I can not see my dear Mag, which leaves me miserable.

 Were she to see me, she wou'd pardon many faults of mine. The heart that only throbs for <u>one</u> must be wretched when absence seperates them. There is nothing new here. I will arrange my business, as I have me <u>an Express</u> from Red Land. I will do all that I can to be off for there. I pray you my Love, to be cheerful and happy! In heart & soul I am thine truly.

 My affection to your Mother, and to you. I can say no more—but that I am—

Thy Husband
Sam Houston

Mrs. M. M. Houston
PS Persons are walking on the floor, and I can not write a fair hand.

Thine

Houston

Cap Blacks[3] family are all sick. The Thomsonian[4] practice has failed.

[1]Houston may be referring to Francis Sturdevant of Washington County. Identified in Gifford White, ed., *1840 Citizens of Texas,* Vol. I (Land Grants), (St. Louis: Ingmire Publishers, 1983), 243.

[2]Nancy Lea and Antoinette Lea Bledsoe.

[3]John S. Black. See Robin Montgomery, *The History of Montgomery County,* (Austin: Pemberton Press, 1975), 171–72 and *Writings,* III, 348n.

[4]A medical sect whose "botanic system was based on the theory that vegetable remedies and steam doctoring provided the heat necessary to cure all diseases. Its followers were against bloodletting and the use of calomel. This sect was opposed by 'regular' doctors." William Ransom Hogan, *The Texas Republic,* (Austin: University of Texas Press, 1969), 236–37. W. A . Newman Dorland, *The American Illustrated Medical Dictionary,* (Philadelphia: W. B. Saunders Company, 1937), defines it as a system of medical practice, chiefly botanic, founded by Samuel Thomson, a New Hampshire farmer (402).

In the late summer of 1840, the Houstons began a tour of east Texas. Margaret became ill with malaria and Houston took her to the home of Antoinette and William Bledsoe to recuperate. He then continued his trip.

Mrs. Margaret Lea Houston
Washington Texas
Care of Captain W. Bledsoe

Crockett Texas
22nd August 1840

My dear,

This evening I came to this place, after riding twenty eight miles in the sun. I am yet quite well, but bled myself last evening for fear of too great pletharge [sic]. I learned that there has been sickness in the East, but is now abating. Indeed sickness has been universal in Texas. I hope it will cease, with the cool nights and mornings. There is no news that would interest you, and I fear that you will not hear from me as no mail is now running. I will write by private hand, with the hope that it may reach you safely.

I am more lonely each day in my estimation. To see you engrosses my greatest desires. But for the while I must be reconciled and pray for your health, safety, and happiness. In two days I hope to reach

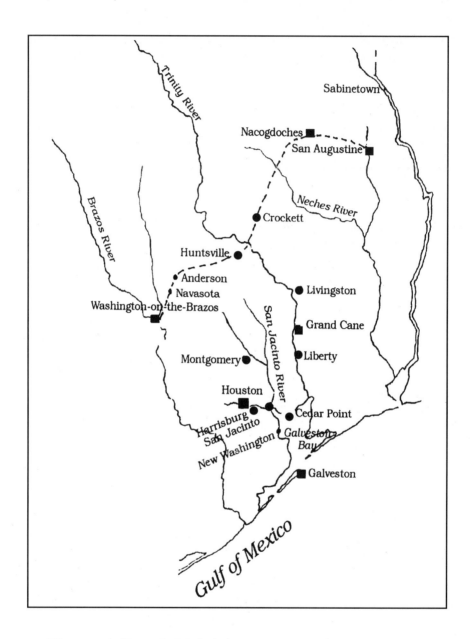

Houston's Travels Mid-August, 1840 to October 4, 1840

Nacogdoches, but in the mean time I will write to you. Walling[1] is still the faithful attentive man, and really without him, I wou'd be at a loss. To my horses, he is everything. They are all doing well, and improve on the journey.

The people all express many regrets, that you are not with me so you may be prepared to play the lyon-ess, as you pass the journey. I hope to have some amusing incidents, when I am so happy as to embrace you; You will not allow me to sing or I wou'd learn to chaunt "Be gone dull care" etc. As it is I'm quite miserable taciturn and sad. Thus you see what a spice of good humour has done, with my musical faculties.

Now my beloved, present me kindly to our dear sis, and the Captain. May Heaven bless thee!

Thine affectionately devoted husband
Sam Houston

[1]Could be either John, Jesse, or Thomas Walling. The three brothers lived a few miles from Nacogdoches. *Handbook of Texas*, II, 858. Jesse was a close friend of Houston's.

Mrs. Margaret Lea Houston
Washington Texas
By Col Richardson[1]

Near San Augustine
28th August 1840

My beloved Maggy,

On yesterday I arrived at this place (my friend Subletts[2]) and found all well. My friends were all "appie," and only deplored your absence but rejoiced at your recovery. News had reached that you had ceased to exist. You are not aware of the sadness caused at this report. When I arrived the joy was correspondent to the depression which had existed. You are looked for with pleasure and anxiety by all classes. I have declined a dinner invitation, but have agreed to address the people in Town, on the 3rd Sept.[3] You will see the correspondence which has taken place. In it "I cry aloud and spare not." It will pay some of my political debts. To some it will be worse than the <u>squeal</u> of "Lynchy" hog. I will enclose to you a slip from the paper of the Red Lands, for your perusal. The spirit to which it is written is very fine, and complementary! In my absence from you, I feel as tho' I was deprived of my <u>better part</u>. I was aware that I would be lonesome, but I really feel insulated, and tho' hope lingers with me, yet I feel as miserable as if you were across the ocean. I never did realize the hope while single that I wou'd find in a wife a perfect companion and one who wou'd be capable, by her wisdom and prudence to sustain me, or one who wou'd endear life to me, and blot out the infelicity of the past. I am disappointed in this calculation. I have supposed that I would be kindly and justly treated by a woman of fidelity, and that I would be all kindness to her, cherish, protect, and sustain her. I thought that mutual dependence wou'd make us agreeable, contented, and diminish the care of life. I only deplore the situation of our country that requires my absence from you! I long to see you, that we may talk over matters. I feel that I have my full consent, to retire and pursue a course adapted to our mutual felicity. I am inclined to believe that public station will not promote our individual happiness! You are highly capable of reflecting and judging of these suggestions. I feel only concern, in the perfection of your happiness so far as temporal matters are involved. The holy religion which you profess & practice will enable you to look with an eye of Hope to the mediatorial cross of your blessed, and atoning Redeemer! This reflection will sustain you in the trials of your earthly probation! You will find no conduct of mine a stumbling block to your path. The study of my life shall be to render you happy in temporal & spiritual affairs!

Yesterday I rec'd a long letter from my niece Mrs. Peland[4] in which she says our relatives are all well, and no misfortune! She urges the subject of Religion with much earnestness, and renders much scripture! In this section there has been much sickness and frequent death—tho' the mortality is not so great as represented.

The great drought, in my opinion, has been the cause of disease. My business is somewhat embarrassed in this quarter, and some attempts to rob me of my rights! "It will be so, awhile at first." My hopes of success and wealth are sanguine, and I hope to see your face long adorned with the smiles of contentment and inspirited by the music of the Guitar, and other little etcetera <u>tones</u>!!!!

You will be grievously tired in perusing the dull, and heavy contents of this letter!—Therefore I will close after asking you on your contemplated trip to the East.

Request Capt Bledsoe to have two good lock chains, a hatchet, ropes and nails—let yourself and sister get out at all bad places. Let the Captain ride before, and for Gods-sake let there be a good driver. The one he had won't do! It will require four mules in the carriage— let the Captain inquire at Cincinatti[5] for the nearest and best road when he crosses the River. The bottom is very bad!—if he should take the wrong road. And when he comes to Bradshaw,[6] let him take the left hand road at least until he comes to Beans[7]—then if he should wish to come by Mr John Durst's,[8] he can get directions. I never passed any difficult part of the road, but what I felt solicitude for your safety. I am here rusticating, and our friend Judge Scurry[9] is now with me. He bids me to commend him to you most kindly. He will have a fine batch of stories for you by the time you arrive.

I pray you to commend most cordially and truly to our dear Sister and the Captain with my solicitude for their happiness and prosperity.

For the future may God allow me to be the careful and successful guardian of your happiness! The day is spent, and the people returning from camp meeting. I must conclude this weary Epistle. You will be tired when you have read it.

Thy husband
Truly affectionately
Sam Houston

[On envelope:]
23rd Sept.—no news since Sunday. A <u>chill</u> is just leaving me and must today God bless thee my love

Thine
Houston

[1]Probably Colonel Daniel Long Richardson, the father–in-law of David Kaufman of Sabine. For information about the Richardson/Kaufman families see Edna McDaniel White and Blanche Findley Toole, *Sabine County Historical Sketches and Genealogical Records,* (Beaumont: LaBelle Printing Company, 1972), 20.
[2]Phillip Sublet was Houston's boyhood friend from Tennessee and a son-in-law of Elisha Roberts. *Writings,* II, 371n.
[3]See *Writings,* II, 350–52, Houston's "Reply to a Dinner Invitation," August 28, 1840.
[4]Pheobe Jane Penland, the daughter of Houston's sister, Eliza Moore. Hearne Collection of Papers, San Antonio.
[5]A small settlement on the Trinity River which was located near the present city of

Huntsville. Bob Bowman, *The 35 Best Ghost Towns in East Texas*, (Lufkin: Best of East Texas Publishers, 1988), 127.

[6]The Bradshaw farm was on the road to Crockett west of Nacogdoches just past the Durst farm. Archie P. McDonald, *Hurrah for Texas! The Diary of Adolphus Sterne 1838–1851*, (Waco: Texian Press, 1969), 59–60.

[7]The farm of Ellis P. Bean, twenty-eight miles from Nacogdoches on the road to Crockett. Ibid., 44.

[8]John Durst settled at Nacogdoches in the Old Stone Fort. *Handbook of Texas*, I, 527.

[9]Richardson Scurry, an old friend from Tennessee, who settled in San Augustine. *Handbook of Texas*, II, 584 and *Writings*, I , 512n.

To Margaret Lea Houston
Washington Texas
My friend Mr Vance[1] care of Capt Bledsoe
Sam Houston

> San Augustine
> 4th September 1840
> $100 cash
> Texas

My Love,

To day by a Mr Cartwright from Washington[2] I heard that you were well enough to be shopping, and this gave me pleasure—It was my first and only news of you since the painful moment of parting. But I heard that our dear sis, Antoinette was very ill. I hope it is a mistake. God preserve her, long and happy.

My affections burn to see you. You are the light of my path; and the only being that can or cou'd cheer my heart. To see you wou'd be joy inexpressible. When this is handed to you, and you should be at Capt B's I pray to get him to see, if there was not some one traveling East, that you may write to me, and not rely on the mail—'tis uncertain and not to be relied upon. As I can not see you, my busy thoughts will pursue you, and fancy makes me wretched. I then rely, for your safety, and happiness upon our God whom you serve, and in whom I believe!!! He will sustain us in virtue, & happiness. Without his aid, we can not be happy or prosperous.

On yesterday I spoke to the people, and they seemed happy, & satisfied. The election will take [place] on the 7th Instant (Monday).[3] Tomorrow, I expect to visit camp meeting, but I do not know what denomination it is. You will know for I hope soon to see you here. "Everybody" is anxious to see you in the Red Lands. I wou'd be right "appie" to see you myself. Mrs. Sublett[4] wou'd be glad to see you to spend some time with them! If your sister can't come with you, and you bring Maria[5] along, <u>don't come</u>, but let me know it. If Capt B, & sis, comes [sic] with you, let him bring four mules in the carriage. They will be needful, and all the caution possible to save the Ladies & the carriage—Get out at all bad places. Come by Cincinnati, as persons are <u>killed</u>, on the upper road— by the Indians!!! I need not write more as the news here wou'd not interest you. My health improves much in my opinion! My stock of fine horses are doing well. I am trading for a fine saddle mare, for you, and a hackney.

The people improve in health, and I hope by the time that you read[,] here all will have recovered!

Mr Vance, the Gentleman who bears this letter, is an old friend of mine from Tennessee! Let him be treated as such!!! I wish my dear wife to become acquainted with Mr Vance, as he will be pleased, and can tell the truth when he returns to Tennessee.

By Mr. V. I send you $100 in Texas money and only regret that I cannot send you a Million in Gold. As Mr. Vance is on the eve of departure, I will only add my infinite love to you, and my affection to our dear Sis, and the Captain.—If necessary for your happiness, send an express to me and I will be with you. All my friends here desire me to present their cordial esteem & estimation.

Do write to me, and should you set out, come by Cincinnati. Be careful. Idol of my affections, Adieu.

Thy husband
Sam Houston

Mrs. M. L. Houston
My love to Sis Antoinette & the Captain. Write to me all about Mother!!!

Houston

PS I have heard that Tom and Esau[6] are safe in Houston. I am glad of it! There is no money here, but don't you regard that. I will have enough for you, if I shou'd <u>rob</u> the highways! or the byways!!!

Sam Houston

Maggy Houston

[on the back]
Mrs. Nancy Lea
Care of Mr. A. C. Allen[7]
Cedar Point Texas
By Mr. Vance

Dear Mother,

I wish you to pay great attention to Mr. Vance, he is a great friend of Gen Houston's and a man of high standing in the states. My health is very low, and God only knows when I shall recover. I am under the care of a Thomsonian. You will see that the Gen. still expects us in the red lands.[8] We have no means of undeceiving him as our letters can not reach him. Mother, if you are in need, would you not borrow from Judge Johnson[9] or some other friend of Gen Houstons in his name? I will take the responsibility myself.

Thy child M. L. Houston

[1]This was probably Andrew Vance, a partner of Vance & Dicks from Clarksville, Tennessee. He died in Galveston November 12, 1840. Silas Emmet Lucas, ed., *Obituaries from Early Tennessee Newspapers 1794–1851*, (Easley, South Carolina: Southern Historical Press, 1978), 377.

[2]It is unclear to which Cartwright brother this refers. Matthew, Peter, and William all owned property in Washington County. Worth S. Ray, *Austin Colony Pioneers*, (Austin: Pemberton Press, 1970), 75.

[3]Houston was re-elected as congressman from Nacogdoches in this election. M. K. Wisehart, *Sam Houston: American Giant*, (Washington: Robert B. Luce, 1962), 363.

[4]Easter Jane Roberts, Mrs. Phillip Sublet. *Handbook of Texas*, II, 683.

[5]A Lea family servant.

[6]Two of the slaves owned by Houston. Lenoir Hunt, *My Master*, (Dallas: Manfried, Van Nort & Company, 1940), 97.

[7]Augustus Chapman Allen, one of the founders of the city of Houston. For a biography see *Writings*, II, 181–83n.

[8]East Texas.

[9]Judge Robert D. Johnson of Galveston. For a biography see *Handbook of Texas*, I, 917.

Mrs. Margaret Lea Houston
Near Washington Texas
To be left at Capt Bledsoe's if the Gentleman can't see Mrs. Houston

Nacogdoches Texas
13th Sept 1840

My beloved,

An hour since I arrived, and on my way this morning [I] had the pleasure to meet your letter of the 1st inst, with the [torn] and the papers enclosed.[1] I snatched them and opened them with intense feeling of anxiety. My distress was great, as I had not heard of you but once since we parted! I was weary of conjecture at your situation. I had written some six or seven letters. The fact of your relapse accounted for—or cou'd I anticipated I wou'd never be seperated from you for an hour. But I am in the Red Lands, and if I leave without arranging matters, I must loose [sic] many thousands. I have eight fine blooded horses for which I paid $9000.00, and they must be disposed of. I have also four or five saddle horses, and must sell three of them. I have advertised 822 acres of fine land near to this place to sell.[2] This means money I must have. The other day my love, I sent you $100 by Mr. Vance, and only regret that I had no more to send. I do not say "spare"—for it was all that I had—the last, and only cent.

I had forebodings that something had happened and that you wou'd not come on, but in the event you did I've sent you every advice. It was best that you shou'd <u>not</u> come, and as I have been so long detained, do not now attempt it, as you may miss me on the road, & the Indians are killing people within 28 miles of Nacogdoches, residing on the main road, by which you wou'd be compelled to travel! Don't by any means <u>attempt</u> to come, but wait for my return with patience—my entire love is with you, my spirit is cheered by the recollection of your charms & worth, and my prayers [are] to the God of the universe are for you. [torn] my anguish, and not hearing from you. I threw myself upon the mercy of the Great Eternal intelligence, whom I have at heart ever adored, and who has in all my earthly trials sustained me! To Him and thee I look for all my happiness on this globe! Heaven will protect and guide us! Dr. Smith[3] wrote to me from on board the Steam Boat— our blessed Mother was on board, going to Cedar Point to see Jones[4] and the hands as she heard they were doing no good! The doctor promised all assistance and protection to her, while there and said that she wou'd not visit you until my return—Now you may rely on my return as soon as possible. I will be careful not to <u>see</u> any Indians on the way because I will have company enough. It will be necessary for me to attend San Augustine court on the 4th Monday Inst, and where I have been offered very large <u>fees</u>.[5] One little one of $500.00. We need all that I can make. I must now tell you that for six days & nights I have suffered with a general disease here—The Diarrhea which has in some cases been fatal. To day [sic] I am better. I never took to my bed, but rode in the sun every day, little more. At one time I did not think that [I would] survive two hours without relief. I will be more careful of my health! I have taken medicine from the Great Wilson,[6] as my friend was not at hand! (Irion).

I thank you for the prayers of affection which you render for me, and I will try to act worthy of the offering! Not withstanding my disease has reduced me in flesh, my colour is fast returning to my former red land hue! There has been much sickness, but it has been the first for fifty years, and may not again occur. As to where we settle, I will talk to you of that, and many things when we meet. My Love, what I told you of Miss E.....[7] was correct. You may think of the matter—but let it be kept a profound secret—be always guarded—you are "Houston's Wife" and <u>many would joy to dash our cup of bliss. My joy is in your life!</u> I have only time to write to you, but no more as the bearer is in waiting. Give my love to our dear Sis and the Captain. Please say to him that I have rec'd the papers but not yet seen Gowans[8] of the subject—<u>Don't</u> attempt to come on. I will write every chance. I wish you could by private hand do let me know how your breast is,[9] and indeed <u>every thing</u>. God bless and keep and preserve you.

Thy Husband truly
Sam Houston

Mrs. M. L. Houston

[1]This letter has not been located.

[2]Houston owned property on the west bank of Sands Bayou. For field notes describing the property see R. B. Blake, "Transcripts of Documents from Records of the District Court of Nacogdoches County, Concerning Individuals Who Participated in the Texas Revolution, 1836," (n.p., 1995), 95. Barker History Center, University of Texas Library, Austin, Texas.

[3]Dr. Ashbel Smith.

[4]Probably William Jefferson Jones, a farmer, lawyer and statesman who lived in Galveston County. For a biography see *Handbook of Texas*, I, 927.

[5]Houston was representing the Galveston Bay and Texas Land Company in several suits. See Wisehart, 362

[6]Dr. Stephen Wilson was a well-known physician who lived four miles northwest of San Augustine. G. L. Crockett, *Two Centuries in East Texas,* (Dallas: Southwest Press, 1932), 261.

[7]Eliza Allen, Houston's first wife. They were divorced before he met Margaret. Apparently Houston is referring to what he had told Margaret concerning his mysterious first marriage.

[8]William Goyens was a free black freight hauler and blacksmith in Nacogdoches. He served as an interpreter in dealing with the Indians. For a biography see *Handbook of Texas,* I, 713.

[9]Margaret was suffering from a tumor of the breast.

[On envelope] This is sent to
Mrs. Margaret Lea Houston
Washington, Texas
by Col. J. Snively

Nacogdoches
17th Sept [1840]

My Dear Wife,

On yesterday I sent you a package by Mr. Gantt.[1] Col Snively,[2] my friend, will start on Saturday next (two days hence) and tho to-day I am not so well, I can not forgo the pleasure of writing to you again. You can have no idea of my troubled spirit. To see you would be happiness, if less the divine, at least extreme. I can not see you, as soon as I would desire, but our mutual interest compels me to remain for awhile in this region.

Every day is an age to me, despite the kindness and respect shown me. Two days since I made a defense in a criminal case and tho' this is said to be the county most adverse to me, you would have thought I was a popular Gentleman!!!

Since then the clients in an important case have called upon me, [and] should I be here at the spring court, I expect in San Augustine and this county to clear from $10 to $20,000 per annum, by the practice. Were I am single man, I would not make these calculations, but my <u>dear</u> I am now Benedict the married man!!! This small item in life will change my course, if not my nature! Oh Maggie, I only wish that I could see you, that I might feel that I was [blurred] companion and an equal—in whose presence I was happy and one who would feel that I was devoted to her happiness—her honor and her future fame and glory! Then I would indeed be happy. You can have no idea when you are absent from me, how much I realize communion with our past hours of mutual confidence and bliss. I feel that when we were united [blurred] and ventured much—too much! But I will convince to the world that even with one who is thought to disregard life, and all its clamor, that woman can redeem him, and bring him within the fold.

Dearest, I pray you my <u>Love</u>, think not for one moment, that I will delay seeing you the instant that I can reach you after my business is concluded in this section. My house in this place is not finished, but is in progress. I paid two years since for it, $5500 for it, but as I always have been treated so I am again. I was to have had it finished two years since. It is a pretty place and an extensive Lot. Fine water and beautiful Garden Places. You would be happy to see this section of the country, and the people will hardly forgive me for not seeing you in this quarter!

I tell them <u>family matters</u> permitting, that you will visit them in the spring. This suits them only as a [blurred] apology. Indeed my love, I wish you had come on with me—but this will of Providence forbad it!

You must say to our friend Bledsoe that his letter and the Doctors has come to hand, and I am happy that he is not involved, but if he wants that, I would help him out, so far as Land would go in the business. My wish is to aid all our family and see them enjoy ease and plenty & character in the country!

You will be weary of my over much writing, and I must write shorter letters. Really the pleasure in communicating to you includes all unhappiness and therefore I must continue writing. I only feel miserable that I can't see you to tell you all that I feel for you! Lovers profess all that they feel, but husbands are not so happy! I feel more than language can express. That you should feel equally the endearments of affection, is but reasonable, and for that reason, I wish to become located, settled and in a situation where we can be united in place as well as in affection. The days which are departed, we can not recall, but we have a right to anticipate the future. In life I have been in the habit of looking forward, and yet I cherish the same hope—With every hope you are blended and identified as the most precious object of creation. I feel that I have given you pain and boundless solicitude. For all this you will pardon me and feel that it was not displeasure to you in any respect, but an error on my part. My dear Margaret, we have a bright future, I hope to look to. One that will secure to us all that mortals should anticipate, and all that virtue can deserve. With you I feel that we are responsible not only to the rules of morality, but to the holy precepts of our savior, Jesus Christ!!! That a believing wife may save an unbelieving husband is my sincere desire. My dear, I must close this letter and with it, I repose my happiness, my fault, my honor, and my all on earth!!! Oh that I could see you but one hour that I might enjoy your smile—But this my dear Maggy, is too trite. I might be so situated that my "face wou'd hurt me" were [it] to be seen by the world!

I pray you to give my kind love to our dear sister and Captain Bledsoe. Assure them of my kind affection and wishes for their prosperity.

My dear Wife, I pray you to be assured of my entire devotion, and that I will not be happy one moment, until we meet! My Love, I am doing all in my power to promote our mutual interest. [blurred] is well and shall bear me to my dear Maggy—look for me by the 10th proximo. I have written to our dear Mother! The old lady requires and deserves all our reverence and love—we must not fail to pay her the homage due to her.[3]

I am truly thy husband
Sam Houston

Mrs. M. L. Houston

[1]William Gant was a congressman from Washington County. He died shortly after this letter was written. For a biography see *Handbook of Texas,* I, 670.
[2]Jacob S. Snively, a surveyor who lived in Nacogdoches. For a biography see *Handbook of Texas,* II, 631.
[3]Houston's letter to Nancy Lea has not been located.

William Bledsoe
Washington
Texas

San Augustine County

21st Sept 1840

My dear Bledsoe,

Yesterday was Sunday and I passed much of the day in writing to my dear Maggy and musing upon the past as well as contemplating the future. My situation has been such that I can not leave here without [ink spot]. I have horses here worth some $12,000 dollars. They cost me in the states $8,500 and some I have added since to my stocks. All these wou'd have gone to waste. I need all that I have to be independent and there is due me on this quarter $18,500—of this. I should have something. I must have money at least enough to meet present demands. All that I care for is to [blurred] Maggy in a style that will at least prevent her from feeling embarrassment. To accomplish this, I must exert myself and I do hope to Heaven she will not [blurred] when she reflects that it is for her more than myself that I wish to secure the property which I have acquired under circumstances of risk and at hazard.

My dear Margaret has too much mind not to appreciate my situation. I feel confident that some one has told my dear Margaret that [I am] in "Sprees" here and this has made her very unhappy and for this she sent to me. I might have thought of this, and find her feelings against report. It is thus that misery is infused into the breast of [blurred] must say that it was unkind as well as untrue.

Why does my dear Wife listen to such tales as render credence to falsehood. I must go to her the first moment in my power, and when she sees me she will be satisfied that I have been slandered. I will not justify myself because I am not accused. Tell my dear wife not to be so silly as to believe every report which she may hear of me. Tell her that I am willing to quit public life and never be absent from her for one week again. I dislike public life as much as she can. With it, I am satisfied, I've done enough for my country and more than it can do for me!

22nd Sept 1840

I am just in an ague and as it is first, I hope it will be the last this season. My love to my dear wife, to Sister Ann, etc.

Ever thine truly
Sam Houston

William Bledsoe
In a few days I hope to set out to see my dear Wife. Today I make

disposition of my blood stock. I have a filly for Margaret, you may say to her.

Houston

On September 23, 1840, Houston wrote Margaret from San August-ine. In the letter he expressed his hope that she would hear no more slanders of him. Although it did not bother him, he was upset because he knew it distressed her. He also promised, "if you hear the truth, you never shall hear of my being on a 'spree.'" For a complete text of the letter see Writings, *II, 352–53.*

Mrs. Margaret Lea Houston
Galveston
Texas
care of Mr. Moore[1]

San Augustine
25 Sept 1840

My beloved Margaret,

To day my anguish was rendered almost insupportable by two reports which reached me that you were worse, but on inquiry I found that the individuals had not been within eight or ten miles of you. This day I care for nothing, if you are worse, or shou'd decease before I can see you; but ruin to those, on whom the blame may fall. I wou'd not hope for happiness again without you!

Cou'd I be assured that you were aware of my situation, and demanded my presence, I wou'd before the God of Heaven, leave here to embrace you! I have owing to me $19,000—I have this day in horses a value $12,000, and I am tendered $4000 in fees at court. This is $35,000 besides my riding horses. 3 are valuable and that I would sell at court. Shou'd I leave for ten days, and abandon all that I have here, we would suffer the agony of <u>poverty</u>. You my dear have always enjoyed abundance, and were you destitute, you wou'd be miserable and myself wretched!!! I know not what to write, nor can I hope for happiness or tranquillity until I see you, and if I shou'd depart and leave my business, so as to loose [sic] my interest in this section, I will never hope for happiness again. My dear you have heard, and will hear reports and should you regard them, you will be miserable, and I must be forever destroyed in my hopes and happiness. I have endeavor'd to sustain you during my absence by writing, but it is all in vain. With the hope of blessing you, I am only more miserable than tho I had been silent! It is vain for me to hope for happiness on earth! I have always believed in a heaven, and an Eternity in which virtue wou'd be rewarded. If there shou'd be none, my loss will be infinite and my happiness incomplete. To be a bankrupt on earth I fear much! and I dread the awful bankruptcy in Heaven! For solvency in the latter, I had hoped assistance from you, but you can not feel faith in me and I must feel the most wretched of mortals!

Oh my love! for the sake of our dear Savior, I pray you to be sustained until we can meet! Were it not for the love which I bear you I wou'd not wish to inhabit earth a single moment! Will you not be composed until I can reach you! Must our ruin be mortal, or will you incur it alone!!!! My Love, I pray you again, do not dispond [sic], do not be unhappy until I come to you. Did I under circumstances, which exist, fly to you, and abandon our mutual interest, I wou'd never be enabled again to smile upon you! I wou'd be unbounded in my wretchedness! I will not be myself until I can again embrace you—Tho business requires my attention, and the most important suits which have ever been tried in Texas, at the coming term will come out, I will not be in a situation to render to my Clients a return for their money! I will wait for the first day of court and [bottom of the page is torn off]

I feel assured what Mr. Vance reported caused the Express to be sent to me!!! This much I was satisfied of by the Express. If my wife and my friends will not confide in me, I must feel too much degraded to wish ever to embrace them! The days which have dealed out to me much misery, have not equaled the few which have passed!!!

Nothing can, nothing ever will abate my love for you, my dear Wife—but oh for Heavens sake, pity me! My Love, I will not wait an instant longer here, than what duty to you and myself will compel me to stay!

Give my love to our dear Sister, and my regards to Capt Bledsoe! To day I saw Mr Gowans, and he says he will go with me to Washington, but if he shou'd not, that he will send the money by me, to Capt Bledsoe.

Ever thy devoted husband
[signature has been torn off]

[1]This probably refers to John W. Moore of Harris County. For a biography see E. L. Jennet, *Biographical Directory of the Texan Conventions and Congresses, 1832–1845*, (n.p., 1941), 143.

Mrs. Margaret Lea Houston
Galveston
Lt. Moore

San Augustine
27th September 1840

My Beloved,

Yesterday, I mailed a long letter for you, and now holy sunday is drawing to a close, and wears the solemnity of an autumn evening. It has been a day of sadness and sober thoughts with me. Tho' persons have called to see me, and consult with me, on the business of court, which commence tomorrow, I cou'd not regard their application with the interest which I wou'd do under other circumstances. The improbable and painful solicitude which I feel for you, precludes every joy, & pleasure but what may arise from my association with you, and the hope that I may soon embrace you again. My spirits are somewhat calmed in the last day and night, but the night before last, I was sleepless and arose in the morning the wretched and distant husband from a beloved wife. On yesterday, I had the happiness to receive your kind and greatly valued favor of the 5th Instant when you had recovered from your relapse.[1] Oh my love, had I not received the Express from you, my joy wou'd have been complete. I was doomed to this place, which I now regard as a prison, and shall until one more week must lapse. I must be here at court, and stay one week. That will commence tomorrow, so that in fourteen days, I trust in God to be with you!!! My health was improving until the express came, and tho' it is now tolerable, my anxiety and inquietude, has not been of advantage to it.

From my dear kindred, I have heard that "Mr Wallace is no more."[2] My Sister Mary is now a widow, but her circumstances are quite abundant, and she is a good manager. The remainder of the relations are well, and send much love to you! The regrets here, that you cou'd not come on to the red lands, is universal. I make every promise of a speedy visit, and appoint next March! I hope that kind Heaven [will] enable us to comply unless <u>you</u> shou'd make an <u>excuse</u> too! My dear, I hope the chills were entirely owing to the change of the Season and wou'd soon cease. Oh my love! you occupy my thoughts and my prayers! That I shou'd ever have given my thoughts to an earthly object, I did not believe even in the Halcyon days of life! That you will ever be less the object of my love I cannot—nay I will not even suppose! than what you now are. Without you I cou'd not wish to live, unless I were a hermit, that now cou'd or wou'd disturb my thoughts of you, and those hours of happiness, which I had passed with you. My heart often, and always, recurs to the scenes of the past, after hoping for the future. Only pity me, for my detention! but for my sake, do not blame me! It was love and duty to you which controlled me! My love when I can see you, and tell you all you will commend my course, and bless your husband!!!

'Tis night
thine ever
Houston

It is now monday morning, and I have come to Town to attend my duties in court. I find a press of <u>clients</u> and my answer is, "I cannot stay until court is over." These hard times, this is really <u>hard</u> upon me! My love, I care only for you. When my worldly wants are met, your comfort will constitute all that I desire. Were it not that the election was over, I shou'd not run. I can not do more, than I have done for Texas; and you wou'd be better satisfied to see me at home. Or where <u>we might choose to be</u>!!! I am happy that you apprehend the situation of our dear Mother is not comfortable. Wou'd to God that I cou'd assist her in any way. I told her of her situation, but she did not credit me! I have written to her, and told her to do as she pleased with the hands at the Point with their hire and those which she has. She cannot want for any thing, but your presence to make her happy! I feel all for the old lady that I cou'd for my blessed Parent were she living. Both wou'd be entitled to my affection and a filial duty! I will not detain here one hour, but the moment that my business is over, I will start, if it is midnight! Night brings back the memory of two sleepless nights, which have passed over me. But as you were the subject of my reflections, I do not regret the want of repose. Be you happy and I must be contented!

I am happy my Dear, that you are gratified at what Col. Butler[3] said, and the manner of it. He wrote me a long letter on that and other subjects. My love, I have seen our friend Dr. Irion & Lady[4] for a few hours, on my way here, but not since. I will see them on my way home. Mrs. Durst[5] was not able to be seen from fever or <u>something</u> else. I may write to you by private hand, but not again by mail after today, as I hope to be off before a second mail will start from this place.

I expect to reach you with all possible expedition, when I set out from this place. Until I can see you do not despair, I beseech you my dear Wife.

You may need funds, and I will do all in my power to reach you that you may want nothing. Don't regard any <u>fibs</u>, which you may hear of me! Be assured that Houston feels and remembers that <u>Margaret is his Wife</u>!!! I will obey you by writing to my brothers & Dear Sisters. I will be happy to send your love and to speak of you as I feel!

I will remember your religious admonitions, and Heaven can bear witness of my prayers for your recovery and happiness.

My love to our dear sister and the captain provided he kept his <u>promise</u> to me! Write to our mother and speak of me! Give my love to her!

Thy devoted Husband
Sam Houston

M. L. Houston

[1]Margaret's letter of September 5, 1840, has not been located.
[2]Col. Matthew Wallace was the first husband of Mary Houston. She later married his nephew, General William Wallace. Hearne Collection of Papers, San Antonio.
[3]Colonel Anthony Butler was a congressman from Washington County. For a biography see *Writings,* I, 248n.
[4]Dr. Robert and Anna Raguet Irion of San Augustine.
[5]There were several Durst families in San Augustine. This may possibly be Delilah Dill (Mrs. Joseph) Durst or Harriet Jamison (Mrs. John Durst). *Handbook of Texas,* I , 522.

Mrs. M. L. Houston
By Mr. Crawford[1]

San Augustine
3rd Oct 1840

My beloved,

Mr. Crawford will leave here tomorrow morning, and I am compelled to write on a plank in the court house. I can only say that business has detained me and may for a few days longer. A trial is now before the court of great importance, and I am the leading counsel in the case.

My love, I wou'd give millions to see you at this moment. I pray you to be assured that nothing detains me but duty to you, as well as myself. The counsel is now speaking, and I must follow—so you will excuse this note. I will not detain an hour longer than I may be compelled! My anxiety is boundless to see you. To day I had <u>two chills</u>. The weather is cold, but I will not shrink from duty, or affection. Dr. Wilson says that he will restore me perfectly, and be assured by the <u>love which I bear you</u>, that I will indulge in no shade of intemperance, and if not well the cause shall not be produced by me.

I had made arrangements about my horses! and will save myself and you a few thousand dollars!

I am almost delirious to see <u>you</u>, and again embrace <u>you</u>, with my affections! I hope to set out to see you in four days. My brain burns with pain, and the <u>fever</u> of two <u>chills</u> is upon me.

My love to Sister & Bledsoe.

Thy Husband,
Affectionately Houston

Mrs. M. Lea Houston.

Genl [James Pinckney] Henderson is sick in town but mending.
H.

[1]Houston is probably speaking of James W. Crawford of Washington County. Ray, 85.

To Mrs. Margaret L. Houston
Washington Texas
Care of Captain Bledsoe

San Augustine
4th October 1840

My dearest Margaret,

From the Post Office, I have this moment taken a letter from Capt Bledsoe dated the 13th ult.[1] I need not—I will [not] attempt to describe my feelings. He states your ill health, and that is enough to agonize me. I <u>will</u> go, and <u>see you</u>, tho' it shou'd destroy me! Every one who knows my devotion to you might be assured that nothing but imperative duty and necessity cou'd detain me one moment from you! My presence shall shew [sic] that I will pretermit both, and leave to Heaven the results. I will start and leave all my interest here to destruction and ruin. I owe you this as you are sick and cannot be impressed with my situation and business here. I was to have had a negro boy, to have taken home with me, but I must loose [sic] him and go home alone! If I can but see you, I don't regard the loss. We may get along without him, but he will be the last item of my loosings [sic]. Do not regard them as my mind is made up, and I do not wish <u>you</u> to think of them!

We have had two severe frosts here the last two nights. I have had the dumb ague, and that three times in 24 hours. I am taking medicine in hopes soon to be well. Yesterday I was engaged in an important cause, and suffering all day from the <u>chills</u> tho' of this I wrote you. This morning I am writing in a room without fire, or fire place [sic] and my hands are cold as ice. You will excuse my writing, as it is very bad, and I am not quite well, tho' not absolutely sick!

I wish to write you a thousand things, but will reserve them till we meet. Oh! Margaret, I must be unhappy until I can see you, when I hope to forget all cares! and if possible render you happy! Bledsoe thinks that I have nothing to do, but to mount my horse, to start from this section of the country. I wish that I had never left you,—I wou'd have eschewed ten thousand pangs of anguish, and wou'd have been more happy, no matter what my losses might have been!

Your peace and happiness, united with your health, are, and ought to be, the objects of my peculiar care, and solicitude. You will believe this,—but should you doubt it, I must be a miserable man! Shou'd this reach you before I can, for the sake of Heaven and our mutual felicity, be contented and cherish tranquility. If you will not, your health must suffer, and my joy will be diminished. Do pray be happy!

I am so chilly, that I can write no more. Last night I remained in town owing [to] the Jurys [sic] not coming in with a verdict. Gen'l [James Pinckney] Henderson is sick with ague. I have been to see him this morning. If I live by the 8th I will start to meet, and embrace my beloved Margaret. Make my kind love to our dear Sister, and regards to Captain Bledsoe.

Thy most devoted and affectionate Husband
Sam Houston

[1]This letter has not been located.

Chapter II

November 10, [1840]–February 3, 1841

November 10, [1840]: Margaret Houston to Sam Houston
December 3, 1840: Sam Houston to Margaret Houston
December 9, 1840: Sam Houston to Margaret Houston
December 10, 1840: Margaret Houston to Sam Houston
December 12, 1840: Sam Houston to Margaret Houston
December 14, 1840: Sam Houston to Margaret Houston
December 16, 1840: Sam Houston to Margaret Houston
December 17, 1840: Sam Houston to Margaret Houston
December 22, 1840: Sam Houston to Margaret Houston
December 24, 1840: Sam Houston to Margaret Houston
[December 25, 1840]: Sam Houston to Margaret Houston
December 31, 1840: Sam Houston to Margaret Houston
[December, 1840]: Sam Houston to Margaret Houston
January 7 and 13, 1841: Sam Houston to Margaret Houston
January 8, 1841: Sam Houston to Margaret Houston
January 12–13, 1841: Sam Houston to Margaret Houston
January 14, 1841: Sam Houston to Margaret Houston
January 16, 1841: Sam Houston to Margaret Houston
January 18, 1841: Margaret Houston to Sam Houston
January 18, 1841: Sam Houston to Margaret Houston
January 19, 1841: Sam Houston to Margaret Houston

January 22–26, 1841: Sam Houston to Margaret Houston
January 27, [1841]: Margaret Houston to Sam Houston
[January] 29, [1841]: Sam Houston to Margaret Houston
[January, 1841]: Sam Houston to Margaret Houston
January 30, 1841: Margaret Houston to Sam Houston
January 31, 1841: Sam Houston to Margaret Houston
February 1, 1841: Sam Houston to Margaret Houston
February 2, 1841: Sam Houston to Margaret Houston
February 3, 1841: Sam Houston to Margaret Houston

Houston traveled to Austin to take part in the Fifth Congress of Texas. Margaret and her mother left Grand Cane for Galveston where they would spend the winter in Nancy's rented house. Margaret wrote the following letter on the trip home.

Houston Nov. 10 [1840]
Tuesday night

My dear husband,

We arrived (Mr. Winfield's)[1] about 4 o'clock this evening. We had a pretty jolting journey, but I feel quite well after it, and not at all fatigued. We spent the first night at Mrs. Dunham's[2] who was exceedingly kind to us, so much so that I wish you always to speak in very friendly terms of the family. The old lady seems to dote on you. Last night we staid [sic] at Burnet's[3] & today came on without any accident. Capt. [John S.] Black called on us this evening. His family is in good health. Jane is mending rapidly and able to sew 2 hours each day. He says Armstrong called at his house to get directions to Cedar point, but we have heard nothing farther of him. The Capt expects to go up in a few days and he has promised me to urge you to return with him if your health continues bad. Oh what would I not give to see you! How I would throw my arms around you and tell you again and again how much I love you! My beloved take good care of yourself. <u>Remember</u> there is a heart whose every fibre is entwined around you. There is one who must live without you, or sink with you! Mother and I expect to leave on the Gen. Houston the day after tomorrow. I have no doubt we will get along very well. Philips[4] and Moreland[5] are in this place, but I have not yet made the collections. If I should fail in them and should find it necessary to make some <u>little extra preparations</u>, I suppose it would not be much amiss to extend our credit a little. However no human being can have a greater horror of it than I have, and I shall not do it unless necessity compels me. I think I shall soon have excellent health. The <u>symptoms</u> are certainly <u>very fine</u>. Oh if I could only know that your health was improving, how happy I would be! How cold and desolate is the world without you my love! Perhaps the day will soon come when dreary distance shall not thus intrude between us, but each hour shall bring its own bright joy, and day after day shall pass on and find me still with him I love, gazing fondly upon him, and listening to his soft endearing voice and—will you finish the picture love? A thousand fancies are flitting across my mind, but you will readily imagine what they are!

I have been told that several persons are expected to depart for Austin early in the morning. For that reason I thought it best to write tonight although it is getting quite late. I am writing in Mrs. Winfield's drawing room, and it is pretty much filled with company. This will account to you for the confused and hurried manner in which my letter is written. Mrs. Winfield[6] sends her compliments to you and says she has a fine looking dog called Sam Houston. Oh and it has a pretty little mate for him named Maggy.

I will write to you again by Capt Black if he goes up and I will endeavor to interest you more than I am able to do at present. Do write to me very often. It is late at night—quite late.

Farewell my best beloved.
Thy own devoted
Maggy.

P.S. Dr. Watson[7] begs to be remembered to you. Oh, if I could only see you! My love you will hear of poor Mrs. Brown's death (formerly Mrs. Mann.)[8] Mr. Winfield sends his compliments.   Maggy

P.S. My dear husband, after I finished writing to you last night, I received a letter from Young[9] containing the intelligence that Sister Royston's little Margaret Antoinette was no more. My heart is oppressed with grief and I feel as if I could scarcely bear it. Oh that you were with me! He says that Sister V[arilla] is almost broken-hearted. Mr. Bledsoe has just started to Cedar Point. He will return tomorrow.

---

[1]Edward H. Winfield was assistant quartermaster of the Texas Army, tax assessor of Harris County, and later lived in Washington County. For a biography see *Writings*, I, 402–403n, and *Handbook of Texas*, II, 923.
[2]The Dunham family resided in Montgomery County. Montgomery, 276.
[3]Matthew Burnett had a plantation on Little Cypress Creek eight miles north or Harrisburg. William Physick Zuber, *My Eighty Years in Texas*, (Austin: University of Texas Press, 1971), 80. For a history of the plantation see Max Freund, ed., *Gustav Dresel's Houston Journal*, (Austin: University of Texas Press, 1954), 162.
[4]Alexander H. Phillips, a lawyer in Galveston. For a biography see *Handbook of Texas*, II, 372.
[5]Major Isaac N. Moreland, chief justice of Harris County. See *Writings*, I, 463n.

[6]Ann Gray Vernon Winfield. For a biography see Annie Doom Pickrell, *Pioneer Women of Texas*, (Austin: The Steck Company, 1929), 108–15.

[7]Dr. Robert Watson, a surgeon in the Texas Army. See "Nomination of Eleven Government Officials," Houston to the Honorable Senate of Texas, December 5, 1837, *Writings*, II, 164.

[8]Pamelia Mann, (Mrs. T. K. Brown). Identified in Grammer, 34. She was proprietor of Mansion House in Houston. Marie Phelps McAshan, *On the Corner of Main and Texas: A Houston Legacy*, (Houston: Hutchins House, 1985), 29.

[9]Young Lea Royston, Margaret's nephew. Hearne Collection, San Antonio. For a biography see Willis Brewer, *Alabama: Her History, Resources, War Record and Public Men from 1540 to 1872*, (Spartanburg, S. C.: Reprint Company Publishers, 1975), 497.

Houston reached Austin in late November and immediately became the principal supporter of the Cherokee Bill. Adolphus Sterne described this as legislation that would have confirmed the title of lands awarded to the Cherokee Nation by the Treaty of 1836. It would ultimately be defeated. [McDonald, 19]

To Mrs. Margaret L. Houston
Galveston Texas
By Colonel T. Johnson[1]

Austin
3rd Dec 1840

My Dear Margaret,

Yours of the 14th ult. has just reached me, and I leave to your fancy to deduce the pleasure which it gave me.[2] I was in the Hall, and wou'd have made a speech today, but had two severe chills before eleven oclock, and did not feel that I cou'd do justice to the Cherokee question. Tomorrow I hope to meet it with some ability.[3] To day the House was crowded to over-flowing—Ladies and Gentlemen—Owing to circumstances I was mortified, but at the moment, I received yr letter and this to me was everything. For two mails I heard nothing of you, and really I was distressed, and pained to the heart. Now I feel happy, and write to you all that I deem interesting to you. No mortal can apprehend how much I love you, and the anxiety, which I cherish to see you. Col Johnson will start to day and is teasing me to finish my letter. All that I need assure you of is my boundless <u>love</u>!!! I note with pleasure, all the items of news which your interesting letter contains. My love preserve your health, for I regard you as the only hope or solace on earth.

You did not tell me how our excellent Mother was. Don't forget me to her. Tell Tilly[4] & [Dr. Edmund] Tucker my regards & you may salute our friends. By the next mail, I will write at length, and by every private opportunity. After yr letter was handed to me, I saw Mrs. and Colonel Flood[5]—they send great love to you, and the Madame says she will write to you this week. She will do so. The Col is cool and much respected. I feel better this evening, and hope to have no more chills. Tomorrow I must speak on the Cherokee Bill. You will hear that I have not been disgraced.

I pray you my love to be happy, and remain assured of my endless love! Bledsoe has written to me, and all well! Col Johnson can wait no longer. I can't look over my letter. Love to Mother.

Thy devoted Husband
Houston

To Margaret
P. S. Col. Johnson was elected Judge today over Tod Robinson[6] 27 to 17. Shelby[7] rec'd 1. I voted for Johnson. This is the last item of news that I recollect of.

Thine
Houston

Maggy
P.S. My letter like a Lady's is all in the P. S. Col., Mrs. Flood and my friends send a thousand kind salutations and good wishes to you. They look knowing at me. H.

---

[1]Thomas Johnson was elected judge of the first judicial district to serve a term beginning January 30, 1841. *Compiled Index to Elected and Appointed Officials of the Republic of Texas 1835–1846* , (Austin: State Archives Division, Texas State Library, 1981), 66.

[2]No letter dated November 14, 1840 has been located.

[3]For text of this speech see *Writings*, II, 354–62.

[4]Caroline Matilda Maffit (also spelled Moffitt), Margaret's friend and neighbor. Elizabeth Brooks, *Prominent Women of Texas*, (Akron: Werner Company, 1896), 22.

[5]George Flood, the United States representative to the Republic of Texas, and his wife Catherine, were close friends of the Houstons. See Houston to Mrs. George Flood, *Writings,* II, 363, and Katherine Pauls, *Gannie*, (Printed privately, n.d.). A copy is in the Barker History Center, University of Texas.

[6]A member of the House of Representatives from Brazoria. For a biography see *Handbook of Texas*, II, 491.

[7]Houston is probably referring to Anthony B. Shelby who had been elected Judge of the First Judicial District in 1839. *Writings*, IV, 430n.

Mrs. Margaret L. Houston
Galveston, Texas
Dr. E. Tucker

Austin
9th Dec 1840

My Love!

I wrote a pretty long letter to you last night.[1] To day while Mr. Kaufman[2] is speaking I must write to you. I will have to answer him. This will not give me much trouble. I have many assailants, but do not be distressed at the news! I will not be defeated. I only say this to you, that you may not be unhappy—it is not egotistical in me I hope. Dr. Tucker can tell you all the news. He has reposed with me, and will tell you that my health is improving every day. This may my dear, assure you of the falsity of idle report which may reach you! My beloved Margaret, you can have no estimation of my anxiety to embrace you. I wou'd rather be with you, than to wear a crown, or wield a sceptre without thee! To me the world wou'd be a waste and misery wou'd ensue to every hope of future felicity. My beloved I am in the midst of so much noise, that I must conclude.

My regards to Mother. My regards I pray to present to your female friends. I will speak this evening!

Thy ever devoted husband
Houston

To Margaret

[1]No letter for this date has been found.

[2]David Spangler Kaufman. Adolphus Sterne reports for this date: "Kaufman had the floor to make an eloquent speach [sic] against the Cherokee Bill." McDonald, 9.

A group of Texians commanded by Samuel Jordan had crossed the Rio Grande and joined with the Mexican forces, led by Antonio Canales, who were attempting to overthrow Santa Anna. Canales made peace with the Centralists and betrayed the Texian auxiliaries. Margaret wrote Houston on the news she had heard:

Galveston Dec. 10th [1840]

My beloved,

I can not believe that my letters will weary you, not withstanding thier frequent recurrence and thier want of variety. In my seclusion I am furnished with very few subjects except the changes of the weather (which in this place are certainly not without variety) and the simple cares and amusements of home, that home that only needs your society to make it my world. Perhaps my stock of information would not be sufficient to amuse a mere formal correspondent, but I am sure the subjects that interest me at all must interest my dear husband very much. And why should they not, for indeed I scarcely ever think of any thing unconnected with himself. The <u>great world</u> however is at this time excited on a subject of which none of us can be totally disregardless—the union of the Federal force with the Centralists. You see your predictions are verified. What do you think will be the result of the combination? Is it probable that the Mexicans will now invade Texas? I dare not suffer myself to indulge such a fear. And yet how uncertain are all our calculations. Whilst we are looking forward to the time when beneath "our own vine and fig tree" we shall rest from the cares of life and dreaming of the happiness that is to encircle our fireside, the dark clouds may be gathering at a distance that is to wreck our sweetest hopes and visions.

Yesterday a man of war[1] arrived bringing 23 of the Texians who had joined Canales[2] and retired on his union with the Centralists and also the body of our minister to Mexico who had been dead 6 days.[3] The passengers were in great distress when they arrived, being entirely out of provisions.[4] The New York also arrived yesterday and brought the news of our recognition by England. The circumstance I am told has affected a change in favour of our currency in New Orleans. Poor Texas may yet rise and occupy a stand amongst nations that even that haughty monarchy herself may envy! "the God of battles" and the "King of kings" is alone to decide. I could wish that our minds were less disturbed by political subjects and

that in some quiet spot of earth we might worship God in the simplicity of our hearts, but that God has so arranged it that even the simple joys of home are in some degree dependent on the public good and society is united by links that must be preserved invisible. Each day I miss you more and there is not a moment of the dull heavy hours that roll slowly away in which you are not present
[incomplete]

[1]The *San Antonio* under the command of Lt. Alexander Moore. *Handbook of Texas,* II, 540.

[2]Antonio Canales was against Santa Anna before the Texas Revolution, but remained neutral during the conflict. He later sponsored a "Republic of the Rio Grande" along with Zapata. Canales became a general in the Mexican Army after he joined forces with Santa Anna. *Handbook of Texas,* III, 141.

[3]James Treat, who died on board of consumption on November 30, 1840. *Handbook of Texas,* I , 798. See also *Telegraph and Texas Register*, December 16, 1840.

[4]For Houston's account of this incident see his speech made to the U. S. Senate, August 8, 1850. *Writings,* V, 212–14.

Mrs. Margaret L. Houston
Galveston Texas
Care of Col Wilson[1]

Austin
12 Dec. 1840

My dearly beloved,

Some days have elapsed since I wrote to you. The reason was, that I had no opportunity to send my letters, and I will add another reason. Mr. Mayfield[2] made a speech of three days and to day I replied for some three hours.[3] To speak of my own acts to you, my dear, by letter I will not, but Mrs. Flood and Col who were present, and formed a part of a crowded auditory say they will tell you all about the matter. She was kind enough to say that you wou'd have been much gratified, and because you were not present she rejoiced for you. I was pretty well satisfied with myself. The main reason was, that I was labouring for the interest of my country. Oh my dear Wife! The only pleasure that I have is to peruse your letters! again and again. You will believe this when I tell you, that all my evenings and nights, are passed in my room! To be sure I have much company, but they are sober men, and my room is a dry one, for there is [sic] no spirits in it.

Mr. Wilson has roomed with me, and by him, I send this letter! He can tell you of the painful anxiety I feel to meet you, and to remain with you! I can not be cheerful, nor happy, until I see you! I even envy poor "sis" the privilidge [sic] which she has of saluting you with affection. Excuse me my love, for such trifles! They are <u>truths</u>, as well as trifles. When I can see you, I will have much to tell you of, and it will amuse you, if it shou'd not edify you! To day I quoted you in my speech—but I did not give the author! Not that I did not deem it <u>high authority</u>! I will write by every opportunity, until I can set out to embrace you, my <u>beloved</u>! My health I hope will soon be fine, and when we meet, that you will find me in health. If you chuse [sic] to stay at the Island, I pray you do so. You will gratify me! My love to my dear Mother! Salute our friends and I pray you to accept my tenderest and most devoted love!

Thy husband
Houston

Margaret

I know nothing of the contents of this letter, but take the liberty of saluting you, my dear Madame, as a brother.

Hockley[4]

The General writes with a bad pen.

[1]Possibly Robert Wilson, an associate of the Allen brothers of Houston. For a biography see *Handbook of Texas*, II, 921–22.
[2]James Mayfield, a representative from Nacogdoches and Secretary of State under Lamar. See *Handbook of Texas, II*, 164. Adolphus Sterne reported that Mayfield spoke for three days against the Cherokee Bill. McDonald, 20.
[3]A copy of Houston's speech has not been located.
[4]George W. Hockley, a long time friend of Houston's who served as his chief of staff at San Jacinto and later as Secretary of War. For a biography see *Writings*, I , 331–32n and Dixon and Kemp, 73–75.

Austin
14th Dec. 1840

My Love,

Col. Wilson did not depart so soon as he intended. Sunday passed and in the evening, I visited Col & Mrs Flood, and passed a short time. I like to be there because they talk of you; and that pleases me. I let the Madame read some of your letters. She praises them very much, and says that I must be happy! "How generous we can be when it costs us nothing." This is the quotation used in my speech, and as the Madame and Col had read it, they understood it and smiled! Oh How happy I wou'd be cou'd I pass but one day with my dear Maggy. I wou'd know that she was well, if it were so, and if not well, I cou'd minister to her in sickness. Oh how tenderly I do love!!! Tho' I have not expressed to you the pleasure which I felt, at hearing that the <u>tumour</u> was disappearing. I never the less felt the highest gratifications—I knew that it would relieve your feelings, and rid you of many unhappy cares. Again it seemed to indicate that my predictions in relation to contingencies touching <u>the future</u> were verified. Do you take? They are talking on the floor and it confuses me a little! as I have a slight pain in my head. I have caught cold, tho' it is trifling.

I pray Kind Heaven to preserve you in the most perfect health, and joyous felicity. When I can meet you, as the Frenchman said, "I will die so appy." I have not indulged in the relation of anecdotes! I used two in my speech the other day with fine effect! and mortified two gentlemen at the expression of a hardy laugh to all present.

One was the "Buck" that "jumped so high," and the other was the "old wastnesses [sic]." One I applied to Mr Vanzandt,[1] and the other was applied to Mr Mayfield. I told a pig story that produced much excitement among <u>some people</u>. "Wounded pigeons will flutter." They had assailed me for several days, and I sat, and calmly looked on without emotion. They have felt the lash and will do so, whenever they call upon me in debate! One matter you wish to learn and that is as to what my course will be in relation to <u>certain</u> Great Matters. I have for the sake of my country, concluded to run for the Presidency, "provided always" that you cheerfully concur in the measure! If not, you have only to say so! The country is in a deplorable state. Lamar[2] has obtained leave of absence to visit the States! Burnet and he 'tis said, have quarreled and Burnet[3] says he will resign— <u>'tis a consummation most devotedly to be wished</u>, for our Country—Dr. Jones[4] who is protem President of the Senate wou'd be President de facto. He is a Gentleman of high intelligence, and worth, and is an able statesman!

Mrs. Flood the other day, said to me, Gen'l Houston, you have a noble wife, and highly ambitious. I replied "oh no. You don't think so Madame." "Oh yes indeed" said she—so I said I had been as fortunate as my friend Col Flood. She laughed heartily. Maggy she may have guessed well! Don't deem me as reproaching you, my love, for if you were to confess the charge, I wou'd not love you less! But you will become weary of reading my tedious epistles.

I hope Martin, Young & Vernal have all reached you ire [sic] now. Col and Mrs Flood, and the little one send you much love; and all my particular friends wish to be remembered to you!

Thy devoted husband
Houston

Margaret

[1]Isaac Van Zandt, representative from Marshall. For a biography see *Writings*, III , 113–14n and *Handbook of Texas*, II , 882. For an account of this anecdote see Alfred M. Williams, *Sam Houston and the War of Independence in Texas*, (Boston: Houghton, Mifflin and Company, 1893), 256–57.

[2]President Mirabeau B. Lamar was ill had and traveled to the United States for medical treatment. Llerena Friend, *Sam Houston: The Great Designer*, (Austin: University of Texas Press, 1954), 100.

[3]During Lamar's absence, vice-president David G. Burnet was in charge of the government. Ibid.

[4]Dr. Anson Jones.

Austin
16th Dec 1840

My Love,

Last evening I was sorely disappointed by learning that Mr. Case[1] from Galveston had arrived with a letter from you. I found him. He handed me four letters, but not one from my beloved Wife! I soon met a gentleman who had seen you at a party at Mrs Maffets[2] [sic]. I asked him if you were well and cheerful, when [he] replied you were! I ask him how our Mother was? He said she was not there!! I asked no other question! Neither as to the duration of the Party or its extent. Nor did I ask who had waited upon! You had told me that you would pay one visit there in company with Mother. This was after a free conversation touching Mrs. M. I was somewhat surprised but did not censure you! I was depressed that night. I had a painful illness—but today I attended the house as usual. It was not the news that produced my illness, my stomach was affected by eating half cooked beets! Not able to sleep, thro' my window I beheld the solitary moon coursing thro' the sweet Heavens. I gazed upon it with melancholy pleasure! I contemplated the blue canopy, and smiled upon the bright stars! (for <u>you know why I love them</u>)!! Tho' variant in a magnitude, they all presented the purest lustre and oh! how my bosom swelled, in view of the rich constellation! I said in my spirit such is the pure association in which the Wife of Houston should appear!! His beloved, and adorable Margaret!! Do you remember the advice of Napoleon to his wife? I love you more than he ever cou'd love Josephine! You are to me the beacon light of happiness!!! You are a talisman of life to me! and I cherish you, in my very hearts core!

But enough of this—I do not desire that you shou'd become a recluse. No my love, such is not my wish. I wish you to be happy, to be cheerful, and to recreate yourself! This will conduce to health and health will give felicity! Oh my dear Maggy, you can fancy nothing of the anxiety which I feel for you. To me, <u>you</u> are a "good thing."

On yesterday I was dared to become a candidate for the Presidency, when met the challange [sic] with a most peremptory, and emphatic assurance that "I wou'd"—at the same time making to myself mental reservations, (if you are willing). Do not let what I have said induce you to yield any objections, which you may entertain. For myself, I have flung away ambition. I wish to retire to quiet and rural life, where I can <u>live</u> and <u>love</u> my dear, dear <u>Margaret</u>! These I look to as days of bliss, of joy, of happiness to us! We can't in this vale of sorrow escape the cares of life. Retirement is the place of holiness and suited to the contemplation of eternal hopes & joys. I pray that God may render us a pious, and holy pair. I sometimes fear, that you will be very unhappy because I am not religious. Remember thy people are my people, and thy God is my God. I seek religion, and my heart is disposed to revere our God, but it is not <u>received</u>. Not to Heaven, nor you, can it ever be <u>deceitful</u>. Cou'd you witness its constant recurrence to you, you never wou'd doubt my idoltry [sic]! My regards and thanks to our dear Mother!

Thy constant and thy most devoted husband
Houston

Margaret

[1]Probably Joel Titus Case, editor of the *Daily Courier.* For a biography see *Handbook of Texas,* I, 305.
[2]Mrs. John Newland (Anne Carnic) Maffitt (sometimes spelled Moffitt), the mother of twin daughters Tilly and Henrietta Maffitt. Mrs. Maffitt operated a boarding house in Galveston. Philip Graham, *The Life and Poems of Mirabeau Bonaparte Lamar,* (Chapel Hill: University of North Carolina Press, 1938), 49. For more information about this family see Brooks, 22–24.

Mrs. Margaret L. Houston
Galveston Texas

Austin
17th Dec 1840

Oh my dear Margaret, how happy I was on last evening by the receipt of your valued letter of the 7th inst.[1] I had been depressed, but your letter again revived me; nor wou'd I feel the reality until I had thrice perused it. Now I am happy, and tho' depressed, I will tell you that yesterday or rather To day, was the first time that I had walked up Capitol Hill without the arm of a friend. To day I ascended it without much fatigue, and felt that I will be well! You can sustain me, my only beloved! You can preserve! You are my life, and love, as I have suggested. Oh I feel that my spirit is revived within me by your letter. The pious and sweet christian spirit, which your letter breathes almost persuades me to be a Christian. (Wou'd to Heaven, I were one). Hear me, my love!!! A Rev'd Mr. Richardson,[2] pastor Rutersville church and chaplain of the Senate, met a friend of mine a few miles from this place on his way "to conference," and asked him as to my health—He indicated some <u>mystery</u> by his looks. My friend asked him if I was regular? and when I left town, I saw him sitting with some persons on a log, and seemed soberer than I had before seen him. Now when I have laid my hand upon his head, and he knew [what] he stated was untrue! But I will explain the matter for your satisfaction. He knew that I had a Baptist wife, and the Methodist wish to obtain an unconstitutional charter for Rutersville College. He and I voted to lay it on the table. This was my offence [sic]! Shou'd it again come up, I will take a stand! The object was to choke all other religions! Now! Tho' you will say you care nothing about these matters, yet you must feel I am the husband of a proud and generous and noble woman! Yet she is woman!!! Adorable! I am in the House writing and a constant noise. I am compelled to write to you! I have discovered a green flower, and as it represents our national emblem, and one that I trust you & I will always love—one to which you have so freely alluded, I will send you many for yourself, and special friends have handed one to Madame Flood. 'Tis the star flower. I found it in my friend [George] Hockleys lot—I think pretty, or I wou'd not send it to my Margaret! You will deem it pretty I am sure! But shou'd you not, you will appreciate the tribute of a devoted heart! It is a trifle Margaret, but it brings back to my heart, past happy hours!

My love, I do not know that I can write you any thing more— and I felt well assured that [you] must be weary, and tho' I will not close my letter until some messenger may leave, you may therefore be teased, by some additions. But in this my love, you must bear with me! I only feel happy when I am reading your letters, or writing my poor epistles to you! I hope ire [sic] this Martin [Lea] and our friends are with you! I too can realise your happiness & our Mothers at their arrival. I will send you some scraps of papers & a letter from our brother Henry—It is old, but you will wish to see it! Our sister S[erena] is not well, but I hope her affliction is not and will not be mortal.

Ladies are liable to qualms and toothaches!

I hope when the spring renders its mild and genial influences, that many blessings will return, or come with it! Oh how tender are the anticipations of future hopes and joys, and little cares!!

18th Dec

To day only renews my anxiety to commune with you, or if possible to be with you! Last evening I sat with Col & Madame Flood until ten o clock,—then retired to my room. To day, you can hear about the streets, that "Gen'l Houston was in a spree last night!" This has often been the case when "Sam Houston" was in his bed. There are two Gen'l Houstons or Hustons[3] here. My shoulders are very broad, and such reports I condemn and defy the authors! Thus wags the world! I only apprehend, that my dear Margaret may feel mortified shou'd such reports reach her ears.

But by this time, my dear Wife shou'd know that there are motives for abusing! Had this not been my fortune thro' life, I had never been in Mobile and of course I wou'd not have had the felicity of seeing my dearly beloved Margaret! 'Twas a wish to let the world see that I was slandered which took me to the U S, when I learned from you, to love the bright star of evening. Oh! How bright and beautifully did it shine on last night! I contemplated its purity and fancied that I again felt your gentle pressure upon my right arm! But when I was wraped [sic] in thought, and my soul was all fire, I realized that I was far distant from my loved Margaret! I hate this common world, and only wish that I cou'd enjoy a world where you wou'd be the bright, and only orb to which my eye wou'd turn, and upon which I wou'd gaze and be happy! The day may yet come, when I will be happy. To that time I often cast the light of my spirit, and when the intensity of hope directs me to the future, I embrace Margaret as the only one who is to minister to the bliss which I anticipate.

My dear I always write in the Hall, for indeed I can not write in my room, as it is a thor'ofare [sic] when I am in it. Therefore you will excuse the confused manner of my diction! A constant prating is going on, and my ears are deafened by nonsense, and sound without reason. I must close, as my intention was not to write a book, but to write a letter, and I am sure you will be weary, ire you have read this long, very long letter!

Thy devoted husband
Houston

Margaret

[On envelope] Very [blurred] love and going to church. Thy devoted H.

---

[1]This letter is reported to be part of the Franklin Williams Collection, but the original has not been located. For excerpts from this letter see William Seale, *Sam Houston's Wife,* (Norman, Oklahoma: University of Oklahoma Press, 1970), 45, 47, 50.
[2]The Reverend Chauncey Richardson. For a biography see *Handbook of Texas,* II, 469.

Mrs. Margaret L Houston
Galveston Texas

Austin
22nd Dec 1840

My dear,

To day I was to have spoken on the great land Bill, but when I came to the House, I found that I had a slight <u>chill</u>,—not severe, but such as to prevent me from debate. I am greatly improved, in my general health, and hope soon to be in better health than you have known me to enjoy. My love, your favour of the 12th inst[1] came to me pleasant & mild as the dews on Heaven. I felt some little regret, as you were not well, but as you said that your illness was not serious, but to be "expected," I felt not so much distressed as I otherwise wou'd have done. The fever is now abating, and I feel better than I have done for days. Oh my Love, if I cou'd only be in your presence, and feel that you pillowed my head, how happy I shou'd be. Yes, when I am with you, I must be happy—I must think myself well!! Where you are not—I feel as though I were in a world without a <u>sun</u>! With you, I hope one day to realize that you are with me, and a <u>Son</u>! I let Madame Flood read your last letter and she was very "appie." They are all well! Mrs. B.[2] I have seen for the last ten days. I do not know how she gets on with her Beaus, but suppose very well! Your pretty little friends the Miss Lees[3] I am told are well. I have never yet been to see them! They stand very fair in society. I have promised to visit them, but to be candid with you my love, I feel unhappy to see females where you are not. You are the only being that I wish to see on this earth. Oh my love, when we meet how happy I will be, when telling you all that I feel, and think of you!

Owing to some matters, I feel much discontent, and may abandon some of my views expressed to you. I am well assured of one thing, and that is that I can never be happy, only when I am with my beloved Margaret!!! Oh how rich wou'd be my joys and happiness cou'd I only enjoy your society. Then indeed, I wou'd feel that I was more than compensated for all my cares & privations. I detest my present condition, and will get rid of it so soon as possible.

I find that all my thoughts, my wishes, and future joys are all centered in you and incidents connected with you!

My Love, when we can be settled on Cedar Point,[4] or Liddesdale, we can be happy. I will unite with you, when you will invoke the blessings of Heaven! I will not allow myself to act in any manner which can distress or torture my beloved Wife!

From day to day, I read and peruse your letters. They are to me a solace, and when I peruse them, I feel, at moments, as tho' I were in sweet communion with you; and heard my Margarets voice. Then I feel again, that I am far distant from the spirit of my earthly hopes! I can not & will not, stay one hour longer than I can avoid. My love, I will fly to you, as the weary dove wou'd return to the Ark of old, when it was wearied and desired rest! Such my love, is the condition of my devoted heart. I fear my love, that I have acted in Texas to little advantage, and that I will have to surrender it, in its present crisis. I love my adopted country. I have periled life for it, but I fear it will be unavailing, and I must look for some new abode—some resting place!

To see men in Congress, who have not been in the country for one year, and they assume to become law givers distresses me! The Sages of antiquity dictated wisdom, and young men listen to the wisdom of others. As it now is the young men governed by passion, decide according to feeling, to interest, and to passion. If I can not send this letter until Lt. Moore[5] leaves, I will amend it—as perhaps I may have something new to write. But my love, I pray that you will not allow yourself to want any thing—no matter whether it is necessary or not. Do you commend it, whether it is necessary or fanciful. I wou'd hate myself if the wife of Houston desired any thing and cou'd not realize, and enjoy it. My love, I will never leave you again. I will truly abandon all the things but Margaret. When we can be at home with our stock—our poultry, and such <u>little matters, as we may claim our peculiar care</u>! I trust we will [be] happy! Then I can feel that I am happy, and sustained by the wisdom and advice of my dear Margaret. Yes! her advice is always to me, a subject of gratification, and I truly trust in Heaven, that it may be a light to my path, and a lamp to my out going!

I always write so much, that I am fearful that you will be weary, and the reason is that my letters are so vapid! The intention, you will appreciate, 'tis simply, that I am communing with my beloved Wife!

23rd Dec. 1840

My dear,—the Bill on which I expected to speak has not yet been considered and therefore I have not spoken. The House is now engaged in post office matters—a dry business! I will send you the last paper.

Some correspondent here in writing to the Houston Star has taken upon him to abuse me in unmeasured terms. On my own account, I do not care for any thing that may be written, or said—But my dear, I regret it on your account—if it shou'd reach you. Tho' you are the wife of a politician, if not a great man! You may suppose that I really do feel on my own account. This wou'd be erronious [sic] conclusions!

You write to me dear of war!!! This is produced by "panic makers" and men who want places! The battle of San Jacinto must be rivalled [sic], and Honor stalk abroad in uniform. This has produced the <u>fever</u>, but we will never be invaded by a force from Mexico that will penetrate our country! 'Tis idle to think of it! If we have to fight, we can always <u>drub</u> them when they come to us. We are too poor to invade a nation, but we are able to defend our soil when we are assailed—It wou'd require $5,000,000 of par funds to fit out an expedition of 5000 men, and less than that wou'd be useless. We shou'd be wise and prudent. The nation is now involved to an immense extent!

I am now in the House of Congress, and Col Flood is at my right shoulder—He is very well, and to day Madame Flood requested me to present her affectionately to you! The Col, with his usual politeness bids me to commend him kindly to you! The family are all well and happy. They have not yet taken a house, for none can be obtained! The houses here are miserable shanties! I am happy that you did not come to this wretched place!

To day I had a very slight chill, and feel well. I have taken medicine, but not calomel! Cou'd I only be at home with my dear, dear Margaret, I wou'd be well because I wou'd be happy!

I wou'd [be] glad to send you some trifle as a memento, but it is so destitute of every [torn . . .] it does not contain many men in whom the people have confidence. I can live a part from the world, or rather have with my dear Maggy, a world of my own! If spared by Heaven, I have much to meditate upon and review of the past. I have much to write, and many errors to correct, if a true history shou'd ever be written of the events of the war of the Texian Revolution. This Love, concerns you as much as it [does] my self and shou'd it not be possible for me to accomplish it, and I should omit it, my friends ought not to excuse me. Shou'd I be detained longer than the first of Feby, I will write you every day! Gentlemen, who sit near me say that if I love my country as well as I do my wife, that I wou'd be the best patriot on earth. This is pretty true! Don't you think so Maggy? [incomplete]

[1] This letter has not been located.

[2] Houston is probably referring to an actress, Mrs. Emma Barker. See Marquis James, *The Raven*, (New York City: Blue Ribbon Books, 1929), 301 and Mrs. Dilrue Harris, "Reminiscences," *Southwestern Historical Quarterly*, 7(January 1904): 215. Adolphus Sterne speaks of Mrs. Barker furnishing the vocal music for the Ball of the Masonic Fraternity. McDonald, 75.

[3] Lydia and Julia Lee were on the ship that brought Margaret to Texas. For biographies of the Lee sisters see Pickrell, 304–12.

[4] Houston was building a home on Cedar Point across the bay from Galveston. His neighbor, James Morgan, described the house as "truly a log cabin of one room about 14 feet square." Feris A. Bass, Jr., and B. R. Brunson, eds., *Fragile Empire: The Texas Correspondence of Samuel Swartout and James Morgan,* (Austin: Shoal Creek Publishers Inc., 1978), 13.

[5] Houston is probably referring to Lt. Alexander Moore.

Austin
24 Dec 1840

My Love,

Last night, I closed my letters to you, expecting that Lt Moore wou'd start this morning. As he will not I can write again, but I have but little to write. Tomorrow will be Christmas, but I am willing to attend to business and not adjourn over. It will be the first time in my life that I have done so. The reason is obvious. I wish to see my dear Wife and every day that I am detained by any means, seems to me an age. For this reason I am willing to sit night and day in this house until we can adjourn, and until I can embrace my beloved Maggy!! Every day only increases my disgust with the associations which surround me, and the duties which devolve upon me.

You can have no idea of my wishes on the subject of being with you. Then you will no longer be annoyed by reports about me. You will see me, and can better judge of me. In your <u>situation</u>, my love, I feel the most intense anxiety to be with you, and sustain you! I can fancy your situation, and I apprehend that you must feel great depression, and were I present I cou'd cheer you to some extent. I cou'd amuse you, by the relation of incidents which have occured [sic] since we parted. They are all moral and sinless! These will amuse you,—I fear that [you] think of me my love, as one whose mind is not sufficiently pure, to combine with your spirit. My love, shou'd we live [to] meet again, I will try and accomodate [sic] myself to your happiness and never to cause you unhappiness, or solicitude as to the acts of my life.

I feel to day, that my inclination, and perhaps my duty, wou'd induce me to leave this place and fly to the smiles and the bosom of my dearly beloved Margaret.

I have not told you that Tilly [Matilda Maffitt] and Judge [Robert Dabney] Johnson had written to me a letter, but I have not answered it. You will have the goodness to commend me to them as well as my other friends! Tell Tilly that I will write to her, so soon as <u>you</u> write me leave to do so! To be candid, I wish to write to no one, but my dear Maggy! To her my entire affections cling! Yes, she is the very spirit, which animates and cheers me! She is the genius of my dreams—They embrace her presence! The frequency of my letters, and their great length will satisfy you, of my feelings & devotion.

The house is about to adjourn, and I will close this letter. Adieu my love!

Houston

Mrs. Margaret Lea Houston
Galveston Texas
Lt Moore

[December 25, 1840]
Austin, Texas

My dear Margaret,

This is Christmas night. To day I was at Church. I waited upon Madame Flood, and M. Saligny[1] was one of the party. This was my only act of Gallantry. I regard this lady most kindly because after sitting until the time of repose, she will kindly say to me, "Gen'l Houston, do not go out to night." This is what you wou'd say to me—this is what my sisters would say! Therefore "I <u>affection</u> her," and her many other virtues! An excellent Mother—a devoted Wife, a generous friend, and a pure Christian. I am happy that you place me under her control! I need a guardian Genius to govern me, and by your mandate I will submit to her Ladyships rule and orders. I wish you my dear Margaret to write to the madame often. When you do I will hear of you and be happy. My love, I can only be happy when I hear from you or of you. My <u>love</u>! I only regret the hours tedious, dull, and hateful, when I see the possibility of being detained from you!

My friend (on battlefields) Dick Scurry is at my elbow and he bids me to salute you, with his kind respects. My friends all command me to render you the salutations of the <u>Season</u>!

My love, I present the wishes of my heart for many, happy Christmas, and new years.

My love, thy devoted husband
Houston

To Mrs M L Houston

P.S. My regards to Mother, and shou'd Martin, Vernal, and Young arrive, salute them kindly for me. Houston
I have opened this, as it is now the 26th Dec and all is well! God Bless thee, my dear Maggy.
Houston

[1]Alphonse de Saligny, the French minister to the Republic of Texas. For a biography see *Writings*, III, 65–66n.

31st Dec 1840

Mrs Houston
Galveston Texas

My Love

I have no letter paper, on which to write you! You in part realize the poverty of the country! I have told you something of this before! This is most distressing to the heart of a Patriot.

My love, your letter with its <u>interesting envelope</u> has just reached me, and you can not fancy the pleasure which I enjoyed in the perusal of your highly interesting epistles. Mrs. Flood had rec'd her letters hours before I rec'd yours. She was kind enough to send it to me by the Colonel! Oh it was a pretty letter! I met the Sargt at Arms to day and when he gave me your letters, I was "so appie."

Bishop Timon[1] left here to day and by him I sent a note (introductory) and a News Paper. You will be amused at the various slanders against me. My dear, dear Maggy, I wou'd not write to you so often as I do, were it not for two reasons. One is that my love can only be gratified by communing with you!! This is the first and most <u>important</u>, consideration. The next is that you may or might suppose that I was in a "<u>spree</u>" and could not write you my affection every moment of my time.

Margaret! 'Tis a sourse [sic] of great distress to me, that you may hear so many <u>fibs</u> upon me! that you will, in your present situation be distressed, and it may influence your happiness. By and bye your letter and its enclosure I hand it over to Mrs Flood to peruse. This I know was a great treason against you, but 'tis done, and you will forgive me, I know! 'Twas family matters I know, but she is a capital mother, and you will excuse me! or at best <u>pardon me</u>.

Your letter to Mrs Flood was deemed so fine and beautiful, that many of the most intelligent have seen it as a specimen of the excellent epistolary correspondence. I deem in very fine! But of this I need say nothing, for whatever my dear Maggy does, it is excellent in the eyes of her devoted husband—i.e. If he has eyes? for 'tis said <u>love</u> is "blind." Oh my dear Wife! if I cou'd only be with you I wou'd be the happiest of men, yes, of mortals.

I am in the Hall, and I can hear Bob Potter[2] (the infamous) abusing me in the Senate! It does not distress me, my love, because infamy can never reach the moral elevation of <u>honor or honesty</u>. The news of "Genl Green,"[3] I am happy to say to you is not true. He is here, and wishes to be Minister to Spain! Poor puppy!! I wou'd pity him if I did not dispise [sic] him! His intellectual and moral qualities debase him so much, that I cannot think of him!

This is a place, that will afford no news to interest to you! I am sorry for this, but sorrow never yet supplied a defect in happiness.

13th Jany. Until to day, I wou'd not close this letter, tho it is of old date—we had <u>no mail</u>, and if things keep on a short time, we will have no <u>Males</u> in the country!! 'Tis 8 oclock PM and we are in secession—doing no good but wasting candles, without credit to buy more when they are burned out!

I can tell you no news.

Thy ever devoted husband
Houston

Margaret Lea Houston

[On the outside] Our excellent friend Hockley, & fifty others pray to be presented to you!

Thine
Houston

[1]Bishop John Timon, sent to Texas by the Catholic Bishop of New Orleans in 1839, was often invited to speak at the capital. Hogan, 203.
[2]Robert Potter, Senator from the Red River District and Secretary of the Navy. For a biography see *Writings,* I , 441–42n.
[3]Thomas Jefferson Green, a brigadier general in the Texas Army. For a biography see *Writings,* I , 515n and *Handbook of Texas,* I , 738.

This letter was not dated but it was written by Houston to Margaret when he was in Austin serving as a member of the Congress of the Republic of Texas circa December, 1840.

As it is not time for me to retire to repose, I will just write as much as I please. I do this because persons will talk less to me, knowing that I am writing to you, than if I were idle, and I can think of you as much as I may chuse! As I may write of everything, I will tell you what I have of Mrs. Barker every day from some beau of hers. She is said to be gay and much admired. I reckon she is a good woman, but too thoughtless from what I learn. I say this much only. I hear nothing culpable in her conduct. That she wou'd fancy to marry, I have no doubt! This you know my Love, wou'd be reasonable—for a lone woman is <u>very lonely</u>. Perhaps she is the black eyed Lady that you saw in the cards. I told Mrs. Flood what you said on that subject, and about the black eyes. Then for the first time I learned that Mrs. B's eyes were black, so you will not suppose that I was <u>ogling</u> with her Ladyship.—If I had, I wou'd have discovered the difference between blue and black eyes.—For the first glance that I ever cast upon you, I knew the colour of your eyes! Yes, I found there attractions that Madam cou'd never present to my prudent affections! Enough of this. I hope she will do well! I do not think that she visits Mrs. Flood often, tho' I think the Madam F. thinks well of her!

The Miss Lee's are the prettiest Ladies that I have seen here! I promised to go and visit them, but have not done so. I think they are provoked at me! I guess it will not be in my power to see them, previous to my leaving Austin, as I hope my stay will be short. I saw them when I was speaking, but I did not approach them when I ceased. I do not know a half dozen of ladies in the city. 'Tis enough, as I cou'd not, by any means, play the beau with them. They will lose nothing by the want of my attentions, as I cou'd not make love to them, tho' even if you shou'd never find out my address to them! I suppose I might say some very civil things to them, but I have thought that I had exhausted all my rhetoric of love in courting you.—At all events, I have used none since! Yes, I have. I have courted you ever since, and wish very much to make my personal address to you again. Oh the beautiful "soft things" that I purpose to say to you will make you smile very prettily! You will think that you are again a Belle!!! <u>You</u> are <u>my</u> Belle of all events, and I assure you my feelings are more tender, and my admiration as vivid as it was the first evening that we met at Sommerville.[1] These were days of vast idleness and dissipation, but they were to me days of hope and happiness. 'Twas there, I saw, admired, and loved my Margaret. Our meeting, our jesting, our promenade, our converse, our gazing on the "Lone star," my confession and the <u>seal</u> of my <u>penitence</u>!!! Then our walk to the flower Garden. Our walks in Bledsoe's Garden—Oh my Love to all those scenes I recur with extatic [sic] pleasure. You too, may sometimes think upon those days with pleasure and delight! We may yet enjoy days, if not as well they may be equally pleasing to us <u>mutually</u>!!!

You see my Love, that I am really in love yet! Yes, I am constrained to love either by nature, or the force of circumstances. I feel that I am not to blame for Oh I have a <u>very fair apology</u> for loving! Don't you think so Maggy? Do you take?

My love, I showed your poetry to a special friend who was greatly pleased with it. I deem myself greatly your debtor for the compliment. I taxed my muse, but it was all in vain—I cou'd not stir up my Pegasus; horses are very poor here! and to that I wou'd have you ascribe my failure! But I know you will prefer that I shou'd write prose—because I am always prosing when I write!

My love, I embrace you, but hope soon to clasp you to my heart! and press you there continually. Salute all that we are in duty bound to regard.

Most tenderly thy husband

Margaret

[1]This passage refers to the night Houston and Margaret met, on May 31, 1839, at the home of Martin Lea in Sommerville, Alabama, and to later visits to the home of William Bledsoe in Mobile, Alabama. See Roberts, 18–19.

Austin, 7th Jany 1841

Oh my beloved,

Happy was I last night when Major Neighbors[1] called upon me with your "Christmas Gift"[2]—met me in a sad and sorry moment, but bro't to me a balm! Yes a balm that all the spices of Arabia cou'd not combine. I had been gloomy from the fact that we have no mails, and I had lost all hope of intelligence from my beloved Margaret. Dear Spirit, how much I had reflected on your situation and upon my own—A being that I loved so much might not be well, and languishing on a sick bed and none to watch her heaving heart and minister to her situation and mitigate her anguish! This I fancied that I cou'd do to some extent, were I with her! By your dear letter I was advised that you were not well, but not dangerous! Even this gave me some relief, tho very imperfect, I must confess to you! My prospect [is] of remaining here, until the last of the present month. It may be that I will be detained here until the 6th or 7th Poximo! [sic]

Therefore you may well judge of my misery of heart, at the anticipation of happiness defered [sic]!

How fondly wou'd I fly to you, were it not that duty detains me, and were I to leave I might be regarded as a deserter from the interest of my country! This I do not wish to do. Nor to incur a charge that wou'd wound the feelings of a friend! [torn] dear Wife will appreciate most [torn] none cou'd more properly do so. I wrote by the last opportunity that [was] offered to me, and have had a letter written on my table for several days!

[At the end of this letter, on the same page, Houston wrote the following:]

13th Jany 41

About to seal this letter with the balance of my many incongruous Epistles which I send you. I must express my happiness at learning this moment, that Vernal has reached Galveston. At this I am rejoiced because you and our dear Mother will be so happy!

I beg you to salute him, with my great affection, and say that I will be proud to meet him. What about his pretty "Flame" of which we have heard! I suppose there was some flirtation in this business. No matter. 'Tis well enough and he is of age! I wou'd like to hear our dear Mother catecize [sic] Vernal on the subject of his "love scrape"! The Old Lady will look grave and solemn on the occasion! It will not only be as to the past and present, but she will cast an eye to the future! Oh how happy I wou'd be, to join the little circle, and be happy with my wife, my Mother, & my Brother.

Thy ever devoted husband
Houston

Margaret

[1]Probably Robert Simpson Neighbors, quartermaster of the Texas Army. For a biography see *Writings,* V , 165–67.
[2]No letter from Margaret dated December 25, 1840, has been located.

Austin 8th Jany 1841

Dear Margaret,

Having written a part of two letters, I must commence a third one because I had no opportunity to send them to you. In a few days I expect to have an opportunity to forward all my communications by Maj. Zavala.[1] This you will see in the 8th of Jany, a "National day" of the U.S.[2] Hence at 12 o clock Col Flood gave a Wine Party. I was there, and gave my salutations to Madam Flood by drinking a single glass of wine! This was due and Houston was not forgotten on the occasion! But, I was not happy! The company was mixed!! I thought of you my love! and you were distant, far distant from the eyes and arms of Houston.—not distant from his heart, for every thought of you swells my bosom with warmest emotions!

So soon as I came to the hall at 3 oclok just before the House met, I witnessed a fight which took place between a senator and member of the House! They were parted by other members! No great damage was done! 'Twas the wine of Col Flood, I presume that produced it in part! I hope never again to witness such another scene!

Oh! but I am weary of public life. How hateful are even its honors! I feel my love, that I can only be happy when I will be with you. I feel my only love, as tho I cou'd only be calm, intelligent and happy when I cou'd hear your voice and enjoy the admonition of your wisdom! I wou'd then be a rational, cheerful, and happy man. Our time woud [sic] pass in rational conversations, in reading, and in exercise! There are days, and years, to which I cast the vision of my spirits. You too my love, I feel assured, look to them with intense interest!

I have not for two weeks seen the fair Mrs. [Emma] B[arker], nor do I expect to see her before I leave this horrible place! I do fondly look to the day when I can embrace the only object of my affection!

13th Jany

I wou'd not close my letter until I might have an opportunity to send it with others to you!

Thy devoted husband
Houston

Margaret

[1]Lorenzo de Zavala, Jr., who took part in the Battle of San Jacinto and acted as an interpreter between Santa Anna and Houston. John Henry Brown, *Indian Wars and Pioneers of Texas*, (Austin: L. E. Daniell Publishers, 1880), 127.

[2] Houston may be referring to the fact that in many places January 8 was celebrated

in honor of Andrew Jackson's victory at New Orleans in the War of 1812. It was also celebrated as the anniversary of the Democratic National Committee. Jane M. Hatch, *The American Book of Days*, (New York: H. W. Wilson Company, 1978), 49–51.

Austin, 12th Jany 1841

My dear Margaret,

Today I am in the Hall, and in better health than usual. To hear all the fearful talks of <u>war</u> wou'd make the sweet blood of your gentle heart curdle, and run chills thro' your veins. You need be under no apprehension, my love, of invasion. If your chevalliers [sic] chuse to make war upon Mexico, they may do so, but they will have more to repent of than to cheer themselves with!

Panic makers are to be found in every country. They now exist in Texas & are in full meridian and beaming splendor. Men who want places and have not got them wou'd move Heaven and Earth to create and occupy them! This my love is the reason of all this tremendous fuss!!! You may rely upon this fact my dear, that you will never be disturbed by the approach of a Mexican force. Certain men want fame and wish to "bang San Jacinto." Let them try it! I will never envy the man who rivals that transaction! But my dear, men are ambitious, <u>miserably</u> so! The man who wou'd wish to excite his country, and with a desire to agrandise himself at the cost of his country's good is a poor, very poor creature!

Texas at this time is in a worse dilemma than it was on the 20th of April 1836. Few can realise its situation, but within less than eight months you will see the catastrophy [sic] which will be revealed to this people! You shall be aloof from all the influences of agitation. We are so poor as a nation that we can not procure stationary. How then can we invade a nation with <u>mines</u> and eight million of souls?

(13th Jany)

My love to day papers arrived from Galveston, but no letters! I am crazy to hear from you. But as I did not, I am left to suppose that [you] are not indisposed. If it were the case, Dr. Tucker wou'd write to me! To day I heard from Bledsoe, and our dear Sister. They are well and happy! I was much gratified to learn the news, but at the same time Col Cole[s][1] said (for he was down at home) that he did not hear from "farther East"—So you see how well 'tis known that my heart is always with you! I do not make a noise about you! My writing and my associations prove that I must have some object of attractions distant from the scenes which surround me daily and hourly. For some days past we have had wet and damp weather. I was getting well very fast, and looked better than you have ever seen me. I hope the weather will soon change for the better! This moment I have been invited to a wedding! 'Tis Genl Harrison[2] to Mrs. McInstry.[3] So you see, she will soon be Mrs. Genl Harrison, and the wife of a <u>noble fellow</u>! I am informed that the Ladies of Austin will be there. I expect to attend, but for a short time. I will not play <u>debonair</u>, nor will I show of the Gallant! My heart and my affections will not allow me to be any thing but devoted husband. A husband who never loved but one object, and that object is his beloved Margaret. But fancy how painful it must be for me to remain at a distance from the only object on earth, that I love or ever can love! Oh how supremely blessed wou'd I be if I cou'd once more see your dear smile and press you to my bounding bosom. I detest the vapid scenes which surround me! I can do no good in this Body. I may prevent injury, but of this I am doubtful.

I have said, we are in a crisis, and I am sorry to review the assertions! It is painful to contemplate, the impending ruin to our country! The murky cloud which hangs over us must burst in a few short months. War is not in the elements (in truth) which compose this cloud. Fearful as it may be, the country will sustain its-self. The Government must dissolve, but the judiciary will remain and sustain the Nation or the people will sustain the judiciary!

I am apprehensive that you will suppose that I design to make a politician of you! This I leave to you my dear, and doubting nothing, I feel that you will make the proper choice on this as well as all other subjects! I trust that you have not been visited by a Norther of late and oh! the fearful dampness which has surrounded you, has distressed me. So much! Until I can see you, I will not be "appie." Today a proposition was made to adjourn on the 20 inst., but was laid on the Table until the 18th. I must break off to Galveston.—I must see my "wee wife" and attend to our interest (mutual). Nothing can ever give me peace and happiness, but my Margaret & my home!

You must salute Mother for me & Tillie, Henrietta & [Dr. Edmund] Tucker. By all means, commend me to Mrs. Taylor & Mrs.

Price.[4] Mr. Taylor[5] is my bed fellow and you doubtless are the bed fellow of Mrs. Taylor! I am never out at night, so you see how dutiful I am to your wishes. I can render you no additional news, only, that Mr. Saligney proposes to give to myself and friends within the present week. It will be pleasant and agreeable, and all will leave there sober. Frenchmen never get intoxicated. I know that you do not suspect that I wou'd become heated, but I like to anticipate solicitude, which might by possibility be awakened. Thus you see the conscious rebuking which former bad conduct has incurred! You will appreciate all these matters. They are on account of my own dear Maggy! They are right and my dear, jest or not jest, it is true. I feel this evening that I can not stay longer! Today I took a plain dinner with Hockley and presented your kindness to him. He was very happy!! as was thy husband.

Major Zavala will be the first person that will leave this place of Galveston and I will write until he may depart. 'Tis my only happiness to think of you, and to write to you. You can not estimate my vast felicity while dwelling in sweet memory of the past. I trust the future will be no less happy and joyful than the past. My spirit, my love, my heart, must abide with you and dwell in your bosom! But oh! Maggy, you in your last did not mention the "tumor."[6] Has it left you? I hope it has, or you wou'd have told me of it. My love every thing mentioned by you imparts to me much interest. Then write to me that I may receive it by the 6th of Feby. Again, my love to our mother.

Thy devoted Husband
Houston

Margaret

---

[1]Colonel John P. Coles of Washington County served in the Senate from 1840–1841. Hollon, 314.
[2]G. W. Harrison. Grammer, 76.
[3]Ann C. McKinstry. They were married on January 14, 1841, in Travis County. Grammer, 76.
[4]Houston is probably referring to the family of James H. Price. Margaret, in a letter of June 16, 1846, mentions staying with the Prices and a visit from the Morgans. Price would later marry Elizabeth Morgan. Grammer, 36.
[5]Ben Taylor, reading clerk in the Texas Senate. Identified in Jennet, n. p.
[6]Margaret was still suffering from the breast tumor.

Austin
14th Jany 1841

My Love!

To day I sealed only four letters to you—all number'd in due form according to date![1]

We are again in the House, and there appears to be no one attentive to business. I wou'd be happy to be relieved from the position in which a sense of duty holds me.

Just as I was on my way to the capitol, I met Mrs. Flood, and she bade me to salute you with <u>great affection</u>. You will embrace her wishes! She is a fine Lady! She loves you so well that I love her some too! The little Girls,[2] when they see me, run and ask about "Mrs Houston" or "Margaret" for they have learned your name.

Oh my love! When others love you, who have but seen you, how much ought I, the husband to <u>love this</u>? Tomorrow the war question will come up, and your husband must <u>do</u> his duty.

The Cicero's of the House, as well as the Hotspurs will be in the field, and no doubt but "seven Richmonds" too will be in the field.[3] I will with the blessing of God sustain myself, and my good Lady's feelings!!! They are to me more than my own individual <u>vanity</u>.

To make you happy is all my desire. To see you cheerful, smiling, and approving my acts and conduct, oh how blessed I shou'd [sic] be. The recollection of other days cou'd never obtrude upon me, but I wou'd feel that all my existence was combined in the consciousness of the presence of my dear Maggy.

I will cease writing for the reason that you will suppose me intending to <u>court</u> you <u>again</u>! One courtship and <u>eternal love</u>! This is my motto. The House has this moment adjourned until 10 A.M. tomorrow, and 'tis only 1 o clock P.M. This does not look like a speedy adjournment of the Body. I say "Body" for it has no <u>soul</u>.

Adieu my love
Houston

Margaret

[1]Houston's four letters to Margaret which are numbered include those of December 31, 1840, and January 7, 8, and 12, 1841.

[2]The Flood daughters were Florida and Laura. Identified in *Daughters of the Republic of Texas, Founders and Patriots of Texas,* v. 1, (Published privately, 1963), 27, 504.

[3]Houston is probably referring to Shakespeare's *King Richard III,* Act V, Scene iv, Line 9. Justin Kaplan, ed., *Familiar Quotations,* (Boston: Little, Brown and Company, 1992), 166.

Austin
16th Jany 1841

My love,

This is one of the darkest days that I recollect to have seen in Texas. Early this morning we had a violent thunder storm! It yet lowers around us. We have had much rain, and in the anticipation of a <u>norther</u> we are all shivering with dread! Gloomy as the day is, I must write to you, and send you the <u>war Documents</u>. You will see how supremely ridiculous the evidence, as well as the report appear! I send you the "Sentinal"[1] and mark a piece which I am sure was written by our good friend Dr. Moore.[2] I have read the <u>pretty effusion</u>, and marked it for your perusal! You need not suppose that I am unhappy! If I were, I wou'd not mark it for your notice! As the piece is untrue, I care <u>nothing</u> about it!

You my love, will smile at the nonsense which malignity inspires. Were I as I am represented to <u>be</u>, my enemies wou'd be satisfied and silent. It wou'd be gratification to see me a "drunken sot!" But my dear, <u>they</u> see that my constitution is daily renewing and my complexion becoming pure and clear! These are painful symptoms to my adversaries. Other causes too obtain to irritate and inflame the base and designing! When it is known that I am to speak, the Hall is crowded and the Ladies attend the debates! When I cease, the ladies leave and the galleries are empty! These facts are calculated to create <u>hatred</u>, and hatred will induce <u>slander</u>! Do not be distressed. I can not forget my love and admiration for Margaret! I wou'd not inflict one pang to your dear heart for Empires!

Maj. Taylor has been, and yet [is] in my room and bed fellow! From him you will derive all the news! I am so happy to hear that Vernal has visited you & our mother! You will now have a <u>protector</u> until I can be with you!

But the <u>wedding</u> that is over and I was there quite grave but very <u>genteel</u>!

I drank one cup of coffee, but not even one glass of <u>wine</u>! Nor any thing stronger as I find that total abstinence will make me all that I ever was in point of health and constitution. But there is more than this to be considered! The feelings of my dearly beloved Maggy—whose only dread is that I may abandon myself (at sometime) to <u>intemperance</u>! Don't doubt me!!! I trust that <u>when we meet, you will be satisfied</u>!

Today De Zavalla was to start for the Island, but it is so unfavorable that I suppose he will not depart until Maj. Taylor will also go, as he is anxious to see Bledsoe. I believe I will pass at Mr. Saligney's party. He says it is intended as a compliment to myself and friends. A Diplomatist wou'd not compromit [sic] his standing & character for a "drunken sot." This is a commentary on the reports against me! You will so esteem the facts! But this is idle and I will only say be happy and assured of my love! This hope shall buoy me! I appreciate <u>all your feelings</u>! Yes correctly and very tenderly!

Give my love to our mother and our brother Vernal, Tilly, Henrietta, Tucker, Judge Johnson, and our Lady friends salute for me! Take care of poor Sis for me!

I am thy devoted husband
Yes thine own truly
Sam Houston

To Mrs. Houston

[1]Austin's *Texas Sentinal* was anti-Houston to the point of printing slander. *Handbook of Texas,* II, 760.

[2]Dr. Francis Moore, Jr., publisher of the Houston *Telegraph and Texas Register,* and an outspoken foe of Houston. For a biography see *Writings,* VIII, 127–28n and *Handbook of Texas,* II, 221.

Addressed to Gen. Sam Houston,
Austin Texas

Jan. 18, 1841, Galveston

My love,

There are so few persons passing from this place to Austin at present that I have determined to write by Tom[1] and get him to send it from Houston. I am not without some hope that you will be with me before it can reach Austin, but you may not be. I think it necessary to write. We have had the coldest weather during the last two days that I have ever known and the land looks bleak and ugly I assure you. Today the norther has abated but the cold is still intense. My husband I hope you are not vexed with me for urging you so much to come home. If you are I do not know what atonement to make, for I can not recal [sic] what I have said, tho' must still beg you to come to me. Bishop Timon called & delivered your letter[2] and has been up once since. I have seldom found an acquaintance with whom I am better pleased. His manners & conversations are entirely elegant. He introduced a friend of yours but I did not understand his name.

The furniture which I sent for arrived this morning. It was terribly abused. I think Harrisburg should be made to pay for it.

My dear it is disagreeable to communicate disagreeable news to any one but above all to my dear husband. Nevertheless I think it my duty to inform you that my beloved mother is in great distress about her lot. Cody[3] has determined to make her pay another hundred in addition to the 600 she has already paid and has employed an attorney for that purpose. I do not know how it will terminate. Bro. V. has employed Mr. Rose[4] to attend to it.

Everyone tells me that your health is improved a great deal. I thank God that is so, and though I may soon recover from my present low state, yet when I hear that you are doing so well I consider myself blessed. If I could believe that you would be with me soon it would give me new strength, but as you say nothing about it in your letters, I do not know when to expect you. Bro. V[ernal] will not decide upon his course until he sees you. He will go to Cedar Point again shortly. Then my Love, if I live, how happy will we be in that sweet place! You shall assist me in planting my flowers and training my vines and we will wander through those sweet groves and be as happy as the spirits of some enchanted isle. And there is another hope which sometimes throws a light over the future.[5] Oh, shall I live to realize it! If I do not you may perhaps and I love to think that you may be reminded of me.

Dearest I know not why I write thus for I would not willingly cause you one sad thought, but the truth is that without you I am so sad myself that my language is necessarily so. Do not let the fear of meeting a moping wife detain you from me for I can not be sad when you are with me. Ma thinks we will go to Cedar point so soon as you get home. This is [torn] to make my health there without you. It is a gloomy day, cold dark clouds are hovering above this city and the streets are covered with ice. It is quite a Norwegian scene. My hands are so cold that I fear you will not be able to read my writing, but my dear husband will excuse every thing. When I look back over the long sundry days that have passed since you departed I can scarcely realize my own identity or believe that the pale melancholy face that the glass reflects is the same who a few weeks ago was the happy wife of Houston and blessed with his society.

I have not seen the Miss Maffets[6] for [torn] while. Matilda is very sick with the croup and Dr. Tucker is attending on her. As she has discarded Judge Johnson, I should not be surprised if the Dr. offered himself.

18th

My dear,

I expect this will be handed to you by Mr. [Edward W.] Winfield who will tell you about Ma's business. There is some aspect of settling it without a law suit. I would write more, but I am not able.

Forever thy own
M. L. H.

[1] Houston's slave.
[2] See Houston to Margaret, December 31, 1840.
[3] This is possibly A. J. Cody, the only Cody recorded in Galveston during the 1840 census. Identified in Gifford White, *1840 Census of the Republic of Texas,* (Austin: Pemberton Press, 1966), 53.
[4] Robert Rose, a lawyer for the Galveston Bay Company. Mary Virginia Henderson, "Minor Empresario Contracts for Colonization of Texas—1825–1834," *Southwestern Historical Quarterly,* 31(April, 1928): 314–15.
[5] Margaret is probably referring to their desire for a child.
[6] Matilda and Henrietta Maffit.

My dear,

I had hoped today to have sent my packages to you by hand, but in this I am disappointed. The day is the most inclement that I have ever experienced in Texas. The earth is clad in white. Last night it snowed finely and tho it is not deep yet the day is so cold that the snow remains. Tho I am by a large fire I am so cold that I can hardly write and have to keep my ink at the fire or it will freeze. It is cold enough to freeze in the pen. Mr. Taylor & myself did not quite chill to death tho' our room is as cold and open as a barn. Fire wood too, is very scarce and our Land-lord[1] is a lordly dog! He is one of the fat gentry of this world, claims nothing himself. Says all belongs to his wife, and wou'd pick strangers of all they have by borrowing, and refusing in Bills to discount what he borrows in the way of cash.

You see I must indulge in mild abuse. Tis the very worst abuse, for tis all <u>truth</u>, and that is the most cruel abuse. Were it false, it wou'd be persecution, but as tis truth, tis <u>cruelty</u>!

Subrosa: I detest this place, and will never love it. I am sure! I may be here again, and you may also, but my dear, I really think that we wou'd be more happy at home in our little family, where our dear mother cou'd direct and superintend us both!

Notwithstanding my wretched accommodations, you wou'd be astounded to see how much my health improves! Tis visible to all and every one congratulates me upon the facts.

Today a consistent & very inveterate opponent of mine for years came and gave me his adhesion, and when we meet I will amuse you by a little narrative. This is a queer world in which we are placed, as a dwarf once said to me, "human nature is human nature still." So I find it.

Members are prating, and I am weary of nonsense. I have not opened my mouth for days—The war question is suspended for the present, and for Mr. Mayfield to prepare the balance of his speech. He is to abuse me well, and from the start, which he has made, he will allow me to explain matters for which I have been so much misrepresented! and abused. I mean the "retreat" and the battle of "San Jacinto." I rejoice that my health promises one ample ability to do myself justice! My speech will be reported, and this I intend for your satisfaction, and the gratification of our friends in Alabama!

This is due to
[incomplete]

[1]Probably Richard Bullock. Houston roomed at Bullock's Hotel during this session of Congress. Patsy McDonald Spaw, *The Texas Senate, Volume I: Republic to the Civil War*, (College Station: Texas A&M University Press, 1990), 103. The hotel stood at the corner of 6th and Congress streets and had been hastily constructed to receive the new government. It also consisted of a series of smaller log buildings. *Handbook of Texas*, I, 244.

Mrs. Houston
Galveston Texas

[January] 19th 11 o'clock at night [1841]

Tonight my love, Mr. Saligney gave to myself and particular friends a party. I left there at 9, and did think to have retired ire this hour. But company kept me up! The party was select and pleasant. I wished you health, but did not drink even a glass of wine! There was good humour but no excess. Mr S. sent you a flower from the summit of the kisses presented to the guest! I enclose it to you with his respects! This I execute with much pleasure!

To day, 'tis said that I made one of the most felicitous of the efforts of my life. I was most satisfied with it myself, or rather I was satisfied with myself!

It was informative, and for that it was the better! Dr. Herburt[1] was present and as he is from Alabama, I was gratified. He was pleased! Maj Taylor, my friend was also present! He said it was fine. This is enough to say about it! My love I fear for the stability of our Government! But Texas must be saved!!!

Enclosed you will find a sketch of San Antonio presented to you, by Maj Bonnell,[2] former editor of the "Centinal" [sic] of this place, that abused me so much! Thus wags!! Oh when we meet, what a budget of news I will have to open to you! But if I write much more, I will have but little to narrate, for never did a devoted husband write so much to a beloved wife, as I have done to you while absent. You will have a weeks reading, and that will do, in place of Books, for the time being. I write to no one, but my own Maggy!

You must apologize to Tilly, Judge Johnson and Tucker for me!

Tell Tilly & Henrietta, that I hear they are as beautiful and bewitching as ever—I hear it with pleasure.

Present me to all our friends. My love to Mother and Bud![3]

My health improves every hour—though I have a slight cold.

May the Almighty God bless my beloved Margaret. I hope we will adjourn on the last of this month.

Thy husband
Houston
'Tis past 12!

Margaret

[1]Dr. Walter Herburt, a son-in-law of James Webb. Identified in Daughters of the Republic of Texas, *Founders and Patriots of Texas,* I, 13.

[2]Major George Bonnell of Austin. For a biography see *Writings,* I, 335n and *Handbook of Texas,* I , 186.

[3]Vernal Lea was sometimes called Bud.

To Mrs. Margaret Lea Houston
Galveston
Texas

Austin
22nd Jany 1841

My love,

I must write. I can not forego my disposition to be prating to you. No matter how trite, my notions may happen to be! 'Tis to my dear Margaret that I am writing. It is but common to look in the frontier for news, but if such [is] your situation, you will be disappointed unless you take for news that we are doing no good for the nation, nor do I think any thing will be done of importance! Land as usual has been the song and slang of the session. It has been the ruin of our country and the reality will soon be upon us. You my love, will not feel but see the beauty and splendor of foolishness! Of this, I will have much to say when we meet. I trust in kind Heaven that you will see me enjoy such health as you have not before witnessed. With the exception of a cold and hoarseness, I do not recollect to have enjoyed better health! I am in better health than I was when I first saw my dear Maggy at Mobile.

From this you will suppose that I am fortunate, living as I have been in a room less comfortable than a stable. You have no idea my love, what my situation has been! Tho I pay high for board—and lodging, yet I have lain under my own blankets—even my saddle blanket! Thank God I have but a few days more to endure this state of things. I count every day, and every hour, that passes. I can not sleep until 5 oclock AM. This is a partial drawback on my health, tho' not serious, for my meditations are upon my love of Margaret & my country. This you will believe. I am sure you will attach faith to. But this is prating and so often said that I fear you will think me some what <u>silly</u>!

We have met after dinner, and I see plainly that nothing can be done of utility to the country. Relief Bills and local Bills, or acts, are all that have been passed this session. I fear that no financial plan will be devised to give us standing as to credit, either at home or abroad, with our creditors! If this is not done, we must remain in a deplorable condition! No appropriation for this current year has been made! Nor do I suppose that any will be made. I look every day to see the House break up without any regular adjournment. The reason is plain—there are only seven members[1] here of the former Congress in the House of Representatives, tho' it consists of forty. Many members have not been resident in the Republic for two years. This is a strange conviction of things. Men ignorant of the history, wants, and facilities, are to determine what has to be done for its benefit and salvation. Little ought I have thought of this state of things since years ago, but it is nevertheless true, that such was my apprehension.

I always believed that Texas wou'd be capable of achieving her Independence, but I doubted the capacity of those into whose hands the Government might be confided to sustain free institutions. This I now realise! The universal distrust in the administration [is] prognosticating its downfall. It can not remain—It must sink or dissolve!

The nation will exist in its primitive element. The people will raise corn and rear stock, and live "fat and full." The burdens of Government will be very light for we will have <u>none</u>. You wou'd be amused to see the casting about among aspirants for coming events. Burnet can not fill his Cabinet[2]—those who have standing and reputation will not hazard it by an identity with the administration. You will think this strange when you reflect that a place in the Cabinet of

Texas was esteemed most honorable and noble! Then, how has Texas fallen! How mortifying is the patriot? to see the cup dashed from her lips! You my dear, will not feel the influences of such calamities, tho you may witness it at a distance without feeling its calamity.

It will, it must be years before this fair land will again experience an exemption from Taxation and every prospect of plenty and happiness restored to it. The day may come, it will come, but not within the present year when we can sit under our own vine and our own fig tree and worship God according to the dictates of our own conscience—There Maggy, we can be happy and feel that we owe every thing to the Great Author of our lives.

To day I called to see Col Flood and as usual conversation adverted to you. The Madam had been to see the Presidents Mansion, as it has been vacant since Lamar's departure. The Madam said that "you cou'd make it a pleasant residence." I asked her if she thought "you wou'd like to be there as a President's wife." She replied with animation "Oh yes! any lady in America wou'd be happy to be there as such." I did not ask her if she intended to convey the idea that I must be the President as the cause of happiness. I was silent, but smiled at my own conceit, which was that if you were there, I must be also! About this my love, I have no ambition. The state or station, wou'd be one of misery and not even <u>splendid misery</u>!

The sun is setting over our beautiful western hills. The day has been mild, and the evening is serene, and the sunset is calm and sweet! I turn my face to the east when I worship because my Margaret is there! My heart turns to the smiles of my Margaret, as the "fire worshipers" [sic] turned to render their homage to the centre of light! I hope soon to bow to your shrine for your bosom is the temple of my affections.

23rd

Just as I ceased writing news came in last evening that Indians were seen in the vicinity of the city and the Brother in law of Judge Smith of this county was pursued by four supposed to be comanchies [sic]. He reported that he had left Judge Smith and his little son about 12 years old in the neighbourhood of the Indians about two miles from the city. Night came on and a party went out to look for the missing. No discoveries were made. The horse and a dog of Judge Smith came in about 9 P.M. The distress of Mrs. Smith I am told was terrible. This morning a company went out and about a mile from the capitol they found the mutilated remains of the Judge and as the ground was marshy they also found where the little Boy was taken from the ground and no doubt taken off a prisoner. You can now imagine the distress of an agonized mother. This is owing to the wretched imbecility of the Executive to whom power was delegated, but the other day power to raise, and employ spy companies, to prevent such catastrophies [sic], as the present. Poor beast, he is but a wretch, foul and polluted![3]

The only care of Burnet is to create a party to sustain him, but all will not do. The poor creature will be execrated in the mouth of Babes. We have nothing to hope from such selfishness. I have just made a speech on the subject of a French Colony. My hand is unsteady because I was a good deal excited during the time I was on the floor.

It is nonsense, or I fear you will think so. I dreamed of you most kindly and fancied that I had arrived at Galveston in the morning & flew to meet the wife of my bosom. You met me, and I was happy, but weary from my great anxiety to meet you and the want of repose for days and nights.

Oh I was very happy and restored for days in peace. You I thought were happy too—quite happy. I will not describe your appearance minutely! But I thought you looked well, very well! The time far approaches when we are to leave here, and then I will hurry home. I will have to go by Bledsoes, tho' it is not the nearest route! I will not long delay, but I feel satisfied you will not suspect me of playing the sluggard by the ways.

I hope to meet a boat at [torn] ready to sail in an hour for Galveston. I need not urge an assurance of my great solicitude to see you! For in my minds eye I can see no being on the Island but my dear Maggy. The Island wou'd be to me a dreary waste if you were not there!

My friends I wou'd be happy to meet, and see those to whom my presence wou'd be welcome. They I am told are many. Of this you may learn something, but not mingling much you must be comparatively unadvised of the state of things.

Every day I see Mr. McKinney and Mr. Williams[4] of Galveston. They are great friends of mine. But indeed my dear, in this place, I do not believe that I have one opponent out of every ten men in this county, notwithstanding the power of the patronage which the Government has to bestow. People here look sad and melancholy and the fact of Judge Smiths massacre has had an additional influence in depressing the [torn] mind! In most of the speeches made to day, allusion to the death of Judge Smith, murder has been alluded to. We are ding dong in land matters and in all that many have come for to this place! God save the country! It will require more than mortal aid. Divine help may save us.

But I do not wish to indulge in any unpleasant anticipations for the reason that reality is bad enough to contemplate. The heart of the Patriot must sicken and languish while hope alone will sustain us. Millions have been expended and independent of the debt which hangs upon us, we are in a worse situation than what we were as a nation two years ago! Confidence is destroyed in the Government, and it has no power to recall what has been loss'd! I may write rather gloomy today because it is a sad one and a [torn]. And tho' I feel better than I have done as health in the last five years, I nevertheless have some head ache [sic] from cold, but nothing serious. My anxiety is so great to leave here that I hope I will have no time to be sick. For some days I have had no "hippo." My spirits are fine, and I am cheerful, but a little cross grained when I am too much annoyed by the impertinence of idle or troublesome persons. But in the main, I am quite "amiable and polite." Night is coming upon us. It is after five oclock.

25th Monday

My dear, I passed yesterday in my room and as you wou'd have wished me to do. I mean in reading and thinking of my dear Maggy. Every hour to me is an age, and my spirit "breaks thro' times barrier and o'ertakes the <u>hour</u>." The hour, when we shall meet. Were it not that we have no mail, I wou'd be [torn] happy because I have received no letter from you since yours of the 31st ult.[5] As well as I recollect, and I have learned that you had been more indisposed than I had before heard of. How painful has been my state of feeling during this session, and indeed I wou'd not detain one hour, if it were not that the Treaties from Europe have arrived and as they suppose my presence of some importance to the present state of the country!

The crisis increases in magnitude, and tho' war seems to slumber while panic makers decrease, yet other matters of grave import rush upon us! We must meet and face them! All alarm about the Indians has subsided, and will be the case until some depredation may again occur. It will not be many days, or I am no judge of Indian hostility. There is but [one] passion here, and that is for office, or rather for cash! Depreciated as our money is, there is nevertheless a fondness for it.

An aversion to labor and industry is the curse of the community. If men wou'd rely upon their own exertion and not waste their time in useless pursuit of office, they wou'd be more decent, more independent, and more moral and proud—Expectation disappointed invariably depresses the mind and deprives the individual of a certain portion of his energy, and self respect. Nothing is so well calculated to exalt a man in his own esteem as to throw him upon his own resources, if he is made of the right <u>stuff</u>! The treaty has not been made public,[6] but may be previous to my closing this letter, and I will send you its complexion and some of its features! I presume that I will be in favor of the treaties, tho' some parts of them, I may not like or approve. Nothing of human formation is perfect. To give you some idea of the great efficiency of the present President pro tem, I will tell you that tho' Judge Smith was killed by the Indians on friday [sic], the war energies of a population comprising at least 250 has slumbered until this morning—they are now about to go out when the Indians are in all probability are [sic] distant 150 miles from this place. They were on horseback. Never had I fancied such culpable dereliction wou'd ever have existed in Texas. The truth is that the perversity of Government defied all calculation and wisdom and forecasts are set at naught.

It is just rumoured that we will not get off so soon as we had hoped. We may be called so soon as we adjourn by the President and you may be assured if I find that my presence is not absolutely necessary, I will not stay one hour in obedience to any dictum of Davy G. Burnet. This Congress has enacted my friend Hockley out of office![7] This is cruel and unjust. An officer, who was at the dawning of the Revolution, and has been useful ever since shou'd not be lightly dealt by and at a time when his services are more important than they have ever been! The arms will all go wreck and ruin and the country will be without munitions of war in the event that they shou'd [be] needful!

We have cloudy and dull weather, but when I am writing to you, you will not suppose me very lazy if I shou'd partake in the character of my composition of the <u>shade</u> of the weather. I feel that I am <u>dull</u> in writing, or I need not write so much!

You I hope will have health and leisure to read much, or at least what I can have time to write. Col Flood and his family are well and all cooped in one little room about 14 feet square. 'Tis a great city! Just such as savages wou'd not live in! As a city its days are number'd and its glory will pass away!

We adjourn for dinner!

26th Jany 1841

My dear, There is nothing new this morning to tell you of. The treaties have not been promulgated by the senate. To day I hope we may hear some news of our relations to the old world! Tho' I must confess that I do not feel cheerful on this occasion. It may be that my depression may pass by and that the illusion that hangs over my spirits may be dispelled!—at least I hope so!

This week I apprehend will pass, and nothing will be done with an eye single to the welfare of the nation. Yes of Texas! But we must look out for the worst and act for the best. This morning I hear an amusing threat against me in the Executive party, if it is sufficiently numerous and respectable to be called a party, have said that they wou'd assail me on some leading measures[,] so irritate me, that I wou'd get into a <u>spree</u> and they wou'd obtain a triumph! In this my dear they shall be distressed for I have and will inflict upon my enemies the most signal disappointment! My health as well as my demeanour is such as to render my adversaries miserable!

It plagues me much when I reflect that my habits in other days shou'd have been such as to require double caution at this period of life. 'Tis past, and let it go! I have not been so well as I am now, for the last five years. My health is restored and my colour is returning! The only inconvenience which I experience is a want of sleep. Before three AM. I never sleep and my only repose is in the morning so that I often rise exhausted. My nights are not [now?] as I have stated, are employed in thinking of my Maggy & my country. Often I fancy that I hear the gentle accent of your voice fall sweetly upon my ear and arouse joy in my heart. But it brings to me disappointment and regret that I ever left you. But my prayers are devout that we shall soon meet again. Meet not to part in life again for so long a period as our seperation [sic] has been of late.

I began this letter with a hope and expectation to have closed and sent it to you long since. I will now close and pray that you will commend me to Mother, Bud, if with you. To Tillly, Henrietta, Tucker, Johnson, and our friends. Tell Tilly that I write to no one, but you and that when I get home, I [will] write her a long letter under your eye!

Tell Maria to take care of you and not let you become unwell. Present me to the Taylors and Prices.

Thy ever devoted Husband
Houston

Margaret

{On outside} My dear, I have not time to read over and correct this letter. An opportunity occurs to forward it.

Thine, Houston

[1]Houston is referring to himself, George W. Hill, David S. Kaufman, William Menefee, Moses Roberts, Cornelius Van Ness, and James Wright. Jennet, n.p. See listings for Fourth and Fifth Congresses of Texas.

[2]Lamar had been granted a leave due to illness and David G. Burnet became the chief executive. Wisehart, 365.

[3]James Smith, Chief Justice of Travis County. The son was later ransomed by John Roland for $60. For an account of the incident see James Holmes Jenkins III, ed., *Recollections of Early Texas*, (Austin: University of Texas Press, 1958), 162–63 and *Austin City Gazette*, January 27, 1841.

[4]Thomas F. McKinney and Samuel M. Williams, partners in a trading and banking company located in Galveston. For information about these partners see *Writings*, IV , 34–36n.

[5]This letter from Margaret has not been located.

[6]Houston is referring to Texas's treaty with England.

[7]George W. Hockley had served as Secretary of War during Houston's administration. President Lamar replaced him with Albert Sidney Johnston. For a biography see *Writings*, I, 331n.

General Sam Houston
Austin, Texas
By Mr. Dawson

Galveston, Jan 27th [1841]

My Love,

Capt. Todd[1] called this morning & informed me that a Mr. Dawson[2] was going up to Austin, and would take a letter for me. I am glad of the opportunity, for although I have written to you constantly, I apprehend that you do not get my letters as I never receive any acknowledgments. I have sent a letter to the care of Judge Moreland[3] which you will perhaps receive with this. I have nothing amusing to tell you, for I have been so ritual of late that the fluctuations of society have left me several degrees in the lurch. I write to you therefore merely because you are very dear to me and because I love to tell you my thoughts & feelings, although they may be tame & uninteresting. If you have rec'd my letters, I fear you are vexed at my urgent entreaties for you to come home. You must not be, my Love, for indeed I am very lonely without you. I ought to have known however that it would disturb you and that the prudent course would have been to conceal my illness & low spirits from you. I confess that selfishness and the desire of being with you prompted me against my better judgment to tell you everything. But my husband will surely forgive this weakness which originated in devoted love for him! If you do not—I have no other excuse to offer, and if I promise you to exercise more firmness here after, you will not believe me— for I made the same promise when you returned from the red lands! It has been so long since I saw you that the past seems almost like a dream but such a dream! so bright—so beautiful. Shall we ever see such happiness again? I trust we shall.

I rec'd a letter from Mr. Bledsoe a few days ago. He mentioned that he & sister A[ntoinette] had some idea of coming down with you. I should be delighted if she could as it would be a great source of comfort to have her with me at this time. Almost every day brings us some new rumour of war. It will at least serve as a subject of conversation and that is what the people often need. It is now several weeks since I have been out of the house. Oh how beautiful and tempting is the blue sky and even the bare prairie! How often in other days has my heart bounced with rapture when I could roam through the balmy woods and breathe the pure air of Heaven! But alas I did not know what a blessed privilege it was until entirely deprived of it. I vainly imagine that while I live the flowers would never cease to bloom—the wild birds to sing for me. Perhaps the sweet spring may bring back the same hopes. I sometimes grow fretful and impatient, but I think I am resigned to any fate that may await me. I have a merciful God to deal with, and though he should bid me go down to an early grave, my spirit can say "thy will be done." But I will not dwell on this subject. My Love do you find time to read the bible? I trust that you do and that its holy precepts may sink deep into your heart. I would have you read the history of our blessed Saviour again & again and to meditate much upon his character.

My love, do write to me oftener. I am so happy when I get a letter from you! But when days & weeks pass away without one cherishing word, my heart feels as if it would burst with grief. Oh shall I ever be with you again and see you and hear you speak! I shall be wild with joy. I am sure if my heart was probed at this time, there would not be found much patriotism in it, for I almost hate the duties that keep you from me. Mother & bro. V[ernal] send their love to you. Dearest do not forgit [sic].

Your own devoted
M. L. Houston

[on outside of letter]

It is 6 years today since my dear father[4] died.
"I know that he's gone where his forehead is starred
   With the beauty that dwelt in his soul!"
but this day always brings to me a loneliness of heart that nothing can dissipate. I mention the circumstances because you have always simpathised with my feelings toward that sainted being. How sad is such simpathy! It enables us to realize "the joy of grief" and the very sorrow that else would render life lonely & desolate becomes a link of union that makes life desirable. Dear noble husband, how often do I need thy gentle simpathy! Sometimes when my heart is filled with gloom, I try to imagine what you would say to me, and there is even pleasure in that. How much sweeter would be the reality! Present me to our friends Mr. & Mrs. Toland.[5] Tell her I am expecting an answer to my letter. Dearest farewell

---

[1]John Grant Todd [also spelled Tod]. For a biography see *Writings*, II , 250n.
[2]This was quite possibly Frederick Dawson, a member of a firm of shipbuilders who regularly visited the sessions of Congress. For a biography see *Writings*, III,

248–49n.

[3]Isaac N. Moreland, chief justice of Harris County. For a biography see *Writings,* I, 463n.

[4]Temple Lea.

[5]Probably Mr. and Mrs. Joseph Toland. For biographies see Ray, 226.

Austin 29th [January, 1841]

My Beloved,

'Tis impossible for me to express the pleasure I experience at seeing a man from Galveston. It was Mr. Brannum.[1] But it was the hope that he had news from my adorable wife—my Maggy!!! When he announced to me that he had letters from you, my spirit bounded with delightful anticipations. I soon realised them for I never quit him until I had in my possession every letter and then, I tore them open, and literally devoured their contents! Oh my dear Wife, what joy was mingled with regret—of joy to hear from you, and regret that you were not so happy as I cou'd wish you to be. My love, you will laugh at the charge which you have implied against me when you receive all the letters which I have written to you and those which I may write.

What a wretched novice our friend Price must be. He ought to have done for you as his wife did—told you something agreeable, but not have suggested any thing unpleasant. Why my Love, I do assure you that never was man so devoted to [a] dear wife, as I am to you. Sometimes I think if the world only knew how much I am devoted to you, that it wou'd laugh at me and say, 'tis strange that this man retains his reason. You are present to me in the burst of dawn—all the day, and you are with me until I sink in repose. I try to fancy how you look. I mean your personal appearance—You know my remarks about Mrs Cady and there is some resemblance in your <u>figures</u>. And like causes will produce like effects. So you must not blame me if I shou'd fancy how you wou'd look in a wrapper, or loose dress! I wish that I cou'd clasp you in one and press you to my heart.

In reading your letters I almost imagined that I was with you and heard your voice. The smile, too, I fancied was playing upon your sweet face which has so often cheered my heart and revealed to me the charmed hope that happiness wou'd yet abide with my Margaret and myself and such <u>additional companions</u> as Heaven may bestow.

Is not this a rational expectation in the present prospect of affairs? My Dear, I hope you will deem it so! If I were to write as I feel, you wou'd, I fear, think me a very simpleton. Like you, I am almost <u>crazy</u>, but have not the pleasure to hear our Mother rate me with the charge. If I cou'd only embrace you, I wou'd be willing to drink composition tea.—Yes, even stronger than the last dose given to me by mother. This is but a feeble illustration of my anxiety to be with my Beloved Maggy.

I often dwell with so much pleasure on our past joys and affection. The kind temper with which you always treated me except at Capt Bledsoes, when you took the "Jockey word" of me about the empress Maggy! This was quite diplomatic in you my dear! I did not intend to reproach you, but only to be very sedate, until I was amused by your tact! There was too much joy in my heart to quarrel at that time, and I wou'd not, sick and generally cross, as I was have mar'd your dear peace for all that I was worth, apart from your affections—for they are my capital. They constitute my wealth on earth!

I am so sorry that your dreams distress you. They are but dreams, and I want you to regard them as you now do: the <u>predictions</u> of your Cousin Columbus![2] You must feel more or less depression in your <u>travail</u>. I think all women who are destined to become mothers experience this state of mind. Take what recreation you can & by no means yield to melancholy. Walk much in the house when you cannot take exercise in the open air. This you will
[incomplete]

[1]W. T. Brannum. Listed in White, *The 1840 Census of the Republic of Texas*, 49.
[2]Columbus Lea of Marion, Alabama, was the son of Green Lea and Peggy Moffitt and was a double first cousin of Margaret. Hearne Collection, San Antonio. For a biography see Brewer, 491.

The following letter is not dated, but appears to have been written by Houston to Margaret on a Saturday before his letter of January 31, 1841:

My dear, I have just returned to the hall at 7 oclk. from dining with Mr. Saligny, and all that I drank was a thimble glass of "absinth" [sic]. This I did because I was absent from you!!! We have to sit at night, as well as day to get rid of business. Thus in a few days we may succeed. It is now raining most heavily, and I fear high waters may delay me, on my way home! We can enjoy here mud, mire and rain! "Tis all that we can provide ourselves."—I am told that Judge Terrell,[1] my particular friend is Sec'y of State, and Dr. Chalmers,[2] two weeks in the country Sec'y of the Treasure. These matters are too new and when we meet I will tell you an anecdote in relation to Genl Jackson,[3] on the subject of things being too new or to[o] young to live! I write more in sorrow than in jest. Indeed, I do feel for my poor, poor Texas. As business is pressing, and pen is bad, and my knife is dull, I must close what you must deem as a tedious epistle. You will excuse me, when you reflect that I have to write in the middle of confusion. I am spoken to every moment by some person wishing my opinion. This is complimentary, but very troublesome when I am writing to you! Since I came here, I have only written a half dozen of letters, save to my Maggy.

I solemnly declare to you that I wou'd not live, as I have done since we parted for ten thousand dollars, another three months.

The war panic is over. I have just seen news from Rio Grande, and the bubble has bursted in perfect ridicule. Felix Don Huston, was sent to raise volunteers. He went to La Grange and cou'd raise none. To save his credit, Davy G.[4] has recalled him. Oh what Glory has been deferred by fate who wou'd not love Glory? It is so cruel not to let the present stamp of HEROES ellipse San Jacinto. It cou'd have been done, as nothing but shadows would have been met on the Rio Grande. But oh! the quantity of Beef that wou'd have rendered the frontier a "scene of carnage." Yes, my Love, carnage and bloodshed wou'd have been the watch word! and reply. Men will find that it is necessary for them to use some honest employment for an honest livelihood. 'Tis pity, aye, wondrous pitiful, that the country shou'd not be able to support those who are too lazy to support the country by resource to industry. Uniform is a very striking and fanciful dress. To a fine person what a set off, and to a bad one, what an imposing decoration!!

You have never seen me with mine.—This I regret, but some wet day, I will dress in it, when I have nothing else to do! It is not blue and Buff, but "Green & Gold." One Gentleman without Law, has received from Davy G. the sum of $10,000, but what has become of it, no one knows; or the Representatives of the people do not! I do declare to you, my dear Margaret, that the corruption of this administration is beyond all comprehension. They have been base, and regardless of every principle of honesty and patriotism!!! But why am I prating to you? Oh because, I cou'd write or talk to you forever!

The Treaty (conventional) with England to give us peace with Mexico has been ratified. This is the only God-send that has fallen in the way of Texas. With peace, we can now get on, if "Poorly" as little James Neely told my venerated mother. But Texas will not ultimately sink, tho she must be greatly depressed for time yet to come!

This item I give you that you may be assured that I will not be called to arms!!! I became a little cowardly, and the reason is, I fear that I love you so much that I do not wish to go into danger, least I might by some simpleton be knocked on the head!

Tomorrow is the sabbath, or Sunday, and I will read the Bible, and try to keep the day holy! Tho I am wicked, I may try to be good!

Tell Vernal, if he is with you, that I thank him for his letter! If he is not with you, I hope to meet him at Bledsoe's. I expect to pass one night there.

Give my love to Mother—Salute Tilly, Henrietta, Tucker, Johnson, the Taylors, the Prices, and all who have been kind to you! Dont treat Maria[5] unkindly, by this I mean dont mortify her. Remember our hopes, my Love!!! I hope she will be needed![6] Maggy, pardon me. If you should blush when you read this, and if others shou'd be present, and you shou'd blush, when you read this letter, don't regard it, for you always (to my fancy) blush very prettily! Farewell my love, you are more kindly endeared to me every day!!!

Thy devoted husband
Houston

Margaret

[1]George Whitfield Terrell, former Attorney General of Tennessee when Houston was governor, served as District Attorney of the San Augustine District. For a biography see *Writings*, III, 52–53n.

[2]John G. Chalmers of La Grange. For a biography see Nixon, 346–47 and*Writings*, III, 239n.

[3]Andrew Jackson.

[4]Acting President David G. Burnet.

[5]A Lea family servant.

[6]This alludes to the fact that Margaret may have been expecting a baby.

The following letter was written to Houston by Margaret and is from the Charlotte Darby Taylor Collection, Houston, Texas:

Galveston, Jan 30th 1841

What shall I say to my beloved husband today? Shall I tell him that he is dearer to my heart every hour that I Live. No, I will not for that would be hyperbolical, But I can tell him that there is not an hour nor a moment that I do not miss his dear presence. I can not say,

"There's not a garden walk I tread
There's not a flower I see,
But brings to mind some hope that's fled,
Some joy I've lost with thee!!!"

for my ill health & present mode of life do not allow me such contemplations, but I can say,

There's not a hue upon the sky,
Nor murmur of the sea,
There's not a breeze than wanders by,
But brings some thoughts of thee!

I have been reading the story of one who loved her husband—devotedly—with all the energies of her soul (in a word as I love my brave & noble Houston!) who poured out her young heart's treasures upon him who in return only gave cold indifferences & neglect. Whilst I almost wept over the tale of imaginary sorrow, I felt that her fate would never be mine, for I surely would not survive the first proof of his indifference. Oh No, I would not live and feel myself unloved by him, for whom I would cheerfully leave kindred, home, friends, every thing that was near & dear and dwell amongst the wildest tribe of Indians! Oh how happy I have been when his gentle looks & words have told me that my deep devotion was returned! And even now during the lonely hours of his absence, the memory of them arises within my heart like a well-spring in some arid resort, but how often whilst our hearts are basking in the sunshine of hope and fancy does some sudden cloud arise and envelope our bright dreams in the blackness of darkness!! Thus while my heart whispers, "he loves me yet," I am happy—oh how happy! But then I ask myself, "may he not forget me?" and a cold shuddering steals over me. I would not live long with such feelings. Oh dearest, do not forget me!

Jan. 31st. By the Maryland this morning, I rec'd your truly interesting Package. I sent bro. V[ernal] over so soon as I saw the smoke of the boat and in the meantime prepared myself for a good comfortable, weeping fit in case that he brought me no letter, but fortunately you deprived me of the luxury, and had your letter not put me into a very amiable mood, after reading the immortal Moore's effusion, I should have felt more like fighting than weeping. As it was I acted with becoming dignity, especially as Dr. Tucker was present—who you know had seen a little of my temper on a similar occasion. Poor fellow! he enjoys the <u>sweet privilege of saying what he chooses</u>, and we are compelled to pass him like the shiny snake that we can not thrust out of our path—for fear of soiling the feet. I will send bro M[artin] the paper which contains the reply to Moore. I think my health is better. Dr. Tucker thinks I will be quite well so soon as you come home.

Neither he nor Mother will suffer me to go out, nor is it my own inclination to visit at present, but bro V. gladly acts as my substitute where there are any young ladies concerned. I do not think there is any danger of him marrying for he is in love with so many that he can not make a selection from amongst them. If you do not come home soon, Ma thinks of taking me to Capt Black's[1] and Dr. Tucker urges it as he thinks the climate would agree with me better. One of Mother's reasons would be that she is paying no rent at present—as her own lot is now a perfect pool and she fears the exposure I might have in getting to Cedar point, but if I <u>have my way</u>, I will go to no private house unless you take me to our own home. My love, if I do not see you shortly, I fear I shall forget all my sentiment & romance for truly I am become a most awfully commonplace person. Ma very often laughs to hear me talking of onions, hoes, and ploughs and all such coarse things and she says she can not imagine what has come over me.

The truth is I am thinking day & night how frugal and industrious we will be, when we get to keeping house. Now you must not think that I love you less from mingling your dear image with such common things, as I have mentioned. No—no! What is there that would not become beautiful and interesting to me from being associated with the idea of my dear—dear husband. Mother says, I am growing so petulant & disagreeable that she will have to send for you to manage me![2]

I must not omit to tell you that recently more that one person has said to me that I am strikingly like you. It is realy not a compliment at any time. Although you would gallantly dispute me much less at present, for I am pale & emaciated and very very homely. Ma & bro. V send a great deal of love to you.

Farewell Love, Hasten home to your devoted Maggy

Feb. 30th
You must excuse this very rough epistle I hope you will have left Austin before it reaches there.

I have been reading Jenyn's internal evidence of Christianity & "Watson's reply to Paine." They contain a great deal of fine reasoning and I hope to have the pleasure of reviewing them with you when you come home.

Present me to Col. and Mrs. Flood and to Col Hockley and whomsoever you wish. Miller[3] remercies to Mr. Saligny pour le jolie fleur, as you say it is from him.

[1]Captain John S. Black. Margaret is probably referring to Montgomery County, where the Black family owned property. Montgomery, 169–70.
[2]Right after this sentence, Margaret crossed out the next ten lines, and they are now illegible.
[3]Washington D. Miller, Houston's Secretary. For a biography see *Writings*, II, 389n.

Mrs. M. L. Houston
Galveston
Texas

Austin 31st Jany 1841

My Beloved,

This is the holy day, and I have been in my own room and not absent from it. The day has been rainy beyond any thing before seen by us in this place. I am disappointed by the rain for the reason that the person who was to bear my letter will not leave to day. So I chuse to add another to the general class of scribbling. I can add but one important item & it is that my friend Judge [George Whitfield] Terrell will not accept the appointment of Sec'y of State. He is wise for his standing on the Bench is enviable for a man of his age, and in the East there is no one to fill his place. Moreover he cou'd not harmonize with such a man as Burnet, a man who has no care but selfishness nor does he regard the countrys weal. Were he honest, he is not capable and will convert all the resources of Government to orate and sustain a Party—Political. The Judge by remaining on the Bench will, I have no doubt, attain the highest honors of that department of Government which I regard as the palladium of pure Freedom— For my dear I make a difference between Liberty and Freedom.— Liberty, I regard as the privilege to chuse in what manner we will be governed. Freedom is to my mind the well regulated enjoyment of Liberty. Nothing so much conduces to this object as an enlightened, honest, and fearless judiciary! Men look to it for the Guardian of their rights of property and person—and the Protector of their lives! Thus regarding it, they feel impressed with a weightier sense of obligation to sustain it than any other Department of Government! The duration of its chiefs being more permanent than the officers of any other department of the Government of Republics! From these considerations, as well as my high personal regard for a <u>friend</u>, I am greatly gratified that he did not embark in a sinking ship!

You see my Love that I must be prosing or prating. Prosing if I wrote about politics and prating if I tell you that I love you or wou'd give Kingdoms to be with you (if I only <u>had them</u> to <u>give</u>). Be this as it may, as I have done prosing, I will now prate. Love! 'Tis true my

Love, that I am a little happy and very miserable too! Happy because we must soon adjourn, and miserable because I am not where my Margaret is! Oh this day has caused me so often to think of you that I have not sent for a Bible. I did not, when I cou'd remain undisturbed, wish to call my thoughts from you. You are my sum and substance of existence. You are my leading star! But now my love, you are the lone star of Texas! You will doubtless regard this as a just comparison! I am sorry that it is too true! But, I wish you to be happy in the confidence that I will soon embrace you.

Had I been at home to day, how happy wou'd we have been. We cou'd have talked over a thousand matters, and the world cou'd not have intruded upon our privacy! Such days and scenes as these, I trust are in store for us. The world will then be worth enjoyment and indeed to us this wou'd be the greatest of earthly bliss. For such delights, I wou'd with pleasure either hoe, grub, or plough thro' the week, if no other employment wou'd justify the enjoyment of my dear Maggy's society.

I did rather suppose when I wrote you a letter on yesterday, that it wou'd be the last that I wou'd write to you soon because I hope to follow it. The aspect of affairs changes like fancy dreams, or the phases of a changeling. I find every thing here changes more or less except my <u>love of you</u> and that you will find, <u>fellowed</u> by one object only, and that is North Stars. It was the only comparison that Shakespeare cou'd find for the decision of Julius Caesar! So I chuse to compare my love of you! Sunday night as it is, I have <u>only</u> five Gentlemen around me conversing, and with me occasionally. To me, this is most <u>painful courtesy</u>. Oh my love, when will I be at peace? Never until I can see, and be with you, and then I hope to be happy!!!

My only care is to make you happy. In that event I must be blessed also. Again I am compelled to exclaim, why am I so constantly writing to my dear Maggy? The only answer or apology that I can find in my mind is that my heart will control my head and hand. You will pardon these <u>petty</u> faults—if faults they are.

Every day this place looks to me more and more dreary. How sad is the solitude of heart. It is more dreary than all the solitude of the desarts [sic] and the wilds of nature. In them there is something striking, and the wind can be delighted, or at least astonished, by some apparent freak of old Mother nature! Prolific in her productions, in the wonders of nature, we can be taught lessons of philosophy and wisdom.—But in the solitude of a crown, how little can we derive of wisdom, instruction, or pleasure when the only being on earth is absent from the eye and only present to the heart. This my dear is my situation and the only one that I can realise in your absence.

My love to all. Thy most truly devoted and affectionate husband Houston

Austin 8 oclock P.M. 1st Feby 1841

This evening my Beloved, I had closed a letter to you thinking it wou'd be the last, until I wou'd see you, but as I came to the capitol, I looked to the west, and saw the <u>lone</u> the brightest star that I ever saw because you were not with me, and the star that <u>we looked upon was eclipsed by your presence</u>. This evening when I saw the star, it was elevated above the summit of a stately Live Oak and the lustre of the star appeared to be sustained and beautifully contrasted with perennial verdure of the oak and its durability. The star may set, and will rise again, but the oak will not change, its verdant character is our love. Gaiety may change, but our affections treasured as they are in the hearts core, we may rely upon their analogy to the Live Oak. On the 4th Inst, we will adjourn, I have no doubt. The members will not stay an hour longer. They as well as myself are miserable here, and must be so as long as we may be detained! To night for a long time, we again see the bright moon. It is descending beautifully. I have just learned that Mr. Meggenson[1] has arrived! and that he has letters for me. I can not find him, but hope he has news from my dear Maggy! Oh my Love! You will think me crazy, I am sure, or a <u>kind Simpleton</u>. Pardon me my dear Wife. If I loved you less you wou'd not be teazed [sic] to read all I write! But you cant read a letter while I can write a page! By this suggestion you may derive patience enough to sustain you in reading all the sillyness [sic] which I have inflicted upon you for the last few days.

This Congress has done all the harm that it can do, I hope, and now it refuses to do any good! God help the country! By and bye, the country will be older and people will be more wise and considerate. The public domain will be disposed of, and land stealing will cease. When this may be the case, we can hope for reflection and just and honest legislation. Until then demagogues will seize upon the worst feelings of the human heart, cupidity, and avarice! and by these means obtain high places. I detest a demagogue and abhor the vulgar cant that "such a man has too much land." And my dear, the worst of the course is that it is the greatest crime to have bought and paid for the land previous to the Revolution and <u>fought</u> and defended it during the war!!

You can have some Idea my love, of the wisdom of Congress from this hint. The courts will be our reliance. They will be honest, and independent & will sustain the citizens rights. I rely with confidence upon the Judiciary of the country! It must save the nation and will be bound to declare all the land laws of this session unconstitutional. This will save the nation! If it can be saved!!! My Love, I must conclude this letter in the hope that you are and may remain happy. My prayers will accompany my hopes!

Thy husband
Houston

Madam Margaret
My Love, I have just had the pleasure and <u>sorrow</u> to read yours of the 18th. All my love to you. I will soon be with you. Thy most devoted Houston.
I am sorry because you are sad and not well!
To My Wife

[1]Probably Joseph C. Meggenson. See *Writings*, IV , 331n.

Mrs. Margaret L. Houston
Galveston, Texas
Capt. Brannum

Austin 2nd Feby 1841

My Dear Maggy,
Again I must write to you and express my deep and feeling regrets that you are so low spirited and melancholy as your last letter indicated.[1] The distress of our dear Mother about her lot has vexed

you. Oh what a miscreant he must be—Cody will come to an igno-
minious death. Every day I hear of some forging of his and now
Hale[2] and others have to pay for his crimes. This is all well enough!!!
[Edward H.] Winfield, who is but little better has written to me, that
he has "satisfactorily settled the matter about the Lot to the satisfaction of the parties." If so I am glad of it. How Vernal ever hit upon
Mr. Rose I cant guess—but my Love, tell him to incur no expense
until I can get home! That I trust in Heaven will be but a few days—
Tho' they will be long and tedious days.

I am not astonished my love that the furniture is much abused. I
am to blame, if any one is —the fault was mine, but not the crime if
any—This I will explain to you. I take the blame to myself, but you
had a harmless agency in the matter. You will be amused at the explanation!!! But I had as well tell you now—If I had not seen you in
Mobile and fallen in love with you, I wou'd have been at Houston
and had it sold. I was to blame for seeing you, and loving you and
you were a little to blame for taking into consideration my love.
Thus I settle the furniture matters. Oh Maggy, we will "make out"
well, I hope, and so long as our love remains unimpaired, we can be
rich and happy.—But why I [sic] am I always writing to you? For
the life of me I cant tell, unless it is that I always think of you, and
think of nothing else! You will be vexed with me for writing so much
to you.

You must have the patience of Job to read and think of all that I
write to you! I am sure never did Lover write so constantly to his
Dulcenia as I do to you! The only reason can be that I love you more
than man ever loved dear woman. But you are to me all that I wou'd
wish you to be, only that you are not always with me. You wou'd
cheer me, and I wou'd cherish and console you! Every little care I
wou'd alleviate as I did at Col Andrews[3] when you had been distressed and were determined to quarrel with me! Yes my Love, you
were in a pit and tried to reproach me agreeably—but your dear
heart soon failed you and you abandoned it as cruel to me. Yes
Maggy! You did do it, and I have often smiled at your want of tact to
manage a quarrel.

My Love, dont think that I recall these matters in malice.—No
they are recur'd to as pleasing reminiscences—all that is connected
with you Dearest, affords me pleasure and delight! My Love! It really seems to me if I do not see you soon that I will become crazy.

Even now, I hardly know what I write. I do know what I feel! I feel that I am the husband of Margaret, and that I do love her almost to madness. Certainly delirium!! Nor do I wish to see the day when I shall love her less. The passion flower blooms but once in the season. So I am doomed to love but once in the season of life.

Have no care my love, that I will be a Candidate for President without your wishes. I will not even say consent to you in [torn] . . . pray you suppose that I wou'd accept any situation on this earth that wou'd withdraw myself from you, and the charms of your society. The most splendid sceptre in the world cou'd not induce me to forego my boundless love of you. No my dear, you are the only human being that ever absorbed my thoughts, my love, my life and all and _every_ hope! Don' think that ambition has one charm for me! You have a thousand!!! I told the Colonel and Mrs Flood of your request in relation to my _candidacy._ They were astounded, and Mrs. F. said "oh! it is not possible, but she can't help it—the people will elect you _any how._" I replied, that you shou'd decide!!! If I were to declare that I wou'd not serve, if elected, I assure you that it wou'd be deemed a national calamity.

I am only sorry for my country, that [torn] . . . most conscious of my infelicity. I wou'd depart, if I believed that you wou'd derive any real advantage. I wou'd incur the charge of dereliction in the discharge of my duty. I had no business here, in the first place, but being here, you wou'd not wish me to be a _deserter_!!! While I may be detained, the grief, and infelicity must be mine. I write to you constantly, but can not hope to hear from you, unless by accident. Since I first came to this place, I never failed to write to you by every opportunity. Many may have left here, of whom I knew nothing; therefore I did not write because I did not know that they wou'd pass by or be at Galveston. All my leisure hours, or even moments, have I devoted in rendering the offering of my affections to you! But I am sure you will not complain of me. The moment that the . . .
[incomplete]

[1]See Margaret to Houston, January 18, 1841.
[2]Houston is probably referring to Wiley Pope Hale of Galveston. Identified in Gifford White, _1840 Citizens of the Republic of Texas, I, Land Grants,_ (St. Louis: Ingmire Publications, 1983), 103.
[3]Col. John D. Andrews. The Houstons had earlier visited in the Andrews' home on Austin Street in Houston City probably in the late summer of 1840. Marguerite

Johnston, *Houston: The Unknown City 1836-1946*, (College Station: Texas A&M University Press, 1991), 48.

Austin 3rd Feby 41

By the enclosed News paper[1] my Beloved will see that I have <u>not consented to become a Candidate for the Presidency</u>! The affection and happiness of my endeared Margaret are more to me than all the Gewgaws of ambition or the pageantry of Royalty.

Shou'd she desire me to do so, I will consent but not otherwise! My <u>Love</u> must decide and let her regard <u>her own</u> happiness.

Mine will consist in <u>Her felicity</u>. The determination of my Love I will abide by. Thy people shall be my people and thy God shall be my God! On tomorrow I suppose we will adjourn.

Thy devoted Husband
Houston

Lady Margaret

[1]The newspaper clipping has not been located.

Chapter III

[March 22], 1841–November 10, 1841

[March 22], 1841: Margaret Houston to Sam Houston
[Spring 1841]: Sam Houston to Margaret Houston
April 1, 1841: Margaret Houston to Sam Houston
April 15, 1841: Margaret Houston to Sam Houston
November 10, 1841: Sam Houston to John Hall

After Congress adjourned Houston joined Margaret in Galveston and they spent some time at Cedar Point. In the spring Margaret remained behind while Houston went on a trip to East Texas to take care of his law practice. The following letter from Margaret is not dated, but was written some time in the spring of 1841 circa March 22.

[22 March 1841]

Addressed to Gen. Sam Houston
Nacogdoches, Texas

I rec'd a letter from brother Henry a few days ago, directed to you, but addressed to us both. He seems to be considerably distrest on account of Sister Serena's low health, but I trust that his fears are groundless. Dr. Anson Jones is in this place and Mr. McKinney told me in the street this morning that he would bring him to see us this evening. I presume his visit is rather an electioneering one. There is scarcely any thing else discussed in Galveston at this time, but the election of him president. Gen. Hunt[1] seems to be rather in the ascendant at present, but perhaps Dr. Jones's visit may turn the scene.

24th

Dr. Jones called the night before last. I was very much pleased with him. He mentioned that Mr Flood and family with Mr. Saligny would be in Galveston shortly. He has had a disagreement with Mr. Bullock and considers himself treated with so little respect by Burnet and others that Dr. Jones fears he will leave Texas in disgust.[2] Wednesday Mr. Webb[3] and Col. Dangerfield[4] called on us. I think they both leave today. The one for Mexico, the other for France. No recent news except the death of Col. John Evans on the 22nd.[5]

I am told that Mr. Waters[6] has returned to Houston, but I can not ascertain that he brought any news of you, except that you had no cold idea when you would return! This of course was not very cheering to me especially as I understand that you have nothing to detain you. I am weary—weary of this place and would go immediately to the point if I thought you would be absent much longer. Dearest I do not think you can stay from me much longer. I am sure I could not from you. Mr. McKinney[7] has declined going east. I will therefore conclude this and get him to forward it immediately. It is the opinion of every one that there will be a call session of congress.

The very thought is sickening to me and if there is, you must prepare to let me go to Marion [Alabama] where I could have the company of my friends, for I could not spend another age in Texas without you. I am spiritless today and therefore will write no more.

Farewell my best beloved.
Thy ever M. L. Houston

My health has undergone a considerable change since you left. I have scarcely ever any cough and my breast seems nearly well, but every other day I had a severe chill and fever. Mother is well and sends her love to you.

[1]General Memucan Hunt. For a biography see *Writings,* I, 525n.
[2]Alphonse Saligny, the French minister to Texas, felt he had been overcharged by innkeeper Richard Bullock. Later when Bullock's pigs continued to eat corn from the stable of the French Legation, Saligny ordered his servants to kill the pigs. For an account of what became known as "The Pig War" see James L. Haly, *Texas —An Album of History,* (Garden City, N. Y.: Doubleday, 1985), 125–27, and George Lankevich, ed., *The Presidents of the Republic of Texas,* (Dobbs Ferry, N. Y.: Oceana Publications, Inc., 1979), 39.
[3]James Webb was appointed emissary to Mexico on March 22, 1841. Lankevich, 39.
[4]William Henry Daingerfield. For a biography see *Writings,* II, 452n.
[5]Margaret possibly was referring to John S. Evans, a Galveston newspaper editor. For a biography see *Handbook of Texas,* I , 575.
[6]A J. S. Waters lived fifteen miles below Houston. Louis Wiltz Kemp, "Glimpses of Texas History," *Post Dispatch* (Houston), May 11, 1930.
[7]Thomas McKinney.

The first part of the following letter from Houston is missing. It is addressed to "Mrs. Margaret Houston, by Col. Bowyer[1] to Galveston" and was probably was written in the spring of 1841.

[Spring 1841]

. . . I found Shepperd & Lynch well and very happy. They request me to present the[ir] respectful compliments to you and Mother, and their love to Tilly & Henny [Henrietta]. So I reverse the manner of salutation—and send to you & mother, Sister & Bud, my love—to Tilly, Henny, Judge Johnson, and Mr. Rose, my kind salutations.

Dr. K.[2] told me that in cases <u>such as we have spoken of</u> that he would prefer no physician on the island to Dr. Laberdie.[3] He has no fancy for Dr. Roberts[4] line of business. This is <u>sub rosa</u>. [He] thinks pretty well of Doct. [torn].

But my Love, I have no unpleasant anticipation about these matters, as I hope to be at home by the time that you may expect me! My spirit and my love are always with you, and I must be prating. You will not be displeased with this as it evinces the portion of my boundless affection for you. You can not fancy my foolish anxiety to be with you again, and sit and see and hear you speak while I can muse on the past and in fancy enjoy the happy future!!!

Unless I cease, you will really suppose that I am courting you anew. You must allow me the pleasure, as I will not have any one to court, or admire until I can render my personal devoirs to your La-dyship. Then you are not to pout with me. You will have no cordial to object to, but I hope you will have no cheeks to slap, if you shou'd become captious!! I was really astonished, when I [torn] to see the change in my complexion [torn]

You can not realize it. All sallowness has left me, and my cheeks are as red as yours. Riding does not fatigue me in the least, nor does walking. I am restored perfectly to my cheerfulness & more than ever satisfied, that my health will be restored to what it was six years ago! I will omit neither care nor attention for its restoration! I have [torn] motives for this course—the first is you demand it, and my first objective is to see you happy. It is not that you demand it in words, but the sacred relations which bind me to you demand this much of me! Moreover, if I live, I must get rich, or at least independent. These reasons, with many others will weigh with me and must prevail. Keep an eye on Martha or she may run away as well as others. Allow yourself to <u>want nothing</u>, and do not let any business distress you.

Thine ever,
Houston

[1]James Bowyer, the Chief Justice of Galveston. Joe E. Ericson, comp., *Judges of the Republic of Texas 1836–46: A Biographical Directory*, (Dallas: Taylor Publishing, 1980), 13.
[2]May be Dr. William Kerr of Nacogdoches. V. K. Carpenter, *1850 Census of Texas*, v.

1, (Huntsville, Arkansas: Century Enterprises, 1969), 438.
[3]Dr. Nicholas LaBadie. Identified in George Plunkett Red, *The Medicine Man in Texas,* (Houston: Standard Printing & Lithographing Company, 1930), 52–55.
[4]Dr. Willis Roberts of Galveston. Identified in Nixon, 341–42.

Margaret may have suffered a miscarriage around this time. She wrote of her health problems in the following letter:

Galveston April l, 1841

My own Love,

I will not attempt to amuse you this evening, for I have been so lonely ever since you left me that I have forgotten all my vivacity, but I must write to you for I am so accustomed to telling you all my thoughts and feelings that it has been almost an involuntary thing with me. Do you ever observe the beautiful language of Medora in Byron's corsair?:

"And he is gone?
How often sudden solitude
That fearful question doth intrude
I was but a moment past and here he stood!"

This may give you some faint idea of my feelings. When the dreadful idea rushed upon me that you were no longer with me, that the eyes whose looks of affection had so often gladdened my heart were then fixed on some distant scene. [blurred] I was not at all well the day after you left and sent down for Dr. Hawkins.[1] He came up and bled me pretty freely much against Mother's wishes however, but he said it was absolutely necessary and I felt that something had to be done. He had a conversation with Mother about me and he seems to think from my appearance that it is all a mistake about my situation and attributes the symptoms to some arrangement of the nerves. I do not know how this could be, but it is certainly a singular case.

Mrs. Hawkins left today on the Neptune[2] and will remain with her relations in New Orleans until the Dr. can join her. Mr. Bledsoe and Bro V[ernal] left us on Tuesday for Washington. Armstrong[3] has been across from Cedar Point. I expected him to have every thing as comfortable as possible as we expected to be at home in the course of a few weeks. Mrs. [blurred] has been up again but I was too unwell to see her. I understand that she declares her husband shall not vote for you but he tells her he will exercise his own judgment in such cases. Capt. Emerson[4] is still very ill and I fear that he is in great danger.

April 2nd

Gen. [Memucan] Hunt called on us last night but I felt so unwell that I did not go out to see him. Today I feel quite well and hope soon to be entirely recovered. It is not [sic] 7 o'clock AM so you see I am thrusting off the insolent habits you have taught me. You can not imagine how much sister A[ntoinette]'s company enlivens me. I do not think I could endure your absence without her. Judge Johnson requested me to say to you that you must not mention something he told you Je ne sais [torn] I suppose you will understand.

I hope you will not be uneasy about me [torn] your absence or leave your business unfinished on my account for if things should result as we at first anticipated, I shall no doubtless have every necessary attention. I trust therefore that your mind will be free and undisturbed about me and that you will not fatigue yourself on your return. I will try to be cheerful and not give in to despondency for I find that it is [torn] to my health.

Dearest, remember that you promised me to take care of yourself. Oh how happy I would be to meet you again in fine health! I need not tell you to write to me by every opportunity for that I am sure you will do. I hope to have the pleasure of writing to you again by Mr. [Thomas] McKinney. Mother and I send a great deal of love to you. Mrs. R. requests me to present her compliments. Farewell my best beloved. May our Heavenly Father protect you and bring you again safely to [torn]

Your devoted
M. L. Houston

[1]Dr. Robert Hawkins, former Surgeon General of the Texas Army. Identified in Marion Day Mullins, *First Census of Texas, 1829–1836*, (Washington, D. C.: Special Publication of the National Genealogical Society, Number 22, 1959), 73.
[2]The *Neptune* was a steamship which ran from New Orleans to Galveston in a trip

which took 40 hours. It carried 30 cabin passengers and 40 in steerage. Hogan, 9.
[3]Jacob Armstrong was a neighbor who owned property on the east side of Cedar Bayou. *An Abstract of the Original Titles of Record in the General Land Office,* (Austin: Reproduced by Pemberton Press, 1964), 123.
[4]F. B. Emerson of Galveston. Identified in White, *1840 Citizens of Texas, Land Grants,* I, 76.

Galveston, April 15th, 1841

My own Love,

I feel in pretty good spirits today and it is such a rare thing of late that I think I had better write to you while the sun shines. I am delighted at the idea of having you with me in a few days. It is now nearly three weeks since you left me and you know your limits will then be nearly out! I have borne your absence with more patience than I imagined I could exercise but it has certainly been very distressing to me. Sister A[ntoinette] and Mrs. Gant[1] expect to leave on tomorrow and meet Mr. Bledsoe in Houston. I do not know how I shall get along without them. The only thing that reconciles me to thier departure is the hope that you will be with me very soon. I have been busily employed in preparing our things for house-keeping (for I shall not consider myself a housekeeper until we get to our own house) and that is the most agreeable amusement I can have at present. I should like to know if you are as anxious to get settled at home as I am. I do not think you can be <u>altogether dearest</u>.

Emma sent me some beautiful flowers from New Orleans, and they are growing quite prettily. The flowers that brother M[artin] brought me are all doing finely. I rec'd a letter from Col. Christy[2] by Mrs. Garat.[3] He mentioned that Mrs. C.'s health was very bad and had been so since Dec. He fears that her symptoms are premonitory of consumption. At the time he says that she was so ill that he was induced to write as her substitute.

Dr. Hawkins is still here and calls up occasionally. I fear that he is treating himself rather badly. It is certainly a great pity for a man of his intelligence. I hope I have seen Dr. Moore's[4] last piece, but lest it should have escaped you, if I can get a copy of it I will send it to you. Well I think I have almost exhausted my gossip for today. [torn] as a last remark I believe <u>a la Price</u> I will write you a little poetry.

<u>My husband's picture.</u>

Dear gentle shade of him I love!
I've gazed upon thee, till thine eye,
In liquid light doth seem to move
And look on me in sympathy!

And oh that smile! I know it well,
It minds me of the one in May
When soft the rising starlight fell
Upon the flowers at close of day!

And first my trembling lips did own
Thy love returned that holy hour
Sure nature smiled in unison,
Through every tree and vine and flower.

As now I gaze upon that form
Against those clouds of threatening mien,
The bold relief, as if no storm
Could ever scathe thy brow again.

An image starts within my mind,
As if a shadow from the past,
On some sweet dream of olden time
Had suddenly my heart o'ercast.

Yes—yes—it must be so the same
Proud form of majesty! the one
That o'er my girlish visions came
And that my heart hath loved alone!

  Cap. Emerson is thought to be a little better. The Dr. concludes that his room was not sufficiently comfortable for him and we gave up the dining room to him. I never knew before how lonely a room of sickness was without the presence of a lady. The poor fellow often speaks with tears of his mother and his children far away.

Saturday 17th

What an age has past since I heard from you! But I have not supposed for a moment that you had suffered any opportunity of writing to pass you. Sister A[ntoinette] and Mrs. Gant left yesterday morning with the expectations of meeting Mr. Bledsoe in Houston. Brother Vernal arrived at home last night. He came down with the expectation of returning with Sis but passed her on the way.

22nd

Today Mr. Edmunds[5] gave me the San Augustine paper containing the account of your reception in that place.[6] I was very much gratified, but less so than I would have been if I had rec'd a letter from you by <u>the same mail</u>! Eh bien, I will write to you always, let my letters be uninteresting as they may. This may seem a little like reproach, but it is not dearest for if your engagement was such that you can not write, I will excuse you.

I enclose a little pensee (in english "remembrances"). The emblem is "Forget me not" and it is my favorite flower. I love it not only for its simple beauty, but for some sweet association of childhood connected with it.

[letter is incomplete]

[1]Mrs. William W. Gant of Washington County. Identified in *Handbook of Texas,* I, 670.

[2]William Christy, of New Orleans, was an old friend of Houston's. Llerena Friend, *Sam Houston: The Great Designer,* (Austin: University of Texas Press, 1954), 72.

[3]This is probably Mrs. Charles C. Garrett of Galveston. Identified in White, *1840 Citizens of Texas, Land Grants I* , 91.

[4]Margaret is undoubtedly referring to an article written by Dr. Francis Moore, Jr., for the *Telegraph and Texas Register* (Houston). Possibly this is the one of March 31, 1841, which announced for Burnet.

[5]Pizene Edmunds, sometimes spelled Edmonds. For a biography see *Writings,* II, 453.

[6]A public dinner to honor Houston had been given at San Augustine on April 5, 1841. Wisehart, 368.

Houston was nominated for President of the Republic of Texas by the

citizens of Harris County. He returned from East Texas and spent most of the summer at Cedar Point engaging in a newspaper battle with David G. Burnet. Houston was elected on September 6, 1841, and Edward Burleson was elected vice-president. The following letter is from the Crockett Courier, *January 31, 1890. In it Houston wrote to his friend John L. Hall of Crockett concerning his thoughts on becoming president:*

General Houston to Capt John L. Hall at Crockett

Cedar Point
November 10, 1841

Dear Sir:

On yesterday we arrived at home and again look upon the beautiful Bay. I am sorry that I will have so short a time to enjoy at home. It is my intention to be on the way to Austin by the 1st of December.

Mrs. Houston's health is much improved since we left Crockett, but is not sufficiently well to risk the climate of Austin this winter. I dislike leaving home, because Mrs H cannot accompany me. The winter would be dreary enough in Austin with all the comforts that could be commanded with a family. Without one, the only resource of happiness will be business. I will be reasonably miserable and should contemplate the time as lost if it were not that I hope to do my country some service. God knows it needs something to be done for it. If anything that I can do will be of advantage to Texas, or by possibility, relieve her from pressure, I will find myself richly rewarded for any pains or cares that I may endure in my trip to the frontier.

Our navy has not yet started, and if it could be of any use to us I would be glad that it should not go. If it should sail, you may rely upon it that it will be the last of our navy. That it will be in the hands of Santa Anna in ninety days, I would be willing to wager a trifle. I would not be surprised if it would turn out that the whole revolution in Yucatan was set on foot by Santa Anna with a view to inveigle Lamar and get the navy in possession. The revolution was a bloodless one and soon ended. Moreover, Santa Anna has a great contempt for Lamar and would be quite delighted to play a trick upon him. Besides, it would furnish Mexico with a navy, which she is not able to purchase, and have our whole coast at her mercy. We will see.

Be pleased to make Mrs. Houston's respects and mine to Mrs.

Hall[1] and the ladies of our acquaintance. Salute all friends for us, and be assured of our best feelings and wishes for your happiness.

Yours truly
Sam Houston

Capt Jno L Hall

Request General [James Pinckney] Henderson and Judge [George] Terrell to be at Austin. The inauguration will take place the 13th December. Say so—privately

[1]The former Elizabeth Oatman. Kemp, 36–38.

Chapter IV

November 30, 1841–February 7, 1842

November 30, 1841: Sam Houston to Margaret Houston
December 1, 1841: Robert Irion to Sam Houston
December 2, 1841: Sam Houston to Margaret Houston
December 5, 1841: Margaret Houston to Sam Houston
December 6, 1841: Sam Houston to Margaret Houston
December 6, 1841: Margaret Houston to Sam Houston
December 9, 1841: Sam Houston to Margaret Houston
December 9, 1841: Sam Houston to Margaret Houston
December 10, 1841: Sam Houston to Margaret Houston
December 11, 1841: Margaret Houston to Sam Houston
December 12, 1841: Sam Houston to Margaret Houston
December 13, 1841: Sam Houston to Margaret Houston
December 15, 1841: Sam Houston to Robert Irion
December 15, 1841: Sam Houston to Margaret Houston
December 21–22, 1841: Sam Houston to Margaret Houston
December 24–28, 1841: Sam Houston to Margaret Houston
December 29–30, 1841: Sam Houston to Margaret Houston
January 1, 1842: Sam Houston to Margaret Houston
January 3, [1842]: Margaret Houston to Sam Houston
January 3, [1842]: Margaret Houston to Sam Houston
January 5, [1842]: Margaret Houston to Sam Houston

January 6, 1842: Sam Houston to Margaret Houston
January 6, 1842: Sam Houston to Margaret Houston
January 7, 1842 : Margaret Houston to Sam Houston
January 8, 1842: Sam Houston to Margaret Houston
January 10, 1842: Sam Houston to Margaret Houston
January 12, 1842: Sam Houston to Margaret Houston
January 12, 1842: Margaret Houston to Sam Houston
January 13, 1842: Margaret Houston to Sam Houston
January 13, 1842: Sam Houston to Margaret Houston
January 14–18, 1842: Sam Houston to Margaret Houston
January 14, 1842: Margaret Houston to Sam Houston
January 15, 1842: Margaret Houston to Sam Houston
January 19, 1842: Sam Houston to Margaret Houston
January 19, 1842: Sam Houston to Margaret Houston
January 20, 1842: Margaret Houston to Sam Houston
January 21–22, 1842: Sam Houston to Margaret Houston
January 25, 1842: Sam Houston to Margaret Houston
January 25, 1842: Margaret Houston to Sam Houston
January 27–28, 1842: Sam Houston to Margaret Houston
January 29, 1842: Margaret Houston to Sam Houston
January 30, 1842: Sam Houston to Margaret Houston
[January 31, 1842]: Sam Houston to Margaret Houston
January 31, 1842: Sam Houston to Margaret Houston
February 1, 1842: Sam Houston to Margaret Houston
February 1, 1842: Sam Houston to Margaret Houston
February 3, 1842: Sam Houston to Margaret Houston
February 7, 1842: Margaret Houston to Sam Houston

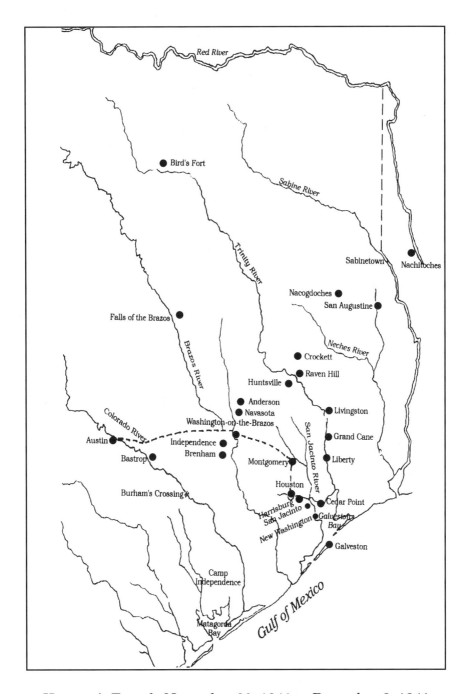

Houston's Travels November 30, 1841 to December 8, 1841

In November of 1841, Houston journeyed to Austin for the sixth session of the Congress of the Republic of Texas, this time as President-elect. Margaret remained behind in Houston City at the home of John and Eugenia Andrews on Austin Street. Houston wrote the following letter as he began the trip to the capital.

Mrs. Margaret Lea Houston
City of Houston
Texas
Major Reily[1]

Maj Uzzells[2]
30th Nov. 1841

My Love,

This day has gone off pretty well and to my great satisfaction there is no Ball to night. The reception given to me was cordial and quite genteel. The whole matter has given earnest [sic] of the feelings and confidence expressed at the last election. This is all well enough and such as must be agreeable to me, but the pageant was marred because you were not a participant in the passing scenes. The Absence of all that I cherish on earth was well calculated to diminish the pleasure which I ought to feel on such occasions—For had the last few months been passed without such constant and intimate association, I might possibly feel less acutely the anguish caused by my absence from my dear Margaret. Do not suppose that I am writing a <u>love letter</u>, or resuming my courtship. I must confess that I do love a good deal and cou'd have no objection to pay my addresses in person to the fair one to whom I feel so much devoted as my dear "Dulcina." You can have no idea my beloved of the solitary state of my feelings—I look around me from time to time and listen for the tones of your voice which have so often soothed the agitations of an excited heart. The intensity of my feelings really produces a desultory state of mind, and produces a train of reflections of the most unpleasant character. The absence, which I am compelled to anticipate, renders my situation truly painful. When I feel that my absence must be for weeks or months from you and distant from every source of joy I am truly unhappy—When these anticipations are contrasted with the last few months and the felicity which I have enjoyed in your society, I must confess that my destiny seems any thing but enviable. The distinction of station is a poor recompense for the sacrifice which is incidental to my absence. In all and every throb of my heart, in every emotion, you are blended with my spirit. What fame I may acquire and every honor which may be confered upon me, wou'd be insipid and valueless were it not that it will enhance your noble pride and gratification.

In summing up my enjoyments of the past, I must assure you that those of the last few months are esteemed by me of more inestimable value than those of my past existence. Their recollection can never fail to awaken in my bosom the purest happiness, and inspire a feeling of gratitude to our God for his matchless kindness. They were hours of bliss to me because you seemed happy, and I was really blessed. They were the result of temperance of reason and of <u>holy affection</u>. Thus you will perceive that I appreciate properly the influence of sobriety upon our happiness, and the necessity of my adherence to a principle which can place us in the possession of every earthly blessing and from which a departure cou'd promise nothing but misfortune and wretchedness! Affection for <u>you</u>, my love, has produced this change and conviction which must and will remain, while affection maintains a place in my heart, or reason can direct my actions. Entertain no fears my beloved, as to my temperance, and propriety of conduct. Had I no regard for myself, the devotion which I entertain for you wou'd control my actions—But I must confess that in an adherance [sic] to these sacred principles, my own pride is awakened and stimulated by a sense of duty to my self and to posterity! <u>In all things</u>, rely upon my devotion to your dear self and be happy—

On the subject of my trip to Austin, I wish you to entertain no fears. The arm of the Lord will defend me, and his grace preserve me! The prayers of the righteous will be heard when they appeal to the almighty, and your prayers will be heard in my behalf. I will not disregard the caution proper to be used for my safety. Mr. Allison Lewis[3] will leave here with me for Austin. All the news that I hear from Congress is <u>not</u> of an unpleasant character. I hope the best for my country, and will omit nothing on my part to render it prosperous and happy.

I have heard from Bledsoe, and hope to see our dear Sister as I pass. Bud is mending, and I trust will soon be well again. I will be very amiable while at Bledsoes. I will not allow one word to escape me that can won'd [wound] the feelings of our dear Antoinette. I will write to Capt [John S.] Black to go down and arrange matters at our place! Maj. Western[4] will hire Joshua,[5] if it shou'd be proper to hire him out, and of this you must be the sole judge! In all matters refered to you, do as you deem best, and it will meet my hearty concurrence!

Col Bennett[6] will take Crusader[7] so I will be rid of our trouble. My idle time will be employed in attending to our home matters. I must try and render available all our means, and be placed in such a situation as we deserve.

I will write to you on all occasions and try to write a better letter when next I write than <u>this</u>—for I really feel mortified at the faults of this letter and wou'd not send it if I had time to write another. Major [James] Reily will tell you all the news. I love him more, as I know him better. He is a noble man. Comment me in the kindest terms to Col & Mrs. Andrews[8] and assure them of my sincere regards. Salute all our friends—may Heaven guard thee my beloved.

Thy husband Sam Houston

[1]Major James Reily, a Houston lawyer who represented Texas as chargé d'affaires at Washington, D. C. For a biography see *Writings*, II, 374–75n.
[2]Elisha Uzzell who lived near Montgomery, Texas. Montgomery, 126.
[3]In the 1840s Allison Lewis published a card proposing to do all of Houston's dueling for him and inviting "blood thirsty gentlemen" to pitch in. Rip Ford reported that no one was sporting for a fight. McDonald, 19.
[4]Major Thomas G. Western, a member of the Texas Army from Goliad, who made the address at the burial of the remains of the victims of the Alamo. *Writings*, II, 512–13n and Best, 283–84.
[5]Margaret's slave.
[6]Houston is probably referring to Colonel Joseph L. Bennet. For a biography see *Writings*, III, 131n.
[7]Houston's horse.
[8]John D. and Eugenia Andrews of Houston.

During the summer of 1841 the Houstons had been concerned about Margaret's health after a miscarriage. Houston had requested Dr. Robert Irion to advise Dr. Walter Fosgate, Margaret's personal physician,[1] how to

restore her health so that she could bear children normally. On December 1, 1841, Irion wrote to Houston:

With respect to Mrs. Houston's health, a subject which gives me infinitely more concern than all the appointments in the world, I have little to add to my former suggestions. I consulted freely with Dr. [Walter] Fosgate on the subject and there was an apparent agreement in our impressions. On reflection I am decidedly of the opinion that the irregularity of minstruation [sic], the consequence of abortion, produced her ill health; & that it never can be restored till that discharge becomes regular. I explained this to Dr. F. indicating, at the same time, the remedies which had been most successful in my hands in the treatment of such cases, and advised use of them without delay, which I sincerely hope he had done.[2]

[1]Nixon, 428–29.
[2]Martha Anne Turner, *Texas Epic*, (Wichita Falls, Texas: Nortex Press, 1974), 131–32. For the reply to this letter see Houston to Irion, December 15, 1841, in this chapter.

Houston continued his journey, stopping near Washington-on-the-Brazos where he wrote Margaret:

Mrs. Margaret Lea Houston
City of Houston
V. B. Lea

Washington County
2nd Dec 1841

My Beloved. Until I came to Washington I did not expect that Mr [William] Bledsoe had started, so I came to Mr. Farquahars[1] who purchased his place. I learn that our dear Sister and Vernal will stay to night at Mr. Niles[2] three miles from here. Tho' it is late, I am waiting until the moon rises to go and see Antoinette, if she is on this side of the Brasos [sic]. I have made Bledsoe another proposition, and will send it to him by our Sister. It is to give him 300 acres of land, and mother 100, if he will settle at the point[3] to give him ten leaves [sic] this year and priviledges [sic] of wood etc. I hope he will accept my offer—It is as generous as there is any use for. If he <u>will</u> go to the Trinity, I will do all that I promised him to do in that event.

I send you by Bud [Vernal] all the news from Austin. It may please you, as you are not forgotten—<u>Lady</u> wou'd be <u>singluar</u> [sic] and wife too—"Family" is <u>plural</u> & therefore more <u>important</u>. I must not disappoint the "big doins" which are to take place on the occasion. I will feel too sensibly that my dear family <u>are</u> not with me. You can have no idea my dear love, of the painful—truly painful emotions which agitated me as I was approaching this neighborhood. The days of bliss so lately passed with you near to my present situation were all recalled and clustered around my heart. I felt that I was indeed lonely and melancholy. The [bottom line torn off] . . . when I reflected upon my absence from you. I really esteemed the sacrifice greater than the honor is agreeable. These things might delight me at another time, and under different circumstances, but when it is probable that you are languishing in sickness, I can feel no joy that is not blended with pain and sorrow—For your dear sake, I hope my apprehensions are idle and that you are rejoicing in health and are happy. Cherish no idle cares on my account. I feel confident that the God whom you serve will protect <u>your husband</u>. You may be assured that <u>your happiness</u> and my <u>own honor</u> shall be my incentive to action and deportment. I will do <u>no act whatever,</u> if <u>truly</u> reported to you, that cou'd cause a blush to mantle your cheeks or awaken one painful emotion in your heart! I feel that to a great extent, I am the arbiter of your <u>peace</u> and your happiness. I will cherish my love as you wou'd desire for one earthly being & for <u>one</u> only—my Maggy! I need not tell you that my arch enemy never dares to approach me! I mean "Grog" in any shape or character.

Col Cooke[4] and others will go with me to Austin from this place tomorrow. I intend to go to Roberts[5] or Fullers.[6] I am told that Judge Baylor[7] will join me on the way and accompany me to Austin. I hope so! I parted with Dr. Tucker[8] to day and he wished to be remembered to you in the most respectful terms. He says that he will be at Austin on the 13th inst. [bottom line is torn off] I will write <u>whenever I can</u>. You I trust will do like wise. By the Bye, I intend not to stay more than one hour at the Ball, if I attend. I feel well assured that I can not enjoy <u>one</u> where you are not. You must not charge me with writing "love letters." So I must now wait until I see what the character of yours will be!

To Col & Mrs. Andrews, and to all our dear friends, I pray you to commend most truly. If you shou'd want money (<u>I don't say need</u> it) I pray you to let me know it. I will have <u>plenty</u> for you! My love to our dear mother, when [you] see her or write to her.

Thy devoted husband
Sam Houston

Mrs. M. L. Houston

[1]James L. Farquahars, identified in Lois Smith Murray, *Baylor at Independence*, (Waco: Baylor University Press, 1972), 27.
[2]A map of Washington-on-the-Brazos (compiled and drafted by Dana Morris, La Grange, Texas, 1974), shows Joseph W. J. Niles occupying Lot 6 (E) Block 12. Copy of map in possession of Madge Thornall Roberts.
[3]Cedar Point. No evidence has been found that the Bledsoes accepted Houston's offer.
[4]William G. Cooke. Identified in *Writings,* I, 343n.
[5]S. R. Roberts ("Squire Roberts") who kept a hotel in Washington. Johnnie Lockhart Wallis and Laurance Hill, *Sixty Years on the Brazos*, (Waco: Texian Press, 1967), 44.
[6]Samuel Fuller of Washington County. For a biography see Ray, 99.
[7]Robert Emmett Bledsoe Baylor was both a judge and a Baptist preacher. *Writings,* II, 438n.
[8]Dr. Edmund Tucker.

There was no regular postal service between Austin and Houston, so both Margaret and Houston had to depend on travelers to deliver their letters. Margaret wrote the following letter after she arrived in Houston City.

Houston Dec. 5th, 1841

My Love,

I have been told that a gentleman leaves this place some time today for Austin, and in great haste I have commenced a little scrawl for you. Thereafter I will not be so hurried, as I intend always to have a letter in readiness for anyone who may get off. I feel quite well today and in pretty good spirits. Dr. [Walter] Fosgate called on me yesterday evening and this morning and he seems quite delighted with my symptoms although he observed that I am a little pale and nervous. But that is easily accounted for by any one who has been appraised of my recent trial in parting with my beloved husband. The Dr. was quite sober and dignified. He left this morning for Fort bend [sic] and designs removing shortly to Washington. Capt. [John S.] Black has called twice to make some arrangements for Cedar point. He expects to be there on next Saturday or Sunday for the purpose of meeting Smith,[1] and making an engagement with him. If he does not succeed in getting any one to take charge of the place, he says Munroe[2] will remain there until your return. I have concluded to hire Joshua here and have not yet decided about Vina[3] exactly and can not until I hear from the island. I intend to write to Mother by the next boat, and I presume she will answer me by its return.

I am this particular because I am aware of your penchant for <u>minute details</u>. And now dearest I would like to tell you all the anguish that I have suffered from parting with you, but I do believe if you knew the extent of it you would be tempted to come home to me immediately. But dearest in this dark hour let us go to our Heavenly Father for consolation. He is our friend. Oh let us trust in him. Poor frail creatures! What a desolate fate would be ours without his sustaining hand! And yet whilst prosperity is around us and our hearts are gladdened with the smiles of affection, we forget that we are "but dust and ashes" and our proud spirits expand with a sense of importance, and our thoughts wander from God! But oh when the hour of loneliness and desolation gathers around us, and we look up for the eyes that we love and a dreary void is before us! and we listen for the voice that once cheered us and dull silence chills our souls! Oh who could live through that shadow of death were it not for the low sweet whispering of hope "trust thou in God!"

Things go pretty much in the same way as when you were here. My friend Mrs. Lee[4] is still here, but expects to leave on the next boat. I answered Bro. Will's[5] letter yesterday and wrote a pretty long epistle. My husband would call it a good letter, but you knew he overates [sic] every thing I do! Dearest I could write all day, but Mr. Lubbock[6] is just come for my letter. Rest assured I will neglect no opportunity of writing and I trust you will not either.
Farewell best and most beloved of husbands.

Thine forever

M. L. Houston

[1] An overseer hired to manage Cedar Point. This may have been someone in the family of Christian Smith who owned the land adjoining Cedar Point. (Not to be confused with Dr. Ashbel Smith who lived across the bay.)

[2] Monroe Black, son of John S. Black. Montgomery, 130.

[3] Sometimes spelled Vinah, she was one of Margaret's slave. See Temple Lea's Will.

[4] Mrs. W. Douglas Lee (Ophelia Caroline Morgan) was the daughter of James Morgan. Bass and Brunson, 105.

[5] Houston's brother William of Memphis, Tennessee.

[6] Francis R. Lubbock. In his memoirs, Lubbock notes that he was in Austin at this time because of his apointment as Comptroller. Francis R. Lubbock, *Six Decades in Texas: The Memoirs of Francis R. Lubbock*, (Austin: B. C. Jones & Company, 1900), 142.

To
Mrs. Margaret Lea Houston
at Col Andrews
City of Houston
Texas
Col Weaver of Selma

At Stevens 6th Dec 1841

My Love,

I write you by Col Weaver[1] of Selma who will call upon you. On yesterday, I lay bye as it was Sunday—I did not know that I had materials or I wou'd have written all day. Nothing gives me so much pleasure as to commune with you. In a few moments I will set out for Austin. I saw Bledsoe, and made a last effort to secure the society of our dear Sister, and mother for you, but with what success I can't say—I saw our sister, Vernal & Bledsoe and tried all that I ought to do to have them locate at the point.[2] Col W. is starting. I must cease. You will find a <u>small</u> bundle inside. You <u>know</u> the <u>subject</u> on which I feel so much pain whenever I think of it, and on which I have <u>advised</u>! My soul is agonized when I reflect upon the probable time that I must be absent, but not an hour longer than I am copelled [sic] to be. Until we meet, my sole and undivided love and truth are thine.

Give my regards to Col & Mrs Andrews and salute all friends. I know you will write always. I will not fail to do so. The 3rd night I intend to be at Austin from last night. 'Tis too painful to think of my unavoidable absence—Take care of your health my love.

Thy devoted Husband
Houston

Mrs. M. L. Houston

My health improves and habits don't fall off—they are unshaken and will so remain—My love for you will prevent any indulgence during life. I will be a man—

Thy Houston

Margaret

[1]Philip J. Weaver of Selma, Alabama. For a biography see Thomas McAdory Owen, *History of Alabama and Dictionary of Alabama Biography,* v. 4, (Chicago: S. J. Clarke Publishing, 1921), 736.
[2]Cedar Point.

To Gen'l Sam Houston, Austin Texas
Mr. [Pizene] Edmonds

Houston, Dec. 6th, 1841

My love,

I have told some of my friends that I intend to do nothing but write to you while you are gone, and I expect when you get this you will begin to think that I realy [sic] intend to carry out the threat. Mrs. Andrews says that I shall do no such thing, and that she does not intend to give me up entirely even to commune with you. Alas I feel so changed since you left that I can not imagine how any one can be amused or entertained by me and I certainly feel very little inclination to be entertained by others. But I will try to shake off this despondency. My health is evidently improving, but I had not ventured below stairs[1] since you left (except once to see Dr. Fosgate) for fear of taking cold. I will however see Mr. Edmonds this evening if possible, as he is to take this, and he will then be able to tell you more about me. Dearest this is the 9th day since we parted. More than a week! Can it be that I have passed so long a time away from him who has made the sun-shine of my existence for many a happy day! Oh my Love, the world looks dreary around me. Day and night pass away alike to me, and the sun's cheering rays bring no more life to my soul than the illumination of the cold tomb can impart to the ashes it contains! I have lost all relish for my favourite amusements. Even my loved guitar is laid aside, a neglected thing. Last night in the Solitude of my chamber, I wrote a little poem upon it, which I will give you, but you must not laugh at it. I send it merely that you may see how closely your image is incorporated with every thought of my heart.

Rest thee awhile my sweet guitar!
I have no cheerful song for thee,
And words of grief would sadly mar
Thine own enchanting melody!

I will not wake upon thy chords,
The sacred scenes of days bye-gone,
The unforgotten looks and words,
That linger in the heart alone.

For memory doth not bring again
The absent loved unto the sight,
And visions woke by music's strain
Shed o'er the heart a joyless light!

Thus far thy notes have breathed alone
The gladsome tale of joy and weal
And never, never may one tone
Of sorrow o'er thy wild chords steal!

Sleep till the cloud hath passed away
That darkens now my spirit's light
And then I'll sing a joyous lay
Of hope renewed and visions bright!

My Love I know you will chide me for thus giving away to melancholy, but rest assured that I will strive against it. Yet you can not blame me. Oh think how lonely I must be! No gentle husband near me to whom I can express every thought and impulse of my soul! Oh I have been so happy! Surely I have loved too devotedly. But if I have I am punished—sorely punished! Dearest do you ever think of our sweet woodland home! Oh what happy days we have passed there! I remember in one of our evening rambles when we had paused to survey the grandeur of the scenery that I looked up and beheld in your countenance a reflection of the joy that filled my own soul and oh my brain seemed almost oppressed with a sense of happiness but those days are passed and the sweet scene that we then looked upon is now clothed in wintry gloom like my own heart. Yet spring will come again and then my love I hope we can retire once more from the cares and bustle of "the great world."

Emigration is pouring into the country. The Neptune on her last trip brought out a large number of passengers and a great many came up on the boats last night. I am much disappointed at brother Martin's not coming and fear that he has declined it altogether or he would not delay so long. If he comes I will send him up to Austin if possible. I have not yet sat for my picture for the reason that I have been looking a <u>little wan</u>. You know we all like to appear as well as possible on <u>canvass</u>. I mentioned to Mrs. Andrews that I wished her and the Col. to sit for us and she seemed highly gratified and flattered. I do not think I have any news for you my Love. I have crowds of visitors every day to see me, but I have denied every one except a few particular friends whom I admit to my room. But I think I shall soon be able to take my station in society.

Mrs. H.[2] has called since I commenced writing and requested to know if I would see her in my room as I was too feeble to go below. I sent her word that I was writing to you and could not see company. She then sent me <u>her love</u> and regretted that she could not see me! Oh what an amiable creature is the fawning sycophant! Especially if you have ever been calumniated by them!

I made an interesting acquaintance today, a Mrs. Gessum. She is an agreeable lady. I did not mention to you that I wrote to brother William that I wished him to bring Isabella[3] when he comes. I trust he will do so. It is now night. My friend Mrs. Reily[4] has been with me this evening. Oh how sweetly we talked of you! I told her I had been happy today for I had been writing to you! But oh my love, once more I must take leave of you! I would say be resigned till we meet again but my own heart is so sad that I have no word of comfort for you, and I can not say dearest that I wish you to be very happy away from me! You must write to me constantly for I derive so much happiness from your letters.

Thy devoted wife
M. L. Houston

[1]The Andrews' home was a large two-story house with a parlor, library, small sitting room and large dining room downstairs and five bedrooms upstairs. Johnston, 22. For a picture of the home see *Houston Post*, October 3, 1937, Section I, p. 16, "Progress Dooms City Landmark to Wreckers," by Paul O. Taylor.
[2]Margaret is probably referring to Mrs. Albert C. Horton (Eliza Holiday). Hugh Best, *Debrett's Texas Peerage*, (New York: Coward-McCann, 1983), 317. See also Houston to Margaret, December 31, 1841.
[3]Isabella Moore, Houston's niece, was the daughter of Eliza Houston and S. A. Moore.
[4]Ellen Reily, the wife of James Reily. Best, 334.

To Jones P O
Mrs. Margaret Lea Houston
City of Houston
Texas
Mr Highsmith[1]

Austin
9th Dec 1841

My Dear Love,

By Hockley your kind and endearing letter[2] came to me on the way up to this place. Oh how my poor heart beat! I was cheered, yet melancholy, and nursed my love to this place. On yesterday I rec'd the most elegant and hearty greeting that I have ever done. Speeches and a party at night! I did not dance and only once passed thro the room. The thousand inquiries for you were most kind, and all regret not to have greeted you [torn] have every promise. Judge Baylor [torn] my room, and sends his kind love to you with the expression of many regrets, but says he will see you so soon as he can.

The mail is closed, but I will send this to Bastrop, and have it put in at that place. My dear I will write to you a long letter to night. You may anticipate what I will say. I will say how dearly and devotedly I love you, and you only. You are the bright spirit of my earthly hopes, and boundless love. Do say to those dear Ladies who were so kind to you, in sickness & sorrow that my heart swells when I think of them.

I can not express my sense of obligation to them, no more than I can my love for you. Present my love to Col and Mrs. Andrews, Maj & Mrs Reily—Write, Oh do write. I will persecute you with letters. I hope our relations have come from Alabama—if so commend to them. Love to Mother and all friends. Send if you can my chicken to the point, but dont trouble yourself about it.

Thy devoted husband
Houston

Mrs. Houston

This is a steel pen, and I cant [sic] write—I have none else. My head is cool, and shall be so—my beloved.

Thine
Houston

[1]Houston may be referring to the Samuel Highsmith identified in Homer S. Thrall, *A Pictorial History of Texas, from the Earliest Visits of European Adventurers to A. D. 1879*, (St. Louis: N. D. Thompson and Company, 1879), 552.
[2]See Margaret to Houston, December 6, 1841.
[3]Cedar Point.

Later that same evening Houston wrote Margaret of his feelings about the Inauguration, the problems he was facing and his fears for Texas.

Austin 9th Dec 1841

Dearest,

'Tis not to redeem my promise that I write to you to night, but to gratify a penchant which I feel for saying something to you. I am in sooth very miserable, tho' very well. To be absent from you renders me a solitary being—not a person, for I am pressed with company, but my spirit is lonely.—I had almost said depressed, but I will not. The hope of meeting you ire a great lapse of time shall transpire yields me some consolation. Every day—nay every hour will be noted by me! Delay I trust will only render our joy more perfect when we meet! Until then, every hope and wish shall be thine, and for thee—and thee alone, and I will write "love letters" very often! Being a candid man, if I do write, I must tell the truth, and to do that I must say that I love you very much. You can not excel my love, for 'tis boundless! But more of this when we meet.

Touching politicks [sic]—They are every thing but pleasant and desirable! Our country is on the brink of disolution [sic], and if I can save it, it will be a greater work than I have before achieved. The elements yet exist, and if I can obtain cooperation, I will redeem it!!! Congress has done every thing needful for its destruction by passing a retrenchment bill, if it cou'd have any effect, but it will be inef-fectual and void! How it will act during the remainder of the session, no one can divine! Corruption to be sure has nothing to feed on, but faction shews its splenetic aspect! I think it will die of the intermettants [sic]. It looks shakish [sic]! Poor Lamar is in a pack of troubles and pity can only save him from impeachment, but is unable to redeem him from contempt & derision! He has made several overtures to me for friendship, thro [sic] his friends, or rather an effort at reconciliation—but I, as you wou'd have me do, repose upon my dignity.—he is too base to be respected and too imbecile to be trusted! Then you see, my Love that the [one who] wou'd be Minister will be held at bay. I have not forgotten your maxim "that it is an easy matter for us to be generous when it costs us nothing." Were I to suffer a reconciliation, it wou'd be at the cost of my honest pride of heart and to answer some sinister end of which I will advise you in my next. But why not now? Well, I will! The appropriation or Retrenchment Bill is now in the hands of Lamar and the five days will not expire until I come into office, but he can if he wishes sign it, or approve it at any time while he is in office! Five days are all that are allowed for consideration, and to veto a Bill or it becomes a law. I wou'd rather have it to veto myself, and he believes so. Now if I were to be reconciled, he wou'd ascribe it to that fact or others might, so I will not only be pure, but above suspicion! If I leave no other legacy on earth but love and honor they shall stand and remain pure and unsullied as the moonbeams which play around our cottage home. Shah! This figure is faulty!! But the association is not. It is imbued deeply with the recollection of happiest hours which flew unnumbered while we sat in happy blessed converse uninterrupted by obtrusive care! How fondly—truly and calmly, do I recur to those happy and peaceful scenes. Oh that the condition of my country wou'd permit, I wou'd never leave them unless with the <u>fairest apology</u>!!! You will believe this, I am sure! If it were not that I fear to write "love letters," I do not know what else I might have said to you, and even now my dear Maggy, I apprehend that you will say I have already perpetrated the offence [sic]. Well I can't help it, for it has always been a fault of mine that I cou'd not retain my own secrets. Well you can aid me in keeping them.

I will now say to you, have no fears on the score of my personal safety. I believe the smoke will, or has passed or, with the influence which produced it—a <u>Glass of Grog</u>![1] I hope my Love, you will be happy. I can not wait until I embrace you in person, for my heart holds you in the warmest embrace! My love to our Mother and to our dear friends. You know whom we cherish.

Ever thy devoted husband
Houston

Margaret
The clock strikes 1 AM Good night!

[1]Grog was Houston's nickname for David G. Burnet. In his newspaper replies to Burnet during the election campaign Houston had written: "the letter 'G' in your name stood for 'Grog.'" *Writings*, II, 379, A Reply to "Publius," August 16, 1841.

Austin 10th Dec 1841

Dearest,

I am just from supper and before the crowd gathers in my room, I can say something. To day I attended the debates in the H.R. and heard the acts of poor Lamar pretty well used up. Mr Van Zandt[1] made a very sensible speech, and in pretty good taste. Mr Wynnes[2] also made a sensible effort, and they were both on the side of the constitution. But my love, it (the constitution) is at an end. Chaos is restored and order has fled! Whatever good that my result from my action upon the country will be ascribable to myself instead of Congress. For <u>they</u> are wild on every subject that they have touched since I came, or if they are not wild, I <u>must</u> be. That the latter may be the case is very possible for my guardian Angel is absent, but her influence as to my conduct is always present. My dearest Love, I feel but one influence, and that is my desire to make you happy—yes! very happy, and then preserve it by the most perfect temperance and rectitude, but more and more the desire and power to preserve my pledge and save you the sorrow and mortification of seeing a man who is devoted to you fall a victim to the influence of a degrading habit! I can see others drink & pass my time with them and not [have] the least inclination to participate with them! And if I were even to feel the desire for a glass, I wou'd only have to recall the image of my beloved wife and fancy her boundless agony at such an announcement. But of this feel no fears—I have no cause for my indulgence. I am as happy as I can be when my dear wife is absent from me. Yes, the seperation [sic] of souls endeared by the most remarkable congeniality of <u>heads</u> and <u>hearts</u>! I assure you that I meet no one of either sex who can respond to opinions, notions, and feelings in a manner like you.—I feel proud, and at the same time grateful to my creator for such a boon and my devotion of heart is the holy testimony!

Col A. C. Horton[3] is here, and is very kind. He talks much of you, and of course he is not a disagreeable companion for me. He brought for you many kind regards of Mrs Horton[4] and with his own, I am desired to present them to you. They are anxious to have you to visit Matagorda and pass weeks and months with them. The Col has been ill, but is quite recover'd at this time. The seat of Government question has not been mooted yet! On this matter, as you will suppose, I say—nothing!

Monday the 13th[5] advances slowly, and I will not make great "notes of preparation." 'Tis not my habit![6] Tho' I was not well this morning, I feel quite well to night. Candidly, after my epistle of last night was concluded, my mind was so much occupied with thoughts of you that I did not close my eyes in sleep until day was breaking! Don't suppose now that I am going to break out in a strain of soft love making professions—no, none of that! Judge Terrell, Mr. Durst, and Judge Sterne[7] all arrived this evening, and a letter from our friend Dr. Irion, with much love from all the Ladies and good folks with a request that I shall present them to you. You have no idea my love of the great wish which has been expressed to see you here. If it were so that the seat of Government were where you cou'd have been present, my bosom wou'd expand with the most noble and manly pride! I hope the day is not distant when you [will] be present on all occasions in which your pride or feelings will be interested. You are always present with my affections and inspire my actions! But this can not complete my bliss. Do be happy, my dearest!

I hope Martin [Lea] and Young [Royston][8] are with you and mother—Give my love to all, and don't fail in expressing my boundless feelings to those who sat by you in sickness and affliction! I will write to my friend Col Andrews in a few days—when the <u>fuss</u> is over.

Thy ever devoted
Houston

Margaret

[1]Isaac Van Zandt, representative from Marshall. For a biography see *Writings*, III, 113n, and Jennet, 184.
[2]A. Wynnes, representative from Harris County. Jennet, 197.
[3]Colonel Albert C. Horton. For a biography see Best, 317.
[4]See Margaret to Houston, December 6, 1841.
[5] Inauguration Day.
[6] Houston usually made his speeches without using notes.
[7]Judge George W. Terrell, Jacob Durst, and Judge Adolphus Sterne, all of San Augustine.
[8]Margaret's brother and nephew.

Margaret wrote the following letter on the night just prior to the Inauguration:

To Gen'l Sam Houston,
Austin, Texas,
Mr. Lubbock

Houston, Dec. 11, 1841

My beloved,

Yesterday I rec'd your letter by Col. Weaver[1] and on the previous night the one from Washington.[2] How shall I thank you for those dear proofs of remembrance and affection! Oh my Love, I could not live without your letters! They impart new energy to my lowly spirits and after reading them again and again through the long day I treasure each expression of affection and at night fall to sleep with the image of Him I love fresh upon my heart. Dearest I am lonely and desolate without you! My thoughts never wander from you one moment. I sometimes almost wish that you may not feel the gloom and despondency that oppresses my soul but oh my woman's heart craves a full return of devotion and if but half is given I know you can not be happy without me. I can not bear to think of the time that must pass before we meet. I will think of it as little as possible and try to be cheerful. My health is much better than when you left me, and I hope by the time you get home I shall be quite well. We have had a crowded house for several days and quite a cheerful circle. Every one seems to be gay and animated and at table I try to unite in the cheerful jest, but my heart is far far away. Gen. [James Pinckney] Henderson is with us at this time. I am much better pleased with him than formerly, and in frequent conversations have discovered the true nobility of character which you have often mentioned to me. But I must confess that his greatest merit with me is his evident affection for my dear husband. He becomes excited on hearing your name and his eye sparkles with enthusiasm. That is just what I like!

It is now past 9 o'clock PM. Major & Mrs. Reily and Mr. [Francis R.] Lubbock came up after tea and the evening has past rather pleasantly. But in vain I try to be cheerful. Oh my Love, my heart is so sad that the voice of mirth is grating to me! When others are gay and happy around me, I long for the solitude of my chamber that I may indulge my own sacred grief. Yes it is dearer to me far than all the frivolities and gaieties of the world for then I can think of my beloved without interruption and recall many a fond word of his long since forgotten by him! How sweet are such recollections! What blessed consolation they bring during the long hours of absence! You mentioned that brother Vernal was to bring your letter from Washington,[3] but it was brought by some other person and I have heard nothing of him. I have heard from Mother once since I wrote to you before. She was quite well.

12th It is now sabbath evening. I wished very much to go to church this morning but the day was so damp and heavy that I was afraid to venture out. I intend to take as much exercise as possible in pleasant weather, but think it is best to remain within doors when the atmosphere is humid. Mr. Lubbock who is to take this will tell you that I am looking remarkable well. My own opinion is that I have never looked so well in Texas. I think Houston agrees with me decidedly! You are at liberty to mention this to any of the members (when the question of moving the seat of government is brought forward) who may feel sufficiently interested in us to be biassed [sic] by it. The ladies of Harrisburg have sent up a request for me to make them a visit and I think it likely that Mrs. Reily and I will drive down and take dinner with them. But I have not exactly decided upon it for you know I have not a very great partiality for the place.[4] Amongst them who sent the request was Judge Briscoe's family![5]

Maj. [Thomas G.] Western a few days ago brought me your letter addressed to him which I read with mingled feelings of pleasure and pain. Each additional proof of affection from you is certainly an additional source of happiness to me yet I can not but be pained to perceive that you are so anxious and unhappy about my situation. Dear noble husband I do intreat [sic] you to entertain no uneasiness about me! My wants are abundantly supplied, and I have never suffered myself to indulge any whim or caprice that would entail unnecessary expense. Oh how willingly would I resign all the honours of our station and retire into some obscure forest if I could have you my beloved always with me. Yes if blessed with the presence of him I love, I could toil cheerfully through the live long day! It is no romantic picture for oh my love the vain plaudits of the crown can not repay us for the severe trials and disappointments which we are compelled to endure, the painful parting, the agonizing fears and the long long dreary hours of absence! How little the obscure labourer appreciates his happiness! I have often mused upon his calm and peaceful lot and wished that we like him might pass ourselves in some quiet valley far away from the noisy crowd! But again I ask myself if I would be willing to annihilate the brilliant needs of my noble husband and bury his genius in the wild woods. No, I could not do that for my heart throbs with pride when I think of his greatness and his immortal fame, but oh I would have him always near me! I can not bear the dreary void of his absence. The world has no charm for me when he is gone, but all is dreariness and desolation. Day creeps on to day and the only joy that mingles with the passing hour is the thought that his return is so much nearer! Dearest it is a fearful thing to love thus! I feel that every hope and wish of our souls and life itself is dependant [sic] on one being! Oh God protect that being! In the dark hour of danger do thou be near him. Guard him from "the pestilence that walketh abroad at noonday and the arrow that flieth by night!"

Oh my love, my soul is filled with a thousand fears for your safety! Oh how long shall I endure this state of mind! I will try to seek consolation where alone it can be found at the mercy seat of God. There dearest of human beings I will plead for you and pray that you may return to me in safety. Oh how intensely I will think of you tomorrow! May heaven strengthen your arm and direct your heart for our country's good! It will be a solemn occasion, and I know you will feel deeply the responsibility that shall be thrown upon you.

In a few weeks dearest shall we not meet again? Oh yes I will think so, and live upon the hope! Since my health is improved so much I am compelled to see a great deal of company, and my friends often mention you with great tenderness. I will not be jealous of Miss Stone[6] for she has become one of my greatest friends. If she were not so I can not say how I would feel towards her for she is certainly a very charming girl. Mr. Waters is returned from Ala. and I suppose there will be a wedding soon, but do not know certainly. 13th Mr. Lubbock is to call this morning for my letter, and I must now bid you adieu. Do write by every mail my Love. The Col. and Mrs. Andrews send you a kiss by Mrs. Lubbock and say that I should do the same, but I would choose to prefer "to deliver mine in propria persona!" My cough has left me entirely for several days, and I am getting quite stout and strong. My dear you must not forget Col Nail[7] [sic] He was here a few days ago, and I am told quite destitute.

Thy own
M. L. Houston

[1]See Houston to Margaret, December 6, 1841.
[2]See Houston to Margaret, December 2, 1841.
[3]See Houston to Margaret, December 1, 1841.
[4]Margaret may be referring to her disapproval of a plan to move the capital to Harrisburg.
[5]Judge Andrew Briscoe and his wife Mary Jane Harris, of Harrisburg. Best, 261.
[6]Margaret "Mag" Stone was the fourteen-year-old ward of Millie and William Fairfax

Gray, who lived near the Andrews. Houston was fond of "Mag" and his later letters indicate she may have had a "crush" on him. For her biography see Pickrell, 270–74.

[7]Colonel James C. Neill. For a biography see *Writings*, I, 333n, and *Handbook of Texas*, II, 268.

Austin Texas

Sunday morning 12th Dec 1841

My Love,

Tho my room is full of company, I do not feel like conversation until I can tell you of the dream which I had this morning. Judge Terrell was my bed fellow last night, and is one of the most profound sleepers that I have known. When he rose at day break, I fell into a profound and delightful sleep. I fancied that you were in my arms, and that we were felicitating ourselves, that all the cares of the world were shut out from us, and that we were as happy as mortals can be! My heart beat high, and my bosom swelled with joy and delight! My delightful vision was disturbed and annihilated by a call to "Breakfast." Then indeed, I realised the absence of my beloved Margaret. Yes, of <u>my wife</u>! Oh how cruel, how painful is absence to me, and add to that the fear of your indisposition, when if I were present, I cou'd soothe or at least sustain my dearest Margaret. Until I can again be with you, I can feel but one round of anxiety and solicitude. I trust the session will not be protracted, but if it shou'd the fault will not be mine. The moment that it adjourns, with leave of Heaven, I will fly to your responsive bosom, resolved never again to leave you on this globe. I have lived for mankind. I will try and live for ourselves.

Today I have promised to dine out with my old friend, Maj. Brigham,[1] in a family way. I will meet a few personal friends there, and so soon as it is over, I will return and finish the Epistle. You need not expect that I will convert it into a "love letter." No, no more of that until you have obtained your mothers and friends consent to our union.

My love I have dined and also returned from a ride with our friend Col Horton. But oh my dearest, I must tell you that ire I dined I had the inexpressible pleasure to receive your blessed letter by Mr Edmunds.[2] 'Tis said by those who have watched me that I only read it three times in two hours. Thus my Love you may judge of my delight when I first perused its endearing contents. I was so happy that I cou'd hardly confide in its reality, and too so closely allied to the illusion of last night! I do now believe it to be reality, and this I have ascertained by the responses of affection. That Mr Edmunds did not see you can not be helped, as he cou'd not go to see you, having to start, and he had the <u>letter</u>! I ought to repose sweetly, but this [I] can not [do] to night. I am so much alive to sensibility that I can not, will not sleep. Tomorrow will have little to do with my meditations or my thoughts—tho' it is to embrace the most important event to Texas that awaits, or has awaited her, in her history. She now gasps for life, for she has been long strugling [sic] in the throws of corruption. News too has just arrived of the capture of the Santa Fe expedition by the Mexicans. It has arrived thro [sic] the Mexican Journals, and is not doubted. I may obtain further particulars, and in that event you shall have them!

Tomorrow I doubt not but what I shall sustain my reputation for speaking—at least I will for patriotism and sense. Expectation is much qui vive, and I must on account of dear Maggys pride and felicity. My own happiness consists in making you so!

My dearest, as I intend to write to you again before I can send to you, I will draw this letter to a close, for really, tho' you may be gratified, nay! rejoiced in hearing from me, I do apprehend, or fear, that you will weary yourself in reading so much as I have, and may write to you. For I am in writing as I was in talking when I begin. And when I write so much, I am sure to prose to some extend. If I were to write to any one but to you my beloved, I know it wou'd be deemed insipid. I thank you for your commands to Brother Will, and you may issue as many for your dear self in another direction. In short, do as you wish my love. I will be Presidential. I will "approve."

Thine own
Houston

Margaret

---

[1]Major Asa Brigham, who would serve as Houston's Secretary of Treasury. *Writings*, II, 310–11. For a description of the festivities see Lubbock, 141–43.
[2]See Margaret to Houston, December 6, 1841.

*On the day of his inauguration as president of the Republic of Texas,
Houston wrote Margaret the following account of the ceremonies.*

Austin
13th Dec 1841

My Love,

I am just starting to the Ball which is promised to be very fine.[1] I
will not detain long for on my return, I will resume the pleasure of
writing to you and cou'd I by my presence inspire every heart with
emotions that should reflect the sweetest smiles from every fair face
in the room, I shou'd not be willing to forgo one moment the duty
and delight of telling you some thing which may interest you!—

Dearest, I have this moment returned from the Ball, and one more
animated, I have not seen on any occasion. All seemed to me to feel
happy on the change of an odious & unpopular administration for
one which seemed to promise well to the nation. There was one alone
who felt that he was lonely and cheerless, tho' he wore smiles on the
occasion—I mean your devoted husband. You were not there my
Love, tho' you were in every mouth, and every one either expressed
regret at your absence, or made kind inquiries for your welfare, with
the declaration of a desire to see and become acquainted with you.
If you were present I have but little doubt but what you wou'd rival
me in popularity. Enough have seen and been introduced to you to
present you in the most lively and agreeable colours. These matters
do not mortify me in the least, but add to my pride, the pleasing
reflection that I have the felicity of being united to one who fills so
large a space in the worlds eye and whose virtues and worth I am
capable of appreciating!

I did not dance, tho' importuned by all to do so. I had a thousand reasons for declining, but I will only cite one, and that is simply that you wou'd prefer that I wou'd not. I refused, and did not
wish to dance for it would have been heartlessness in me to have
done so when you perhaps were prostrate on the bed of sickness
and rather than yield, I told all of your indisposition, and that on all
occasions checked their troublesome importunities.—You know how
I feel about these matters. For instance Genl Thompsons wedding!!

The day and its ceremonies had passed off—At 11 AM the Travis Guards marched to my quarters and escorted myself with the Vice President[2] to the Presidents House. There were no refreshments either for the committees of both Houses, the Guards, or spectators. For the first time, I met poor Lamar and restrained my contempt so far as to be proudly civil. The procession proceeded to the Capitol where seats were prepared for the Ladies and an area for the Gentlemen in which they had to stand. This was in rear of the Capitol, for it cou'd not contain one half or fourth of the multitude present. Lamar made no valedictory. The oath was then administered to me (after prayer by our dear friend Judge Baylor) when I made my inaugural address. It was an hour or hour and a half long! It pleased every person but myself, and indeed I was not pleased with it. I sustained my reputation well to be sure, but I did not think it extremely felicitous. It was less so than if you, my beloved, had been present to have inspired me with your looks of deep solicitude on such occasions. The procession when I had concluded repaired to my quarters, where I had refreshments prepared, and enjoyed themselves for an hour or more. All passed off well, and the inhabitants are now wrapped in the arms of Morpheus after a day of joy to them! The day was lovely, and indicated the favor of a benignant God to this people.

To night I learned that it had been presented that I wou'd get into a "spree" before all was over—but they were wide of the mark. I "Touch not taste not, and handle not (nor want not) the unhallowed thing."! My Love I must tell you a jest, and one too which made the "cold chills run over me." The oath of office was administer'd to the V. President when he said "Fellow Citizens! as I have prepared an address to deliver when I take my seat in the senate, I will not make one now and only return my thanks for the votes of a grateful people." While this was done, his right hand was pressed upon his heart, and when it concluded his hand was extended with the palm up and a school boy bow cut short the ceremony! This my love is for you, Mrs Andrews, and Mrs. Reily, and you may let the Col & Major Reily take one laugh at it, but only one, and then—"Mum is the word." My dear this is no Jest when all is considered. 'Tis nevertheless true. 'Tis now 3 ock A.M and I will try and get a nap by morning. I will not go to the White House to live.[3] Tomorrow, I intend to have an Invoice of the furniture taken,[4] and Congress may sell it, for I never will use it. 'Tis nearly all destroyed $8,000 worth only. I hate the pollution! and there fore will never touch one article of it! Baylor, Hockley, Hemphill,[5] Jones, Terrell, and a host of others desire to be presented to you.

You Dearest, will know to whom I wish my regards to be presented.

Thy ever devoted
Houston

Margaret

Sixteen suns have set since we parted. To me it has been an age of solicitude!

Your Ode to your Guitar,[6] my Love, is a pretty thing indeed, and lest I might be mistaken, I showed it to several <u>candid friends</u> of known taste, and they pronounced it very fine!

I did not want their judgement, but I was so pleased with it that I wished to exhibit it. Don't scold!

Thy
Houston

[1]The Inaugural Ball took place in the Senate Chamber. Friend, 103.
[2]Edward Burleson. Best, 281–82.
[3]Houston chose instead to live at the Eberly House. Friend, 102, and Lubbock, 142.
[4]For this inventory see *Writings*, II, 409–15.
[5]Judge John Hemphill. *Writings*, II, 438.
[6]For this poem see Margaret to Houston, December 6, 1841.

Houston replied to Dr. Irion's letter of December 1, 1841, in a note which may be found in the Irion Collection of Documents, Archives Division, of the Sam Houston State University library, Huntsville, Texas.

Austin
15th Dec 1841

My dear Irion,

I can only command a moment to thank you for your valued favor. I was truly happy to hear of Madams & your welfare. For the suggestions and advice you gave in relation to Mrs. Houstons case, I render to you my devoted thanks. The news of the transactions here, you will hear of by Mr Durst. Mrs H is not here. She commanded me to present to you and Mrs Irion her kind affection. Be pleased to salute your excellent Lady with my devoted esteem and kindest wishes for her happiness.

Thy devoted friend
Houston

Dr. R. A. Irion

Oh, write often?

Austin
15th Dec 1841

Dearest,

No letter came from you by last mail. I hope you did not know of its departure. As no one but Major Reily wrote to me, and he said you were quite well, I will believe him, for I wou'd be more miserable than I am if I did not.

My Love, my task is more than I can perform, but my failure shall incur no censure. I wou'd rather resign and retire to our home. A Congress, sent to aid me, you will see, has placed every embarrassment in my way. My destiny is a queer one, and I must see it out! The people sent to Santa Fe[1] are destroyed. I will send you the first printed detail that I can attain!

I can write you nothing more than that I love you more and more every hour of my existence. This is coarse and you can not think I am composing a love letter, tho' I often reperuse yours, and wonder at myself that you have not had (or your letters) the power to inspire me with the faculty. Believe me, I feel all that is inexpressible of love and my dearest Margaret.

Oh my Love how devoted I am thy adoring—Houston

Mrs. Genl Sam Houston
City of Houston
Texas
Oh, do write to me always?
To the Andrews & Reilys—Give my love and to our dear mother.

Thine Ever
Houston

[1]Houston is referring to the ill-fated Santa Fe Expedition. For an account of this expedition, see Wisehart, 382–91.

The following letter to Margaret was dictated by Houston to his secretary Washington D. Miller:

Austin, Dec 21st 1841

My Dearest,

You will discover that I address you by my friend Mr. Miller[1] as my amanuensis. That no idle feast may be entertained, or apprehensions arise in the mind for my welfare, I will tell you without ceremony that I am rather on the order of invalids. My ancle[2] [sic] has plagued me so much, that for two days past I have moved about, when I moved at all, on my crutches. Without being at all dangerous, it has been most esquisitely [sic] painful. Moreover, my nights have been entirely sleepless, but by-the-by, that was no great inconvenience to me, as it afforded me ample time to meditate upon my dear Margaret. Last night, particularly, I was "very satisfied" because I had the pleasure to receive your dear letter by Mr. Lubbock, embracing the incidents of three days.[3]

Dec. 22nd, 1841.

Being prevented from closing my letter on last evening, I have now resolved to continue the communication. As Congress adjourned over from yesterday until tomorrow, today I have no doubt I have received upwards of an hundred visits, some on business, and a great many through personal regard—as all enquired how the ancle [sic] came on. Pretty well was the answer, but I have not slept but a few hours in the last forty-eight. Yet my general health is better than when I had to regret to part with you. Leaving you in the situation I did at Houston, in the feeling agony of my heart, it certainly formed an era in the history of my affections.

This evening, by Maj. Western and Gen. Hunt, I had the extreme felicity of receiving your letters[4] about three hours since, and I have only perused them each twice. I am in the habit of carrying your letters in a breast pocket of my hunting shirt by way of reference. The use of them I fear will have a tendency to destroy the delectable manuscript and disappoint the novelist in a specimen of very pretty epistolary correspondences. Amongst many other agreeable incidents mentioned in your letter, I could not avoid smiling at the philosophical display of affection indicated in the remarks of our friend Mr. Huckins[5]—such things do happen, but really they form no reason why we should be assimilated to others in these matters. I believe the first time I see him, I will call upon him and know if he has a panacea and if I can obtain it. If I had more apathy and less devotion of heart, I would enjoy more sleep and experience much less anxiety.—not, my Love, that I have any inclination to regard you less tenderly than what I do. But then you know that philosophy gives such a charm to dignity. However, if you are not satisfied with this plan of happiness, I will endeavor to assimilate my letters to my affections, and write while ever I have room and can filch any time from the annoying circumstances which surround me. You speak of your companionship with my likeness. I will contend that I have the advantage of you. The dear original would be constantly present to my mind, if I were separated from you by the Andes or the Pacific. The recollection of you is so vividly impressed upon my mind that it seems to me I hear your soothing whisper in tones of gentlest admonition say, "Dearest husband, do not forget my devotion to you, and do not fail to be—a clever fellow." To which I respond, "Do not doubt me." I am aware, my Love, that you feel much anxiety about predictions which will be certain to reach you, and the kind speculations which my enemies are pleased to make on the future. I pray you will not allow them to annoy you in the least. I never believed that trouble was any excuse for tilting headlong upon ruin. The great merit of true philosophy is that it sustains the noble soul in adversity; and inspires it with purposes which point to the exaltation of character and confirm a high destiny. The man that is not capable of bearing misfortune has little to do in the great business of life. In untried circumstances, he might have a passable reputation, and might attract the passing notice of mankind, but the incidents of his life would never be striking nor command either the admiration or reverence of posterity. I am now placed in the midst of circumstances untried in their character, for no country has ever been similarly situated with Texas. If my exertions, united with those of my friends, (for they are the salt of the Earth,) should prove triumphant in combatting [sic] the difficulties which surround us at this moment; it will at least illustrate two things: first, that Texas is fortunate, and second, that I will be to some extent instrumental in the illustration of her good.

None my beloved, would enjoy with more extatic [sic] pleasure and felicity the success attendant upon my efforts than yourself. Every pleasure which I derive from the anticipation of success is blended with my devotion to you. To be honored—to be renowned—to be the benefactor of mankind, and an ornament and blessing to this nation, were you not to be a participant, would be matters of duty that belong to a due sense of character. But without the delightful emotions which your approbation would inspire, would deprive me of half the joys anticipated. In your letters, my Dear, you have spoken of your love of retirement and seclusion, and that you were only reconciled by the necessity which separates us. Dearest, believe me that no other consideration on Earth, but necessity would induce my absence from you for one single day. The greatest perfection of my happiness on Earth is your presence. Without your presence is continually coupled anxiety, regret and painful solicitude. Your health is precarious; your continued liability to indisposition are matters of intense and vivid interest to me. No circumstances, my Dear, shall induce me to remain separated from you. I take great pleasure in assuring you that I expect and fondly anticipate an early adjournment of Congress, my Dear, about the 15th of January; and with the blessing of Heaven, the hour of its adjournment I intend shall find me on the way to Houston. Saxe Weimar[6] is in fine trim— fat and frolicsome; and I entertain no fears but my ancle [sic] will be in a state of perfect solvency. I shall feel very ambitious to make a short trip and a quick surprise.

O! by-the-by, I have'nt [sic] told you; I communicated a message to Congress the other day.[7] It is said to be very clever. That's my private opinion. Mr. Miller, my Private Secretary, says its very clever. I am satisfied that he did think so; for if he had deemed it very faulty he would have been sure to have taken sparing. He has sufficient pride to have felt deeply mortified at any failure. You can judge of his personal regard from his letters which you have seen. You have heard Vernal speak of his literary pride. When I see you, my Love, I will tell you of a promise I have made Mr. Miller. He blushes at the very suggestion now; but I will not inflict the distress upon him of telling you what it is.

Well, but my Dear, the Message, as I was saying. There was just satin enough in town to have you a copy struck on it. That I take great pleasure in sending to you. Pray don't think, my Dear it was to propitiate you by any means. I do it merely to flatter a small spice of selfish vanity on your part. You can determine its merits. It contains no rhetoric. It's a plain common sense document—"sensible to the last." The <u>invocation,</u> my Dear, is indeed not hypocritical. It's in good faith, if not in good taste. I will send you two on colored <u>silk</u>— one for Mrs. Reily and the other for Mrs. Andrews. Then you can exercise that agreeable faculty you speak of, my Dear. You know "how agreeable it is to be generous" etc.

As it lacks a few minutes of twelve o'clock at night, I shall begin to draw this letter to a close, but I must tell you of a ball that has taken place to-night, given to poor Lamar.[8] It was a forced-put. His friends are trying to shake off the odium that attaches to him. Congress has whipt and cleaned him once or twice. The plea urged in his behalf was sour pity, and that inspired contempt enough to shield him from the penalty of his crime. I did not go, though invited. I learn there were not half the number of ladies there that were at the inauguration ball. Bob Potter and he made speeches at considerable length, I understand. His majesty has still a penchant for the Court of St. James. I cannot consort with rich scoundrels. He is a bad man, and utterly impure.

I have not time to tell you the numerous amusing incidents connected with my visit to the place and the solicitude expressed by his friends for reconciliation.

By accident I have heard that Bledsoe has concluded to go to Cedar Point. I hope it is so. But if not, I will hope the best. I got a very fine letter from our brother Henry that I enclose to you. Dear noble Fellow! I wish we could see him once happily situated in Texas. I admire his nobility of feeling; and the expression of his regard for us was truly grateful to me. I know it will be truly gratifying to you.

Maj. Reily, and Lubbock and Western and many friends are here. The holy days of Christmas are on hand; but Mr. Miller and myself will not participate in them. You must commend me with great affection to Mother. Salute Mrs. Andrews and Mrs. Reily with a kiss. Commend me to all our friends, and tell them I will write to you whenever I can.

I have been at the marriage of one member of Congress[9] a few nights since—I am invited to one in the country tomorrow evening. I have a carriage at my command; but if I should go, I'll take the crutches along.

Now I don't know what to say about that little enchantress, Maggy Stone. Tell her that on your behalf, I will love her just as much as you do. Being your other half, if not your better half, I ought to love no less than half. Tell her I am very sorry to hear that she was indisposed and did not accompany you to Harrisburg. If you should be unwell, (but Heaven avert it) don't let her give you any medicine. Tell her I say so. You've heard of spiders being put in dumplings!! Every day I am reproached for not having brought you with me. My apology is, I am going for you the moment Congress may adjourn. It is well enough for my reputation that I didn't bring you along; for I have no doubt you would have had the credit of all the crack compositions that I have produced. 'Tis generally believed here, that you are entitled to all the credit of my reformation; and that's a most famous work, for it was more than all the world beside could do. And for the sake of my dear Maggy, I will not act the scamp lest it might tarnish her deserved renown.

Now I think, my Dear, this will pass for a <u>poser</u>. My beloved in closing, I take great pleasure in presenting my friends old Millers best respects to you and if you see Vernal present W Miller & myself to him. Salute Col Andrews with my best regards.

Thy ever devoted
Husband
Houston

Margaret

[1]Washington D. Miller was Houston's private secretary. See Houston to Miller, October 12, 1841, and Houston to Miller, December 13, 1841, *Writings,* II, 388–89, 398.
[2]Houston's ankle had been shattered in the Battle of San Jacinto, and he had trouble with it throughout his life.
[3]See Margaret to Houston, December 11, 1841.
[4]These letters have not been located.
[5]The Reverend James Huckins, a Baptist minister in Houston. Harlan J. Matthews, *Centennial Story of Texas Baptists,* (Dallas: Baptist General Convention of Texas, 1936), 83.
[6]Houston's horse.
[7]First Message to Congress, Second Administration. *Writings,* II , 399–408.

[8]For a description of the Ball see Friend, 103, and *Daily Bulletin*, December 23, 1841.
[9]The wedding of Congressman Moses F. Roberts and Nancy Murray, December 20, 1841. Listed in Grammer, 76.

Austin

24th Dec 1841

My dearly beloved Margaret,

This moment my heart was greeted by your letter favor'd by Mr Harris.[1] Every endearing thought of you had been cherished by me as they will ever remain. But I did not anticipate a letter at this time. My whole heart rejoiced to learn that you are cheerful, <u>in funds</u> and fine health! Oh my Love, these these [sic] assurances render me—I had almost said happy, but no they can not, for you are not present!!! I am gratified that you will be in easy circumstances until I can once more embrace my beloved. I was unhappy from a fear that you might wish to possess something not in your power to command. The apprehension too that you might be again attacked by sickness and I wou'd not [be] present to wait upon you, and comfort, and solace you. Even the days of your affliction and sickness afford me some pleasure when I recur to them. You said that my attentions were kind and afforded you relief in your distress. Every evidence of affection rendered by me and regarded by you must ever remain dear to me. To sum up my affection for you, I can only say that with you, I am happy and without you I cou'd feel no happiness. My Love is boundless. My dear, you say that you passed a night with Mrs Reily, and that your theme was your husbands etc! Maggy <u>we are clever fellows, you may be assured</u>. We love back again. Last night, we were at a wedding[2] ten miles in the country and passed there for <u>first rate</u> Gentlemen. The Major was my aid on the occasion and I had one crutch with me, so I was well sustained. Mr Smith the Bridegroom was a genteel man and well to do. The Bride was a pretty being (nearly). Her hair was dark & her eyes. Her cheeks were ruddy and her hight [sic] and form the perfect representatives of—Oh! I wou'd say my dearest Maggy! In life I have not seen a greater resemblance [sic] in figures. And what do you think? This morning, she presented herself in a dress made and in colors just like your silk dress worn by you the day after our union! I thought of your brother Henry's <u>greeting</u> to you. Now under all these circumstances how do you think I felt? Curious enough, you may be sure! Her resemblance to you was so impressive and her modesty so much in character that I did want—yes I did want to kiss her! That I wou'd have done there is but little doubt, had I been previously acquainted with her and her husband, but I had not been introduced to either! Today I dined at his Fathers with the wedding party & many from this place. The distance was about three miles and the "eating doings" were first rate throughout! You were a subject of universal inquiry. Males and females asked your health and added "When will you bring Mrs Houston to Austin? We want to see her." Never was I so kindly treated. All were affectionate to me, and my lame ancle—that was a subject of simpathy [sic]. But my ancle—it is nearly well!

Now my dear, I will respond to you on the subject of politicks [sic]. I have ordered the Navy in to port some days since, but kept it a secrete [sic], as I do not wish to alarm their fears while at sea or until I can get them within my control![3] You will take the hint. There are some in command that I wou'd not like to trust, if they saw their advantage lay on the other hand. As to the seat of Govt, there are many reasons, I am told, why that has not agitated! Talk of Austin as the finest place in the world, if you think so, but say nothing to the contrary my dear, and when we meet, I will tell you the reason!

I read your remarks on the Navy[4] to some members of the Cabinet who were present and they were pleased and amused at your <u>quiping</u> [sic] tact. They think you are in reality like myself, and Major Reily says that you will be the next President. To day Dr. Jones, Hockley, & Terrell were all confirmed by the Senate.[5] On tomorrow or when the Senate meets again, Maj Reily will be also. Mr Gail Borden and Mr Lubbock[6] were confirmed in their several stations!

This letter was commenced with a hope that I cou'd send it tomorrow, but I now heard that I will not have an opportunity! So you may suppose I will add a good deal more news to what it already contains. Dont my dear wife be uneasy, about the Lady who resembles you so much. I never expect to see her again and if I were, and admired her, it wou'd only be an evidence of my love for you. I can love no being but you and no other image can ever command my love and admiration. So whatever presents you to my thoughts must claim my remark and recall recollections dearer to me than all the other scenes of by gone existences.

My resolution is taken that if I live to embrace you again, I will never leave you, nor cease to love you. Absence to me is torture, and I almost fear that I love you too much. But this fear if possible only renders you more endeared to my affections! Love, Christmas times are on hand, but your devoted husband will not join in them. No my dear, I am thy <u>husband</u>!!! As I regard thy happiness, so shall I bear myself! I feel cheerful when I reflect upon my mastery obtain[ed] over intemperance and that thru it I have added to your sum of felicity. My friends too are all joy and cheerfulness. Indeed, every patriot in Texas, I believe feels rejoiced at the change while even malignity is render'd harmless. You my Love will appreciate my cause of satisfaction as much as any one—or I will say as much more as any one!

You will see by the papers that I am on tomorrow to make the Grand Masonic invocation. On this matter I have had no reflection nor preparation. I must do the best I can. My only dread on these matters is that I may fail and you will be mortified. But, I know you you [sic] cou'd account for it, or if you can't I can. I think <u>too much</u> about you to think of any thing else <u>enough</u>. What say you to this? Is it not correct? I say this, in half jest & earnest. Tell me what you think on the subject?

I will cease to night as it is 12 M. and if no opportunity occurs tomorrow, I will employ the most of the day in finishing this epistle!

It is now one o clock Christmas day, and I resume my epistolary work.[7] I was mistaken about the day and its exercises.

The 27th will be the day and in the meantime, I may have some leisure and make some preparation, at least try and meet public expectation whatever it may be! To day I feel sad & melancholy. My ancle has pained me which is one cause. Last night when I retired I thought that I wou'd enjoy a pleasant nights repose, but I was wofully [sic] disappointed. A portion of the night I was delirious, and this morning I arose feeble and unwell. But as I had promised to finish to day this letter to you, I wou'd not my love forego so great a pleasure, tho performed in much pain. I think too, that I am mending as I progress in the completion of a task so agreeable as laying my complaints before my dearest wife. Dont take sick because I am not as well as I wish to be. This morning I have had many visits, notwithstanding a notice on my door that the morning until one oclock my time will be employed in the duties of my office. It will then be open until six at night for calls. From six until midnight, I will again have time to labour in "my vocation."

You will perceive my love, from this hint that I have but "little to do"! This will only be the case until the adjournment of Congress. For my dear wife, I will most assuredly resign before I will again remain seperated [sic] from you for one month hereafter. Had I the control of the Government, I cou'd save the country, but now I do really distrust the effort. I will not say that I despair of its future existence, but my mind is by no means free from apprehension, for its safety and success. My measures are not to be carried out in my opinion, and if they are not we may look out for ruin!!! If not individual ruin, we may look out for a suspension of the functions of Government—and then anarchy. It does appear to me that no mortal power can avert the ruin impending over Texas. Every convulsive throw only leaves her more prostrate in her condition. Her resources are wasted and the body politick is weakened so much that even my sanguine hope is beginning to languish! The ways of God are past finding out, but indeed my love, no mortal forecast with my present means can avert the impending evils!

My dearest, it is useless for us to repine. We can be happy in retirement. We have seen our happiest days in life glide by at Cedar Point. We were happy there and happy we can be again! I will not, my dear decide my course until I can have your sage advice. You well know that I have borne with my country and that my struggles in its darkest gloom and despondency have saved it! I wou'd yet freely peril my life to save and establish its Liberty on a firm foundation. My destiny or some wayward fatality will not allow me the delightful anticipations which I have so fondly cherished! Don't you despond. You have no need to do so. You shall not feel the miseries of anarchy. With my habits I could go any where, and by my profession we cou'd obtain all the needful comforts, and have the protection of law with all the blessings arising from orders! So my dear I wou'd be sorry that you shou'd permit your dear self to be unhappy. I wou'd be perhaps more kind to you if I were not to say this much to you on this subject, but defer my remarks until we meet. But the truth is my Love, I do not wish to think or feel any thing that I wou'd conceal from you. You are entitled, richly entitled, to all that I am or to all that I may possess. I thank you as the kind and ministering angel in the hand of Heaven that has restrained me from vicious habits and rendered me the rational husband of my amiable and lovely wife! 'Tis possible that others might have possessed the charms, but upon this subject, I will ever remain a skeptic! For this simple reason—you are the only dear object that I ever loved with my whole heart and existence! That love can never change unless you shou'd deem me unworthy of yours! That can not be anticipated—Therefore <u>we will love</u>!!!

Since writing the foregoing part of my letter, or a large portion of it, I was in the mood which it wou'd indicate! I was a little, very little, in the dumps—But some Senators and Representatives have been to see me, and I believe they will try and sustain me, but to what extent, I can not say.

Dearest it is 10 PM and I have not been out of my office to day. I have received many kind wishes of the season and returned my felicitations to my visitors. I had nothing to extend to them, but my hand. There was no liquor, no egg nog, nor have I seen one drop of any thing in that <u>time</u>! I do not remember a Christmas when I cou'd have said as <u>little</u> for it. You will say it is <u>just</u> enough! Well agreed. My friend Reily has been here to see me twice to day! and I read a paragraph in his Ladies letter in which she says many kind and true things of you!

I see that you have got the start of me if I were elligible [sic] to a reelection and I wou'd have no objection my Love as you will see by my letter that I am not much charmed with my situation. I read a portion of this letter to two members who called to see me after I had written it, and they stared a good deal and implored me to see you before I came to any solemn conclusion! So you can judge, as they were men of good sense how far matters are thought of at Austin.

This day at least as much depends upon my firmness and sagacity, as did on the 21st of Apl [sic] of 36. Then I was able to save the country because I was supreme! Were I so now, I cou'd do it without an apparent effort—or the least oppressions. The time is on its march, I fear when neither nor both will succeed without a convulsion of the most distressing character! <u>I wou'd save my country if I could!</u> but I fear it will not let me save it again!

<u>Fortune</u> becomes weary in pursuing us if we do not embrace her occasionally! She woos us now, but I fear she will not receive the

proper attentions to insure the benefit of her smiles or the continuance of her favors. As it is 12 at night, I will close for the present, but not seal my <u>short</u> letter until I see if I can't add something else before I can send it.

26th This morning my Love, I am much better and feel as if I wou'd soon be well, but in as much as I will be compelled to remain here longer than I have any wish to do! As the day passes I will recur to this letter.

My dearest, I send you a "New Years Gift," and you can retain or dispose of them to your liking. I can obtain nothing here that pleases me. For really I wou'd not present any thing common to you! But we must be as we can, tho' not as we wish to be, in Austin. My love you may confide in the trust that the seat of Government can not and will not remain at this point. 'Tis reported in town this morning that Indians were in and prowling about last night!

Other news of an unpleasant character has also reached me this moment. The mail from Bexar has not arrived—it was due on thursday, so it is delinquent three full days. So soon as the news reached me, I ordered Col Hockley to sent out the requisite number of men to examine, to act, and report! Indians have been seen within twelve miles of this place, and on the road between, and Bexar on the route by which the mail rider had to pass. That he is killed there is no doubt in the minds of those who ought to be judges.[8] 'Tis not improbable that some of our members may have been caught on their way to Bexar. Mr Morris, with Van Ness[9] and others, went over to take Christmas. I hope they may not have been surprised on the way!

This is the Lord's day and my dear, I must confess to you that I will be compelled to transact business of my office. This you may deplore, but it can not well be avoided. If others had attended to business, I wou'd have less to do, and the country have been in a much more prosperous condition! Giving you news, I must tell you that a Ball was given to Lamar on the 22nd by those who had been fed at the expense of the Government, and those who wished to give him a puff. I did not attend, but induced my friends to do so lest he might suppose that I thought enough about him to design any thing connected with him. In the Ball room I learn, he was addressed by "Bob Potter" in a long speech, and made one in answer—

par nobile fratrum! Allusion I believe was made to the <u>bosom of his family</u>—This will do! Congress had just "whipped and cleared him" as they wou'd say in Tennessee, and even this was the result of hard begging and pity. He deserves punishment, but contempt may shield him.

My dear, I can not tell to what length this letter will be <u>spun out</u>. It may not get off until Major Reily starts—If it does not, I will continue to annex amendments to it so as to have it at least long enough. It shou'd be so, and thus make amends for its defects. I wish Congress wou'd adjourn!!!

27th Dec.

My Love! To day I am in my office, but was too indisposed from cold to attend the Masonic procession and make the Invocation.[10] Judge Hutchinson[11] will no doubt make a very fine address on the occasion. I regret much that I could not attend. I am very hoarse and my mouth is pretty much as it was on our way home from Nacogdoches. Whether it may arise from my using inferior Tobacco I can not say. 'Tis certain that when engaged [in] writing to you I do cut my Tobacco rather fine as I do whenever excited on any subject!

You may be amused at this—it is nevertheless very true! Do you recall at Cedar Point on certain occasions how particular I was to have the <u>mats</u> near me when writing? It is truly a hardship that I can not find a conveyance for this letter to you. Hereafter I will send my news in small parcels and not impose upon you so great a task as to read a history without even a resting spell.

The sun now shines brightly upon the hills of Austin, but my heart is sad. I am far, very far distant from all that I love on earth. I am a prisoner of Hope—but I fear it is that hope which maketh the heart sick. Heaven I trust will again permit us the pleasure of embracing each other, never again to be seperated, and endure all the miseries of anxiety and solicitude. Never dearest will I consent again either to endure or to inflict wretchedness such as results from absence! How much I love you, Heaven only knows! My friends say that 'tis well for me—that my habits are reformed, even the habit of swearing which has been so difficult to repress! I trust my Love, that you will never again have reason to reprove me—For the future I will use my best exertions and indeed employ all my energies to forego a practice so ridiculous as swearing! Whatever beneficial influence my example may have upon society I will firmly accord to my country! But my Love, there is a consideration much nearer to my heart and that is a desire to <u>render you</u> happy.

I feel too, to a much greater extent than I ever have done or at least of late years, that the immortal spark will be cherished by a course of Godly walk and conversation. My dearest, I was not formed in mind or heart for vice or vicious pursuits. They bring me no joy, but leave an aching empty voice of unsatisfied thought.

My friends have set for me the commencement of a New Year to abstain from all "strong expressions." I too, my dear, will appoint that day, but I will from this time put a stop [to] the evil if I can! Nous varrons [sic]!

To day the news has arrived from the scout sent in quest of the mail rider that he was found in a dreadfully mutilated condition & the wolves preying upon him. The mail was gone, and the trail was almost effaced as four days had transpired! Congress at the last session gave the protection of the frontier to the Chief Justices, and had deprived me of the means of rendering my aid to the country. Again there is no money—no Government stores, no ammunition nor arms! A fine condition for a "New Country." But of this I will prate no more about these matters, as it can do no good! I have made my arrangements to get as much money as will pay my way home! So this subject I will dismiss.

Judge Baylor has just been in my office and as usual my dear Maggy was a subject of our chat. He is a most worthy Gentleman indeed! Maj Reily was Grand Orator of the <u>Fraternity</u> to day, and I am informed made a beautiful address. He has just been to see me, but I did not then know that he had so much cause of felicitation as I now do—So I will have the pleasure of rendering him my congratulations, which will be shortly. My Love, "how easy it is to be generous when it costs nothing."

You see that I do not intend to become weary in well doing. Having leisure I will tell you that our friend Maj Western is in my office pouring over a news paper. I fear to avoid my teasing him about you, with a thousand inquiries! Do you when you see him, tax him with the fact. See what a fine apology he will make! He threatens me with heavy complaints and accusations to be made to you against me. You must allow the major some latitude in his statements! His veracity I know to be good, but then all Gentlemen who travel are fond to deal in the marvellous [sic]. So if he states any thing in the character of accusation against me, you I am assured, will suppose that he is <u>exercising a travellers license</u>! Major Reily also threatens me very boldly. I will not retaliate if he shou'd—Thus passes a portion of our time when leisure will allow!

'Tis night my Love, and I am just from a Masonic party—Major Western, Major Reily, and Genl Terrell came to my room, and wou'd have me to go with them to the Ball Room. I did so, and have returned to my office. I passed round and saw all the Ladies. Many of them came to me and saluted me very kindly. I was on one crutch which I hope soon to lay aside!

Many injunctions were laid me to bring "Mrs Houston. Oh. we are so anxious to see her." Nothing can afford me so much pleasure as to introduce you to her—the moment that Congress adjourns my horse will beat the door and I will start to see her Ladyship is my reply! I feel very much like an exile, even in the midst of what is called a very fine party! Heaven save from the torture of such parties, when you are not present! Judge Eves,[12] the charge d' affaires, was there, and very happy. I wonder at it. He had a Lady on his arm, a little matter which has not happened to me in Austin. I saw Mrs Mayfield—she was a busy as a Bee in a Tar barrel, and really seemed as tho' her husband was not a defaultee to the amount of $39,000. Nevertheless this is a fact! Just think of this corruption—$29,000 were expended in a few months that he played Sec'y of State, and $10,000 as an <u>army</u> gentleman.

This is the way that the people's money has gone, and the reason involved. 'Tis said that the darkest hour of night is just before the dawn. But this is too much to say of the base and the unprincipled!! The efforts of those in power were all employed to sink the country so low that if it shou'd dissolve upon me to make an effort to say my country, the effort wou'd be unavailing. This is my candid opinion. They may be mistaken and wou'd be if I cou'd only have my way.

28th Dec—My Love, to day Mr. Walton[13] assures me that he will set out in a few hours—if he does, I will be ready for his departure, and calculate on writing again by Major Reily who says he will start tomorrow. You need not look for any more long letters. I will cherish all the love for you that you can imagine or desire. I know you are not so cruel as to wish me altogether miserable, and unless you do, you will not desire me to feel more acutely the pangs of absence.

I have written to Col Andrews, but did not request the letter to be shown to you! As he is a Gentleman of fine sense, he will hardly show it! You may, and I request it, kiss Mrs Andrews & Mrs Reily for me—and if you chuse you may pinch your little namesakes cheek for me! or bite her ear—Yes—you may kiss her if you please. Present me kindly to all our friends, and may God of his infinite mercy and kindness bless and protect you!

Thy ever devoted husband
Houston

Mrs M. L. Houston
City of Houston
Texas

[1]This letter has not been located. It was probably brought by William P. Harris or his brother John R. Harris, both of whom lived near Houston. Identified in *Writings*, II, 260n.
[2]The wedding of Alfred Smith to Nancy Ann Mills. Listed in Grammer, 76.
[3]The Texas Navy under Commodore Edwin Moore had set sail for an invasion of Yucatan. Lankevitch, 41.
[4]Margaret's letter containing these remarks has not been located.
[5]Anson Jones, Secretary of State; George Hockley, Secretary of War; George Terrell, Attorney General. Wisehart, 377.
[6]James Reily, minister to the U. S.; Gail Borden, collector of the port at Galveston; Francis Lubbuck, comptroller. Ibid.
[7]Because it was difficult to get mail out of Austin, Houston often composed one letter to Margaret over a period of several days, numbering each page as he added to it.
[8]On December 23, 1841, Indians supposed to be Wacoes and Towaccanies attacked a settlement between the Guadalupe and Colorado Rivers and killed a mail rider. L. W. Kemp, "Glimpses of Texas History,"*Post Dispatch* (Houston), August 25, 1929.
[9]John D. Morris and Cornelius Van Ness, representatives from San Antonio. *Handbook of Texas*, II , 237 and 831–32.
[10]The Austin *Daily Bulletin*, December 24, 1841, reported that Houston made the invocation. Friend, 104. (This would appear to be an error.)
[11]Judge Anderson Hutchinson. *Writings, III* , 524.
[12]Judge Joseph Eve of Kentucky was chargé d'affaires of the United States to the Republic of Texas. *Writings*, III, 135–36.
[13]John Walton of Galveston. Identified in White, *1840 Census of Texas*, 54.

To
Mrs Margaret Lea Houston
City of Houston
Texas
Mr Green

Very Dear Maggy,

As Major Reily will set out on tomorrow, I will commence to night a letter not knowing how long it will be spun out. By the time that you get thro my last, you will have this to commence! I will send you a News paper in which you will find and [sic] <u>old acquaintance</u>. Look in 3rd page, 3rd volume, and you recognize it! The only incident to day of note is the death of a young man by the name of Anderson. He died of consumption, and was very clever! Poor fellow he died far, very far in a land of strangers—tho' he received every attention until he was laid in "the narrow house."

My Love, I have not sworn to day, but was in the act, when I caught myself! We don't know how good we can be until we try in <u>good earnest</u>. I hope to do much in the way of reformation—but I will not brag until a twelve month has passed as you are to have all the credit! Judge Terrell and my self intend to accompany Major Reily as far as Mr Durhams[1] tomorrow evening, if we can. It is only nine miles from the city! There we can get good eating for at least our supper, and a breakfast—that will do us at least for one week until we can visit him again. His is a poor little cabbin [sic], but I assure you, the eating is first rate!—it can't be beat any where! I am now waiting in my office for Maj Reily to have a diplomatic confab with him, previous to his departure for the U States!

You will my Love, suppose that if I were present, I wou'd annoy you most superlatively with my chat, as I evince such an outrageous penchant for chatting to you at a distance. You must excuse me for I can't help it. This you know, is the excuse for all bad <u>habits</u>. You may doubt whether or not this is a <u>very bad habit</u>?

I was pained that I did not get a letter from you by mail! 'Tis true I had the happiness to get several from you on recent dates, but then I cou'd read always while you are the authoress! Because your <u>Novels</u> are always new, no matter when they were written!

The people here look cheerful, dark as the prospect seems for the country. They say "Houston can save us." The[y] may be right, but it will be a very "tight squeeze." So long as they think so, they can't be loss'd, but they may be a good-deal bewildered!

I again anticipate the pleasure of seeing the Congress adjourn by the 20th of January—Nothing can give me more pleasure than this fact, but to see my "dear wee wifie" and this wou'd be a grand move towards the consummation of the latter! So soon as Congress can raise the wind to get off, I think they will vacate the city of the Hills, and fly to the Lowlands for refuge and homes!

> Oh! sacred hour!
> How fond, endearing is the thought,
> That all my treasure, and my love are there!
> How fleet life currents course
> When moved by pure affection
> And aroused by all the lust,
> Emotions of an ardent heart.
> A heart which beats with kindest love
> Must ire recur to the shrine
> Of all his hopes and cares!
> There true devotion, will it offer up
> To the bright Star which guides
> Its destiny—(which is my dear Maggy)

You see this is set for Poetry whither it is or not. By it you will at least discover that my heart is with you!—if I am not. I wou'd however like much to be with it for all times to come!

My Mr Miller says "Mrs Houston will criticise it to death." I wou'd send it, with all its defects and require you to send me a criticism upon it if you please. Don't spare me, for I had no business to attempt Poetry after a days incessant labour! I will cease for to night— So, good night my Love!

30th This morning I have not seen Major Reily, and do not know whether or not he will get off to day! It is a very cold morning, and I do assure you upon my word after seperating [sic] from him at half past one o clock this morning, I never closed my eyes in sleep. We had talked of national affairs and what was more we had talked of Love and home! To day I have [to] make many communications to Congress on various subjects! So you may imagine that I will neither enjoy tranquility nor satisfaction! I am informed that there is a probability of Congress adopting the system of Finance recommended in my message. If it shou'd, I will yet save the country! Unless Congress shou'd play the fool on other very important subjects. The Indian policy is next in importance. Our chance too, for invasion by Mexico is greater than it has been since 1836. God avert it! But if it shou'd come, I will meet it, shou'd I live!

My Love, while I think of it (and the thought [which] arises from that of invasion), I have to day laid away my crutch and feel well. I thank God, very well!—

My Love, this was to go by Maj Reily, but he can't get off until Saturday. Do let Mrs Reily know it. He does not know that old Green[2] is going. So I have to close my Epistle in so much haste that I can not correct this letter.—It may be best so if I were to do it I might not send it. My Love to our friends.

Thy devoted husband
Houston

P.S. My dear Mr Green will let you know when he will return! Treat him civilly.

H.

To Mrs. Houston of Houston

[1]George J. Durham. For a biography see *Writings,* VIII, 107–108n and *Handbook of Texas,* I, 257.
[2]Houston may be referring to George Green, who was in the employ of James Spillman. Gifford White, *They Also Served,* (Nacogdoches: Ericson Books, 1985), 55.

Mrs. Sam Houston
City of Houston Texas
By Maj Reily
Minister

Austin
1st Jany 1842

Dearest,
    With pleasure I Greet you! A happy New Year! That you may enjoy many my Love, is in accordance with my most devout prayers!

Maj Reily is just on the eve of departure for Houston. I have had trouble to get him off for the want of money! I regret too, that I can only write to you a note in place of a "poser"—You must supply, every thing not expressed by me. This your dear imagination can do, from the past. You know my increasing devotion! The past will prove it. Oh my ever dear Maggy, day after day passes, and the only happiness which I feel, arises from my recollection of you. Last night I was at a private party, where Maj Reily was one of the guests. It was pretty pleasant for me, for every Lady there either spoke to me of you or sat by me and conversed about you! To set you here; there is great feeling! I tell them <u>that I will be absent from here some four weeks before I return with you</u>!!! Yes, it will be, at <u>least</u>, four weeks before I will be enabled to settle my business and return to this place from Houston! I know you can prepare to come so soon as <u>I may wish</u>!!!

I reiterate to you my Love, that the moment Congress may adjourn, I will have my good horse, Saxe Weimar, at the door,—and then I will set off in an hour. Major Reily can tell you all the news, and really my Love, I have no time—I usually leave my office to sleep, at 2 o clock in the morning. Last night I rested better, than I have done since I was or have been in Austin. I wou'd if possible write to you any thing if I had time to do so. Every moment I look for Judge Terrell, and Maj Reily to start as an escort, with the Major as far as Col [George] Durhams, only ten miles. The carriage is here— I embrace you my ever dearest Wife Maggy, with all my love—yes, my boundless love!!!

Present me most affectionately to Col & Madame Andrews— and Howda yr [sic] friend Mag Stone!

Thy ever devoted
Houston

General Sam Houston
Austin, Texas

Houston, Jan. 3rd 1841 [1842]

My own Love,
I have only five minutes to spend in writing to you but you will

excuse the roughness of a hasty scrawl. I enclose a letter to you from Antoinette,[1] which I took the liberty of opening as I knew it was from her, and I was anxious to hear something of her. I rec'd yours of the 15th on yesterday, but it had taken a trip to Galveston in the mean time being sent by mistake. I also rec'd one from bro. Vernal by the same boat. He went down the Trinity to Galveston. He gave me some of his plans, but as Sis has written you all about them it will be unnecessary to repeat them. Mrs. Andrews' daughters arrived on yesterday. Mrs. Taylor[2] and Miss Thielman.[3] They are quite an addition to our circle, very sprightly and intelligent. Dearest my spirits and fortitude are all gone. I do feel as if I could not live longer without you. If you can not come to me, write me something that will console me, for my heart is very sad.

Dearest thy devoted wife
M. L. Houston

[1]This letter has not been located.
[2]Barbra Tighlman Taylor. Information on the Tighlman (sometimes spelled Thilman) Andrews family may be found in the collection of Mrs. I. B. McFarland in the Peabody Library, Sam Houston State University, Huntsville.
[3]Bettie Tighlman (also spelled Thilman).

Margaret was anxious for the capitol to be moved to another location where she could be with her husband. She expressed her feelings on this subject and other political matters:

General Sam Houston
Austin, Texas

Houston, Jan 3rd. [1842]

Dearest Love,
I rec'd your invaluable letter tonight by Mr. Green,[1] and although it is way past my usual hour for retiring I must answer it tonight as he will be off in the morning. I wrote to you this morning by a Mr. Fisher,[2] but the letter was really so hurried and incoherent that I am now ashamed of it and at this time I am so out of spirits, that I can hardly write at all. Mr. Green tells me that congress will not adjourn within less time than six weeks, and this is my grievance. Surely my

love your patriotism is undergoing a severe test and doubtless will come out like the refiner's gold. Mine has been pretty much shaken by recent events and I must confess that my predominant thought has been that my husband was wasting his time and energies upon an ungrateful people! But perhaps it is wrong to indulge such feelings. If you think so Love, I will try to overcome these. Many thanks for your poetry. Your muse is certainly very amicable to visit you in the midst of the turmoil and impractical bustle which must necessarily reign in Austin at this time, and I am certainly much indebted to her for reminding you of your absent Maggy. If she is so fortuitous at this time, what may we expect when we again roam through the sweet wild woods around our home! Indeed Love, I was delighted with the sentiments entertained in your lines, particularly the conclusion! I had hear of "jumping at conclusions" but I must confess I thought that a pretty sudden leap. Nevertheless, I was highly flattered and I now consider my Husband a poet as well as a hero, statesman, and I believe a philosopher, but I do not know exactly about the latter! Nous verrons [sic]!? The good people of Texas have certainly determined to ascertain.

I hear nothing of the seat of government being moved and it is a subject in which I am not altogether uninterested. It would be a source of consolation to me to know where in the future our home is to be that I might draw plans for it and indulge visions which though they may never be realized would at least amuse me for the moment. But even this is denied us. We are slaves of the public and must await its pleasures. My Love I am almost sorry that I have said so much. I know that it is my duty to soothe you in your deep disappointments and trials as much as possible, but at this moment I am so indignant at the recent acts of congress that I can not restrain my feelings. If the seat of government should not be moved, I must confess to you candidly that I wish you to resign immediately. Of course this will not decide your course of conscience in a case of such importance, but I need to say what I think and Feel!

If you are to serve the people for nothing[3] I think you ought at least to have the privilege of performing the labour in safety and in some civilized spot. But dearest if you are satisfied it will all be right with me for your happiness is mine. My Love, can it be that there is a real probability of a Mexican invasion!

May Heaven avoid such a calamity. Oh my husband I can not

endure the thought. It is too dreadful! I can not be happy until I see you again and hear from your own lips that the danger no longer exists.

Dearest one portion of your letter gives me more pleasure than any others. It was that you were striving to rise above the dreadful practice of swearing. Oh continue those efforts. I entreat you Love by all the sacred happiness we have enjoyed together, by every hope of future happiness do not profane the name of him who has been so merciful to us. Are we not more blessed than others? In vain we look around for that communion of hearts that God has suffered us to enjoy. And oh do not in return ask his name as an expression of anger or to embellish the unjust! Dearest husband, my constant prayer to God is "that you may be saved." Oh that I knew some argument that would drive you to the feet of the saviour! How freely would I yield this fleeting breath and lie down in the cold grave if it would purchase your salvation. But it can not be. If you will not fly to Jesus for refuge there remaineth no more sacrifice from sin but a certain fearful evoking for of judgment and fiery inauguration which shall devour the adversaries. Oh How can I rest one moment while my husband is exposed to the wrath of God! Cold luke warm heart of mine, too long hast thou been swayed by earthly hopes and drawn away from my Heavenly Father by the blessings of his own hand! Dearest each night and morn, I will pray for you with my whole heart and at these calm and peaceful hours, will you not "visit" with me? and Oh I entreat you to throw aside every worldly thought at such a time and pray with a heart free from distractions!

It is late, very late at night and hearts more joyous than mine are lulled into gentle sleep and yet I would write until the east again puts on her rose tinted morning garb for how can I sleep? My heart is troubled like the stormy sea, and no gentle husband is near me to hush by his bright looks of affection, the darkness and clouds from my spirits or by his soft words to still the boisterous words of grief. I am figurative you will say but dearest it is no exaggerated picture. I do feel as if my heart was bursting & deep midnight stillness is reigning around me. My own one thou are not here and oh how silent is the spot in which thy voice is not heard! How dark and dreary the scene, if I behold thee not! Dearest my heart finds relief in the expressions of its deep feelings and I know you will not treat them lightly. Last night I was happy for I dreamed much of you. We meandered arm-in-arm through a lovely country and thick hanging bows above our heads were filled with a thousand bright birds and our path was fringed with innumerable strange and beauteous flowers. We meandered on and on but felt no fatigue for we were happy. Oh may it promise a vision of our journey through life. Dearest talk no more [torn] sacrifices for your country. It must not be. You are mine and mine alone and you must not—oh no you can not leave me again! I am constantly surrounded by friends, but oh I feel desolate for you are not with me and oh what solitude is like the loneliness of a crowd! Write often dearest and oh do hasten home.

Your devoted wife
M. L. Houston

[1] See Houston to Margaret, December 29, 1841.
[2] Margaret is probably speaking of Henry F. Fisher (also spelled Fischer), a book-keeper and salesman in Houston who was seeking an appointment as a consul at Bremen. *Writings*, III, 379 and Johnston, 35.
[3] The Republic of Texas was in deep financial trouble, and as an economy measure the salary of the president was reduced by half. Friend, 380.

General Sam Houston
Austin, Texas

Houston Jan 5th [1842]

My beloved husband,

Maj. Reilly arrived tonight and brought me your highly valued letter.[1] I have been two days and nights with Mrs. Reily,[2] having been detained by rain, and our time has passed as pleasantly as it could be without our husbands. Your letter came to me in the most singular way, for within the last day I have rec'd the packages by Majors Walton and Goodall[3] since receiving the one by Mr. Green. I will account to you for my writing nothing to you about your lameness for I knew nothing of it. How cold and heartless you must have thought my letters! Not one of them containing a word of sympathy in your feelings! But my husband knows me too well to suppose that I would not feel deeply for his affliction. The Maj. tells me that

Congress will adjourn in three weeks, but even that period seems as if it would never come. Three weeks! Oh what an interminable age of anxiety.

I was pleased with your account of the wedding and the lady who is so much like me. Take care you do not fall in love with "the shadow for the substance," the resemblance for the original. Maj. Western writes me that you are becoming a great gallant, but you may tell him that he is forestalled by your warnings! and Maj. Reily too has told me so many good things of you. However, you must thank the major for his letter and for his information, as it has not made me <u>very unhappy</u>. My Love they are not doing much at Cedar Point, and Capt. [John S.] Black has not been able to go down yet. I read a letter from Armstrong[4] today which I dislike to send you as it contains disagreeable information, which I fear will make you unhappy, but I am at a loss what to do and you must excuse my sending it.

Dearest, I fear you take too much exercise. Oh do be careful of your precious health. No one can prize it so much as your own Maggy. Do you not think you must have walked too much on your ancle [sic]. Take good care of yourself Love, and I trust that happy days are in store for us. It is very late at night dearest and I must bid you Farewell.

Thy devoted Maggy

[1]See Houston to Margaret, December 24–28, 1841.
[2]Ellen Hart Reily.
[3]Albert Goodall, the son-in-law of General James Davis. White, *1840 Citizens of Texas, Volume I Land Grants* , 96 and Hearne Collection, San Antonio.
[4]Jacob Armstrong owned land on the east side of Cedar Bayou in the vicinity of Cedar Point. *An Abstract of the Original Titles of Record in the General Land Office—*, (Austin: Reproduced by Pemberton Press, 1964), 123. This letter has not been located.

Mrs Houston
City of Houston Texas
By Mr Shaw[1]

Austin
6th Jany 1842

Dearest,

My friend Mr Shaw will hand you this note, and tell <u>you the news</u>!

I wrote last night & rested pretty well, and to day, I feel like a new man.

Mr Shaw is a very clever young man and please treat him politely.

No news to day. The seat of Government I am told will be adgitated [sic] to day or soon! I say nothing about it, and my dear don't mention it.

My Love, Commend me very kindly to out friends.

Thy ever devoted
Houston

Margaret

You can write to Mother and give her my love. H

[1]This probably refers to James C. Shaw of Galveston. For a biography see Ray, 205, and Best, 351.

Austin
6th Jany 1842

My dearest,

Mr Shaw has been detained some longer than he expected. Had I known it I cou'd have written you a long letter without much in it. I have just galloped Saxe Weimar some two or three miles! I found it of great advantage to me. It has aroused me into action, and I feel quite Well! I will ride every fine day an hour or so! When I have as much time. Indeed my dear, I have very little. I have no good news. Judge Blake[1] begs to be kindly presented to you as does Hockley, and the many others. Again present me to Col Andrews, his noble Lady, and to our excellent friend Mag [Stone] and Madame.[2] Kiss Ella[3] & "Donny" Reily.[4]

Thy ever devoted husband
Houston

Margaret

PS Mr Miller[5] sends his respects, and wou'd send them to Sarah Ann,[6] by you, no doubt (if his modesty did not prevent.) Please play Mr Shaw a pretty tune of [sic] the Guitar, if you please my dear—

Houston

[1]Judge Bennet Blake, chief justice for Nacogdoches. Identified in McDonald, 4.
[2]Margaret Stone's aunt, Mrs. William Fairfax (Mille Stone) Gray.
[3]Samuella Andrews, the daughter of Eugenia and John D. Andrews. Identified in the McFarland Collection, Huntsville, Texas.
[4]Donny Reily, the son of James and Ellen Reily.
[5]Washington D. Miller.
[6]Sarah Ann Royston.

General Sam Houston
Austin, Texas

Houston, Jan 7th 1842

Dearest husband,

As I shall have an opportunity of sending you a letter tomorrow, I have determined to write tonight, though I am not very well, having had a severe chill and fever today, and am now suffering intensely with the headache. But you must not be uneasy about me dearest, for my general health is excellent, and I have scarcely had any cough since you left. I am still with Mrs. Reily, the streets being so horrible muddy, that I can not get home, but it has certainly been a very agreeable captivity, for the Maj. has entertained me with so many accounts of you, that my time has been passed quite pleasantly, and Mrs. Reily sympathises fully with me and appreciates the anxieties of a wife. The Maj. tells me that bride whom you think so much like me is awfully ugly! So you see he is realy taking a traveller's license as you predicted he would do! I am determined to believe that she is pretty in defiance of him. At all events I will believe that you <u>think her pretty!</u> I delivered your kiss to Mag Stone yesterday evening, and she was delighted and desires me to send you one in return. I hasten to do so as I would rather it should be delivered by proxy, though I apprehend that you would like to go upon the credit system in this case and defer the immediate payment of the debt. But I will be very obliging and become responsible for all debts of that kind which she may contract with you. With what readiness do we undertake the <u>pleasant tasks</u> of our friends, especially when thier own performance of them would not be very agreeable to us! There is a new adage Love, and here I might very well bring in my old one. How generous we can be when it costs us nothing! for I fear you will say I have not expended much wit or wisdom upon it, but it certainly augurs some knowledge of the world, and as age brings experience and time doth add <u>age</u>, I think it very proper that I should express myself by an <u>adage</u>!

I suppose there is no prospect of moving the seat of government immediately. What are we to do? I can form no plans for the future in the event of thier retaining it in Austin. Maj. Reily desires me to say to you, that your friends in Houston do not wish you to bring censure upon yourself by any attempt to have it brought to this place independent of congress. I suppose you saw Maj. Western's letter to me. He wishes me to use my influence with you in favor of Harrisburg. This I can not do for I would not like to see <u>Houston</u> put down, especially by some of the proprieties of Harrisburg! Nevertheless it would give me pleasure to oblige a friend so highly esteemed by both of us, if I could do so, without such a sacrifice of feeling as it would certainly cost me to comply with his request. I thank you dearest for brother H.'s[1] Letter. You will readily imagine with what delight I read his expressions of esteem and affection for you. He is a dear noble brother, but I really believe that I like him a <u>little better</u> since I find that he loves you so well and appreciates you.

Mrs. Andrew's daughters are quite an addition to our society and have attracted considerable attention. The gentlemen are getting up a ball for them. I was very much amused at Mr. Power[2] last night. He requested the honour of attending me to the ball, and when I replied that I would not think of going to any party without my husband, he exclaimed, why Victoria would go without Albert! It was said with so much seriousness and sincerity that realy I had not the heart to laugh at the ludicrous comparison, and embarrass the poor fellow by revealing the absurdity of his English notions. Oh my Love, you can not imagine how delighted I am to know that you have left off swearing! I feel as if a new light had dawned upon my existence and at this moment, sweet visions of future happiness are floating through my mind. A weight is taken from my heart—a griev-ous weight, and I trust it will never return. Dearest you have con-ferred so much happiness upon me that I know not how to express my joy and thankfulness. Should Heaven spare us, a life of unchang-ing devotion shall express them for me. It is near midnight, and I must now retire, but I fear it will be to a sleepless pillow, for my thoughts are all with you, and my heart pines for you. The Maj. says "give the Gen. my best love," and Mrs. Reily and Anna Lubbock[3] send thiers to you.

Farewell most beloved of husbands.

Thy devoted Maggy

[1]Henry Lea. This letter has not been found.
[2]Charles Power, a merchant from England. Madge W. Hearne Collection, San Anto-nio.
[3]The sister of Francis R. Lubbock. Dorothy Knox Houghton et. al., *Houston's Forgot-ten Heritage*, (Houston: Rice University Press, 1991), 25.

To Mrs Margaret Lea Houston
City of Houston Texas
By Maj Smith

Austin
8th Jany 1842

My dearest,

Maj Smith[1] will start to day for Galveston, and by him I write to you, but no pleasant news. Major Kaufman[2] was shot by Mayfield[3] on the 6th inst. He is not dead, but little hope is entertained in favour of his recovery. Poor fellow, he suffers much in body and mind I fear! I have written to his father in law[4] and rendered my condo-lences to his dear wife! I have written the best letter that I could do, under circumstances of so delicate a character! This moment Dr. Jones[5] tells me that Major Kaufman is better! I sincerely hope that he may recover. He is in the hand of an Almighty God! who tempers the breeze to the shorn lamb!

My dearest! I hope you will not feel unhappy at this news, tho I am assured that you must feel very unpleasant! And distressed! We must look to the <u>author</u> of our existence, for safety & preservation!

My Love! I feel that there is a Spirit which pervades all space, and illumines eternity! Upon that <u>spirit</u>,—we will rely. My dearest, I have maintained my resolution, as to "swearing," and the vice of intemperance has not one charm for me!

It will, I feel assured, gratify you to hear the news from me, because you are aware, that I will never deceive you, even in trifles, much in less in matters, which involve both your happiness and character,—for it is certain that the wife must share the destiny of her husband, so far as his character is to regulate his position in society! I regard the destiny of the husband, as much dependent upon his relations to the dear object of his affections! If he is noble, generous, and manly, he will always regard her feelings and happiness—while she on the other hand, will consult his feelings, and preserve his honor as the richest jewel in life's casket!!!

Dearest, Every night my prayers are offered to Heaven, for your <u>preservation</u> and <u>happiness</u>! I will never cease, through life, to invoke the favour of the Almighty!

My ever dear Maggy! Nothing has yet been done, about the seat of Government, but one thing you may rely upon! I will never occupy any situation that will require me to remain apart from you! Seperation [sic] from you is the most painful of all my endurance! If spared to embrace you my dearest, I will not again leave you until you bid me go! And say to me "My love, Your country demands your services in the field! Go and defend her." This event I hope, will never occur. Therefore I may say, that I will never leave you, nor forsake you!

This evening, I intend to ride out to Col [George] Durhams with Judge [George W.] Terrell, Judge [Joseph Eve] Eves and several more, to stay until Monday, and obtain some rest. My labor here is not so great as it has been! The disposition of Congress seems more kind to me than it has done! I hope it may be realized, for it will be so much better for the country! On my part nothing shall be wanting to promote, and maintain the best state of feeling, so long as my prerogatives are respected! You wou'd wish me to go no further, I am sure my dear!

I can write you no more, except that I will not fail to remember that "Maj Cocke[6] <u>writes</u> a beautiful hand. etc.

My dear, I will do any thing in my power for him! You did that <u>beautifully, most beautifully</u>. Well, my dearest, I only love you the more, for so doing! I will omit no opportunity of telling you or indicating to you, a small portion of my boundless love for you!

You will, I hope present me very kindly, to our dear friends. When dwelling in thought upon you my dear, and deploring your probable indisposition, I cannot but embrace Mrs Andrews, Mrs Reily, and yr friend Mag Stone, in the group of your kind, and generous attendance! You must render to them, a portion of gratitude. I can never express its measure!

Do not fail to commend me to Col Andrews, Maj Reily and our friends! My Love, I will write by mail, if but one line! to say "My Love! I Greet you!" In the mean time write much to me—or as much as you can with convenience!

Send my love to Mother, to our dear Sisters, and brothers, when you write to them! I look for many letters from you, and hope to meet one or more this evening as I am to travel the main road! My Love, if you want money, call upon Mr Ruthvan[7] or Col Andrews. Maj Western is here. I don't know what he is doing, but I reckon, for Harrisburg[8] strongly!

Thy ever devoted husband
Houston

Maggy

[1]It is unclear to which Smith Houston refers. John H. Smith is identified a resident of Harris County by Dixon and Kemp, 104.
[2]David Spangler Kaufman.
[3]James Mayfield. According to reports Mayfield spoke on the House floor on a judiciary bill and mentioned Kaufman in a severe manner, calling him by name. When the House adjourned Kaufman was waiting for him armed with a cane. Mayfield then shot Kaufman twice. Hogan, 272. The story was reported in *Telegraph and Texas Register*, January 19, 1842.
[4]Col. Daniel Long Richardson of Sabine, the father of Jane Richardson Kaufman. White and Toole, 21.
[5]Anson Jones.
[6]Houston probably is referring to Major William G. Cooke.
[7]Archibald St. Clair Ruthvan was the bookkeeper for Rice-Nichols firm. He later became a well known merchant in Houston. For a biography see *Writings*, VII, 555n.
[8]Houston is referring to the fact that Major Thomas Western was lobbying to have the capitol moved to Harrisburg.

Mrs Sam Houston
City of Houston Texas
By Mr Harris

Austin
10th Jany 1842

My dearest,

Yours of the 3rd instant, I met last evening nine miles from the city,[1] where I was passing my time from Saturday until this morning. I was very happy, yes! Love, I was rejoiced to receive & peruse it again, again! I also learned from Mr. Green who saw you, that you were well. I have a letter for you, but cou'd not send it, as Maj Smith went off without my knowledge. Mr Harris[2] is now waiting on me for this hasty note.

On yesterday I read the Bible, and passed the day in peace and tranquility, a thing that I cou'd not have done in Austin! Maj Kaufman is thought to be out of danger. I am rejoiced at the prospect!

I can only say to you my Love that I think of you <u>constantly</u> and love you without measure. Yes my love, None but you can ever warm this heart into boundless affection! Oh my dearest, don't be <u>unhappy</u> about the seat of Government! About this <u>matter</u> I say nothing! I do not drink, nor swear, and only think of our mutual happiness, and of Virtue, and purity of my life—except, thoughts of our country. My regards to our friends—all!

Thy devoted Houston

Margaret

[1]At the home of George Durham.
[2]Houston is probably referring to a member of the family of Louis Birdsall Harris, who lived in Harrisburg. Best, 353.

Austin
12th Jany 1842

My Dearest,

Your very welcome epistle,[1] by the mail, came to me last night— I say "very welcome," but I need not do so, for all your letters are to me endeared by association to reflect, while I peruse your letters that only a few hours past, you breathed upon the sheet which contains the breathing of affection, and yet I can not even behold the beloved object of all my love and devotion! Yes, my dear <u>one</u>, I deem the privilege of the senseless paper a happy one, for you can bestow a smile or smiles upon it, and whisper the sweet accents of thought, as well as impress the recollections of other days! Days which ever be sacred to me, <u>to us</u>! They are days of "Wildwood" memory. You can not my Love cherish those hours of holy love and affection with more lively sensations than myself. I was delighted with your dream, and the sweet description of past hours—Oh! With what a consuming, and maddening anxiety do I look forward to the moment, when I shall again press my beloved to this lonely heart! Love! You feel, and express the most painful solicitude for my return—I too feel, but cannot express, in terms such as you can, the emotions common to us both.

This moment I have learned that there is a prospect of a speedy adjournment of Congress—I pray that it may be the case. I have "Saxe" well shod, and keep him in the city ready to be off with the first to depart. This evening I will ride out to the country, and pass the night, as the physicians say to me the great advantage that I derive from exercise shou'd be kept up! My food, and the relaxation of business, are of great advantage to me! I will not until we meet describe to you the way in which I subsist in this awful City. Yes "most awful"—When we meet, my beloved, I will take great, yea! <u>vast</u> pleasure, in giving you the details of my "obitium cum dignitate," at Austin!

You may by chance, see a publication in the paper relative to the seat of Government! This is gratuitous, but I will let it pass! The people here are very kind to me, and say "Houston is a very clever fellow. I will support his administration."—So you see my dear how strong self interest is in the mortal feelings. Yes! You and I are selfish—I love you because I deem you superior to all others, in virtue, and excellence, and therefore, I wish you to be mine only,—for, by you, I am happy and prov'd I am blessed, and to be happy & blessed is surely selfish in us! You are selfish, because you do not wish me to love another; because it wou'd disparage you, and you cou'd not love me, but wou'd be miserable. My dearest, you will see that I am greatly hurried, and excuse the inelegant mode of expression used by me!

I will write every day that I can send you a letter, if but a single line to say "Dearest Margaret, _indeed_ I love you." I have just seen Genl Wood and Col Nail.[2] The Genl sends to you and our Mother, and to you all love!

I presented you to both gentlemen—and they were delighted. I will try, and do something for the old Colonel. I told him how much you were delighted with his publications, and I thought He wou'd go into _fits_!

I did not rave at Armstrongs[3] letter, but will send it express soon to Cedar Point. But lest I may not, please get Col Andrews to send for my horse forthwith, and let him be put at the stable of Mr Floyd[4] in Houston. If the Col shou'd have to pay money $20.00 to get the horse brought to Houston, I will repay it with pleasure, when I come down. Do let him be sent for by all means. He cost me $5,500.00.

In great haste. My Love I am ever thy devoted husband.

Houston

Margaret

[1]See Margaret to Houston, January 5, 1842.
[2]George F. Wood and James C. Neill.
[3]Jacob Armstrong.
[4]Elisha Floyd owned the City Hotel on Franklin Avenue between Main and Travis in Houston. _Writings_, I, 341n and White, _Citizens of Texas, v.1, Land Grants_, 84.

Margaret had met the British historian William Kennedy in Houston. She wrote a letter of introduction for him to take to Austin along with a personal note to her husband.

Houston Jan. 12th [1842]

I take great pleasure in presenting to my dear husband, Mr. William Kennidy[1] whose work on Texas has interested us so much. He has my assurance of the high estimation in which you hold him and the gratification it will afford you to form his acquaintance. I hope the very favourable impression he has produced abroad with regard to Texas, will be bourn [sic] in remembrance by the citizens of Austin, and that they will render his visit as agreeable as possible.

Ever thine
Margaret Lea Houston

Gen. Sam Houston

Thursday 13th [1842], Jan.

Dearest,

I have a boon to ask of you. Can you not give Mr. Kennidy a line about the task which we once assigned to Dr. Irion: As you may not understand me—in a word, I wish him to write your biography! I have set my heart upon it Love. Do not suffer me to be disappointed. I know no pen that could so richly portray the thrilling incidents of your life. You will not deny me Love.

Thy Maggy

P.S. I am perfectly well this morning

[1]William Kennedy was confirmed as consul general from Texas to Great Britain on February 3, 1842. He resigned a short time later to accept the position of British consul for the port of Galveston. While he never did write a biography of Sam Houston, he was the author of a history of Texas in two volumes published in London: *The Rise, Progress and Prospects of the Republic of Texas. Writings*, II, 450.

Mrs Houston
City of Houston Texas
By Judge Hart[1]

Austin
13th Jany 1842

My dearest,

Yesterday, I wrote to you, and then spent the evening three miles from the city at a Mr Smiths, where I had milk first rate, and hominy. I slept pretty well and this morning I am quite well, as I thought of you for hours after I lay down. I am not displeased with my reflections. You are the sole of my thoughts, and the bright star of my hopes! This morning, I can only say a word to you, as Judge Hart is now waiting in my room, and will set out as soon as I close. I have written to Colonel Andrews by Judge Hart and directed him what I wish done with my horse. I dislike much to think, that you will be troubled with any business of mine! Don't be uneasy, I pray you. I will take care not to be vexed at anything, so as to make myself ridiculous!!! To day, I have a vast deal of business to transact, and must do it! Time passes, and I must confess that my principle [sic] business will do me to recommend useful measures and prevent mischief! I will not have the pleasure to approve anything beneficial, I fear, for poor dear Texas. But cheer up my Love! We will have better luck next time. You will see Doct Moore[2] perhaps and if you shou'd my dear, treat him kindly. I have buried the Tomahawk with him, and 'tis well to do so. I am at war now with no one and only pass Mayfield[3] without notice! I will only try to get home, and see my love, and live happy. Yes, happy with you, with my dearly beloved Margaret. Oh my Love, my heart swells with emotions most painful, when I look out my window, this morning, and see the bright sun of Kind Heaven cheering all nature, but my lonely heart.

My regards to all our friends, and do believe that my heart is incapable of entertaining affection or love for any being on earth but you Maggy!

To Day a report has reached [me] from San Antonio that 70 Indians came to a Rancho below the town, some 30 miles—wounded as many. I will make a message to Congress, on these matters to day!

Be happy and rely upon my devotion and boundless love. Dearest Adieu.

Thy Houston

Lady Margaret

[1]Judge William Hart.
[2]Dr. Francis Moore, Jr., editor of the *Telegraph and Texas Register*. For a biography see *Writings*, VIII, 125n.
[3]Robert Mayfield.

Austin
14th Jany 1842

You can have no idea my dearest, of the pleasure which your very agreeable letter gave to me! Mr Allen arrived, and I heard that he had a letter from you.[1] Immediately I sent for him and the letter!

Indeed, I perused it with uncommon haste! The only portion which gave me pain was that which announced to me your indisposition. Oh, those miserable chills & fevers do annoy and distress you so much! I hope you will soon escape their influence and become entirely well! Were I with you dearest, I wou'd not be so unhappy on their account, and for other reasons, I wou'd be ten thousand times more happy! I would have a noble heart to sympathise with me, in every care, and in all solicitude.

Tomorrow Dearest, I intend to visit the country and stay until monday morning. Judge Baylor will preach there and we will go down together—It is the house where the wedding was, but the Bride[2] does not live there. So don't think that she is the attraction— for tho invited by her husband,[3] I have not seen her since the wedding.

I grant that Maj Reily may have intended a compliment to you, but he surely did slander the lady! She is not ugly, at the same time I will not admit that she is by a good deal, as pretty as your Ladyship,— nor do I love her, so well by an <u>infinite deal</u>!

(15th) Dearest, I reposed last night well, and feel to day as tho I was on the mending hand. All my friends say—they have not seen me look so well in Texas! So my dearest, I hope as your general health is so good, that we shall meet, both, (and both of us) in cheerfulness, and prepare to make our rambles at Cedar Point.

To day Love, a man came to me to be employed in building me a house where ever I might desire—so I will send him to Houston if he leaves here, and let him put <u>us</u> up a house either at my Rancho,[4] or at the Point,[5] as <u>we</u> may think best. I intend to have it Rough-cast, (white, or any colour which you may chuse) I will have it very neat if we live.

While writing, my mind flys [sic] in advance, to happy days, days yet to come! My Love, I do not forget, that our breath is in our nostrils and that our destiny is in the had of our Creator God! On Him do I rely for every "good and perfect gift."

My dear you will see, that I have issued a Recommendation to keep a Holy Fast on the 2nd day of March next. How this may be regarded by <u>some persons</u>, I do not know; nor my dearest do I care. Had I been chary, I wou'd not have been Sam Houston, but being Houston, <u>I will not be foolishly in dread of what the world may say,</u>

or think of my actions; being satisfied myself that they are right, I will maintain them so! My Love, You I know will approve the measure highly and truly! This wou'd be enough for my satisfaction! I have done right!!!

18th

Dearest, I went to the country with Hon Baylor, Terrell, General Hunt, Hockley & others. On sunday we had preaching tho not by Judge Baylor as he was too unwell! We passed the day very quietly, and that night, Judge Baylor and myself had an argument about man's accountability, and I, of course thought my views most orthodox. We differed but did not quarrel! The Judge is a good man, but no Calvinist. I did not know your view on these matters, tho' the question arose! These matters we alluded to once, but you may not remember it!

Many thanks dearest for your various letters by Mr Kennedy.[6] The one introductory was very pretty, and very proper! For the others, Love, I am obliged to you very much!

I will "not refuse your request," about the items of History for Mr K, but I will defer a compliance with it, until we can meet, & then my dearest we will determine, as to the most delicate and dignified mode of doing the thing.

I have every disposition, Dear Wife, to comply with your wishes, because they are always sensible. They [are] just such as the Idol of my heart shou'd entertain, and such as a devoted husband shou'd be proud & happy to gratify—This my dear, is a part from the pleasure of contributing to your vanity which I truly confess is more on account of myself than on our account. You will think I intend to be smart? but no I only design to be facetious, but it may require a look to give the proper effect.

Your letter Love, on the subject of "addages"[7] made me very happy, and as I let a friend or two see it, we were all amused, and were pleased, that it indicated at least a clear & healthy condition of mind, tho the chills and fevers afflicted your body! You speak of what Major Reily told you about the "Bride." She was on a visit to Col Durhams on last saturday, with her dear husband! So I read to her, and Mrs Durham the part of you letter concerning her, and as you said that "you would believe that she was pretty" etc. I thought she wou'd faint with pleasure! Oh she was so pleased, and the old

Lady too! She will always be happy, and remain satisfied with her-self. But Love, you will remember, that I did not say she resemble[d] you in features. Oh no! that won't do! She is not pretty but her form, and gait or step, are very much "like my sister Eliza's."

You I tell you [sic] that you remind me of her at times.—I do not compare you to any other—They may resemble you in some things, but not in all. You (as you believe) are my <u>nonpareil</u>. I am happy that your faith in this is perfect—If it were not, I should doubt my own worth, and honor, tho dearest, on this subject, I have never been sceptical [sic]. Could you but see the emotions of my heart reflected you wou'd [not] doubt, that all earth compared to you in my affections is a very nothing, and even my mind extends in my love for you to an eternal round of being. Yes my Dearest though the <u>speculation</u> is enshrouded by my impervious mystery, yet it is not sinful to hope, and aspire in soul, to the contemplation of such sub-ject—Did I do so, in derision of Gods [sic] attributes, I wou'd be sinful, but I do so with reverence, if not with a "perfect heart."—I know that nothing less than virtue can guarantee the sweet visions of Hope!

My dearest, I will cherish virtue, and all my exertions shall be directed to secure an interest in Eternal life. This my <u>dear</u>, must [be] under the dispensation of heaven, by virtue of Christ's atonement. You my <u>dearest</u>, may rest assured, that I will never trifle with pro-fessions connected with the institutions of Religion or the adoration of Jehovah! <u>I am done with the vanities and frivolities of life, so far as I can judge of myself</u>! My cheerfulness, I hope, will retain unim-paired, or rather improved! I hope my ever Dearest Maggy, that when we meet, you will have reason to be cheerful! <u>I pray Heaven, that we may soon meet again, never to be absent from each other, one single week thro' life</u>!

Dearest, You speak of Maggy Stone—Now don't you tell her that I will be certain to kiss her, if you are present when I see her, but "my private opinion" is that I will really give her a buss, or pinch her ear! This I intend to do, for the love which she has borne you, in my absence! Tell her that I say she is a "little Captain."

My Love, I was happy to receive dear Antoinettes letter.[8] I fear she is not happy, but I pray that my apprehensions may be ground-less. She ought to be happy, a being so pure, and sweet should be happy! I do regret that <u>they</u> did not settle at the Point. It wou'd have been of great advantage to us both! I will not say so to our Sister, and as for Bledsoe, I will not write to him! I hope he may prosper, but indeed I fear, that he will be unpopular wherever he resides, and this will render Dear Sister unhappy if she shou'd know it! For her, I will do every thing in my power. Why they did not prefer the Point I cannot say, tho' I might guess. My offers were so liberal, that no one cou'd object who had good sense! I am sure it was not the fault of Sister!

I am glad that you have seen Vernal and think strange that Martin has not been over to see us. Poor fellow, I fear that he feels his embarrassments. I wou'd be very happy, if it were in my power to relieve all his wants.

Vernal may do well at Liberty—tho' I did not wish him to settle there, as it is regarded to be the most sickly village in Texas. I offered my advice to him, touching Montgomery, but he did not like it. Should he even enjoy health in Liberty, his friends will feel uneasy about him. Had he been settled, I cou'd have appointed him solicitor for some District.

Whenever Vernal asks for my advice, in obedience to our Dear Henrys request, I will give him my advice and suggestions, but not otherwise! He lacks confidence in my judgment, and I regret it sincerely! I never the less shall feel a deep interest in his welfare and success!

Dearest Maggy, I am fearful that you will think I am in a pet! Well I may be so, for to day I have been pestered out of all measure, and it is very late at night. I hope early in the morning to send you this letter by Mr Doswell,[9] and by mail I may write also.

I have nothing funny to write to you, nor any thing pleasant. I do not know when our wise men will get tired of earning $8.00 per day, in good funds. They appear to have a penchant, for such labour. They (or a part of them) seem to like the business, & I think they had best do so, for I sincerely hope it will be the last time that many of them will have a chance to serve their dear constituents in Congress.

This evening Love, I rode out with Mr Kennedy, and we had much to say to each other. I think when he rivises [sic] his work, he will be in possession of more information touching Texas matters! He thinks Congress is not so wise as they think themselves. He is in the English sense a very "clever man." I am much pleased with him, I assure you, and he seems to think my hunting shirt quite comfortable & Respectable!

I am sure you will weary by the time that you have perused this letter of many days! I feel more happy when communing with you, even by letter than at any other time, while I am absent from your dearest Love! Reflect then, what my happiness would be, if I cou'd only <u>embrace, press you to my heart</u>! I hope the day is not remote, when we will <u>meet</u>, and my dearest you will obtain the consent of your Mother, to our union, for really I do feel as tho' I had written nearly "love letters" enough for one courtship! But "nous verrons"— if you shou'd reject me dear Lady, I will never address another <u>Gal</u>, you may be sure. So you see I am in good earnest and no joke, shou'd Kind Heaven permit us once more to meet.

You must always present me kindly to our dear Mother, and relatives when you write to any of them. I can only write to you, and that chiefly at night!

You know best, in what phrase to present me to our friends—so I delegate to you Love, full powers!

How the seat of Government will be determined, I cant say, but I learned there is much feeling about the matter—To live apart from you Love, while we do live, I will not submit to, if I have only left to me the power to resign all the office [sic] that I now hold!

Congress must adjourn by the 30th instant, but I hope much sooner. It is doing no good I assure you! The people will not thank them for what they have done, in my opinion!

Dear, My only pleasure is in reading your letters, and I thank you greatly—truly for your frequent letters. They can not come too often! I will not have time to read and correct this letter.

Thy ever devoted husband
Houston

Lady Maggy

[1]See Margaret to Houston, January 7, 1842.
[2]Nancy Ann Mills Smith. Identified in Grammer, 76.
[3]Alfred Smith. Ibid.
[4]Houston owned property on the southwest outskirts of Houston near the home of Hadley and Obedience Smith. See Houston to Margaret, May 14, 1842.
[5]Cedar Point on Galveston Bay.
[6]See William Kennedy's letter of introduction and Margaret to Houston, January 12, 1842.
[7]See Margaret to Houston, January 7, 1842.
[8]This letter had not been located.

[9]J. Temple Doswell, a Houston merchant. Identified in Houghton, 66.

General Sam Houston
Austin, Texas

Houston Jan 14, 1842

Dearest Husband,

I returned this evening from Maj. Reily's and I am now in my room with the lonely widow of Mr. Butler, who shares it with me since her husband's death. Oh my Love, it is a sad office to cheer the bereaved in heart! for what can we say to them? We can not say he will come again when the clouds and gloom of winter are past, and the spring returns. Oh no, he is gone to his long home, and will come no more! Nor can we say that home is a happy one, for the mysteries of eternity are hidden from mortal sight. Poor desolate one! Would that I could offer her some consolation! I enjoyed a melancholy satisfaction tonight on leaving the gay and crowded parlour below, for the purpose of curing her solitude, for I felt that it was a sacred duty.

Dearest I am deeply deprest [sic] tonight and realy ought not to write you in such spirits, but as some gentlemen are going up tomorrow, I must say a word or two to you. I rec'd your letter today by Mr. Shaw,[1] but you said nothing about coming home, and as he did not deliver it himself, I had no opportunity on questioning him about the probability of an adjournment. I feel as if I would not live without you any longer. My friends are very attentive to me and exert themselves to amuse me. Almost every day I have an invitation to dine out, but my health does not often suffer me to go out. Tomorrow I expect to dine with Mrs. Norwood[2] and on tuesday, I think Mrs. Reily, the Maj. and I will go out to Mrs. Hadly's.[3]

My Love I can not write more tonight, for it is quite late and I am feeble and unwell, but I will write again by Dr. Smith[4] who expects to set off in a day or two. Do write to me often dearest, for you letters are my comforters.

Thine devotedly
M. L. Houston

[1] Houston to Margaret, January 6, 1842.

[2] Margaret is probably referring to Mrs. Nathaniel Norwood (Margarite Adele Ewing). Identified in Best, 351.

[3] Piety Smith Hadley, the wife of T. J. B. Hadley of Houston. Identified in Karen Thompson, ed., *Defenders of the Republic of Texas*, v. 1, (Austin: Laurel House Press, 1989), 24.

[4] Dr. Ashbel Smith.

General Sam Houston
Austin, Texas

Houston Jan 15th 1842

My beloved husband,

I wrote to you last night and promised to write again by Dr. Smith. I believe that he goes up tomorrow, so that this will reach you by the time you have quite finished the former scrawl and you will be called upon for a new trial of patience. But no, I should not say that—for my husband's letter are such sweet consolers to me that surely mine must interest him rough as they may be. It is not his beautifully rounded sentences that impart so much joy to my heart, but his gentle expression of continued love and remembrance. Your letters have been less frequent of late and my spirits have been far less buoyant. I have a continual weariness at my heart, and the very sight of company is irksome to me. I converse without knowing what I say, and smile yet feel no joy. I believe I am growing selfish, for I can not sympathise with others when they are happy, and almost wonder to see them so, expecting them to feel my own gloom and despondency. I did not dine with Mrs. Norwood today, as I told you last night I would do as I felt sad and averse to seeing company.

Capt. [John S.] Black called on me today and brought very encouraging news from the Point, but he has written you everything so that it will be unnecessary for me to repeat it. Oh how I regret having annoyed you with Armstrong's letter! But my dear, I sent it because I feared it might put you to some inconvenience hereafter if I kept you in ignorance of the real state of things. But enough of this. Oh my Love, I can give you no cause of my utter prostration of spirit! I remarked to one of my friends today that I felt the same gloom that opprest [sic] me the week you left me. Since that time I have lived upon hope with the assistance of some fortitude, but now I am without either. It seems cruel to tell you so much of my sorrow, although it is caused by my absence from you, but dearest I must pour out my full heart to you. If not to you—who is there in this wide world that can feel my grief! Thy generous bosom has ever been ready to yield its sympathy and I wish no other alleviation. I might rush into the vertex of fashion and gaiety and forget my loneliness awhile, but no—in the absence of my husband—that loneliness is sacred.

Sabbath morning—16th

I feel in better spirits this morning and would write you a long letter, but Dr. Smith is just starting. Bro. V[ernal] left yesterday and requested me to ask you to write to him at Liberty and he wished some introductory letter amongst others—one to Mr. Uzzell.[1] Dearest I am pining to see you. Oh do come home.

Thy devoted wife Maggy

[1]Elisha Uzzell.

To Mrs. Houston
City of Houston
By Mr. [J. Temple] Doswell

Austin
19th Jany 1842

Dear Margaret,
This morning I feel quite refreshed again with sleep. Two nights, I have rested more than in any former period in the same time since my arrival in this City. I look hourly for Mr. Doswell. I use him to send letters by him, but not that he has been or is a "Houston man." The reason why I feel more tranquil, than usual is that I hope soon to be relieved from this place and be where I hope for Happiness, for love, for joy, but not for peace. Peace cannot be mine Dearest while I see my country depressed as it is at this time!
My Love, You wish me to say if we are to have war, and that you will rely upon my opinion, or say so. I can only say my dear, that Mexico is in a better situation to invade Texas, than she has been, since 1836. Now whether she is yet in a condition to make a cam-

paign against us must be determined by ourselves. This <u>miserable</u> <u>Congress</u>, I do not mean all, is calculated to destroy the country if anything can do it. (this is sub rosa). But of this the rest when we meet. The bearer will be here in a few moments, and I must close with offering the embraces of my most tender and devoted affection!

The session of Congress and Supreme Court at the same time, is what prolongs our Session to such a useless length of time. A majority of the Lawyers compose Congress, and they have business in Court likewise!

Dearest, No application has been made for leave to march troops thro Texas from the U States, nor to invade Mexico, or if it has been done, I have not heard of it.

My regards to our friends. Many blessings to Maj Reily, Madame, & Donny. I will send letters to the Major.

Thy most devoted husband
Houston

Mrs Maggy

Margaret Lea Houston
City of Houston Texas
Mail

Austin
19th Jany 1842

Dearest

I am just ready to ride out this evening and get a morsel to eat, for here my love I can get nothing fit to live on. Indeed I would pity a dog who was situated as I am. I have no bed to sleep upon. All was, and remains waste that belonged to Government. I am indeed destitute, but thank my God, I will soon be released from this miserable place, again and again, and again see you My Love—To see you, and not to leave you! nor forsake you. The Barouche is at the door!

Thy ever devoted
Houston

Maggy

Mr Kennedy, Generals Hunt & Morehouse[1] will be with me! In the morning I will return.

[1]Edwin Morehouse, Adjutant General of the Army. For a biography see *Writings*, I, 521n.

General Sam Houston
Austin, Texas

Houston Jan 20th 1842

My Love,

I have had the extreme gratification of receiving your letters by Mr. Harris[1] and Judge Hart.[2] The former I did not see. The Judge called on me yesterday. The poor fellow still smarts under the remembrances of his dereliction from duty. I endeavored to make him as easy as possible, but every thing that was said seemed to remind him of his former inconsistency and called forth an apology from him. He tells me that congress will in all probability adjourn today, so I am writing to you half expecting that my letter will pass you on the way, but I will risk it. I do not intend to look for you without any strong reason, for I do not think I could bear a disappointment at present. It would certainly be very painful. My heart beats almost to suffocation when I think of meeting you. If I play the silly child Love, you must excuse me, but I will try to act with becoming dignity! Dearest, you tell me that you can not express your affection for me. And do you realy love me more than you express? If so, I am blessed indeed! I myself—though I have not told you so, have often felt a sad dearth of language, and in reviewing my letters, they fall so far short of my devotion to you that they seem cold and lifeless, and I fear you have thought them so. I regret one thing—that they have been so gloomy and calculated more to depress than to cheer you, but how would I be gay when seperated from my beloved husband?

It is a cold and gloomy day and the ladies are dull and spiritless from last night's ball. They all went from the house except my poor friend Mrs. Butler and myself. I spent the evening in religious conversation with her, how much more happily than if I had joined others in the levity and frivolity that gilds the way to darkness and death! Mrs. B. is naturally a lighthearted thoughtless being, and before her husband's death often chided her for speeches which I considered irreverent and sinful, but now she is humbled and subdued and much interested in religious subjects. Oh how affliction bends the proud spirit! Dearest, the desolate situation of my poor friend has caused me to think much of the few past months of our wedded happiness and to ask myself solemnly if my heart had not been too strongly bound by earthly ties! I would not wish to love you less than I do, but oh I tremble, when I remember how completely every thought, hope, and feeling of my soul was absorbed in that love, and how forgetful I have been of that great eternal being who bestowed so much happiness upon me! Could I have questioned the justice of God, if he had taken you from me, and left me like others in this dark world, heart-broken and hopeless? Ah no, my guilty conscience could have whispered that I had neglected your eternal interest while you were with me and suffered my affections to create an earthly Heaven for themselves and deserved the despair that had fallen upon me! Dearest husband, you are yet spared to me, and if my eager hopes denied me not—your heart has been touched by the Holy Spirit. Ah do not grieve that Spirit—but yield to its gentle pleadings. Dearest I have never attempted to give you a full expression of the happiness which your recent sacrifices of habit have conferred upon me, for how could I express it and even if my language were adequate, perhaps you would think it an unreasonable degree of joy for such a cause—for no human being can appreciate my feelings in this case—no not even my dear husband who has never failed to sympathise with any other emotion of my heart. But there is a being, whose all-seeing eye has marked any variation of my soul's deep feeling.—That God who has heard and answered the wife's prayer!

I have no interesting details for you, or I would write them. You may rely upon my discretion in speaking of Austin, and every other Governmental affair. A word from the wise is sufficient! The Maj. and Mrs. Reily are busily preparing for thier departure.[3] He complains that you have not written to him. Dearest I take leave of you with the hope of having you with me soon.

Ever thy devoted wife
M. L. Houston

[1]Houston to Margaret, January 10, 1842.

[2]Houston to Margaret, January 13, 1842.
[3]James Reily had been appointed as the Texas minister to the United States. They were preparing to leave for Washington D.C. Joseph William Schmitz, *Texas Statecraft 1836–1845,* (San Antonio: Naylor, 1941), 178.

Austin
21st Jany 1842

Ever Dearest Maggy,

Two or Three days have elapsed since I wrote to you, and I absolutely feel lonesome. To day I rode out for an hour with Mr Kennedy, and every day he calls to see me. I am very much pleased with him, and we converse very finely when ever we are together. On tomorrow, I am in company with him to visit the country and stay until monday. You have no idea Love, how much the air and scenes of the country improve my feelings, as well as my health. Cou'd I only enjoy the presence of my dear "wee wifie," and it was any where but on the frontier, I feel as tho' I wou'd be truly happy. Since I have quit swearing (for I really have quit) I feel much more tranquil, and equanimity has taken the place of passion and temper. I do feel my dear, at times, that I wou'd be willing to cast every thing aside, and start to see you, and be happy.

As to the removal of the seat of Government I am told it has been submitted to Congress by various applicants, representing different places.—That they have all been refer'd to a committee, which will report on the subject in a day or two. I have no idea what the report will be, as I take no part in the matter! My duties are truly arduous and if it were not that I sometimes get to the country, I cou'd not sustain myself, tho' all say that my colour, and health improve daily. Some even say, that you will not know me, as my health is so much improved. So I hope, as you will look so well, that when we do see each other, there will be a wedding and for this reason, I have said, obtain your Mothers approbation to our union. My mind is settled on this subject, and I do not expect to change! I only regret that you will have so long a time to deliberate, but as I don't see you fickle, I will rely upon a favourable decision. I hope Congress will not long interpose its session to the consummation of our wishes! I am told, that it has been said that it will adjourn in some eight days to which say amen if not before!

They will not wish to stay much longer I hope, and believe from the fact that I send them messages which make my enemies, and those of the country mind. To day, I sent a pretty smart one to the House of Representatives.[1] Mayfield, I am informed, said it was insulting to the Body—He has no great number to think with him. They will get others, yet stronger. The one to day was pretty able! It was prepared in too much haste!

Congress has passed an exchequer Bill which has become a law, and I learn that a Tariff Bill has passed but it has not reached me. The less they do for the remainder of the session, the better for Texas! The action of a body of men is very uncertain and to be frank Love, not infrequently very injurious to a people.

I must tell you, that I am much pleased with Mr Kennedy.—He is a gentleman of very correct moral feelings, and clearly intellectual! To day I placed some papers in his hand, which have never met the public eye! They were in relation to Santa Anna's liberation by me. One was a veto upon a Resolution of the Senate. The other was a letter from Santa Anna to me[2] and his autograph with which Mr K was much pleased and Mr K thinks a very able document upon the subject. He will see the other papers here important to the history of those times! I will show him my prophesy about the Alamo & Goliad! I presume he will go down with me to Houston when I go, unless he shou'd go to San Antonio de Bexar. I have not told you my dear, that Mrs Col Seguin[3] of Bexar sent me Peloucet[4] (I think it is called) sugar and some charming bread! I am greatly pressed to visit them Love, but I will not go unless you are with me!

You will hear that I have got opposition in Congress, but do not be dismayed, my Dear! It will all come out right, but it may be when the people have exercised their benign influence at the polls! At least you may be assured that your husband will preserve his honor and maintain the dignity of his station. If not in dress, he will in address! I have many things to say Love, that I will not write. You know that I wou'd not make a fine historian, but am a better speaker, therefore I hope soon to speak them all to you! Yes, talk you to sleep as usual! Don't think this is an attempt at smartness, for indeed, tonight I cou'd not be smart if I were to try ever so much! To day, I had been bothered quite too much, if I cou'd help it! 'Tis late and I will try, and get some rest! In the morning dearest, I will doubtless resume my epistle! so I will say "pleasant dreams"!

22nd Dearest, 'Tis morning and a pretty one too, but cold. My repose I thank God, was pleasant and refreshing! The good "Cits" are about breakfasting, and until I can ride out this evening, my time will be much occupied!

Until I can get off from here, I will be pressed by a constant increase of business. It is always the way, about the close of the session.

My Love, as you are my Premier, I must tell you a secrite [sic], and that you may not be kept in suspense, it is this! My friend Col Anderson[5] can not go into the Treasury because he is compelled to come back to the House of Reprs. 'Tis all right that he should do so, and his private circumstances require that he shou'd stay in the East with his family. He regrets the necessity, but must yield. I am satisfied, because I retain his confidence!

To fill the station proposed for him, I will select Col Dangerfield[6] of San Antonio. He is a gentleman of perfect honor, fine sense,— indeed genius, and has borne himself this session like a Prince, and an able gentleman! With those which I have in the cabinet, I move on most harmoniously, and hope beneficially for the country, if it is not too far gone to save it!

I do not know of any smart thing to write, and can only repeat the oft' made declaration, "I do wish that I was with my dearest, my beloved Maggy"—then catch me away again, if you can.

Major Western is here, and one of the most busy Gentlemen on the globe. He is always moving, and his plans, so profound in his plans, that every one knows it about the time that he has planned it! Judge Terrell, Hockley, and perhaps Dr. Jones will accompany Mr Kennedy & myself. There will be some half dozen of us, in all, and I will read the Bible on Sunday, my dear, and on Monday, I hope to return in good health, and spirits, for the business of the week.

Arduous as the duties are, I feel much pleasure in their performance when I can suppose they will result in advantage to the public good. I again promise not to prate on the subject, as it cou'd do no good, but to distress you. My Dear Maggy. With good temper, and temperance added, I will try and move on as calmly as possible.

My Dear, I had the pleasure to receive a letter from Vernal, & was very well pleased with its contents. I say pleased, because he is pleased, and I will write to him, but at the same time I do not hope it will do the least good! I invoke him by everything dear, and sacred, not to settle his negroes on a farm, but to settle in the village of Montgomery, hire them out under his eye,—live upon their hire, having one to wait upon him, and that he cou'd live like a gentleman, until his profession wou'd give him means. If not in the village of Montgomery, any other where he prefer'd locating. I knew and told him, that on a farm he must support them for years, and his mind will be diverted from his profession[7] and every trifling occurrence will now require presence with his negroes. This will cost him some $300.00 per year. They will make no portion of the amount—they must be fed and clad—and this will require money—I do not advise him to change his plans nor will I do,—as a brother and one whose bosom swelled with affection while I was talking to him. I suggested these things, and if he wou'd not pursue them, he wou'd not like to adopt them, until he is compelled by necessity to change his plan! I love Vernal as a brother,—he feels as near to me, as does my own brother Will, but they both have deemed their own judgement best! My reason for the great anxiety which I entertained to have our kinfolk at the <u>point</u> was that Vernal cou'd then settle where he pleased and pursue uninfluenced, his profession and attain to that distinction, which his genius, education, and family, as well as family hopes have assigned to him. Young Royston is younger, and is now rising in his profession, and must be a man of distinction. By Bledsoe settling on Trinity Vernal is induced to locate in Liberty, to be near Sister! Yes, this is the whole matter, and I love him, for his affection for her, and bless her dear Spirit, she deserves it all! Had B settled at the Point, Mother too wou'd have been there, we wou'd have been there, and Vernal cou'd have made a location uninfluenced by feeling, but for upon his judgement, and his will. Now both are controlled by feeling, and my dearest (for indeed my eye is not tearless) I must be assured that Vernal has chosen the last county seat in Texas, at which I would reside, tho' it is a pretty place. I have seen more sickness there in one day, than I ever saw in an Army for the same time! Where B has gone to settle it is not so, but Trinity or Liberty—from its location I do dislike. There it was my noble friend Col Lynch[8] departed.

Death will assail us in every clime and surprise us in every situation, therefore no place can be exempt from disease. "Bud" may have his health there, but I fear it. Do not alarm him about it, if he prefers it, he may enjoy health, and if he had located at Montgomery he might sicken and die!

All that we can do is hope and pray for the best. When I have the happiness to embrace you my Beloved we will talk all these matters over, and take the direction, which your happiness will require! I find dearest, in all things, your advice is sound, and calculated to promote our mutual happiness & prosperity. Nothing of happiness, and honor, and fame or even Glory can be entertained by me, unless you form the most prominent feature in the Picture!

So my very dear Wife, If I have said any thing that may affect your feelings, I pray Love that you will ascribe to me no unkindness, nor a disposition to inflict, upon your noble and generous nature! No Love, I never can for one moment entertain a thought of giving you one moments pain or anguish. But the Subjects on which I have been writing are not pleasant, and now I really wou'd rather approve than disapprove where I can do so in candor. You will at least give credit to my heart, if I have been rough in my expressions.

I will not have time to review this letter, and you will please to supply defects. I doubt not—they are many no doubt. I will write to our beloved brother Henry and probably Martin in a few days. I surely owe Henry a very kind & sensible letter! Independent of his very kind letter to me, I always entertain for him the kindest regard and attachment. Yes, and I reckon the secrete is about this—He is the brother, dear brother, of my dearly beloved Margaret! Do be happy Love until I can be with you! To day I learned (inter nous)[9] that the seat of Government will be removed. Maj Western is busy & has some good aids! I think he will take it to Harrisburg if it goes to any one particular place! The power of removal may be accorded to the president.

I hope my dearest that you will commend me in kindest phrase to our friends, and love to Vernal if he has not left you! Don't let him know any thing that will increase his discontent! He is not of a happy mood, and I hope he will do well!

Kiss Mag Stone for me and if she says one word please bite her ear or her cheek, or her neck! I will write a short note, to Major Reily as I have but a moment!

Thy ever devoted husband
Houston

Mrs. Maggy

Mr. Green[10] goes express, and will hand this in person.

[1]See *Writings,* II, 434–38.
[2]Houston is probably referring to a letter from Santa Anna dated July 22, 1836, or one on November 15, 1836. Copies of both are in the Madge W. Hearne Collection, San Antonio, Texas, and originals are in the Barker History Center, Austin, Texas.
[3]Mrs. Juan Seguin (Gertrudis Flores). Identified by Frederick C. Chabot, *With the Makers of San Antonio,* (San Antonio: Privately Published by Artes Graficas, 1937), 128.
[4]A form of brown sugar formed into a cone.
[5]Kenneth L. Anderson of San Augustine, Speaker of the House of Representatives. For a biography see *Writings,* III, 424n.
[6]William Henry Daingerfield. For the nomination see *Writings,* II, 452.
[7]Vernal Lea was a lawyer. Madge W. Hearne Collection, San Antonio, Texas.
[8]Probably James Lynch, who died in 1840. Ray, 53.
[9]The words "is this right" are written in the margin at this point.
[10]Houston may be referring to George Green, who was an associate of James Spillman of Harris County. White, *They Also Served,* 55.

Austin 25th Jany 1842

Dearest Wife,

Your valuable letter[1] reached me a few hours since, and tho' it is very late at night, I will not deny myself the pleasure of recording the fact. The Post Master was absent from his office from some cause, and I was in suspense, and tomorrow I think the gentleman will, in all probability, meet with a rebuke!

But my Love I am so happy to hear from you that I am disposed to forgiveness. There is in your dear letter a shade of gloom which I can not but feel, and appreciate with great tenderness and sympathy. Indeed my bosom swells with emotions, which I can not essay to express. You are gloomy and sad in heart, my Love, while I am distant from you and can not sustain you by consolation! But dearest, we must look to the future, when we shall meet and with the assurance that we are not again to be seperated in this world, as I truly and verily hope!

You ask me my Beloved, if indeed I do love you more than I can express? Indeed I do. But I ought not to say so, for you will justly charge me with writing "love letters," and you know that you are rather inclined to do that at times. Don't think dearest that I mean this as a taunt. No, not by any means, tho' I don't know that I can express the idea on paper, so well as I cou'd were I present with my dear very dear Maggy! I cou'd then say it, feel it, and manifest it, by looks, by words, and gestures.

Your reflections on the "past," with the lesson which you teach me, are not disregarded my Love, nor can they ever be laid aside, so long as my faculties of mind remain unimpaired or my heart retains its best impulses. I know that we have to die, and after death the judgment. For both these events, eternal in their consequences, I will by all means in my power, endeavour to prepare. 'Tis true of late my mind has dwelt with more reflection and earnestness upon these important subjects than it has ever done, and upon this vast and boundless theme of eternity. I wou'd not flatter, neither mislead, nor trifle with any created being, but I do believe my Beloved, that you are intended by Heaven as the dear being, who is to call home my heart, which has been so long estranged from God, to a sense of my great dependence upon his goodness and his almighty power! If this is not to be done, by the mediation of a blessed Savior, I hope at least that I am so far impressed with proper feeling that I will never violate, in any degree, the most strict proprieties of life!

I feel that we are indeed, but the passing incidents of time in our mortal career, but when I gaze on the blue heavens, and the bright evidences of a Creator God, I am assured that the very intelligence which I possess, and which enables me to admire His works, is but a part of his reflected essence, for God is intelligence, and must be goodness, therefore I will adore Him and admire His creation.

If we live to meet dearest Love we can talk freely, and much upon these subjects, so important to our peace here and happiness in eternity! I do not fear that any reflections of mine upon these subjects will depress you in spirits because you are familiar with them.

26th

Dearest, I ceased writing last night at one oclock, or rather this morning, and enjoyed sweet repose until this morning when thank my God, I feel well refreshed and resumed the very agreeable (I will not say "task" but) employment of continuing my epistle to my dear "wee wifie" Maggy! Of course you can not suppose that I have any great occasion of news, as the time has been inactive and my mind when awake employed in business reflections.

Congress is drawing to a close in its session, and the members say they will adjourn tomorrow. This I know is not possible, nor do I hope, truly that they will adjourn before the 30th or 31st instant. Then the matters most important to the country will have been passed over, and neglected, while others of minor (or rather no) importance have been attended to with great <u>care</u>. You will suppose my dearest that I am not in the best humour possible. This will be a just supposition & one that I regret to say, will be fully sustained by facts. Wretched and blind has been the entire course of legislation pursued by the present Congress and during the present session. The Government must stop. I will no[t] say cease, for that I do not believe so long as <u>I live</u>!

My Love Col Andrews writes to me that my horse matters are easy, & Capt Black writes me about our wee home, poor home.[2] I love it, for the happiness that we have enjoyed at it, and for the hope that we are yet to be happy there! Yes, dearest! I do look to it with hope, as a succedaneum for us in other days. Days when we can enjoy the shade and the fruit of our own vine & fig tree, and worship our God, in all the sincerity of faithful hearts. Faithful to each other, and faithful to Jehovah, the God of Hosts! My Dearest, I will no longer attempt the expression of my affectionate devotion to you. That I shou'd entertain devotion to you is reasonable, and I trust not impious. To whom shou'd I render all my earthly homage, but to You my Love, with whom I am so happy, and without whom I am so miserable! You have to me been the Star of hope, the guide to happiness and peace when I am with you. I am not courting my dear, and don't you suppose me "as trying" to inspire your <u>young heart</u> with anticipations that you are not to realise, so far as I may be enabled, on my part, to insure their consummation. No, nothing of this is to be fancied. And as an earnest of what I say, you are [at] liberty, and even requested, to obtain your excellent Mothers leave to our union, so soon as we meet, and preparations for the nuptials can be in readiness. So you see I am not my fair one, disposed to trifle with your feelings, nor to wound your young and tender affections.

Don't let Mag Stone see this letter, or she will wish to be one of the Brides maids, and I think we had as well dispense with that trite custom.—But as she is a friend of yours, and a clever "little Captain" you may consult her, but it may be as well that you shou'd consult our dear friend Mrs Andrews. She may entertain some very proper notions on on [sic] this subject! "Nous Verions."

Our friend Black was wofully [sic] mistaken in promising 40 acres of land to Smith[3] on the Point. I wou'd not take $800 dollars, and really I think leave to live there and raise what he can is very good recompence [sic]. But of this Love I will say nothing until I get home, and then you may be assured I will say nothing unkind nor out of temper.

As you will be glad to hear it, I will tell you what I learn by others—and I suppose it is true—I am rising in the estimation of Congress, or rather becoming more popular with their majesties!!! Now how much, my dear do you think I care about this matter? not one fig. To feel, and know that I do right is enough for me!—'tis all I wish, or desire. Verily, they shall have their reward, and that will be rendered by the people. I am determined by no means to fall out with the excellent Representatives, Oh! most excellent!

Dearest, I do not know what to say that will be pleasant or agreeable to you.—I will for the first time, lay a command upon you! You are not to write to me any more, at this place, until I see you, after you receive this letter. I do not intend that it shall be my last to you by any means. Our friend Mr [Francis R.] Lubbuck will set out doubtless on Saturday, so I must write by him! I send you a newspaper with which you will be amused when you reflect, as I am told it was written to alarm poor Lamar. I have marked two pieces for your notice. One is touching the "Recommendation," which I assure you was not published with an eye to popularity, but as a matter of principle!

My Love, I have read with deep and heartfelt sympathy your remarks relative to poor Mrs Butler.[4] Her situation must be disconsolate, and her bereavment [sic] profound! From her disposition, as you describe it, she must have experienced all the wildness of grief. It is with the Almighty alone to "temper the breeze to the shorn Lamb." The bruised reed he will not break, nor quench the smoking flame!

I am not disappointed Dearest, in your kind ministration to her melancholy and depressed condition. I know that you will always be the kind, generous, & noble friend of the virtuous in affliction and sorrow! Oh my dear, if I cou'd only embrace you and press you to my swelling heart, I wou'd impress upon your lovely cheek a thousand evidences of my tender and frank affection for you! Yes, I would express more affection for you dearest than words can ever convey to your mind!

By this time you are half provoked Maggy at my disregard of your anticipations at our <u>meeting</u>. When that happy moment arrives Love, you may <u>whimper</u> a little, and if a fugitive tear should be detected, stealing over the pure damask of your cheek, Love, I will be rude enough to arrest it with a kiss. So I will excuse your <u>weakness</u> if you will pardon my <u>rudeness</u>! Do you not deem this a very fair ground for a good understanding between us dear? For fear you may become weary love, I must close my letter. If you shou'd really wish a longer letter, you will only have to read this again. You see my Love how economical I am becoming in matters of family. By the bye Love, I hope to have some Gold to present you with on arrival at home! Home, ah! Home my dearest—Don't think that I will inflict the criticism of another ode upon you, but I must do one thing in despite of my self—I must "jump to a conclusion" of this letter as the mail must close in a short time.

I am ever thine Love
Houston

Lady Margaret

[1]Margaret to Houston, January 20, 1842.
[2]Cedar Point.
[3]Houston had two close neighbors at Cedar Point, William Smith who owned adjoining property and Christian Smith who owned property on the east side of Cedar Bayou. See early map of Chambers County, n.d., in San Antonio Genealogical Library.
[4]See Margaret to Houston, January 20, 1842.

General Sam Houston
Austin, Texas

Jan 25th 1842

Dearest

The gentlemen by whom I expected to send this letter have declined going and I have broken this seal for the purpose of making some little alterations. I have been informed that Maj. Neighbors[1] will leave in the morning for Austin so that I have determined to say <u>one more word</u> to you although it is 3 o'clock AM. The party is just dispursed, [sic] and a very agreeable one it was. Our amusements for the evening concluded with two songs from Jeff Wright,[2] and his grimaces were inimitable I assure you. Dearest you must come home! <u>It is out of the question</u>. I could say a thousand things to you, but my eyes are heavy with sleep.

Loved one farewell

Maggy

[1]Robert S. Neighbors, Assistant Quartermaster of the Texas Army. *Handbook of Texas*, II, 267–68.

[2]Jefferson Wright was an artist and portrait painter who had a studio in Houston. *Writings*, II, 191n and *Handbook of Texas*, II, 938.

Austin

27th Jany 1842

My very dear Maggy,

After sending my letter to the mail last night, I rode out about three miles with several gentlemen to get a good sound sleep. I thought my appetite for sleep was first rate, and so it was, no doubt, but when I retired my mind wandered to the place of its earthly abode—the bosom of my own dear Margaret, and the shrill clarion of the cock, the sentinel of domestic life, proclaimed the approach of dawn ire it was recalled or my eyes closed in repose!

Indeed my Love, I have great reason to chide you, or to quarrel with you, if I did desire [blurred] to be amiable in your estimation! Or had we lived in olden times, I cou'd have sustained the charge of witchcraft craft [sic] against you on the ground that you had be-witched me and owing to that fact, I can not sleep in consequence of the spell which you have thrown upon me!

Now my dear, what do you think of this accusation? When we meet I will endeavor to enforce it most <u>impressively</u>. The Lipan In-dians have just retired from my office. I had a long <u>talk</u> with them to night.[1] It commenced at 8 oclk, and it is now 12 M. So you see, the spell is yet upon me, dearest! One reason why I write to night is that I hope by Mr Lubbuck, to send this letter in a day or two. Every moment of my time is occupied with business. As usual for me, much of my time is taken up in writing vetos [sic].[2] This was my former habit, and as poor worthless Lamar & Burnet made none, it does not sit well on the stomach of the present <u>body</u> of Honorables. This my Love does not vary in the least my feelings or course of conduct. I will pursue the even tenor of my way, and fear shall never deter me from an honest discharge of official duty. In the "glorious uncertainty" of Legislation what to day may call down denunciations may tomorrow command elogy [sic] and encomium.

I have made this digression in the belief that you may hear that I am unpopular with Congress. This is not so, only with those who have either selfish or corrupt ends to answer! Neither my Love, shall ever meet my countenance. No, not even tolerance! This is indeed no egotism my fair one. It is what I am and just what you wish me to be! This is Thursday night and 'tis said that Congress will adjourn on Monday morning. This is a matter most devoutly to be wished! The country will be blessed by the event, and I hope to be equally blessed or doubly so, as I will hope, and try faithfully to <u>embrace</u> <u>you</u> dear Maggy in as little time as Saxe can reach Houston! I saw him exercised to day, and he seemed to anticipate the renewal of my especial attentions to him!

Mr Lubbuck will tell you all the news if he should not loose [sic] all his senses about his dear wife.[3] He is quite crazy! And he can't love her more than half as much as I do you! To day my Love I made a movement towards the Santa Fe <u>prisoners</u>! If any thing can be done, my course will insure success. As to marching troops and release them by force, that is farcical. If a force were now within one hundred miles of the City of Mexico, it wou'd avail nothing to them. It wou'd doubtless insure their instant execution. They wou'd be subject perhaps to the frenzy of a mob, or they wou'd if not destroyed instantly, be transported to the interior of Mexico, and secured in some mines! You will see my dear if the expedition is understood at Washington that the Government of the U. S. will not be half so brave as you now suppose! They have nothing to do with the matter, and you will find that the general feeling and enthusiasm of the people will subside, and if they shou'd survive, that negociation [sic] will be resorted to by the United States. The meetings now held in various parts will be forgotten soon, and the philanthropists who are now all ardour and valour will think of pitching crops for the present year. They will find out that they will require much means, and "times are very <u>hard indeed</u>." Yes "can hardly make out to live"—"Why was Lamar such a fool as to send men on such a wild goose chase?" All these things will succeed to the boasts of conquest—sitting on the <u>throne</u> of the Montezuma's and such like pretty things. The Americans are like the English, a people of words, but they are people of reflection until they get as far south as Texas and here the sun, as well as the Moon, has a surprising influence upon the brain. But we will see! You will wish to know my plan for the release of the poor fellows, and my Love, I will tell you "sub rosa" Mr Kennedy has written to Mr Packenham, the British Minister at Mexico, and if any thing can be done for them, it will be thro' this medium.[4] Am I not right? Why my dear, with the forces of the U. States now in the army, and their entire navy, they cou'd not reach the city of Mexico with all their resources added under four months! Then how long wou'd it require for a mob, for such wou'd be the character of those who wou'd go upon their own hook to reach Mexico? They wou'd <u>never</u> do it! Furthermore the U. S. wou'd not permit a force to be raised within her Territory for any such purpose. Mexico is to them a friendly power, and Christendom wou'd arm in her behalf! These my dear are the true grounds on which to view this subject.

Very Dear Wife, 'tis now the 28th Jany and I am up early, and bound to finish or progress with this epistle. You wou'd if you cou'd feel no deep interest be amused at the fuss some gentlemen are making to get off so soon as Congress may rise. Among them is Dr. Jones. His Lady[5] is on the Brasos [sic] near Washington, and with her a fine noble chubby boy, which is called "Sam Houston" for a friend of ours (much farther from <u>Houston</u> at this time than he has any wish to be!)[6] Well, is not this good reason why he shou'd wish to be at home, and hereafter to stay with his wife or have her to stay with him.

Poor dear Wives, but they have a sad time, if it is only half as bad as that of their husbands in Austin. Why my Love, you can, in Houston, obtain something to eat.—Some oysters, some fruit, or some bread that is palatiable [sic], but here we are destitute and miserable in mind as well as body!

The privation, which the soldier feels or endures for his country is rendered tolerable from the fact that he can do no better and that stern necessity imposes upon him a certain amount of privations. It is different with us, who all feel that it is no sacrifice which we are making to the country, or for it, but that every sacrifice is made to corruption and speculation to the advantage of a few selfish men who care nothing for the general good! Such my Love, were the considerations which led to a removal of the seat of Government in the first instance, and it remains here only because selfishness can not locate it at some new point or return it to the old one! Do not imagine dearest, that I am framing an apology or intending to render a reason for my future absence from you! No Indeed I am not, for all that I have promised has been done in good faith, and my heart, as well as my lips, assure me of the integrity of my promise! I can not, will not endure the idea of being seperated from you or remaining one day absent beyond the calls of stern necessity. The constant action of my memory, as well as my heart, assures me of a truth so interesting to me and I need not enforce upon you Dearest, that I do love you too much to remain absent from you! You will say "Poor fellow! I know that he is candid, or he wou'd never have teased me by writing so many and such long prosing letters as he has done since we parted, if he had not loved me most <u>miserably,</u> for I am sure it is <u>misery</u> to him!" Am I not right in this matter my Love: But I see as the day advances that hours are passing, and I hope they will soon bring me to my dearest Wife, my friend, companion—yes, my Maggy!

Here again I catch myself composing & actually writing "love letters." Now just for one moment, suppose that my letters cou'd meet the eyes of the world, do you think the wise people wou'd ever again suppose that I was <u>fit</u> for a President of a nation? Not they my dear! But they wou'd think that if I were not <u>fit</u> that I certainly wou'd have a <u>fit</u> when we meet!! Even the "Little Captain"[7] wou'd say to herself "Well I am astonished that General Houston shou'd be so silly as to make such a fuss about his wife, as if no other husband had to be absent from his wife." Now the first time that you see her ask her if she does not suppose me "bewitched" by you and if she says yes, slap her, but if she does not why then—why you may kiss her!

After transacting much business to day, I must close this letter. Every day I will write if I can send the letter, and if when on the road I shou'd have a good chance and a man were to out travel me, I am not so sure but what I wou'd again write. Can you beat this my Love? If you can, you can beat me!

Mr Kennedy has just left my room. He was here on business. He has Become a great pet with me, and seems truly pleased. I am glad that he happened here this session. It will be well for the Country, and it will be no hindrance to History. He has said to me, and he is quite modest, "Genl, you have not only had your share of abuse, but you have been more misrepresented that any other man." He says that he felt there was a gap in his History, but he cou'd get no information, only such as he derived from the few private Documents published in relation to my public acts. These you know are but few, and form but little History. He will have a better opportunity my dear, and I suppose I must "grant" your "request."[8] Oh! Maggy, you meant, I do in my heart command? Now did you not my Love. Frank L[ubbock] can't wait longer.

Now dear Wife, commend me with great affection to Col Andrews & his dear Lady. Kiss the wee ones, and if Major Reily and the charming madam are there, commend my best and "kindest salutations," to them. To our other friends, present my Greetings.

Thy Ever Devoted
Houston

Lady Margaret
Judge [Joseph] Eves is to go down with me! He is a [blurred]

---

[1] For Houston's orders concerning peace efforts with the Lipan Indians see *Writings,* IV, 72, Houston to L. B. Franks, February 1, 1842.
[2] *Writings,* II, 445–47.
[3] Adele Barron (Mrs. Frank) Lubbock. Identified in Ross Phares, *The Governors of Texas,* (Gretna, Louisiana: The Pelican Publishing Company, 1976), 99.
[4] Richard Packenham offered his services to Santa Anna as a mediator in securing an armistice between Mexico and Texas. Wisehart, 350–51.
[5] Mary McCrory Jones, identified in Grammer, 76.
[6] Dr. Anson Jones named his son Sam Houston Jones. Several years later when Houston fell into disfavor with Jones, the boy's name was changed to Samuel Edward Jones. Herbert Gambrell, *Anson Jones: The Last President of Texas,* (Austin: University of Texas Press, 1964), 425.
[7] Houston's nickname for Margaret Stone.
[8] Houston is referring to Margaret's request that William Kennedy write his biography.

General Sam Houston
Austin, Texas

Houston Jan 29th 1842

Dearest Husband,

I can not resign the pleasure of writing to you so long as I am disbarred from the blessed privilege of being with you. My last was written with the firm impression that it <u>would be</u> the last of the <u>present series</u> at least. Yours by Mr. Doswell[1] received on yesterday was a source of great pleasure from its expressions of affection, but put to flight the sweet hope of seeing you immediately. I thought at first my courage would have failed me, but after reading your dear letter again and again my spirits revived and I determined not to yield while I had one grain of philosophy to bear me out.

You flattered me Love, by noticing my dream so much that I am almost tempted to tell you what I <u>dreampt</u> [sic] last night. However I will only tell you a part of it. I was in [sic] a few miles of you but could not get to you, and as my exertions one after another were defeated I awoke in an agony. It is said that "Dreams are but our waking thoughts." You will think dearest that my thoughts must be sad indeed and you will not be far wrong. Oh when shall this weary aching head repose once more on that faithful bosom, never again to be exiled. My heart pines for quiet and retirement. This busy world with its boisterous scenes of mirth and its wily snares is no home for me. My spirit is turned to the murmur of wild streams and the song of forest birds! How sweetly could I pass the remainder of my days in uninterrupted communion with the sharer of all my griefs and joys! Dearest, methinks that we would soon forget that earth had any happiness beyond ourselves or that such a thing as sorrow existed—allowing that your devotion is equal to mine!—but I do not think it is quite. However I will not argue the question until you can speak for yourself, and if you convince me that I am mistaken, I shall not be "Convinced against my will!"

Mrs. Andrews' daughter Mrs. Taylor[2] and her husband[3] are very fond of each other and a <u>leeth</u> [sic] ostentatious in that way. He often asks me if I do not think them cruel to remind me so much of you by thier own happiness and display of affection? I told him yesterday that I needed no memorial. I might have said to them that our <u>wedded love</u> was a year and a half older than theirs! but I forborn thinking they could not triumph much longer! It would be well for society if it had more emulation of the kind. Mrs. Andrews gives a large party tomorrow evening and every one expresses disappointment that you will not be present. I expect to mingle with my friends and will endeavor to be as agreeable as possible, but my heart will be joyless and desolate for the only being that can impart happiness to me is far far away.

This will be handed to you by Mr. Castro[4] who comes on some embassy which I have not ascertained exactly. What from Gen. Hamilton[5] being evidently connected with it I presume it is some new scheme of his and have a presentiment that you <u>will not relish it much</u>. If my apprehensions should prove real, dearest you must not forget your habitual <u>politeness</u>! Perhaps I have no right to say such a thing to you who knows so much more of <u>public matters</u> than I do, but my dear husband, you know how earnestly I desire that you should be loved and admired by every one. Positively I have given you a <u>lecture</u> before I was aware of it, but I hope you will not be the <u>less attentive to it</u>.

Oh my Love, I wish you would come home! I have written you so much stuff that I am ashamed of it, but the truth is—I have nothing else to write for my mind is in such a state that I can barely read or think. Sometimes I almost forget every thing except that you are not with me and that my heart pines for you. I have a constant sense of loneliness that no company or amusement can dispel. Nor do I wish it banished for it is a cherished sorrow which the world shall not take from me.

Mr. Lee[6] arrived here this morning from Col. Morgan's.[7] My dear friend Mrs. Lee[8] and her sweet baby are well. I have not heard from Mother lately. No news lately from brother M[artin]. It is a dark dreary day and the chill blast is moaning most dismally around us. I am beginning to sympathise [sic] with the gloom of nature and lest I should say something to make you melancholy I will quit writing. Oh my Love surely another week will not pass before you are with me. Come home if the country must be sacrificed by it for I do not see how you can save the people against thier will.

Thy wife,
Margaret L. Houston

[1]See Houston to Margaret, January 19, 1842.
[2]Barbara Tilghman Taylor.
[3]William Taylor.
[4]Henry Castro, a French emigrant who became a U. S. citizen and later established a colony on the Medina River. *Writings,* II, 441–42. For a description of Castro's trip to Austin see Cornelia English Crook, *Henry Castro: A Study of Early Colonization in Texas,* (San Antonio: St. Mary's University Press, 1988),15–16. For Houston's letter concerning a contract see *Writings,* IV, Houston to Messers. Kennedy and Castro, February 5, 1842. A copy of the contract may be found in Crook, 187–91.
[5]General James Hamilton, Governor of South Carolina. For a biography see *Writings,* I, 32n. For information on Hamilton's relationship with Castro see Crook, 14–15, 58.
[6]W. Douglas Lee. Identified in*Writings,* II, 313n as a developer of the City of Sabine.
[7]Col. James Morgan of New Washington on Galveston Bay. For a biography see *Writings,* I, 407n.
[8]Ophelia Morgan Lee. Identified by Grammer, 34.

During his administration Mirabeau B. Lamar had appointed James Hamilton as Commissioner of Loans. Hamilton had traveled to Europe to seek funds for Texas. As Lamar's term drew to a close Hamilton tried to negotiate a loan from Belgium. Houston was not in favor of securing another debt and had the law authorizing the loan repealed. He wrote Margaret of his plans to dismiss Hamilton.

Austin
30th Jany 1842

My dear Love,

Tomorrow I have fondly regarded as the day of liberation from corroding anxiety and solicitude. I did hope that I wou'd have been released, and on my way to embrace the treasure of my love and all my manly affections. Last evening Cary[1] came with an express from General Hamilton, requesting the delay of Congress for his arrival! What a course they may adopt I know not, but this I do know, that with my consent there will be no detention. This flummery I am tired of. The country shall be no longer humbugged with my approbation.We are now languishing under the withering influence of speculations and speculators!

I am provoked out of all temper, but do not evince what I do feel. I hope the nation will no longer suffer voluntary degradation, whatever it may be compelled to endure from stern necessity arising from the acts of imbeciles!

Texas yet has every thing to expect from a wise course, but I am fearful that the course of propriety will not be regarded and for the want of cooperation the executive will be left alone to sustain the country in a state of wretched despondency! I will not pretend to make this a "love letter" Dear, but will content myself with being cross with every thing around me, but not with <u>you</u>!

Congress shou'd adjourn so soon as possible, and save whatever we may have of means, credit, and character left with us. 'Tis but little, aye, <u>very</u> little indeed.

It wou'd be vain my Love, to attempt the impression of my feelings at this moment! 'Tis hope defered [sic] and expectations disappointed that I have now to anticipate. My countenance will wear no smile until I can leave this place for the solace of your rational and bland society.

The other day by some means, I know not how it was, but the idea that you were <u>my friend</u> flashed upon me with great force. That you were my wife, that you loved me, and that I loved you, that you were my companion with many other ideas were all familiar to my meditations, but the reality that you were <u>my friend</u> had never been <u>powerfully impressed</u> upon my mind, apart from love & all the tender endearments of our association. Thus you may suppose how wonderfully strange it was to me when a thought substantive and conveying the idea of <u>friend</u>, independent of all other relations bursted upon my mind—a thought new yet delightfully pleasing to me! To feel that in this sordid world, I cou'd claim and possess the friendship of one pure and enlightened being was really a pleasing sensation! This wou'd have confirmed me, had any been necessary, never again to depart from my Lovely Margaret, if we are so blessed as to meet again.

I am writing on the 5th page, and when I began I did not think that I would finish two or more.

Carey will go down tomorrow I expect, and I wished to give you the news, and to say something, for as I have told you, I have no pleasure apart from you. I would be miserable were it not for you, and you as you are! Nay I might and no doubt, but what I wou'd be dissipated. As things are, I cou'd not, nay, I wou'd not be so! To day I must write some four vetos for the Hon'ble Congress by tomorrow.[2] They require much attention—So I will write no more until Cary [sic] is ready to set out!

I snatch a moment to close this note. Carey tells me that he will set out very early in the morning so I must close and resume my business. I do not expect to retire before one oclock to night if then. My duties are very pressing, and I deplore the fact that my duties will not end tomorrow, as I fear they will not!

This moment I had the happiness to get your letters by Mr Castro,[3] but have not had the pleasure of seeing them. He is to see me tomorrow.

My very dear Love! You need not suppose that I will fail to retain my wanted address and composure which I find much more easy to do, than I did when I indulged the shameful habit of swearing. That my dear is ended, and I will not resume it in life I am sure! No my Love, this is not only a silly, but a vicious practice! Genl H. will be informed on his arrival that he has been recalled, and has to settle his accounts. I hope he will have no difficulty, in the business & if so, Congress need not be detained to a long time! I do not feel pleasant, my Love, when I reflect upon the gross impositions which Genl H. has practised upon my poor country.[4] I may feel all the force of this, but I will neither speak nor look it. I will be all that you cou'd wish me to be! I cherish <u>you</u> too fondly in my heart to do aught that cou'd inflict upon you the slightest pang or ever jeopardise your happiness tho' you shou'd see my every act! To night I am not happy. Wou'd that your last dream had been as pleasant as your first! But this is no cause of depression nor ought not to be so.

A theme more pleasant is the hopes that Heaven may grant that we shall soon meet, and evince to others and to ourselves that we too can be happy without impairing the happiness of others! Tell Mr & Mrs Taylor[5] that I can love more than he can, that I have <u>longer experience</u>!!!! I was sorry that you cut out a portion of your letter. You knew me well enough Love, to be assured that I ought to see any thing that you wou'd write to me. I thank you for what you have written, and the balance no doubt wou'd have added to my sense of obligation! But of this you were the best judge. Dearest, what [is] making you talk of "snares?" The wise and the pure can avoid them! The vain and silly alone are caught in them. When you refer to the first part of this letter you will see in what light I regard you, and you shou'd always be with me, as I am with you! You will find that I esteem you as a friend most capable of advising me, and upon whose advice I wou'd place the most immeasurable price of all others—Therefore, why cut out the piece?

If you are not confident in me, what am I? Nay Love, had you said ever so much, I wou'd have regarded all that you had said as an emanation of the purest love!

I feel sorrowful from this cause only, and that I can not see you, I fear, so soon as I had hoped to have done. But 'tis said, "the darkest hour is just before the break of day." I hope a bright dawn of happiness will soon burst upon us and upon our country. Oh I do wish that I cou'd cheer you, and make you happy Love, by some gentle influence; how blessed I shou'd be! Our God will bless us, and then we will be truly blessed. I have spent all my leisure with Mr Kennedy, and I find him a man of fine moral sentiments and a gentleman most perfect in all his principles. He loathes the vile and polluted of his species! I send you a scrap, which I attribute to him, but do not know that he wrote it. I also send you a news paper, which may interest you! 'Tis marked! The author is a good writer, but as it is not myself, I can't say who it is.

Dearest! You never acknowledged my message, nor Gloves, nor any thing I sent to you! I fear you did not get them! I sent them by Walton,[6] Mr Shaw[7] and some one else I think.

I will continue to write at every moment that I can command, & send by every chance. I hope you may still have continued to write, as I may be detained. This is the solemn Sabbath night, and I am alone communing with the only object on earth who has possession of my heart and control of my happiness. You and my God shall command my thoughts and my hopes. Commend me to our friends all. This moment a friend tells me that Congress may not adjourn until Thursday, or even Saturday! Oh! is not this most cruel? Love bear with this cross—for to me, it is most cruel! Dearest, if this letter is not pleasant, do I pray you pardon me! For Love, do be assured of my boundless affection. You are the only tie which binds me to society; I may almost say to life!

Adieu my Love
Thy Houston

Mrs Maggy Houston!

[1]This is probably Seth Carey of Galveston. For a biography see Ray, 34.
[2]*Writings,* IV, 456–59.
[3]See Margaret to Houston, January 29, 1842.
[4]Hamilton had offered an unauthorized proposal to Santa Anna that Mexico acknowledge the independence of Texas in exchange for payment of five million dollars. James, 323.
[5]The son-in-law and daughter of Eugenia Andrews.
[6]John A. Walton, the mayor of Galveston.
[7]James Shaw.

Houston wrote Margaret a second letter later the same evening, or rather, very early the next morning. It is not dated, but is with the previous letter and numbered "two" in the series. The letter that follows this one is numbered "three."

[Jan. 31, 1842]

My Love,

It is half past one oclock, and I have written a veto,[1] so my <u>fumes</u> are somewhat off me. I must try and get some rest to night, but I fear the effort will be vain, as I know my thoughts will wander to the bosom of her I love. Oh that bosom, I wish it sweet peace! That head I wish again to <u>pillow</u> on a<u> bosom</u> that can feel no rest until it feels the gentle pressure and the palpitation of a responsive heart!

Love! you told me to say sometimes to you that I was "temperate." So far as abstinence from wine and every other drink, (milk excepted, that at a <u>bit</u> a bottle,) I am truly so. I wou'd be the veriest sinner, if I were to indulge, for indeed my Love I have no propensity to taste one drop of any thing on earth that could excite or intoxicate me!

My health I have not spoken of lately. I thank our Heavenly Father that I am in fine health. Better than you have ever seen me! I draw the very pleasing inference that you are in fine health, or you would have said so to me!

I must cease, retire, and reflect upon my dearest Margaret.

Thy own
Houston

[1]The veto is probably one of those in *Writings*, II, 456–59. January 30 was a Sunday, so Houston may have dated them January 31, 1842, the date they were presented to Congress.

Austin

31st January 42

My Love,

'Tis morning, and I promised rightly last night for surely my rest was but weary rest! Tho' I am blessed with a bright morning, and feel quite well. The Messenger has not set out, as had supposed, therefore I will write to the last moment.

One matter I will tell you of that may be a subject of gossip. It is Dr [Ashbel] Smiths affair. Chalmers[1] the braggadocio has not been out of his shell, I am told since he learned that the Doctor had come to town, but now says he will go to Orleans and fight Bailey Peyton.[2] What a dust <u>we</u> raise, as the fly said riding on the ox's horn! I hope. It is reported here that Lamar and other dignitaries are on their way here with Genl H.[3]—I can not myself arrive at any conclusion, but this you may rely upon, as rumour says. If Lamar shou'd come, Genl [Memucan] Hunt will call upon him for certain slanders circulated in the "Sentinel" last summer charging Genl Hunt with an attempt to supplant Genl Henderson[4] at London as minister etc. This was false and Genl Hunt called for the author. Chalmers was given up to him, when he called upon him by his friend, C gave up Lamar as the story goes, so I am now told that Genl [Memucan] H[unt] will call upon Mr Lamar, and they will have to adjust the matter. So much for this! Next my dear wife, I must tell you another piece of news, or really I may as well say <u>truth</u>. A letter was put into my hand by Colonel Love,[5] sent to me by Mr Burnley[6] which had been written to him by Genl Hamilton,[7] in which was contained this ominous expression, refering to the <u>loan</u> and as I suppose, <u>party</u> influence. "Stand by your post, and keep the forces together until we come up." To my mind "this is very nice." I was astonished that Love, who is a <u>cute</u> man, did not perceive the bearing of the expression and keep it from me! For to me my dearest it spoke volumes.—It betrayed at least a conspiracy to carry, if needful, a measure by combination, which the Executive might not wish to sanction! What think you

[of] it, my only Love? We have fallen upon evil times. Genl Hamilton while in London as Minister, Loan agent, etc, with others, got up an agency to sell Texas lands and to give it effect in London, occupied an office in Exeter Hall, next door to the room in which the abolitionists held their meetings. I learn that Dr Levy Jones,[8] Col Love, and many others were interested in the matter! Now my dear, you can see what cause I have to be "out of sorts." Yet this shall not induce me Love, to loose [sic] my self control.—No! I will be myself, for "Richard is himself again!" To reflect that a man, paid by Government a large salary should forget every thing but self, and that too, when Texas required every man connected with her to do his duty.

This moment, Mr Green placed your letter of the 26 inst in my hand.[9] I have perused it hastily, and regret very much that your indisposition has returned. I was fearful Love, that you had sat too late at the Party, but I wou'd not say so, lest you might suppose me selfish. Oh my Love, I am crazy to see you. How I am to live without you, I can not tell. I am miserable indeed. But our God can comfort us, and sustain us!

My regards to Col A, Lady, and family. Do you my dearest kiss Mag and tell her that "little Captains" shou'd cut no capers. Bite her on the chin a little!

My own Love
Farewell
Thy Devoted
Houston

Maggy
I will remember Henry [Lea], and comply with your request.

---

[1]John Chalmers, Secretary of State in 1841 under acting president, David G. Burnet. *Writings*, III, 239n. During the Houston-Burnet feud of the summer of 1841, Ashbel Smith got into a debate with John C. Chalmers, who published an article attacking Dr. Smith on personal grounds. Smith then accused Chalmers of poking his nose into "a bachelor's kitchen" to divert public attention from his own misdeeds and threatened to put before the public proof of Chalmers's guilt as a swindler if the insults continued. At this point the matter was dropped. See Elizabeth Silverthorne, *Ashbel Smith of Texas,* (College Station: Texas A&M University Press, 1982), 69–70.
[2]Sometimes spelled Balie Peyton. He was an old friend of Houston's from Tennessee and a brother of Houston's landlord, Angelina Eberly. For a biography see *Handbook of Texas,* I, 540.
[3]James Hamilton.

[4]James Pinckney Henderson.

[5]James Love of Galveston, an outspoken foe of Houston's. For a biography see Best, 324.

[6]Albert Triplett Burnley was acting in conjunction with Hamilton to secure loans for the Republic. They had negotiated a loan from the Bank of Pennsylvania. Schmitz, *Texas Statecraft 1836–1845*, 101.

[7]James Hamilton to A.T. Burnley, November 18, 1841. Sam Houston Papers, Catholic Archives of Texas, Austin, Texas.

[8]Dr. Levi Jones of Houston. For a biography see *Handbook of Texas*, I, 925.

[9]Houston may be referring to Margaret's letter of January 25, 1842.

Mrs. Sam Houston
Houston
Texas
[by] Mr. Williamson

Austin
1st Feby 1842

Dearest Love,

This moment I can write a line to you on the subject of news. General Hamilton and his company arrived this morning and I learn that he is chop fallen a good deal. [torn] is so too, and in part by his [torn]. At 2 PM I am to have a visit from him. I will be very polite, you may be assured my Love. His presence will not in my opinion detain Congress—surely not so far as I am concerned, and my consent. I must see you my Love; that to me is every thing on earth.

I have only time to say that you must sum up all the Love that I have ever expressed for you, and make it an hundred fold, and be assured that you will only estimate a portion of my love! Thus you may if you please term this a "love letter" too. I will deny it, for I alledge [sic] that from me it is purely matrimonial. I will look with painful anxiety for adjournment of Congress. My heart is animated by the purest affection, my dear Margaret.

Oh! for the day of our meeting. May kind Heaven shield and protect you, my every hope, and every joy.

Commend me to our friends and bite Mag Stone for me.

Thy devoted husband
Houston

Lady Margaret

Austin
PM 3 oclk 1st Feby 1842

My Love
Genl Hamilton is now in my office. Our interview has been pleasant but too much said to write all, which I hope soon to tell you in person. I will <u>bear myself in all things</u>, as <u>you</u> dear wou'd and do desire.[1]

To gratify you, my dearest, I will say that Mr. Kennedy shall have the information, which you desire he shou'd have. Hockley, Dr Jones, and every person wishes to be presented to your Ladyship.

Thy ever devoted Husband
Houston

Maggy

[1]For Houston's message to Congress concerning General Hamilton see *Writings*, II, 471–72.

The following is the last known letter that Houston wrote to Margaret during the sixth session of the congress.

Mrs. Sam Houston
City of Houston
Texas

Austin
3rd Feby 1842

Dearest
The mail is just closing, and I will only have time to write a line. To day I wrote a long letter to our brother Henry, and told him what a <u>sober, decent</u> man I was. Also how much I loved you, nay how truly I am devoted to you, and abused Congress for not adjourning—when it will I can't say, but I hope in two days. Oh Love I am very distressed at this, but I must bear it. You must too my Dearest

Love! I can't ask you to be patient, for I am not, nor can I be so. I show no temper, but every day throws some new light upon the acts of Genl Hamilton. He won't do, but you may be assured that I won't show it in my intercourse. I wou'd have written you a long letter to day, only I had to write an important veto,[1] and it was ably done! so say those who heard it read. My vetos are growing in popularity!

Oh my Dearest! My every thought embraces you with all the ardour and affection of my nature! My heart beats high with every tender and painful emotion! It appears to me that I am the greatest martyr to my countrys service.

You must allow me to express, I will not say weakness, but the wildness of my affection. Dear I feel sorrowful that you will experience so much disappointment, for I know my own sufferings & solicitude!

Send my Love to our dear Mother. I will write to Sister A[ntoinette] and Vernal. Do write to our dear Sister Eliza [Houston Moore] and to brother Will[iam Houston].

I will not seem too melancholy, but deep as are my regrets, and painful my disappointments, I will beg you to bite Mag Stone either on the chin, or the ear. If you bite her as hard as you did a friend, she will never forget it, or if she does, I am sure your friend never will! Commend me to our friends.

Thy ever devoted husband
Houston

Maggy Houston

[1]*Writings*, II, 466–67, 473–74.

It is possible that Margaret's last letter did not reach Houston before he left the capital. Congress adjourned on February 5, 1841, and Houston immediately left for Houston City on a mule called Bruin, making the trip in two hours less than four days. For a description of his trip home see the letter from Houston to Washington D. Miller written February 15, 1842, Writings, II, 484.

To General Sam Houston
Austin, Texas
Mr. Moore

Houston, Feb. 7th 1842

Dearest husband,

You <u>commanded</u> me not to write to you any more, but recollect Mr. Crawford[1] did not make me promise to obey you, so that you can not charge me with rebellion. The day is so cold and my hands so perfectly frozen that I believe if it were not for the love of showing my independence, I would not write to you. Now my good fellow, take care how you command me here after. Brother Vernal came up last night and went out with me today visiting and shopping. I met Mr. Moore[2] at the Houston house[3] and he told me he would set off for Austin this evening, so I hurried home to write to my beloved, notwithstanding his injunctions to the contrary. Dearest it was a foolish thing in me to excite your curiosity of taking out a part of my letter, but I assure you it was wholly unintentional, and I had no idea of the enormity of it until you presented it before me, in all its hideous colours. I will do so no more!

The truth is I had detailed to you some very extravagant compliments that were paid me by a foreigner who visited this place in company with Mr. Castro, among which was that he had seen Victoria,[4] but Mrs. Houston was far superior & I thought it was a good joke, whilst I was writing them, but I afterwards concluded that I would not risk the imputation of vanity from you, but I regret now that I did not, for the delay and discussion gives it an importance which it realy does not deserve. I dined today at the Houston house with Mrs. Butler who is staying there at present, but returned in time to see Gen. Lamar at Col. Andrews's dinner table. He looks like a great clumsy bear. Poor fellow! Unfortunately the conversation at the table turned upon beauty and grace and I gave it the direction myself, but without the slightest design of disconcerting him I assure you. But my Love, I could not suppress a smile as he arose from the table and hobbled along before us to the sitting room. I was polite enough to conceal my amusement from the company, and I think I deserve some credit for that. You will say I am in good spirits today. Well realy I am, and I can not account for it unless it is that I have my dear brother with me. I have had dear affectionate friends all the while, but they are not like kindred. And my spirit has been so long lowered to the earth by your absence that since seeing brother V. and hearing that Mother was well, I have been a new creature. I do not know when to look for you and the suspense is intolerable, but I will not sink! I had a charming letter from bro. Will a few days ago, but I will not send it to you for fear it might be lost. My Love come home, and I will be happy again.

Thy Maggy

My health is good, and I have had several supplies of money from Galveston. Joshua is here, but I have not been able to hire him, so Col. Andrews keeps him employed.

[On envelope]
Dear Gnl
   I only have time at present to add a word to what Maggy has said. I have some messages for you from Genl Combs[5] which he requested me to deliver in Person touching the policy as regards our Navy. I think I shall not go to Liberty before I see you which I do hope will be soon.

affectionately
V. B. Lea

[1]Reverend Peter Crawford who officiated at the wedding of Houston and Margaret Lea.
[2]Margaret was probably referring to John W. Moore, sheriff of Harris County.
[3]A hotel in Houston City. Hogan, 106.
[4]Queen Victoria of England.
[5]General Leslie Combs of Kentucky. For a biography see *Writings,* IV, 450–51n.

Chapter V

May 5, 1842–July 5, 1842

May 5, 1842: Margaret Houston to Sam Houston
May 5, 1842: Sam Houston to Margaret Houston
May 8, [1842]: Margaret Houston to Sam Houston
May 6–16, 1842: Sam Houston to Margaret Houston
May 13, 1842: Margaret Houston to Sam Houston
May 21, 1842: Margaret Houston to Sam Houston
May 21, 1842: Sam Houston to Margaret Houston
May 22, 1842: Sam Houston to Margaret Houston
May 24–31, 1842: Sam Houston to Margaret Houston
May 31, [1842]: Sam Houston to Margaret Houston
June 3–8, 1842: Sam Houston to Margaret Houston
June 3, 1842: Margaret Houston to Sam Houston
[June?] 1842: Dr. Nathaniel Fletcher to Margaret Houston
June 14, 1842: Margaret Houston to Sam Houston
June 25, 1842: Sam Houston to Margaret Houston
July 5, 1842: Margaret Houston to Sam Houston

In the late spring Margaret sailed from Galveston on a trip back to visit her family in Alabama. Restless Texans were clamoring for an invasion of Mexico to rescue the Santa Fe prisoners. Houston was struggling to maintain an army without funds to pay for it. He sent a number of agents to the United States to ask for volunteers who could equip themselves at their own expense with clothing, a rifle or musket, ammunition, and food for eight days. Houston had a short visit in Galveston and then returned to Houston. The following letters passed between the couple during the summer of 1842.

Steamer New York[1]
General Sam Houston

Houston, Texas
May 5, 1842

My Beloved,

Two stormy nights are past and we are now within a few hours run of New Orleans. The boat jars disgracefully but lest I should not have an opportunity of writing in the city I will at least begin a letter here. Dearest we are far apart and I can scarcely realize I am a breathing creature and thus far from that being in whose affection I have lived so long. Oh how my eyes have ached with unshed tears! and my heart has been heaving with such fresh sensation, but it is for you Love, that I am seeking health and no effort shall be wanting on my part to secure it. I have found Mrs. Fuller[2] an interesting companion. We are both baptists and have amused ourselves today by arguing with a Catholic lady on board. I have just showed Mrs. F. the immense bundle of letters that you wrote me from Austin, and she laughed very much.

I have had some conversation with Col. Gillespie[3] about the removal of the archives. He seems to think that the western people would be satisfied with Washington as a location. Dearest you know best[.] My health has improved constantly since we parted. Night before last I was dreadfully sea-sick. Bro. M[artin] has suffered a great deal too, but poor Martha[4] was worse than either! We had some interesting scenes I assure you! Rather on the order of comical tragedy!

The Capt. and Mrs. Knight[5] are amongst the kindest friends I have ever met. The Capt. amused me very much yesterday in speaking of the "Love[6] meeting" they had in Galveston a few evenings ago. He says he never before took part in any political meeting but as it was expected your name would be handled pretty roughly, he and his clerk Mr. Philips both attended armed with bowie knives and pistols intending to use them if the scoundrels gave them the slightest provocation. This spirit should not be encouraged yet I can not but prize the friendship that is willing to risk everything for you.

9 o'clock at night New Orleans,

We arrived this morning about 6 and have concluded to remain on the boat. The mosquitoes are awful, but I will write in spite of them. The Creole[7] leaves tomorrow at 12, and we must be ready for her. Mr. [Pizene] Edmunds was up to see me tonight. He is the only acquaintance I have met. Oh how lonely I feel in this vast world of strangers! I will see Mrs. Christy[8] if possible according to your request. If we remain long enough in Mobile I will write to you again from that place. But my Love do write to me constantly. My heart is very heavy. I can not live long away from you. <u>Do not condemn me to a long absence</u>. I would implore you and postpone my return past July, but I fear you will weary of my entreaties. Farewell dearest, oh fare thee well.

Thy devoted wife, Maggy

[1]For a description of this ship which sailed between Galveston and New Orleans see Mattie Austin Hatcher, *Mary Austin Holley*, (Dallas: Southwest Press, 1933), 79.
[2]This is probably Charlotte (Mrs. Nathan) Fuller who helped found the First Baptist Church of Houston. B. H. Carroll, *Standard History of Houston*, (Knoxville, Tennessee: H. W. Crew and Company, 1912), 143.
[3]Colonel Barry Gillespie had been appointed general agent of the government for the Mississippi Territory to appoint subagents worthy of confidence. For Houston's instructions to Gillespie see *Writings,* IV, 113–14.
[4]A Lea family slave.
[5]Margaret may be referring to James Knight, a merchant in Ft. Bend County who was from Alabama. Mrs. Knight was formerly Mrs. Bacomb. *Handbook of Texas,* I, 970. Another possibility is Isaac Knight, who is identified as a lawyer from Galveston in White, *First Settlers of Galveston County Texas*, 6.
[6]James Love in Galveston was a leader of persons opposing Houston. Best, 324. For a description of this meeting held at the Merchant's Exchange in Galveston see Joseph Milton Nance, *Attack and Counter-Attack: The Texas-Mexican Frontier, 1842*, (Austin: University of Texas Press, 1964), 163. For a report of this meeting see *Telegraph and Texas Register*, May 4, 1842.
[7]The steamship Creole ran between New Orleans and Mobile.

Mrs. Margaret Lea Houston
Marion
Alabama

City of Houston
5th May 1842

My dearest,

Until objects on the Boat grew small & dim, I gazed after my departing love, yes indeed my wife—my Margaret. My prayers, my soul ascended to Heaven for your safety, for your happiness, for your return to the embraces of an adoring husband! But you will be safe, you must be happy, and you will make others so too. We came up on yesterday & made the trip in one day. I found all things here much as I left them—all quiet and none that I have seen in bad temper! There is no important news from my quarters. Some noise of Indians, but not very satisfactory! Genl Davis[1] will start on tomorrow morning for Corpus Christi & I hope for some good things to "come out of Nazareth." Genl Somerville[2] is here, but I have not had time to converse with him. I hope he may have an excuse!

The enemy will not cross the Rio Grande in any force, I feel confident. It will not be until we can get more arms from the U States, that we will advance upon Mexico. You need not fear that I would be willing to play you the slip & break off to war. If I had to go I guess I should rather move from a sense of imperative duty, than from inclination or choice. So dearest have no fears:—for I will try sending, as I consider it <u>undignified</u> to go on <u>trifling errands</u>! But of this enough.—Once for all I pray you my Love to have no uneasiness. Whilst you are on earth my leading star, you need not fear that I will act regardless of your happiness. From all quarters I learn that the people are united in support of the Executive and his policy. My dear I must tell you that I saw you at your window as the Boat rounded to, and I think you called Martha to stand there, that I might know where you were. It was needless. Affection pointed out No 5 and I saw you, or my fancy told me a story. From thence I went to the Tremont[3] and dined with Hockley.[4] I did not return until evening to our room, and when I opened the door, and looked in—Oh! how

solitary and sad it seemed to me. My eyes were bedimmed with —
but I soon left the apartment, and in a few minutes went to Mothers,[5] and stayed until after nine. Young [Lea Royston] went home
with me for the night, and at 3 oclk we retired. Day light found me
sleepless, and I felt no one to hail with the usual <u>salutation</u>! "Do you
take?" a kiss. No! indeed, I was lonesome! But I am here as busy as
ever. I must finish my letter as Mr Sydnor[6] is going down for the
Neptune. I send you a letter from Sister [Antoinette]. I will write to
her and send her all love. I have seen no one here. I staid [sic] at Mr
DeShains.[7] He had a room & invited me to stay with him. I do not
know where I will stay most, but I think in the country. I did not go
to Col A's[8] nor have I seen Miss Mag [Stone].[9] I will <u>for you</u> and to
hear her talk of you.

Do pray render my love to all, and embrace them for me. Do not
forget our dear Aunt Lea.[10]

Tell Martin of his frogs & shells—they <u>can't</u> surpass the merry
bells which ring thro' Marions hills & dells. But render him my fra-
ternal regards and Sister A[11] my affection.

Most Devotedly
thy husband
Houston

Mrs. Maggy

[1]James Davis was appointed Acting Adjutant General of the Army on May 2, 1842.
On May 5, 1842, Houston ordered Davis to proceed to Corpus Christi to take command of the troops there. Wisehart, 400.
[2]Andrew Somerville. For a biography see *Writings,* II, 493n. The name is also spelled
Sommervill, Somerville, Somervell, and Somervill. In March, 1842, Mexican forces
under Rafael Vasquez crossed the Rio Grande and captured Goliad, Victoria, and
San Antonio. The invaders did nothing more than occupy the cities, raise the Mexican flag and inspect Texan defenses, before withdrawing. On March 18, 1842, Houston sent Brigadier General Andrew Somerville to San Antonio with orders to drive
the Mexican forces out of Texas. In the meantime Edward Burleson, without orders, had gathered three cavalry companies and rushed to San Antonio with a group
eager to follow him across the Rio Grande to avenge the Vasquez raid. When
Somerville arrived, the volunteers informed him that they would serve only under
Burleson. Somerville withdrew without attempting to oust Burleson who, upon
reconsidering his insubordination, also withdrew. The troops were then left without a commander. David Nevin et. al., eds., *The Texans,* (New York: Time-Life Books,
1975), 216; *Writings,* II, 509–11; Wisehart, 401–402.
[3]The Tremont Hotel in Galveston. For information on the hotel see Hogan, 106.
[4]George Hockley.

[5]Nancy Lea's home.

[6]John Sydnor. For a biography see *Writings*, III, 49n.

[7]Possibly the G. G. Deshon identified in White, *First Settlers of Galveston County, Texas*, 10, 34.

[8]Colonel John D. Andrews.

[9]Margaret Stone.

[10]Margaret's aunt, Peggy Moffett Lea, Nancy's sister who was married to Temple Lea's brother. Madge W. Hearne Collection of Papers, San Antonio.

[11]Apphia Lea, Martin's wife. Ibid.

General Sam Houston
Houston, Texas

Mobile Saturday 8th of May [1842]

Dearest Love,

We have been about 10 minutes in port, and several gentlemen of my acquaintance have called on me, amongst the rest Col. Walton[1] and Capt. Penneger.[2] Mrs. Levert[3] has left the city.

This instant Col. Washington[4] and Mrs. Megginson[5] called. We expect to get off at 5 P.M. and it is now about 11. Last night for the first time since we parted I had a severe fit of coughing. I had some difficulty in finding my <u>smoking implements</u>.[6] I searched my dressing box, but could not see them. I then opened my <u>bag basket</u>—as you term it and the rich "treasures of the deep" were poured into my lap in the form of <u>shells</u>. After a useless search through them, I returned to my dressing box and found them. Apropos of <u>shells</u> what beautiful things they are—that is I mean what <u>beautiful tormentors</u>! You have heard of them, have you not? I never comprehended the expression before.

Bro. M[artin] says he has not taken a drop since we took leave of you. I believe him, and with that, seems to have vanished his inordinate fancy for shells so that they are left quietly on my hands. But he has taken excellent care of the baggage and you must give him credit for it. However I believe I will recommend him to purchase a work on conchology and begin regularly to study the science. The horned frogs were left, and I am afraid to laugh at him about them lest he should think I had something to do in liberating them.

Dearest I must hurry as the boat by which this goes has rung its bell. Oh how I long to be with you, but I will not leave my post. Your rule is never to re-appoint one who does so without leave, but that will not be my restraining motion, for I do not think I will ever accept another <u>appointment away from you</u>. Mrs. Christy says she is afraid to trust you away from me, but I told her she need not be. Write often.

In great haste
thy Maggy

On board the Creole, about starting. I have been introduced to several very agreeable passengers. I could not find Edmunds. My health is good. Farewell

Maggy

[1]Possibly George Walton. Identified as a resident of Mobile by Pauline Jones Gandrud, compiler, *Marriage, Death and Legal Notices from Early Alabama Newspapers 1819-1893*, (Easley, S. C.: Southern Historical Press, 1981), 270.
[2]Margaret may be referring to James Penicar of Mobile, the only name in the 1840 census which comes close in pronunciation. Identified in Federal Census of Alabama, 1840, Mobile County, 428.
[3]Octavia Walton LeVert, the wife of Dr. Henry LeVert of Mobile. Ibid. For a biography, see Willis Brewer, *Alabama: Her History, Resources, War Records and Public Men*, (Spartanburg, SC: Reprint Comapny, 1975), 395.
[4]Col. Lewis M. H. Washington, the Texas agent in New Orleans. See Houston to Washington, May 1, 1842, *Writings*, IV, 91–92.
[5]Mrs. George D. Megginson (Sarah Hill). For a biography see Owen, IV, 1184.
[6]It was a common medical practice at this time to prescribe the inhaling of burning stromonium leaves for the relief of asthma. Dorland, 1208. See also Dr. Nathaniel Fletcher's "Prescription for Mrs. Houston", n. d., in Franklin Weston Williams Collection, Woodson Research Center, Rice University, Houston, Texas.

After putting Margaret on the ship for Alabama, Houston returned to Houston City. He wrote the following letter over a ten-day period:

Mrs. Margaret Lea Houston
Marion
Alabama

City of Houston
6th May 1842

My beloved,

Last evening I called up to see Colonel Andrews & family, whom I found well and was kindly welcomed with many regrets and much condolences for your absence! On my way down I came by with Genl [George W.] Terrell, and saw Miss Mag [Stone]. She was pretty well, and we talked altogether of you. I told her how kind you were to me and why it was. She replied that you had guessed very well. I took leave with a most superb bow and went to the supper given to Mr Thomas Lubbuck[1] on his arrival. There were at the party about two hundred guests as I supposed. Many sentiments were given when I was called on for a catch as I supposed, at least intended so by some. Well, I gave "the Santa Fe Prisoners! Texas is pledged to redeem them from their manacles. Union and valiant hearts can do it." The applause was tremendous, tho' all were sober! You see they made nothing. At nine oclk I slid off slily [sic] and retired to business until 12 M and then was sleepless until near day. Jeff Wright was my room mate. I will write some every day!

7th May

Yesterday passed and no important results. All was quiet and I did not hear of the illustrious scrub Mosely[2] but once. I have said [no] important results. In this, I was wrong, for I received a beautiful present for you. It is a Mexican reticule, and the prettiest little thing that I have seen, and not so little either. When Young goes on, I will send it to you, as I am sure you will be pleased with the tribute. It was presented by a Mr Baker of Monclova in Mexico. He wishes to present me a horse, but I have not consented to his acceptance. I called in company with Genl Somerville and took Tea at my friend Mr. Levys.[3] The old Lady had a thousand regrets, as well as him, for your indisposition and many prayers for your happiness and safe return. They very kindly appreciate my loss of your society, and do all they can to amuse and rouse me into cheerfulness. A beautiful fancy cake was presented to me, and I would have kept it, and sent it to you, but I did think it was carrying the joke too far, and would be as bad as our dear brothers "frogs and shells."

8th May

After I had ceased writing yesterday, there was nothing in Town that took place—But there was a horse race at Harrisburg and Monroe Black[4] was compelled to shoot Nimrod Hunt[5]—son of Mrs Mann,[6] who was lately married to Mrs Pages daughter.[7] He began the quarrel and Monroe declined a difficulty, but it seemed that fate had determined the result. Monroe started home, and the other followed him with arms and threatening to commit violence upon him. They were on horses and Monroe shot at him, and struck his hand. The other renewed the attack & fired at Black. Black fired at him again, and shot him thro. the heart. Tomorrow is Monday when Monroe will come into Town and give himself up to the authorities. All appear to justify the act and believe that Monroe was compelled to do the deed. The captain [John S. Black] is some what distressed, but is consoled by the assurance that it was unavoidable.

My dearest since you left I have been much affected with cold. My head aches grievously notwithstanding which I have commenced my allotted task. I have read six chapters at the commencement of the new Testament.

On my return to Houston, I found less press of business than I have experienced since the first of March! From this cause, united with my solitary state of feeling produced by your absence, my mind, or spirit, or soul, for I can only express it, as an intellectual exercise of my faculties, has been newly and strangely exercised. My thoughts were drawn to the scene of death, the termination of all things temporal, and of irrevocable destiny. The uncertainty of life, and the awful certainty of death and eternity. Thus did I reflect upon my situation and the utter impossibility of attaining even one moments respite when the final summons cometh. My apprehensions and feelings were such, as I had never before experienced, and since that moment they have again returned to me, and my understanding says to me "Hearken [sic] to the voice of salvation." My dearest, I may be awakened, but I am not yet renewed in heart, but be assured that I will not quench the spirit, but seek thro' mediation of Jesus Christ that repentance which is not to be repented of.

I feel confident my ever dearest Margaret that you too will offer prayers to God for my salvation. And that as we have lived united on earth, so we shall exist in Heaven. I will not cease to present my prayers at a throne of Grace, until my pardon is sealed and my acceptance is sure, thro' the mediation of a Savior or I am rejected as unworthy of His atonement! I will be earnest & continued in prayer! I know my Love, that you will be distressed and gratified also at my situation. So far as you will be happy, I will be gratified. But I pray you not to be unhappy on my account. It is true my Love, that tears of affection, as well as those of contrition bedim my vision while I am writing to you, but they are the pure effusion of penitence for having so long neglected the duties of religion, and to a great extent, indulgence in the fooleries and vices of the world, which can not be an abiding place for us. All its honors and its vanities are less than shadows compared to the least conception of Eternity. On earth we see numberless trifles, but when we reflect on Eternity, none but the Great Johovah [sic] and His Emaculate Host are there! I will endeavour to obtain even the Humblest place in the presence of my God, thro' the blood and atonement of Jesus Christ my Savior!

10th May

Tho' yesterday was our celebration, or was to have been, of our wedding day, I must assure you that was a day of great suffering to me. I was attacked at Galveston with a bad cold, and it increased after my return until I was attacked with a pain above my right eye (to which you know I am subject) when every remedy failed altho' I had Doct Fosgate (who is very decent) with me. I had recourse to blood letting, which relieved me entirely, and to day as usual, I have been busy. You will perceive that I did not celebrate the "9th of May"[8] as cheerfully as I cou'd have desired. I can only pray that hereafter such occasions may be more in keeping with their original cause.

Lamar & Genl Hunt did not fight[9] tho' Lamar had the aid of the infamous Col Milton[10] as I learn on the occasion. He has come to join the corps of his own kidney in Texas.

Yesterday Smith[11] brought up part of our furniture and I had it stored until he could go down for the balance and so soon as it arrives, I will have it moved to our house. Smith got tipsy and gave me some trouble to get him off again.

My Dearest, when I reflect on what seemed to be your inclination about returning to Texas before you started and the anxiety which you may, and will feel, were you to stay until the latter part of July as was in contemplation, I have resolved to say, my dear, come whenever you please. My arms and heart will embrace you with joy inexpressible. Yes my Love! Do as you please!!! I need not say that I am selfish to some extent in this suggestion, but should you remain my Love, it will be approved by me. I do not see how you can visit your relations with satisfaction much short of the time proposed.

I find one thing to be certain.—My better half is wanting! For I am more than one half less happy than I was while you were with me. Indeed my Love, I do feel that I am alone in the world when I can neither see you, nor hear your voice. I could have said <u>melodious</u> voice, but that would have sounded like a "love letter!" Well I don't care if it had, for to be candid, I do really love you, or I do not understand what love means! Well now my dear, should you return soon, or before July, you would be very lonesome, if you were to leave all your kindred, so I enjoin it upon you my dearest, to bring Sarah Ann[12] with you. It is out here, that you are to bring a niece just like yourself, and to several Beaux I have modestly named to circumstance. Mr Bagby[13] rather asserts some pretensions, as I lay sick in his office & he was greatly pleased with our <u>little</u> Nephew Young L. Royston. You are to bring the young Lady at all events, and I will recommend to her none but the most worthy! Our friend Gov Runnels[14] is with me, and will set out on tomorrow to Mississippi, and return by the time proper to make a move upon our friend Santa Anna. When that will be precisely, I have not yet determined, but as you are my privy counsellor [sic], I intend before I cease this letter to let you know enough to guess the balance. It is important that I shou'd hear from Alabama and Georgia[15] as soon as possible! I hope Genl Pickens[16] is doing well in the way of Emigrants! This is tuesday and saturday we expect news from Orleans. I will send you any papers.

11th May. My Love to day I am not well, but hope to be better, as I have taken some bitters of our friend Price.[17] He has sent me a bottle, and directs me to take a spoonful (Tea) each morning. You must not let what I have said induce you to return sooner than you may wish. It is not an injunction, nor even an invitation. I leave you free to consult your inclinations which I so ungenerously denied you when we parted. If it will conduce to your health, stay as long as you deem proper! You need not fear that I intend to deceive you and go to the army—no my Dearest, I will never dissemble to you, nor [sic] while I have you to confide in! If I were, I should dislike my self, & feel self condemned! You could not respect me, tho' you might pity me much!

I will let some of our new warriors take their wire edges off on the enemy before I will move to the battlefield!

Today it is reported that poor Van Ness,[18] the member of congress from San Antonio, was killed by the accidental going off of a Rifle in the hand of a friend with whom he was riding in Town! No design, nor blame attaches to his friend! Thus pass my enemies from the earth. I do not hate them, nor do I rejoice at their death. While living I condemn them, and dead, I deplore their fate! It has been so from my youth up to age! Van Ness was a wise man in matters of the world, but as I believe, he cared not for the things of Eternity.

The general news of Texas wears on pretty much as it has done! Judge Lipscomb[19] went home to prepare for his trip to Mobile and found two of his children too ill to leave! He will not go on, so Martin will communicate with Genl Smith[20] who is, and will be the agent at that place!

Today I intend to go out to Capt [John S.] Blacks, but may not, as I may have business to transact for the public. You will [hear] that Mr Andrews,[21] the abolitionist agent to New Orleans, has come out with an expose of his mission, and abuses your "dear husband" in the usual style! "Verily, he shall have his reward," but kindly. I become more and more patient every day. Genl Johnston[22] published the correspondence of which I gave you a copy. So much the better! He touches very lightly, and if he had not, why he should have had the whole story! The volunteers at Corpus Christi will cut up some capers as they have done, but they will be of no serious injury to the cause of Texas. A few malcontents have attempted to destroy the hopes of an army, and even to create mutiny in the Navy by circulating false reports about pay. The fact was discovered and plans, I hope defeated! They are few in number, but true to their mischievous purposes. They are such spirits, as would rather reign in hell than serve in Heaven! They will not dim the star of Texas. They try to obscure its lustre, but it will be vain, and they will receive the execrations of all friends to human liberty and regulated government. Even mad democracy will execrate their memory!

I will (as I know my Love you believe) pursue the even tenour [sic] of my way, and tho' I am weary in well doing, I will not faint by the way. I may be sick and feeble, but my purpose will not be faint, but strong while I love my Wife, my County, and my Reputation, or mankind. In all these trials, virtue & honesty will sustain me!

Martin need not come with you if you should return before the 15th or 20th of July and bring Sarah Ann. Young or Robert[23] can accompany you. I do not want Martin, or the Troops here before the 20th of July, or the last, and I wish them all to come near one time well prepared so that they will not be delayed on their arrival, but advance at once upon the enemy. Do not let this news go in the papers, but I wish it known to leaders! and those who are entrusted with our cause!

Martin will be of great use in Alabama, and until active operations, he would be of none in Texas![24]

I hope his every action tells
Thro' Alabama's hills and dells

Do please ask him not to look cross at this but try and smile. I have not said "frogs and shells" once! He must laugh! If he don't, why you will, I am sure! But of this enough!

To day I have been at Mr Bagby about the house and lot. The lady, he says is moving out to day, so this does look like getting the house, and so when the furniture comes, I will have it in the house, but don't think I will live there! Until you return I will visit the place, and see that it is all right and proper![25]

My horse and mule are out at Captain [John S.] Blacks on the grass. I am not able to find them. I expect to hire out Vincy[26] at $15.00 per month, and what will become of the money is uncertain! Speaking of money, if you need, or want any my Love draw on me for any amount that you desire. I may send by Young some titles tho' I hardly expect that any land can be sold in Texas at this time! The machinations of the malcontents has [sic] a bad influence on every thing Texian! "What's done can't be helped." "No use in crying." Poor Jacob did not live in these days, or his philosophy would have been tryed [sic] and he wou'd very often have said, "better luck next time."

About here, I think you had better take a nap, my dear! and read the balance after some repose!

It has just occurred to me that in the multiplicity of business I have not written to my friend Genl McGehee. You I hope my Love, will kindly commend me to him, and to all the kind friends, whom you may meet. Don't forget Genl Thompson, and my brother Martins "Round about" friend the Doctor. If you see poor Mrs Cody,[27] do my dear present me to her, and I know you will not be unkind to her on account of the conduct of her <u>felon husband</u>. You must exercise your generous disposition—it is mercy!! You will see Aunt and all our kindred, and from them I am sure you will receive all kindness.—Tell them so soon as the campaign is over they must all come to Texas, and see us, but I wou'd prefer that they should reside here. It has been to me a land of promise, and will be, I fear, as it has paid me poorly! Therefore, or "ergo" as Mr Andrews has said, it is a land of promise!! But indeed I wou'd above all things like to have our relations in Texas! You I am sure wou'd be delighted with such an arrangement!

If it were possible, I would retire, and never again be heard of only as a private & peaceful citizen, but that day has passed by and I am in for the plate! While you are my counselor, I have no fears of your sensible and friendly advice, and sustain myself if you will only keep your temper. But you know my dear, that you will get provoked at the unruly folks of Texas.

To day I was bargaining about building a house on my place[28] to suit you and such company as might come to see us. It will if I close the bargain be large enough for comfort or convenience. It will be half way on the cottage plan. Two lower rooms and a hall. It will do for Texas. I am to know in a day or two if I can run the risk of paying for the house. I am to have no trouble—he finds and does every thing, and when it is finished he will hand me the keys, and I pay him the cash! I know you wish a house, and not more than we need one. It will be our house! Won't it Dear?

12th May

Last night my Love, I went out to Capt Blacks with Genl Somerville & Col Hadley.[29] I talked little, thought much, and as I felt so lonesome, I concluded to come into town this morning. You have heard of Keepsakes, Boquets [sic], etc. I can tell you of something rather amusing than otherwise. I rode out with <u>your bridle,</u> and even from that very trifling circumstance I derived pleasure and must confess that I mused more than I chatted on my ride. It shews [sic] the influence of trifles upon us in our affections, cares, and even the important business of life. I look some for Young to day, but shou'd he not leave until after the New York sails, I will send this letter. When it comes, I think I will go as far as Morgans,[30] or even from thence to the Island to meet news from you! My anxiety is almost insupportable. You may have been ill, or a thousand things may have happened, and I not there to relieve my beloved! I will seek for consolation from a source above all earthly power. You I know will rely upon that when you advert to the foolish threats which have been made against me. The shield of Jehovah will save me from the machination of mine enemies! They are base men and viler than dogs! The dog is faithful to his master, but <u>they</u> would betray their country. Hence they are viler than dogs!

To day I intend to write a letter to the U States, that will put at rest all speculation about the time.[31] If the good friends of the U States must have the secrete [sic], they shall have it, and we will see how they will sustain Texas at the present & for the future! I have told you already so they shall know it next. Santa Anna may be obliged to me, but no odds for that. We are not chums any way!! I am not induced my dear thro' dread of public opinion, or the clamour of demagogues, but those who have come from the U States, we are not able to sustain with rations nor are we sure at what time means will be sent to us to keep them quiet.—I will employ those who are so anxious to distinguish themselves. I do not calculate upon the extravagant advantages promised to Texas by our friends in the U States. They believe all the promises which they have made, but many were made without calculation or reflection. I feel aware of their generous sympathy and willingness to aid us, but they are embarrassed and we must look to Mexico for remuneration and my impression is that Texas, to a great extent, will have to sustain the war herself. We can succeed single handed, and alone if we can only obtain ammunition.—The rest we will supply ourselves with, and if we alone sustain the conflict, which we must do, if not aided by the promised succour, and then, the glory and all advantages will be ours. It will give to the Texans new claims to Glory, and the administration of Christendom! "Nous Verrons."

We may encounter serious obstacles, but I assure you my dearest, if I could go at once, I would not hesitate [to] say, that our arms would find one difficulty in the way of conquest, and I would feel satisfied to risk my liberty on the event of making Monte Rey [sic] my winter quarters if I did not chuse to advance in the cause of conquest! I predict that all our misfortunes will arise from <u>insubordination</u>. I will denounce it whenever it may present itself to my condemnation! As I am now begining [sic] to prose, I will change my employment, and lay by this sheet!

'Tis after supper, and my friend the Great Western[32] is now with me, and telling me some doleful tales.—Tales of sorrow, how people talk, and what they say, and how wrong it is, "and the likes." I must tell you of the beautiful, and interesting trifles. You know how much they interest and edify me, and how much I care for them!

To day I have been employed in part, preparing documents to send to St. Louis Missouri, to authorize Emigrants from that point to advance upon, and take possession of Santa Fe, and the circumjacent region. So you see my dear, that I will employ every means to annoy and reduce our enemy. I will not be all talk, unless it is so willed by Providence! and that I hope is not the decree!

When you have read my letter, I hope you will not find much in it that will cause reflection for the reason that it contains very little that can be agreeable, tho' much of it [blurred] to you. Things are nearly at a stand here in the way of politicks. Mosely [Baker] the illustrious, is coming round at times & "finds much in Houston to approve." By & by it will be admiration and open praise if the wind sets fair. 'Tis said he will run for the senate! If he does—, I—don't know who else will run, but some clever man, I hope. I have written so much that I will have to read over what I have written, or I will begin to repeat. If the house builder undertakes the job, he says that by August, he will have it done! In the meantime, we will be in the other house, and I hope very happy. I sigh for the happiness of last summer at Cedar Point. Dear Maggy, we were happy there in very truth! I pray that Heaven may have many, very many such days for us when you will enjoy health. Then we can meditate and praise our creator—Grateful for his favors and his mercies! Since writing the above,—I have been to see Miss Betty,[33] and in company with my friend Bagby so you know my visit was welcome. We found Mrs and Mr Ruthvan[34] were there, and we sat until 9 oclk. Miss B. had much to charge me with about Miss Mag, which happens to be—all a mistake. Much love was sent to you by the family, and Madam said at parting "Say to Mrs Houston not to stay two months if she will take my advice." Now you can draw your own inference! I told her that you would never suppose that I cou'd forget you! No, she said, we ladies have vanity enough, but tell her I say come home in less than three months. I have not seen Miss Mag but once since my return and then only to give your message! Now 'tis late, so good night my dear and angels guard you.

13th May. Good morning dearest. It was very late before I slept last night, and this morning I rose late and feeble. I will really change my habit and retire early, so as to rise early. It is more healthy, and one will be more cheerful certainly! This is not a pleasant part of Town, and I will remove to the office, at our house, so soon as I can. This morning all is still in Town, not a whisper, not even the chirp of an insect, but I do hear the rap of a hammer, as I suppose repairing some old building for a new tenant, for so it is that people are moving to Houston since the seat of Government! It will be strange if a day passes without some interesting mischief or excellent falsehood. The illustrious <u>Mosely</u> had gone to his farm, and I am told, said many fine things of me, and among them, that I was mistaken in him, for he was a friend of mine. So might an incendiary of an assassin say, but when asked for the evidence, he cou'd only point to some object of destruction! I will never ask Mosely for one, I assure you, nor will I take any of his "soft soap" for logic. I hope in a few days that I will be thro the press of business until active operations commence, and the field for rumours and wrongs is opened. The times remind me of the Banks, issues are made, whether upon solid or fictitious capital, it makes no matter. 'Tis certain that the issues will never be "redeemed," but no matter. They have passed for so much, and must fall in on the hands of somebody! The greatest hindrance to Texas is that of super abundance of great men. Too great for the proportion of the unambitious. I will thwart the base and malignant few who are striving to ruin the country rather than fail in destroying the man whom they hate with an impure and imperfect hatred. I will now wait for something else! to make out my short epistle!—But ire I do, I must tell you a serious matter. I sent to Miss Mag "the cake" which I told you of with a note. I sent it as your cake, and so next morning as to you she sent a pretty boquet [sic] to me on your account, and tho' many days since, I have not even said thank you for it so now I thank you for it. Betty says, this is too bad, but I told her that she should have Robert when he came over with you, but did not mention Sarah Ann. You know that wou'd not do so well, as a body might suppose. Miss Betty does not invoke competition, and for that reason I was mum. Do not let Sarah Ann be alarmed at difficulties, and as you are my better half, you can assure her of "Executive patronage," all of which will be at your disposal! Now I will set to something else! Mr Miller[35] will have to answer my question of "What next?" He says "dinner, as the Bells have Rung!"

I have dined, and met Gov Smith[36] at dinner, the same honest and noble patriot. He told me of a meeting at Brazoria to take place on tomorrow.[37] It was at first designed to bring the cast of Jimmy Love meetings, but he says the wooers change their tone now. I suppose Lamar & his friend Milton[38] will be there, as I have understood they were both abusing me at Victoria, tho' Lamar denied to bro Martin the fact as to himself! They (my enemies) are always too fast or too slow. Mr. T. Jeff Green, alias Genl is willing to accept rank under the President, so you see "the stock is rising." Good creatures! How vastly patriotic they are!! It is a wonder that my admiration does not overcome me at times. But having so many, and so much to admire, I reckon 'tis that which relieves me, and my Love, you too, have to claim a large share or rather, it has been rendered, even beyond demand, tho' you pretend to require more! Well dearest, when you return, we will settle that matter!

If you should write much before you return, I wish you to tell me all about the kindred. Bro Roystons, Martins, Henry's, and all the families. Tell me how our dear Lucy Ann[39] progresses.—As Sarah Ann is to come with you, she can answer for herself. Tell her she is not to be a Coquet [sic], but a being far above such anguish creating trifles.—True admiration arises from generosity, virtue, and magnanimity, and the coquet can possess no generousity [sic]! I do not pretend to say that a Lady shou'd love because she is loved, but I do say that she ought not to trifle with the feelings & happiness of those who may love her. She can treat any gentleman well and convince him that she does not love him if he is smart, and if he is not, she can be more plain and tell him so. For if he is not smart, he will soon ask her "the question," will you marry me? There a candid and noble mind will give a suitable response! This my Love, is not intended as a <u>lecture</u> to you, for you know what I insist was the case of our courtship, tho' you will to <u>some intent</u> contradict my position. No matter, that is over, and you know I am <u>very yielding</u> in my disposition particularly so to you, if not to "vigilance and safety committies [sic]." To them I can not be pliant, nor to "wou'd be Generals!" I am a little fearful that my dear Niece Lucy Ann will have some disposition to play the Flirt. Tell her of my opinion, but it will not be needful for her in less than ten or twelve years—But she may think me rather too liberal in my allowance of time. This for the present will do for her to reflect upon, as well as to act upon! Before it will be necessary, I hope to see her and then I can consider my decree and knock off several years, if she should be very anxious to make some[one] very clever, very happy! The case of Sarah Ann may be of earlier consideration. When she comes, my Dear, you must bring a power of attorney from her Father & Mother authorizing us to dispose of her if we may think proper, or can do so to manifest advantage! But I hope before one year passes that I will have the pleasure of embracing all the family in Texas! Provided Young is pleased, my heart is set upon their coming, and the coming of my dear Sister Eliza [Houston Moore], and her lord[40] and flock with her! This done and I would be willing to withdraw from all public matters, and let Texas wag on as it might or would!

'Tis pretty late, and the musquitos [sic] are so bad that I must cease for the night. No I can't. I must say more—When I have any leisure on my hands, I am arranging the plan of a campaign, but really I feel greatly in want of means or rather I have none. Any one cou'd act with means, but it will display genius to do much without means! Caesar & Genl Jackson stand in my opinion, unrivalled [sic] in the creation and development of resources, as well as their application. Their[s] is a field open in Texas for a fair experiment.—But success of our enterprize will not be taken as proof (by some of our wise men) as any evidence of extraordinary capacity. Others could have done so too, or even better & it was only luck at last! So good night, my Dearest.

14th May. This morning I am pretty well, and have been busy in various employments. Among them is writing to our dear Sister Antoinette & to mother. I wrote to Sis some three full pages, principally about you & I said in conclusion that so soon as you came home, that we would be happy to see her & Mr Bledsoe. I could not say less, and so far as to her dear self, I was sincere, and rather than not to see her with you again as a dear Sister, I wou'd even be glad to see him, tho' I can never respect the poor fellow. Well Mr McDonald[41] my friend from Austin, has been to see me this morning.—I asked "what news." "None! (said he) the town is quiet & no rascality going on." This is the rarest news for Houston. Its continuance is very uncertain, but I hope it may be of some duration that a pure atmosphere may continue for the time to come! Of all plagues, anarchy and sedition are most to be deprecated!

To day I am again bargaining about "our House" on the Rancho. I may close the bargain and he says if I do, he will do the work by the month of August certain. It is probable that I may make the agreement. It wou'd be very pleasant, and then our country neighbors would Mrs Smith[42] and Col Hadley. This wou'd be pleasant, and we cou'd be quiet & no doubt happy! Nothing do I so much admire and desire as peace, unless it is the pleasure of seeing <u>you</u> again. I am fearful that you will suppose me disposed to urge your return, whether you desire to come or not. No indeed my Love, for however anxious I am again to embrace you, I prize your health and happiness very far above all sinister wishes or feelings on my own part! Do not suppose that I wou'd insinuate that your happiness would be less than mine at our meeting, but you shou'd take into view that you are on a visit and can not guess when you will be enabled to make another, and that might furnish reasons for delay. You know my Dear, that I always make much parade about my disinterestedness, and you know that Mr Price says woe to the man who may trade with Harry Hill or myself!

I see by advertising to the New York, that she will leave Orleans the 7th and 22nd of each month, and should you return my Love, sooner than was anticipated, you can so suit your departure from Perry[43] that you will not be detained in Orleans. Tho' it may be as the New York will be alone in the trace this year, that she may make some changes in her time of arrival and departure! To this you can have a regard! When I can see Young, I will have a chance to talk of matters, & leave them to the exercise of your discretion, but as you will be assured, feeling every interest in the case possible, that matters may so turn out perfect[ly] agreeable to you, my Love. Tomorrow I hope to attend church and the residue of the day, if spared, I will read the scriptures. Further I design after each meal to read a chapter in the New Testament. Thus I will gratify you, and I hope, derive instruction and edification of a temporal as well as a spiritual character.

16th

Dearest, I went to church on yesterday, and read in the Book of Matthew. I found it truly interesting, and edifying to me. To day I heard from Sister & Bledsoe, and to gratify you, I enclose the letters. I will make no remark, but leave this to your reflection! Today I mailed my letter to our dear Sister. I was very kind, but I did not mention receipt of her last letter, tho' I did the one written to you!

My Maggy dearest, your two letters made me truly happy this morning. All that you say was grateful to me. You now my dear can come just when you may please to do so. My "arms and heart shall embrace you." Col Christy writes to me that you have agreed to stay some days on your way home—Provided I will meet there. Indeed I am so anxious to see you, if could that I would even be the bearer of this letter, even to Marion and properia personae, hand it to its address! I hear that Mother has not been well, and I will go to the Island this morning as I can't tell when Young and Vernal will be down. I will send this letter by my aid de camp, Major Wood, who will bear dispatches to Alabama. My dearest, in all things act as you may deem best! My heart embraces you with the truest affection. Embrace our kindred for me! I truly embrace you for writing when I know you had so little time! I may add a postscript at the Island if the New York is not on the start. I will return by the next Boat to Houston.

Dearest I started to the Boat as it was to sail at 12 M. precisely, but found that the Capt was waiting as he said for the passengers tho' he had refused to wait a half hour for despatches. Now my Dearest, you may suppose what my indignation at his conduct must be. What I most regret is that I am compelled to go on his Boat or not to go at all! But no matter my Dear, as I will be traveling in the direction of my Love, why I dont care so much,—but when I stop Oh! but I will feel lonely for I will be and see where we parted! I will go into your state room and there behold where you were. Even that will be some company however melancholy I may feel. I will go to see our dear mother the moment that I arrive on the Island. Oh my Dearest, I have ten thousand things to say to you, and at least nine hundred of the most tender and affectionate characters.

But I hope the day is not distant when I shall have the inexpressible joy of pressing you to my care troubled bosom!!! Then, but not till then will I be happy, tho' I may hear from you, but I can not see you nor can I hear you my Love. But you will I apprehend think that

I am writing "love letters," and this you know I am not to do by agreement. You would not talk matrimony and say "well! I have refer'd the subject to brother Henry and he says that he has no objection, and for my part, I am willing to be united to you for better, or for worse."

Indeed, I feel very much like taking to myself a wife, if you are willing. Yes, those dear letters of yours had a wonderful effect upon me! They are just such things as will keep me in love, and gratify for a moment, and leave me miserable a while—at least until I become reconciled to the idea of distance from society and isolation of place! If this be true, I am in the wilderness of thought and heart even when I am in society. The thought of you presents distance to my mind. My heart is the abode of desolation! You must not entertain a belief that I am begging you to return—no my Dearest, if you are happy, or can enjoy your stay for the term expected when we parted, do not make a fuss, and run off home. For if you do, the kinsfolk will laugh at you and be provoked likewise. I do confess my dearest, that when we parted, I did not then expect active movements so soon as I now intend to have them! The armies of Volunteers will induce action sooner than was anticipated by me! Thus far I have yielded to circumstances, but have not been forced by Faction! The cry is still "Houston must lead us," and many add "or we will not go" and "who else can lead us?" I suppose it has arisen for our old Ladies who do not wish their sons to go, and wives who love their husbands! You can judge which you think the most numerous. You will say the <u>old</u> Ladies are!!!. By the bye, my Love, I have heard you speculate <u>upon</u> this subject!! But to the war and soldiering, my Dear, I am not committed upon this subject, nor will I be until I can again embrace and confer with you! 'Tis a matter of serious import. I doubt not my own one, but what I could gather plenteous Laurels and stores of wealth, but these could never recompense me for the loss and want of your society! I have all the Laurels which I had when you accepted me! With your agency, I have gained other and new victories to which a moral grandure [sic] attaches! To secure these and possess your affections and society are sufficient to gratify my ambition. You say that you have but one <u>earthly</u>—Then dearest as I know what that is, I can say it shall be gratified so far as I can conduce to it.

No ambition, you are assured, could ever induce me to repair to the martial field. Patriotism, aroused by the calls of my bleeding country, have [sic] twice been responded to by me, and you would condemn me were I not to fly to her aid, and redeem her again from oppression and from suffering! You would say—"Go my husband. I will pray for your safety, but Oh! save our country!" Yes Maggy, your nature would speak out—You never could live the wife of a recreant. You may suppose an excuse for you and myself, but you would, in the hour of trial, find the expedient utterly insufficient! But of this I hope we will have opportunity and ample time to discourse ire it will be supposed necessary or probable, tho' at some time it may [be] indispensable.

It is now 2 oclock in the morning on Cloppers bar,[44] tho' not aground, and on board the miserable old "Burleson." Major Wood and your devoted husband were both very anxious to get to the Island previous to the departure of the New York. I hope to have time to write to my dear brother Martin, but if I do not, present him my Love, and tell him to do the best he can for Texas, as I know he will!

I am sorry that Eusaue[45] did not go with you, or that you did not take Martha, if you could have done so from Orleans to Alabama. I fear that you did not try owing to something which I might have said, and if so Love, for my sake, do pardon me. I have been unhappy lest it might be so! But indeed my dearest, those frogs and shells did pester me very much.

I am so happy and so proud that my noble brother did not drink any that I will not plague him any more about his fancies. Ask him if he can't now quit the evil altogether? If he can I should be very happy, and I am sure he will be more so than if he continues to indulge. I do not condemn him, but my suggestion is prompted by the purest affection!

Mr Huckins[46] is at the table with me. He can't sleep, and has risen to read a while. What will he think now, when he knows this is page 42! My health is now very good indeed! I am satisfied that this letter ought to put you out of all patience, and if it should not, it would be wrong to impose further upon your good humour!!!! I need not assure you "my own one" that I will write every opportunity!

Come when you will; come when you may! You shall be <u>welcome</u> any day! This is poetry! You have heard the anecdote of the

Dutchmans sign intended to represent a man, and a horse! Lest there might be some mistake as they were not well done, he wrote above them "Dis is de man, and dis is de orse!" So I just thought that I would call your attention to the poetry, and I venture to say there is as much honest sentiment and feeling in it as any composition of modern times! Yes, I will say there "is more truth than poetry!" Now this is placing ones moral attributes above his grieving. You may call a man a "rascal," and it will offend him much less than to call him a "fool." So in this you must say I am peculiar.

Don't think from the length of my letter that I am trying to persecute you and compel you to come home to avoid the infliction of my letters! No it is to tell you every thing so that you need not come home to know what is passing in Texas!

Judge Terrell has gone to move his family to Houston so that you will soon, I hope, have the pleasure to meet and embrace his excellent and pious Lady! Almost all of your many friends wish me to present them kindly to you!

Dearest, I must close, and may the Great God of the universe preserve, guard, and protect you in happiness!

Thy ever devoted husband,
Houston

Margaret

[1]Thomas Lubbock, the brother of Francis R. Lubbock. For a biography see *Writings*, II, 89n.

[2]Mosely Baker.

[3]Houston is probably referring to S. A. Levy. Mrs. Levy had opened an establishment where she served pastries and ice creams. For more information see Pearl Henricks, "Flavor of City Sam Houston Knew in Early 40's Gleaned from Dim Pages of Pioneer Newspapers," *Houston Chronicle*, January 24, 1937.

[4]Son of John S. Black, a neighbor at Cedar Point. Identified by Montgomery, 170.

[5]Nimrod Hunt was also known as Flournoy Hunt. William Ransom Hogan, "Pamelia Mann, Texas Frontierswoman," *Southwest Review* 20 (Summer 1935): 363.

[6]Mrs. T. K. Mann, owner of Mansion House in Houston. Identified in Grammer, 34.

[7]Ann Wilkerson married Flournoy Hunt on March 19, 1842. Grammer, 36.

[8]The Houstons' wedding anniversary.

[9]A feud had arisen between President Lamar and Memucan Hunt. Two articles appearing in rival Austin newspapers contained assertions that Lamar and Hunt both believed untrue. Hunt held Lamar responsible for stating that Hunt had attempted, while Assistant Secretary of Navy, to recall James Pinckney Henderson as Minister to France with the idea of securing the appointment for himself. William

Ransom Hogan, *The Texas Republic: A Social and Economic History*, (Austin: University of Texas Press, 1969), 285.

[10]John Milton. Charles Adams Gulick, Jr., and Winnie Allen, *The Papers of Mirabeau Buonaparte Lamar*, v. 4, (Austin: Von Boeckmann-Jones Co., 1924), 13. Milton to Lamar, May 3, 1842. For more information on the Lamar-Hunt feud see 6–18, Ibid.

[11]This may refer to a member of either the Christian Smith family or the William Smith family, both of whom were neighbors of the Houstons at Cedar Point. (Not referring to Dr. Ashbel Smith.)

[12]Margaret's niece, Sarah Ann Royston. Madge W. Hearne Collection, San Antonio, Texas.

[13]Thomas M. Bagby, a Houston merchant. For a biography see *Writings*, III, 172n.

[14]Hiram G. Runnels, a former governor of Mississippi (not to be confused with his brother, Hardin Runnels, who would later be elected governor of Texas). For biographies see *Writings*, IV, 100n.

[15]Houston is referring to the agents sent to the United States to raise volunteer troops.

[16]General Andrew Pickens of Alabama was attempting to bring one thousand men to add to the army of Texas. Houston had offered to make him a Brigadier General. *Writings*, IV, 92.

[17]Dr. James Howe Price, Houston's friend from earlier days in Nashville, Tennessee. Montgomery, 150–51.

[18]Cornelius Van Ness.

[19]Abner S. Lipscomb, the General Agent of Texas for the State of Alabama. See Lipscomb to Houston, May 10, 1842. Sam Houston Papers, Catholic Archives of Texas, Austin, Texas. For a biography see *Writings*, IV, 30.

[20]Houston to General Walter Smith, *Writings*, III, 30.

[21]Stephen Pearl Andrews, *Handbook of Texas*, I, 48.

[22]Albert Sidney Johnston.

[23]Margaret's nephew Robert Royston, the brother of Young Lea Royston. Madge W. Hearne Collection, San Antonio, Texas.

[24]Margaret's brother, Martin Lea, was on a mission for Houston to raise money and manpower for the Texas Army. Houston to Martin A. Lea, May 2, 1842, *Writings*, IV, 93.

[25]Houston apparently was planning on renting a house in Houston City from Thomas Bagby.

[26]Vincy, a female, was a Houston slave. Madge W. Hearne Collection of Papers, San Antonio.

[27]Probably Mrs. A. J. Cody of Galveston. See Margaret to Houston, January 18, 1841.

[28]Houston was considering having a house built on the property he owned in Houston City.

[29]Colonel T. B. J. Hadley.

[30]Morgan's Point, the home of James Morgan in the settlement of New Washington. For a biography see *Writings*, I, 407n.

[31] See *Writings*, IV, 102–107, various letters of May 12, 1842, from Sam Houston to John Barrington, Robert Livingston, Walter Smith, or Henry Watkins Allen.

[32]Major Thomas Western.

[33]Betty Tilghman, the daughter of Eugenia Price Andrews.

[34]Jane and Archibald St. Clair Ruthvan. For a biography see *Writings,* VII, 555n.

[35]Washington D. Miller.

[36]Henry Smith, provisional governor of Texas in 1835. Best, 336–77.

[37]For Houston's comments to the chairman of this meeting see Houston to Timothy Pilsbury, May 18, 1842. *Writings,* IV, 110–11.

[38]John Milton.

[39]Margaret's niece, Lucy Ann Lea, the daughter of Henry C. Lea. Madge W. Hearne Collection, San Antonio, Texas.

[40]Samuel A. Moore.

[41]Alexander McDonald. Identified in Grammer, 36.

[42]Mrs. Obedience Fort Smith. Col. T. B. J. Hadley was married to her daughter, Piety Smith. They lived nearby, southwest of Houston City. The Smith home was later given the address of 2616 Louisiana. *Ancestral Biographies,* published privately in 1991 by Miss Ima Hogg Chapter, Daughters of the Republic of Texas, in Houston, 61–63.

[43]Perry County, Alabama.

[44]The mouth of the San Jacinto River located near Morgan's Point was obstructed by a sand bar called Clopper's Bar. Dermoth H. Hardy and Ingham S. Roberts, eds., *Historical Review of South-East Texas,* v. I, (Chicago: Lewis Publishing Co., 1910), 263.

[45]A Houston slave.

[46]The Reverend James Huckins. Hogan, *The Texas Republic,* 198.

Gen. Sam Houston
Houston, Texas

Marion Perry Co. Ala. May 13th 1842

My own Love,

We arrived here on Monday evening, our wedding day, as I predicted. I devote to you the first moment that I could claim from my friends, for we have had a constant jubilee ever since we arrived. I can give you no idea of the cordial greetings with which I was met and if I could be happy away from you, there is nothing wanting to make me so, but I can not be—oh no, I am not happy without you! I have taken my room at brother Henry's and as they keep 7 servants at the house, I am at no loss for attendance. I have not been very well since I arrived, but if you could only see the kindness of my dear relations, you would have no fears for me. I dined yesterday at Gen. King's[1] with several of my friends and we enjoyed ourselves very much. The Gen. and his lady[2] have known me from my infancy and they declared that it seemed scarcely like reality to see me at home again. They made many inquiries about you, and manifested a great deal of interest in our country's cause.

Marion is a perfect earthly paradise. I have never seen anything so beautiful as its green hills and blooming gardens. Oh that my beloved husband were here to share with me the happiness that is around me! But he is far away toiling and oprest [sic] with cares, and I wish I was with him, for it is nonsense to think of being contented without the presence of him who engrosses every thought and wish of my heart. Dearest I still calculate on your writing for me in July. Do not disappoint me if you can avoid it. I expect sister Royston[3] and I will make Aunt Lea[4] a visit within a few days. Cousin Waine and Columbus[5] have been to see us, and wish us to go down immediately, but I think it will be a week before we set off. They tell me Aunt is in very low spirits, and seems almost heart-broken since uncle's death.[6] I long to see her and cheer her, if it be in my power.

We did not come through Selma as we expected, when we left Galveston, finding it more convenient to get home from Cahaba.[7] On my return I will see your relatives if possible. Many changes have taken place since I left. The little girls are young ladies, and many of the young ladies are married and mothers, and some are gone to their long homes! Yes the destroyer has been here—even in these quiet shades, and the young and beautiful are fallen before him. Mrs. Roots the widow of Sister Serena's brother is staying at bro. Henry's. She is an interesting lady, and altogether we make a pleasant circle. Lucy Ann is grown a great deal and much advanced in her studies. Henry, the youngest, is one of the loveliest children I have ever seen. Sister Royston's youngest child is quite as pretty. They make a host when they are all together and indeed I have never seen a more interesting assemblage. Bro. Martin's boys are also fine fellows.[8] Bro. Henry and Sister Serena expect to make us a visit next winter and they tell me if I will stay until Oct. they will return with me, but I can not consent to that.

The exchange for the 250 dollars which you gave me only amounted to 155, but it is quite sufficient for my expenses. I do not think Capt. Wright[9] treated me quite well about Martha. When we arrived at New Orleans he pretended not to have known that she was on board until the boat had left Galveston and I thought his conduct rather un[torn] Will you be kind enough dearest to ask him the price of passage and pay him, as I did not attend to it myself. My

Love, do write to me constantly. Have you rec'd a letter from Dr. Fletcher?[10] He says he has written to you. When you write to Maj. Reily remember me to them, and tell Mrs. R. I intend to write to her soon. Tell Mag Stone I have mentioned her name very frequently to my friends here. If you see Mrs. Andrews and Betty, give them my love. Please write to Ma, if you have time as I shall not be able to write by this mail and tell her I hope to be quite well when I return. The congestive fever has been so fatal in Marion during the two past summers that they are a little afraid of it this season. If it begins, I expect we will go to some of the springs. But I trust it will not be necessary. Have no fear for me dearest. The only anxiety I have is on your account.

Thy own
Maggy

My dear do not part with the horse unless you desire it particularly. Brother Henry bought him for you especially.
We heard last night that Cousin Columbus's wife[11] had given birth to a dead boy.

[1]General Edwin D. King. For a biography see Owen, III, 980.
[2]Ann Alston Hunter King, Ibid.
[3]Varilla Lea Royston.
[4]Peggy Moffitt Lea, Nancy's sister.
[5]Margaret's cousins, the sons of Peggy and Green Lea.
[6]Green Lea.
[7]A small settlement near Marion.
[8]Martin had three sons: Robertus b. 1834, William Jones b. 1836, and Henry Clinton b. 1838. Madge W. Hearne papers, San Antonio.
[9]John L. Wright, the captain of the *Neptune*. L. W. Kemp, "Articles on Early Texas History,"*Houston Post Dispatch*, January 19, 1930. The fare for passengers was $25 for staterooms, $20 for lower cabin and $8 for negroes.
[10]Dr. Nathaniel Fletcher of Marion. See "Prescription for Mrs. Houston," n.d. Franklin Weston Williams Collection of Sam Houston papers, Woodson Research Center, Rice University.
[11]Elizabeth Parker Lea. Identified in Pauline Jones Gandrud, comp., *Alabama Records*, v. 182, (Easley, South Carolina: Southern Historical Press, 1980), 97.

General Sam Houston
Houston, Texas

Perry Co. Marion Ala. May 21, 1842

Dearest Husband,

I have suffered one mail to pass since the reception of your dear letter which was to me "far above the price of rubies." The reason I did not reply to it immediately was that I was not able to do so, having suffered several days with a violent inflammation of the glands. Dr. Fletcher pronounces it bronchitis and thinks it a favourable turn for my health. You speak of your loneliness after my departure. Oh my Love you could not feel more lonely than I did, and even now I can not be resigned to your absence. Sometimes when the children gather around me and tell me how dearly they love me and how much they want to see "Uncle Houston" thier sweet prattle makes me feel something almost like joy, but still my heart retains the sad recollection that my husband is far away. I have been several days at bro. Royston's and if I could be happy without you my dear gentle sister and her sweet children would make me so, but there is no happiness for me in this world apart from my husband. Bro. R is extremely anxious to set off for Texas in the fall, but I fear he will not be able to arrange his business for it, as he is not yet released from the bank. I hope bro. Martin will make some provision for him that will enable him to get off.

Yesterday I looked over your Austin letters and read some of them aloud to sister Virilla. It would have given you pleasure to see the happiness that illumined her meek countenance at every expression of tenderness.

22th Sabbath day. I was not quite well enough yesterday to finish writing, but I feel much better today. I have had a letter from Aunt Lea and she begs me to go to her immediately. I expect sister Serena, sister Virilla and I will go down next week. I intend first to go over and spend a night with Aunt Eiland.[1] Cousin Columbus spent last night with us. He is busy electioneering having come out as a candidate for the lower house.[2] Br. Henry refuses to run this year as his private business requires his attention.[3] If my health is sufficiently good, I hope to enjoy myself very much with my friends but dearest, I can not stay longer than July. No one will suffer me to speak of returning sooner than Oct., but oh my Love, I can not be seperated from you so long! I believe I would go mad! In reviewing your dear letters from Austin, I discovered your frequent promises never to leave me again. And can it be that I have left you! Yes dearest, and the sacrifice was made for yourself alone. I never could have had sufficient courage to leave you on my own account, but for your dear sake, I will try to improve my health. You did not mention in your letter that they were preparing a house for us, but I can not believe that they will suffer us to remain longer without a home. Bro. Henry and sister Serena expect to make us a visit in Oct. and I hope we will be able to entertain them at least <u>pretty comfortably</u>. They will not consent for me to return until they are ready to go with me, but I would rather be there a few weeks <u>before them</u>, not because I think you incapable of preparing the house, but because I am crazy to be with you again.

Sarah Ann is grown to be a tall elegant girl. I expect she will accompany me for my return. If Young has not set off when you get this, you must hurry him home, for his Father's business can never be straightened without his assistance.

Tuesday 24th Br. Henry drove out to bro. Royston's sabbath evening, and brought me in. Yesterday I dined with a large company of my old friends at maj. Townes's.[4] They had a splendid dinner, and besides the pleasure of meeting many whom I had known and loved long long ago, I became acquainted with an old friend of yours. Judge Phelan[5] and lady[6] were there. He was at the university at Nashville, when you were Governor of Tenn., and roomed with you and one of the Whartons in New Orleans in 1832.[7] He speaks of you in the most exalted terms and says I must tell you he is now living here at Marion, half Judge and half farmer and in the whole doing pretty well. After all the memories of the day were over, I came home and made Sarah Royston and Lucy Ann play and sing "Oh doubt not" for me, and oh my Love, I wept until my very heart seemed poured out. I am engaged to three other large dinners, so dearest, you see I am quite a lioness! I think they ought to call me the "heroine of San Jacinto!"

My Love do not ask me to stay longer that July. I do believe my heart would break for all the amusements friends may provide for me here can not cheer me when absent from you. Tell Ma that some of us will write to her this week, and please say to Antoinette when you write to her, that she may expect a letter from me very soon. Tell Mag Stone she must talk to you a great deal about me, and say pretty things of me, but not to say them too prettily! Send some message to Mrs. Andrews and Betty for me. Remember me to Capt. Black, and also to Gen. Terril, Col. Hockley, and all my good friends. Did Gen Terrill see me cry on the boat? I have not yet written to Mrs. Reily, but intend to do so very soon. Dearest do write to me very often, and do not prolong my exile beyond July.

Thy adoring wife Maggy.

Tell br. Vernal I have heard all about his conduct in relation to Miss J. D. and I consider him bound by every thing that is honourable to return and fulfil the expectations he has excited. He will never marry a finer girl or one who can be more devoted to him than she is, but I will write to him before long.

Your adoring wife
M. L. H.

[1]Gincy Moffett Eiland, sister of Nancy Lea. Madge W. Hearne Collection, San Antonio, Texas.
[2]Columbus Lea was elected to the Alabama Legislature in 1844. Owen, III, 1021.
[3]Henry Lea served in the Alabama Senate in 1839 and the House from 1847–1851. Ibid.
[4]Major S. A. Townes had toasted the couple after their marriage and called Margaret "the Conqueress of the conqueror." *Marion Herald*, May 16, 1840.
[5]Judge John Dennis Phelan. For a biography see Owen, IV, 1356.
[6]Mary Ann Harris Phelan, Ibid.
[7]John Wharton, Houston's friend from Tennessee, had a law practice in New Orleans in 1832. Wisehart, 63–64.

To Mrs. Margaret Lea Houston
Marion Alabama

City of Houston
21st May 1842

My Very Dearest,
    Since closing my last to you, Love, I have been quite ill. On my arrival at the Island[1] I went to Gail Bordens[2] office and wrote until I sunk down from exhaustion. For two nights, I had not slept only two hours in forty eight. When I sunk down, I lay on the floor of the office for an hour and slept a troubled sleep for an hour. When I

awoke, I was found to be cold to the knees and elbows. He bathed me in warm alcohol, and gave me a half wine glass to drink. I was then with much difficulty removed to Mrs Maffits[3] and placed in the south room up stairs on a comfortable mattress and suffered greatly with head ache & fever. Our blessed mother came to see me so soon as she heard of my situation, and with sorrow & anxiety sat by me until I went to sleep! But not until my feet and hands had been well bathed in "number six," and a dose of "nervine" administered! In the morning I found myself free from pain, but very weak. I remained in bed a day and a half when I arose and went to business as usual. On yesterday I came up, or [sic] we arrived here this morning. While I was confined, I was attended by my friend, Mr Crump[4] (22nd) Mother, Mrs Maffitt, Miss Tilly & Miss Henrietta.[5] So you see dearest I did not stand in need of more.—Unless, you had been there, and if you had I shou'd have been more happy, and less happy. I wou'd have seen you and heard you, but you would have suffered from anxiety, and you would have exerted yourself beyond your strength to have relieved me from suffering.

Tilly used to laugh and say to Mr Crump, if cousin Maggy saw this she would be provoked[6]—this was when she would be bathing my head with cologne for I sent and purchased a bottle and was well bathed, or my temples in it, while my lower extremities underwent the application of "number six" with equal advantage to my situation!

This moment Young, Vernal, & Bledsoe have all come to my office and left our dear Sister well at Col Morgans.[7] They say that [they] will start today, so that I must be busy, and tell you all the news that may present itself to my notice, or at least so much as I may wish to commit to paper. Don't think that this is done to excite your curiosity and induce you to return to learn the balance. Truly my Dearest, I would be happy to see you, but not until you are satisfied with your visit. Some may write or have written in despair of my health.— Well it did seem to be very bad—it was so too,—but for the want of rest I think—and repose, I could not sleep and did wish to do so!

I have had the Furniture brought up, and Smith & his wife are moving in the house today. The poultry too are up, save four sitting hens left with one sentinel! I will leave the arrangement of all matters to Mrs Smith for really I do not expect to be there three times until my Beloved Maggy returns. I will walk over to the house with

Young & the others, that he can tell you something about matters when he sees you. He must tell you most of the news, as it will not be in my power to write so long a letter as my last, and I am fearful to write too much lest I should babble and tell you too much.

We have just been over to the house to see how matters are coming on. We all thought the[m] very finely indeed. The house looks quite smart. All the furniture is not yet at home, as some of it was stored, which came up first! I do not expect that Smith will stay any longer than matters are arranged, as he wishes to live at the Island. I may move home and bring Vincy home, and get her lord to come up from the Island and wait upon me. If I do this, I will hire out Joshua, and board myself as I now think. I have seen none of your female friends for sometime in this place. Indeed I do not wish to see them much because after seeing and conversing with them about you, I do not sleep—I can not sleep. If it were possible, I would inflict a most agreeable surprize upon you! Yes, if I had the strong pinions of the Eagle, I would be with you, most surprisingly quick! Indeed I would, if it were not for the present state of affairs in Texas, I would go by the first boat. But oh! I can not go nor leave my post. I have much to say to you, or that I cou'd say if I had your ear, as well as your eye! I feel very much like leaving Texas to its fate, and with you retire to the Trinity. Young & Miller are greatly pleased with the land, and I will make such an arrangement so that Bro Royston can send the negroes if he does not move out this fall.

You will bring out Sarah Ann when you come, and she can stay until her Father moves out. You need not suppose that this is an arrangement for me to go to the army. I do not entertain any ambitions in that line. All the laurels on earth will not give sweet peace of mind and hope of a happy immortality to an expiring Hero! The shout of victory may be pleasant to the ear of one who feels conscious that he falls in his country's cause and has achieved a Glorious work. This tho' will not insure a happy eternity—nor insure the favor of the Eternal God! This I would prefer to all the gewgaws of that poor existence! It is only enriched by my associations with you, my dearest Love. Truly nothing else can give me felicity nor do I ever expect to see or enjoy an hour of happiness unless you are embraced within the compass of my thoughts. Of this tho' more when we meet! I must not write "love letters," or you would feel being in Alabama, that I was really courting, and that we were not married!

Therefore you wou'd not come to Texas, but stay until I wou'd go for you, lest someone should say that you had come after me! This wou'd be a dreadful mistake! My dear, You can come and may be assured that no one dare say a word on that subject. I will be responsible. I treat Bledsoe kindly! Sister will stay at the Island some weeks and 'tis possible that Mother & her will come up to see me, and I will try and get them to stay with me until you can come home! I feel pretty well, and hope that I will have no more sickness this season! My mouth and nose are broken out! My lips swollen, and all very sore! Of course, I do not look <u>vastly</u> pretty! I will write to sister Eliza [Houston Moore], and know if they can, and when they will move out. I wish them to settle on Trinity, and I yet fondly hope to enjoy some repose and society. I doubt not Love but what we will settle there if we live. I have come to this conclusion, with a hope that you will there enjoy your health there [sic] better than any where else in Texas. These tho' are matters in which you will have a say so, nor will, nor need I resolve until I can again talk to my dearest Maggy.

It will not be in the range of my power to write you as long a letter as I did by the New York. That was out of all consideration. You could not otherwise than think so. I do not expect to be at Galveston until I can hope to meet you there. I certainly am by no means happy there nor am I very happy here! This is Sunday and Smith drunk so that I have trouble on my hands, and my business is most pressing. These thing will all pass off! Young can tell you all that I have not written!

People may write to you that my health has been worse than what it really was, and say that I am worse than what I am! Truly I am feeble, tho' I think clear of disease. I took no medicine while sick, as I do not love physic!

It might be too late for you to stay until the last of July unless you should wish, or deem it needful for your health to stay until November next. I intend upon mature reflection and urged by the crisis to call the Congress together in June, tho' I have not issued my proclamation to that effect. I think that I will do so in a few days.

My Cabinet are all with me but Col [William Henry] Dangerfield & he was here since you left, but went back by N.Y. on business. Come when you will, my Dearest. By all means bring with you our dear Niece Sarah Ann & Bob, or whom you wish. I will write my Love, as often as I can, and a little more than will be interesting!

I pray God for your health and happiness. Present me kindly to my male relations and friends.—Then embrace with a kiss all my dear Aunts, Sisters, and cousins, and nieces.

Thy devoted Husband
Houston

Margaret
I have not examined and corrected this letter

Thine, Houston

[1]Galveston.

[2]Gail Borden was a surveyor, inventor, and agent for the Galveston City Company. For a biography see *Writings*, IV, 147n.

[3]The boarding house of Mrs. John Newland Maffit (also spelled Moffitt and Mofitte). Brooks, 22.

[4]William R. Crump, Acting Secretary of the Treasury. See Houston to William C. Crump, May 17, 1842, *Writings*, IV, 54–55.

[5]Matilda (Tilly) and Henrietta, twin daughters of Mrs. Maffit. Brooks, 22.

[6]The Maffits were apparently kin to Nancy Lea, but no documentation has been found to explain the relationship.

[7]James Morgan.

To Mrs. Houston
Marion Alabama
Mr Y. L. Royston

City of Houston
22nd May 1841

Dearest,

The Boat has declined going this day & as some thing may occur and I have a piece of poetry to enclose to you, I send you a brand new letter. I believe all the land matters are settled. I was right in supposing that Bud controlled the first arrangement about Trinity and the Point.[1] I am satisfied with matters as they now are because I think you would not be healthy at Cedar Point, and that with me is a <u>desideratum</u>! I have had a thought that I would propose the sale of my <u>point land</u> and "live upon it" in that way. We need a little cash in our family, and I will have it. It can be obtained honestly. I am weary of being needy! It is too bad!!!

23rd

No news Love. The time will not allow me to write more. Young can tell you all—I can only say how much I love you. I am the most anxious being on earth to see you! I can only say my regards to all, and to you my Love,

Farewell,
Thy devoted
Houston

Mrs. Houston

[1]Vernal Lea had decided to settle on the Trinity near Grand Cane, despite Houston's urgings to choose Cedar Point.

To Mrs Sam Houston
Marion Alabama

City of Houston
24th May 1842

Dearest Love,

When I will be able to close and send this letter I can not guess, but doubtless by the N York, on its return. That will be at least one week from this time. On Sunday Young, Vernal, & Bledsoe were here, and I did not ride out in the country to Capt [John S.] Blacks, and read the scriptures. Last evening I rode out with Doctor Jones[1] and today rode in about eleven o clock. Soon after I arrived there I went sound asleep on a chair, but being hungry, I did not retire until I eat [sic] supper. I again took a short nap on a chair, retired, and oh! how I did sleep until 7 AM. A thing not known to my habits. You see if you remain away, that a revolution will be the consequence. I only mean as my habits of business, but not in my affections! No Dearest, that can not, could not be. You are the only shrine at which I can make my offerings on earth. Tho' I am free to confess that my meditations of you are often diverted to the least amusing of all matters, say politicks. Yes my own Love, I have to look to them, and in accordance with what I deem important. I have ordered Congress to convene on the 27th of June.[2] This is not done to bring you home Love, but to see if they will do any good, and if not to saddle them with their own sins and short comings. This will take place before the Troops of Texas men need be in the field. So you see, I am right, as the Congress will have a say on the matters, and it will have no influence from the Rendezvous of the Emigrants from the States which takes place one month after [blurred]. The Proclamation has gone out to day, and I will send you a paper containing it on the first opportunity.[3] I will feel lonesome until I see you, and the more so as poverty will draw me home. I have ordered Vincy in from Captain Blacks, and expect her & Joshua to cook for me! You will pity me, but you need not for you know how little I care about good eating, and as for drinking—the water is fine. To be sure, if you happened to come home, I would not be angry with you my Love. For that would be ungentle and uncivil too. Well! You may come when you please! I will cry contently [sic].

To day I don't know what else to write other than to tell you that the Seditious gentlemen at Corpus Christi are quieted by Genl [James] Davis. This event has not met [George] Hockleys wishes and mine! 'Tis strange that no one, out of my sight, can obey plain and positive orders, but must disobey <u>them</u>, but they <u>think</u> it best and so destroy all my plans! This is not intended for your case Dearest, tho' you say that you will never accept another appointment which will remove you from me! Love I will never tender you another, tho you are the only one who has shone [sic] a disposition to obey orders, until you cou'd apply for a modification of this or a change of import! Oh! if I could only see you! Dearest I have a world of civil things to tell you of. They will all amuse you or interest you in some way. I have seen no Ladies, so I can't say any thing to you of them, or the little scandals which may chance to be afloat in the land or more properly in the city. I will close for to day by telling you that Mr. Tankersley[4] had a severe fist fight to day with the keeper of a Livery Stable, and I am told fought <u>very well</u> and tho the other had a stick and struck him repeatedly, he was near flogging him tho he was deemed very stout & a fighter.

And more you may say to Sarah Ann that [Thomas] Bagby has his genteel person stretched on a sofa near to me at this moment and I tell him if he does not have our lot <u>paled</u> in two days that he shall not have her if he is "silly" enough to fall in love with her when she comes to Houston. So I will not embarrass her by any promise of mine. She shall have a fair promise of all here if she does not leave

Alabama engaged! but if she does, I will not, you know, encourage any <u>flirtations</u>! You know that I married once on purpose to break up the practice—at least you are aware that I tell you so, tho you pretend to deny the fact! Well! I will give it up if you say so! Almost any thing to keep peace my Dear! Only come home, and we will arrange all other difficulties. When you come, I hope to have peace with the world, and then we will have more leisure to quarrel, if we chuse to do so. Which probably we will <u>not</u> chuse!!!

25th Last night, Genl Terrell, Dr Jones, Genl Hunt & myself went out to Captain Blacks. The exercise was of great advantage to my health. Tho I do not think I will have time to ride often to the country, tho Doct Jones desires that I should do so on the grounds that it restores my complexion and renders me more cheerful, and indeed increases my capacity for business. All of these things are important, but as I attribute it to repose, my improvements I think I can obtain that at our house! At least I must make the trial! I will have some one to stay with me—Miller or Jeff Wright I presume.

We will as I suppose live rather badly until—I was going to say until you returned, and if I had, I should be apprehensive that you would think it a hint to leave in a hurry! I do feel very lonesome, I assure you—nor would you believe me if I were to say, nay ever swear that I did not. By this I mean to say that you wou'd suppose I thought so, but was mistaken! I feel like a <u>very young personage</u> that told me of, I think, a little niece of yours which had been absent for some weeks from its mama. Were you to return, tho your absence seems an age, all my recollections would return and I should feel that time and space which now exist to a painful extent would be annihilated by the pleasure of our embrace to bid you to my lonely spirit! You are the only being on earth who can respond to soul & thought and make me happy!

I would not for worlds, that you cou'd or wou'd think me selfish. I do not think that I am so only in this that I intend to regard our happiness so far as not to be the slave of my country, & toil in hopelessness and despair. I have sought to exalt and bless my country, but it will not be blessed. My heart sickens at this prospect, and now some thing must be done! "Nous Verrons!" I must now to work until night! I learn the Neptune has sailed!

Dearest, This morning I returned from a visit of four days to Col Morgans while my health visibly improved. I read nearly all my time, and [ate] very little. I was kindly treated and the Col and my-self occupied the two largest chairs on the porch! To Day I would go to church, but I slept none last night on the Boat and must sleep to day, but intend to read the Scriptures this evening. On board the Boat were several Santa Fe prisoners, who had escaped from prison, and made their way home. I was interested in the details which they gave me of matters!

Dearest you will see that I have mended my pen and resumed the pleasure of writing to you. I had laid aside the sheet and was reflecting, or rather I was meditating upon the future when my friend Miller began teasing me about the conquest of Mexico. I told him that I would not undertake it in person for no consideration! He then said that he would give up all hope of success! I said would you have me to send Mrs Houston to her relations or to a Convent until I should conquer Mexico! Yes, said he, I would just have you to do so and say to her if you please, that is just what I would wish you to do from my heart! So you see my dear, I will have conflicting opinions as to my course to be pursued! About this matter you and I must have something to say. You may think better of the idea of such a course on your return to Texas. Until then I will give no pledge of committal in favor of such an exile—To be seperated from you even for a little season is a melancholy exile!!! My heart is desolated and indeed I find my heart a dreary wilderness!

Memory passes over it, but not to cheer the gloom and add cheerfulness to hope, but it recurs to what was boundless felicity and then points association to my present cheerless condition! You mention Love, the month of October, and the springs for a summer visit. The month of October is the month of yellow fever in Mobile and New Orleans. If you should conclude to stay until then, I would by all means advise your stay until the month of November. If you will be happy Dearest, or contented and wish to pass the summer at any springs either for health or recreation, by all means do so! You will find by former letters from me that you can come home just when you please. And that my arms and heart will all embrace you and strain you to my bosom.

I say <u>home</u> for I can tell you that I called at our cottage before I went to Col Morgans and you would be truly delighted if you could see the neat and tasty arrangement of our house. The matting on the floor so clean and every thing adjusted in pretty style—A place too for the Piano. The round table[5] and in short every thing are fast. Even the bed chamber invites to repose! I looked in that present loneliness. I looked in, but left in company with Mr Crump and have not returned since. Joshua tells me that Vincy has come to town and is there. I have not yet resolved whether I will board at home or not until your return. One reason Love, why I suggested to you the month of June, if you should wish to return soon was that storms are less frequent, or rather that they rarely happen in that month, whereas they are more frequent in July and August. Happy, nay as extatic [sic] as would be my delight at your return, I wish you to understand that I am not urging your return if it were even possible that it could abridge your enjoyments! It may be selfishness in me, but I confess (tho' some might deem it hyperbole) that tho' I could look forward for the thousand years to such happiness as we have enjoyed, that I would only regard it as a single day! Such is my estimate of chaste & virtuous love. Love such as received and such as I give! Virtue and piety alone can render us association in Eternity!! Religion (the religion of Jesus Christ our blessed Savior) is all that can reunite us in the society of the pure spirits who have been redeemed thro the atonement of our blessed and adorable Savior! Dearest, I do feel as tho' I would not, could not survive unless I have some hope in the atonement of the son of God. I am assured that tho' I admit the awful realities of eternal life and eternal death, yet I do not realise that confident & abiding hope that I will be accepted of my God & thru His death be happy hereafter! One consolation to me is my Beloved, that I am communing with a being on earth who will not ridicule my expressions or withhold the kind sympathies of a Christian believer in Christ Jesus! I will try and meditate upon His Holy and Divine character, His boundless and almighty love for mortals, His wise and sacred precepts. Yes, the soothing influence of his mild and holy and spotless example!

Dearest, I would be truly happy on earth while in the possession of your love, and confidence if I could only feel assured that I possessed the favor of my God into everlasting life! I will seek the redemption promised in the Holy Scriptures. 'Tis all that I can do.— For I know that death will come and after death the judgment. I know that if I obtain pardon from God, I must not faint by the way! I must persevere in well doing. I must atone for I have passed much of my life, if not in crime, at least in carelessness and a disregard of that circumspection which would have directed my mind and feelings to a holy walk and a Godly conversation. But instead of this, I have blasphemed with my lips and levity has usurped the place of contemplation and calm reflection. I know Dearest that I have your prayers daily and hourly and to them I will add and renew mine. But every hope is vain unless Jesus will interpose in my behalf!

Dearest, If I could only see you and converse with you, I would feel some solace in my present state of mind. I would realise more of hope in a happy change from death into life. No one do I converse with and indeed, I do not wish to do so. One reason is that I am somewhat fearful lest I might begin to argue with them and become excited so far as to blind my reason and become diverted from my search after truth and holiness—and thusly defeat the very object which I wish to attain. An entire submission to Christ and obtain his forgiveness. I hope my Beloved, that we will yet live to see the day when I shall enjoy the delightful influence of true and Evangelical Religion. I feel that I am now in the presence of a God who might be justly incensed at me as a rebel against his holy Land. At the same moment, I am assured the He is a God of boundless mercy! I am fearful that you will not easily understand me! But I am confident if it is so, that you will readily bear with me, and would soothe me, were you here!

Do not my Dearest reflect on yourself that you are not with me. You ought to be just where you are for you wished and it was my earnest desire. Therefore feel no unhappiness!

When you may desire and are here, then my bosom will swell with grateful emotions to Heaven and boundless affection for you. Do not my Love suppose that your presence is necessary to inspire such feelings. They are always cherished by me. At times it does appear to me that I can not exist without you and I reflect so intensely that I really feel quite stupid and a deadness seizes upon my senses until I am aroused, by some circumstance which says to me, "awake from your reverie."

I awake, but I am alone in society. My Wife, My Love, my Friend, is not here! How can I be happy? I am not. I would not send this letter, only I feel a presentiment from your letter written at Mobile[6] and the tenour [sic] of my several letters that you will wish to come home soon. I have thought that I never would write my feelings— when they might create unhappiness in others. But often as I come to this conclusion, I am sure to violate it. Had I not before been able to sympathise with you when you used to write to me when absent from you! I would now be quite competent. I never loved Marion much, tho' I thought it quite a pretty village—I can assure you that when the declining sun casts its rays eastward I fancy how lovely Marion must appear! This is by association, for I fancy that you are dwelling upon some scene and blending with its recollections of Texas & Sommerville.[7] I view with rapture our favorite star.[8] It is still the star of affection to me, for it seems to grow more bright and beautiful with time. It is the pure emblem of our affection. It is the Banner of our nation, I hope the one will shine throughout Eternity while the other will only survive with things temporal!

30th May. My Love, Monday has come again, and I have resumed my chair in the office more & more satisfied that I can never be happy whilst you are absent. I am in office—Unless I can enjoy private life, and your society not subject to caprices. I will not, can not be happy! Had I not often shown a disposition and wish of this character, I wou'd now suspect some what that I was influenced by my great anxiety to see you and be with you. What I say is "good earnest" and I will adhere to it, if not in practice, I will in principle and de-sire!

Dearest, the Gray horse has gone, but had I suspected what you tell me, I would never have parted from him. Say so to dear gener-ous brother. I pray you my Love to render to our brother Henry every assurance of my sincere regrets and thank him kindly for his presents. Previous to any knowledge of the fact, I had sent to Cor-pus Christi for a splendid Mexican blanket to present to him, when-ever I could send it safely, and one for my dear Maggy to make a Piano cover.

You may quarrel about this if you will, but I really intend to all that I say at present. Whether I will bring the Piano until you come home, or not, I am not positively determined. If you do not return and send me word what you wish done, I will obey you.

I hope you will be resolved to bring Sarah Ann with you. Tell her Mr Bagby is very anxious to see her, and so am I. For many reasons do I wish to see her, but one will suffice to state and that is that you will be with her when she does come! Dearest, You make me unhappy when you speak of the sickness of Marion. Do Dearest, not stay there if you apprehend sickness. I would become mad if I heard of your sickness. Love unless I could be with you, my heart wou'd break with anguish. We ought never in life to part again. I will not be accessary to our seperation again. I was so once. I have repented. But it was right. You have seen your dear relations and I have nearly sunk under official duties! They are more light than formerly and my complexion improves, but I am like the lean kind of Pharaoh, the King of Egypt! Say to Young that he may be satisfied that he shall have just such land as he may wish, and to come on. I have written to Sublett,[9] but no odds he must come and shall be suited, whether Sublett wills it or not for I have my interest there and Young or his father shall be suited. Vernal was huffed at me. He had said that he wanted only 450 acres, and he had taken 800, and some odd acres, and so much front that our leagues would not give front on the river to three settlements. I advised him to let Young have the place which he had selected and take the balance of the front of one league. I was sorry, but Vernal has been so badly petted that he really thinks every one is bound to nurse or pet him. I love him, but I love others of my dear kinsfolk equally well who have more on their hands. When I was a single man, I would have given up a place to kin [the words "a brother in law" are written above the line here] if I had . . . [illegible] but one on earth! Dearest, I only live for you and my relations. For my country I have done enough and I will not long try to save it unless I am sustained "To [blurred] to muse."

Upon the gathering ills we see! So I will seek rational enjoyment and to such things as will not need to be repented of!

On last evening with several Gentlemen, I walked up to our house & had you been there it would have been truly delightful. I returned by Col Andrews and presented you as directed to all, but love to Madam & Miss Betty. I did not sit for tea, but came by Mrs Grays[10] and gave Miss Mag your Love and told her what you said. She was very much pleased and I have but little doubt if she thought I would be a widower soon that she would discard every one of her Beaux—tho Major Nichols[11] who was present did not look as if he thought so! I hope you will soon see her and then you can ascertain the fact. I don't think she would wish a chance and discard her beaux for she seems devoted to you and it may be on your account entirely that she treats me kindly or as my attentions are so rare to Ladies only having been to two houses twice in the place since you left me, she may suppose that my attentions to her would be construed into an impression of very fair taste. You can best judge the cause! But she says that she does love you and would be rejoiced again to look into your sweet face! Guess how I would feel when Mag could feel joy at such an event! I would be much the happier of the two! I wish to see my dear Wife and Mag to have a clever husband. This is all as it should Be! Don't <u>you</u> think so!

My Love, I wrote to Mother and Sister so soon as I read your letter and told them about Marion and the kinsfolk. I wrote to Mother about Aunt Leas depression of spirits, and that you and sister Royston intended to visit her soon! To Day I suppose Young will reach home! You will then git [sic] a reasonably short Epistle! If it were possible, I declare to you that I would forthwith set out for Alabama. Yes, by the New York. I would go and see you! But my Dear, this gives but a faint idea of my anxiety to know that you are well and again to embrace you to my heart! But I can not leave Texas at present! I must not do it! 'Tis vain to think of it. For a while, I will yet make sacrifices to my country! But I do assure you that I will not again sacrifice our happiness by holding office or performing services which can make me no return, but abuse & slander. Look at 28th page.

My Love, How many "long yarns" will I have to spin before I can see you? Do you suppose? I hope not many!

Genl Hardin[12] has just been in to see me and to make kind inquiries about you! He says all the manuscripts are made out, but he forgot them! I believe it. He is anxious that you should have them all! I really did want the "Vision Muse" to send you for our friends. It would beat the muse of the "Cane Brake" hollerer. I wish Columbus had it. It is truly rich, and would wear well! It treats Byron smartly! The Dayton[13] is looked for to night, so I must think of closing this interesting letter.—I feel confident that it will be so to you when you look at it, and think that you have to read the whole letter. Our friend [Thomas] Western says that I should have crossed this with red ink.[14] I think so likewise. Don't you my Dear?

31st May. Good morning my Dear! That seems so familiar and yet so agreeable that I do really almost fancy that I hear a response. But no, it is not so. You are not here! I am alone. You are far away! My Love, when will you be here? But I need not ask! You will be here when you can, and then I will be happy. I will throw away the cares of life if possible, and see you, and be with you, and you only. Oh, but I will be selfish! I will afford Mr Morris[15] reason to condemn me again for my devotion to you!

I am so solitary at times that my mind recurs to my exile in other days, for I have no one to sustain me and solace me in my moments of rest and my reflections will ever recur to my Beloved.—These now I likened in my feelings to days of desolation of heart, when I felt that a world condemned me, and I stood along in the midst of it too proud to receive pity, and too manly to indulge hate! The clouds passed off and my star again appeared at Sommerville and has been bright and pointed me to happiness since that time.

I hope my dear that you have had much enjoyment with your dear Friends and Relations. I would regret that my situation should be a serious drawback upon your happiness. I am fearful that Major Woods told the fact of my serious indispositions. I swore him to secrecy on his departure and bound him not to mention my health or to say it was good, tho' I was fearfully indisposed. Now I am quite well—but you will see that by the length of my letter. The reason why I fear the Major Wood or Daingerfield told I was very ill, friends in Orleans wrote to me letters of condolence & sorrow with prayers for my recovery. All in Texas who love Texas, I believe, wish the restoration of your health and a speedy return. Embrace all our Female relatives & my salutations of regard to the men and Boys for me. Bring Sarah Ann with you, as you may be at times lonesome when I can not be with you!

Thy ever devoted Husband
Houston

Margaret

¹It is unclear whether Houston is referring to Dr. Anson Jones or Dr. Levi Jones.
²For Houston's written orders see *Writings*, III, 58.
³Ibid., 59.
⁴Benjamin F. Tankersley, a Houston lawyer. For a biography see *Writings*, IV, 133n.
⁵Houston describes this table as the only relic of his first administration. See Houston to Margaret, September 1, 1843.

[6]See Margaret to Houston, May 8, 1842.

[7]The home of Martin Lea where Houston first met Margaret.

[8]For an explanation of the significance of this star see Roberts, *Star of Destiny*, 19.

[9]Phillip Sublett of San Augustine.

[10]Millie Stone Gray.

[11]Ebenezer B. Nichols. He and Margaret Stone would marry August 7, 1842. Grammer, 36.

[12]Houston may be referring to Franklin Hardin of Liberty.

[13]The steamship Dayton ran between Houston and Galveston. Hogan, *The Texas Republic*, 72.

[14]Houston is referring to the fact that he was now writing across the first pages of his letter.

[15]Houston may be referring to Richard Morris of Galveston. Identified in *Compiled Index to Elected and Appointed Officials of the Republic of Texas*, 86.

Mrs Margaret Lea Houston
Marion
Alabama

31st May [1842]

Dearest,

To you Mr Teulon[1] sent from N. York city by our Consul[2] five numbers of the Musical Library of Ladies. It is a pretty present, and will be taken great care of for you! as it is to you. Mr [Alexander] McDonald & Miss Margaret Roberts are to marry on the 15th Inst at Mr Dantroys, and I am invited to the wedding. Were you here we wou'd go, I suppose! As it is, I will not!

1st June

My Love, I have not seen Captain Wright,[3] and of course I have said nothing! When you return, I would rather that you should come on his Boat, altho' he has acted badly. This is a matter that I will leave to your wishes. Love, when will you come? Oh, How very, yes, inexpressibly anxious I am to hear from you on the arrival of every Boat, and anxious for their arrival!

From my letters and their unmerciful lines, you will suppose or might suppose that I thought of nothing but my dear Maggy. If I had my wish, I would think of but little else earthly! But you know I must not write "love letters." If I do, you will begin to talk of matrimony, and that you know will make some people blush. It sounds like "a bride" only three months married! Did you ever hear of this before, my Love? If I recollect you were present on one occasion when it was discussed, or <u>barely</u> mentioned. This is a matter to be <u>settled</u> at our meeting.

The Dayton is to start in a few hours, and I must close. <u>Draw on me for what money you may desire</u>. Dearest I wish you to have every thing that you may wish. My Love to all our kin. Mr Norwood (of Mr. Dawson)[4] has this moment told me that Miss Virginia Tenant, a Belle of Baltimore, has sent to you by him a very beautiful silk dress which will be presented to you on your return. It is a new kind of silk, not before seen in Baltimore. In return I requested Mr. Norwood to kiss the young Lady for us! as an acknowledgement of its <u>acceptance and very agreeable character</u>!!!

My heart <u>embraces</u> you with an <u>affectionate</u> Farewell.

Thy ever devoted
Houston

To Mrs Margaret of Texas!
PS I am quite well, thank my God!

Houston

Oh present me particularly to Dr Fletcher and lady, and say I will write soon.

[1]George K. Teulon was the editor of the *Austin City and State Gazette*. For a biography see *Writings,* III, 532n and Joseph Milton Nance, *After San Jacinto,* (Austin: University of Texas Press, 1963), 299. Teulon describes the gifts as "a musical magazine and 'Ladies Companion' packet workbox." See Teulon to Houston, June 25, 1842, Sam Houston Papers, Catholic Archives of Texas, Austin, Texas.
[2]John H. Brower was the Texas consul at New York City. For a biography see*Writings,* IV, 164n.
[3]Captain of the steamship New York.
[4]Frederick Dawson, a naval contractor of Baltimore, Maryland, was a great help to Texas following the revolution. Mr. Norwood was probably one of his representatives. For a biography see *Writings,* II, 454–55n.

In spite of Houston's instructions concerning the equipment needed by volunteers, unequipped soldiers from the United States flocked to Texas.

Problems arose when the troops complained of hard conditions and poor rations and on occasions refused to obey orders. Houston wrote Margaret of the political climate in Texas at this time and of his fears that he would have to take control of the army.

City of Houston
3rd June 1842

My Dearest,

'Tis but a little while since I closed my last (short note) to you, and now it appears to be an age almost! I will quit complaining to myself of my solitary feelings, for I find it is of no use to me! The truth is I must be miserable until you may return. I wou'd not be so plaintive in my letter if I did not feel that you would wish to return by the time that it can reach you! The withdrawal of my orders not to return until the last of July left you free to return so soon as you may deem fit & proper! I never felt alone on the earth before, nor can I look to any event which will relieve me from my sad and depressed feelings until you return. Heretofore I could look to some event that would promise me some satisfactions or I was absorbed in business. The want of your presence has taken every resource from me. Again, I had never considered you an identical & important part of myself. That is not so much as I now do!

One thing which distresses me to some extent is the fact that it may, and I am fearful it will become necessary for me to go to the army and assume command. If such should be the case my Love, you will be capable of appreciating my deep and inexpressible anguish of feeling, as well as my honor. If fortunate, I will be absent for a length of time, and if unfortunate I will never expect to return. It can not be expected that I would (under any circumstances) have to leave you before the 15th of August or the 1st of September. Nothing can induce me to leave you short of the necessity of Salvation to my country. The joy—the happiness which your society affords me is <u>worth</u> all the <u>plaudits</u> of the world or all that I ever have, or ever could receive. With you, I enjoy the souls calm sunshine and unbounded happiness. Did you not exist to render me happy, I feel satisfied that I would again return to Exile or would, for life embrace again the profession of arms! 'Tis painful to be solitary & alone. All around me seem to have their minds filled with business, and are cheerful enough, but I am sure, they have no idea of my feelings.

There is unsatisfied and constant agitation of my heart. At times my brain burns with thought most intense, and all most maddening. I fancy that you are pining in sickness and calling upon me to bathe your scorching temples. <u>My dreams of you are constant</u>! I can not go to see you. If it were possible, I would do so! <u>Public duty</u> is all that prevents me from flying to you.

You can not think me trifling nor insincere, and pray do not suppose me capricious or weak & silly. The subject of my anxiety, if possible, has been increased by my writing so much to you. I wrote too much, and I am sure you be weary of perusing my long and (I do verily think) tedious epistles!

Doct Anson Jones has just been in my office and assures me that I will be called on to take the command of the army, if I will consent to do so. He thinks Congress will, and if it does not, that the people will. As to the latter, I have no doubt & the former may.

In the villages, the people are growing rather quiet, and in the country my popularity is greater, in my opinion, than it ever has been! The workers of inequity are fast finding their level in the abyss of contempt! They are regarded very much as the discord. Love,[1] and his corps among whom I class Mr Walton[2] of Galveston are very lamb-like. I will take the fleece off some of them, and let them run at large!

Times are so hard here that I really do believe the good people are satisfied that, while the glow of their patriotism was up, they have done enough for the whole war. The valiant loafers find that they will not have the pleasure of riding "pressed horses" and hence they are right smartly disgusted with the policy of the President in war matters!

I believe we will have a very good turn out to the call of Government!—Upwards of 3,500 men of Texas will be called by the first requisition! After that as circumstances may require! So long as War wears the charms of novelty, and the cheerfulness of a frolic, Oh it is most charming, but when it assumes its iron visage, it is most ungainly in appearance! The fatigue of the march, the inclemencies of the season, the vigilance of sentryship, the crises of the wounded, and the full onset of battle are such ungentlemanly circumstances that most men of fashionable laziness view them with real disgust! I say "real" for I feel satisfied there is no prudish affectation in the business.

Well Dearest, I do hope we will see how all these matters will terminate. But as to their termination, it must all come out right. We have entered in the race and we have appeald [sic] to "wager of battle"—We must remember that "the race is neither to the swift nor the battle to the strong." The Mexicans have sown the wind and they shall reap the whirlwind! They have forced us to war. We will compel them to peace! I have no fears as to our ultimate success, but my Love, I do not anticipate its termination short some disasters. Were I to commence and conduct the invasion, I should dread none, I assure you! Insubordination and pillage are what we have to guard against. The latter will irritate the inhabitants, & the former, after having led to the latter, will expose the soldiering to the fury of the people and effects of their despair. One or two examples in the out-set would prevent all these evils.—But I fear they must happen be-fore our troops will learn wisdom. I will direct every precaution, nor will I feel tranquil until I know of the first action of the cam-paign. If it is fortunate, I will be happy, and if it is not so, I must find a remedy. We must & we will conquer! The inferiority of our means will only illustrate the Glory of successful appeal to arms! After times will present the fairest complexion of events which the clouds of hatred & malignity have sought to cast around the present and the past!

With such a Congress, under such circumstances, no nation or community ever had such a task before to accomplish. Yet it will be for good, and not for evil.

Were you here my Love, I could talk with you upon these sub-jects freely & fully we could enjoy a communion which I find not in my power to do while you are absent. My Cabinet are much en-gaged and when I am with its members, 'tis on especial business. With you, I cou'd freely converse every day. I could command hours of leisure to be with you, and at least would be happy! You should if I could render you so my dearest Love.

While I am writing my friend Miller is at the opposite side of the table recording in a beautiful volume my official communications since I came into office.[3] At every leisure moment his mind is fixed on war, and he contemplates identity with me in the conquest of the Palaces of the Montezumas and many Grand Feates [sic]. You may say to Sarah Ann that there is no hopes of catching him until the war is at an end!

My Love, you & Mr Miller are to quarrel so soon as you get home, or you are to surrender your command of me (as you know the world says you have it completely!) I will be a mere passive agent, but if I were to consult my wishes before you and my blessed God, I would prefer with you domestic quiet—with my friends, my farm, my stock of fine blooded animals and pretty poultry. With these comforts, while your dear society gave zest to every thing, I would be happy. Yes, more happy than if I had conquered and made millions miserable! Let us hope for rural quiet and the serenity which is the companion of pious souls on earth! Dearest, I do wish you would give me your calm and solemn opinion as to my commanding in the approaching invasion. This request is made upon the supposition that you may not return until the last of July. I can not have too much to reflect upon. It gives me relief to have great variety of Subjects! I wish to know something from you while absent on this important matter. 'Tis one of deep interest. To be sure I hope kind Heaven will grant us many interviews before such could be the case, but I should like to know what you think while Texas is far from you, or at least, none of its perplexities can influence your decision! Mr. Miller feels so strong upon the approaching state of things, and to grant relief to his enthusiastic feelings, I have requested him to write to you upon the subject of my service! This is done upon the condition that I am not to see, nor hear his letter. This bargain is made to last until you return, when we are to compare his views with those of my own! I need not say to you what my wishes are, but I wish you, if you should not soon return, to answer his letter. 'Tis true the crises is one of moment to Texas. It must influence her future destiny!

All these matters, I present to you, and why I can't say, only that I love you & wish you to know everything! But I can not make a business <u>confession</u> unless I am to say some civil thing. You will suppose that I am trying to write "love letters!" And you know that I would not venture such a thing for any trifling consideration. 'Tis true, I some times feel as tho' I were very much in love, you know it has been said that love lasts until matrimony has succeeded to courtship. You do not say this, but some do! In writing letters, what do you think of a page and a half? If two of my letters were to arrive at about the same time, I am sure you wou'd become a proselyte to the Doctrine of short letters! No matter! I will write as much as I please.

You are not bound to read more of it than you may chuse!

I think the world of your <u>pretty little letters</u>! and almost devour the paper on which they are written! I kiss them and the tear of affection blinds my vision. You are the light of my path, and the sunshine of my hopes! or rather you are the star of my existence. You lend light to my Hopes as "the bright star of Sommerville" gave lustre to <u>our</u> western horizon! In Texas we have again gazed upon its sweet brilliance. May it long shine in its peerless purity, and render bright the twilight of life's evening. But my Dearest, I am becoming rather too poetic! So I will "make a smash" of all my fine fancies. You can judge how much I have provoked my charming muse. She will forgive me when it is understood that I am just about to ride out to Capt Blacks with Doct Jones and & Col Hockley! More when I return!

5th day of June

On yesterday, my Love we returned from Captain Black's, and throughout the day I was engaged and when evening closed, I went to see poor Moreland.[4] He is fast sinking under consumption, and it is believed that he can only last a few days, or perhaps a very few hours. Judge Scott,[5] who had lain for the last three years from the effect of a fall from a horse[,] deceased yesterday and will be interred today at 11 o clock. Today we have no Preaching in Town. I will read the scriptures and hope to derive some benefit from meditation. Their precepts will teach us how to live and how to die! Since Thursday, no Boat has been here since Thursday last, and one has been, & is hourly expected. For the convenience of reading, I have concluded to cross this with red ink. But about the Boats, I have had some faint hope that you might come by the next. Not, my Love, that I expect you, but that I would be so perfectly happy. You know that we often desire that a thing might so happen when we have no reasonable grounds to expect that it will do so! Indeed I am very lonely! Last night Mr Bagby & myself, after ten oclock walked out in the Prairie. Thinking of you, I could not rest, but my spirit became weary. Today again I am sad, and my mind is so solitary for the want of converse with you that in the fullness of my affection for you, I am miserable! For all this, pray do not suppose that I reflect only you. Oh no, Dearest, it is myself. I am the one who bears all the censure, if any there is to be born. I thought your absence was needful for your health, and that I might with greater facility perform my duties. Unexpectedly they have been much lightened, and in proportion to my exemption from business my anxiety increases. At times I feel wild as the day of my exile! Every thing around me cloys, and I will not, can not, have recourse to the society of Ladies. Were I to do so, I would only [blurred] them more and more unhappy. They would only have a tendency to assure me more vividly of my situation, and with all your fondness for the monopoly of my affections, I am sure if you could read my thoughts as they arise and exist, you would wish me on my own never to love you less than what I do! Dearest! You may conjecture how much I do love you, but I am sure that you will not realise the painful throws [sic] of my anxiety to embrace you again and pour out the full measure of my love with the full throbbing of my heart. But Dearest, Hope will not bring you to my bosom. It will only render tedious the hours of absence.

If it would not cast too great an effort I might try to think less about you, but as it is, I must yield to the superior influence of love. I indulge in expectation that you will be home by the 15th or at the farthest the 25th of this month. If you should not be, I will not answer for my forthcoming. Not Dearest, that I will violate my policy and go to the army unless you should stay much longer than I can anticipate at this time! But what I mean is that I should run away to the wilderness so as to avoid the trouble of society when I can feel none of its joys. Could you experience but an hour of my solicitude, I am sure you would wonder that I could endure it. There is no means by which I can avoid my situation. You have all and every thing but my presence to induce your stay in Marion. I am compelled to stay here unless I resign & leave my country without hope or prospect. I must stand at my post until your presence can relieve me! Hours, days, months and years have passed by me and the oppressive hands of care and ever deep afflictions seem to glide more rapidly than my present hours and days and nights. They are, in truth, hours of sadness.

The world has calmed down into repose since the still silence of creation is hushed into noiseless quiet and to rest. Yet I can not rest. My heart is with you, and I sigh for the joys of your companionship! If I am in the midst of society, I am alone and my thoughts have no community with the beings around me. How long I will be enabled to endure this state of feeling, I will not pretend to say, but lest you should think me deranged, I must cease to complain.

Had I wished you to return before you were ready, I would, or rather should, have informed you, but <u>I was very happy and did not wish you to return.</u> Don't you think my Dear, that this would have brought you home? I think it would! You would have been curious to know from what cause I could be happy, and my Dear Maggy absent. This would be a delicate question, particularly to your feelings, for as you have often told me that you did not wish me to be too happy when you were not present! You need entertain no fears on this subject, I can assure you. I have concluded after this letter to write no more "love letters" but merely those of a business cast. Then you will have less to reflect about and more time to fancy what I could have written. I have written you so much love in my letters that it will, or would become trite to you if I were to continue reiterated declaration and you might question my sincerity. Tho' if you could only visit Texas at this time you might again assume the Bride! My dear Love, I did not think to ask you home to see me. If Kind Heaven spare me to meet the Congress on the 24th of June, I do wish you could be home at that time.[6] It might be another great moment to me & to the nation!! You are assured that you are a very important personage and so regarded as having a control over my actions of policy etc where you would be supposed to wish the adoption of a measure, it would bring all your influence into the scale! This at the commencement of the session would give a direction to matters and might be of real importance to the adoption of measures which may become a desideratum to the welfare of Texas. This is not attaching too much importance to the actual consideration of your country. Every resource must now be called into action.

I can tell you nothing about the Ladies of your friendship or acquaintance, only that I hear they are all well. This morning, or rather it was last evening, Miss Mag Stone sent me a Boquet by Mr Bagby and said it was on your account, so you see it was rather a cold bath to my vanity. I am so much provoked that I will not wear it in my breast. On looking at my posey buttonhole in my coat, I found some withered remains of some pinks which our dear mother gave me when I was sick at the Island previous to Youngs going to Marion! I will not promise to go and see Mag until you come home, that is if you come soon or should now perchance be on your way.

I am told that her and Betty [Tilghman] are quite jealous of each other & both claiming a preference in your estimation as well as my own. I learn that poor Mag is in low spirits. It may be that she is about to marry and feels like the poor Girl that was so embarrassed the night of [faded] wedding. You recollect I told you of that. It may be that some other cause may exist. She may not wish to marry or may have been crossed in her affections. I do wish both Mag & Betty were happily united to two clever fellows, not that I do fear them as competitors of Sarah Ann when she arrives. By the bye, I am bantering a little on her and tell all people that she resembles you and about the rival of beauty, I can't determine, but 'tis said "that she can excel you in music." I intend to send for the Piano and Guitar when I am assured that you will be home! I do not need any thing to remind me of you or to say—Sir your beloved Margaret, your friend & wife is absent. I will sufficiently feel your absence without such monitors!!! I am weary and will now read. My whole time is employed and a large portion of it in thinking of you my Love!

8th June

Dearest the Dayton came two days since from Galveston, and brought me letters from the Neptune, but none from you, my Love, from what cause I can not imagine. It may be that [Pizene] Edmunds took out the mail by hand and omitted to send it. I am anxious to infer this by what I heard by passengers who came on the Neptune. They did not see, nor cou'd they find Edmunds when the boat was landing, tho' he had promised to see them previous to its sailing. It is almost a month since you wrote to me. I have not had a letter from you since the 10th of May. You can not, I am sure, imagine the state of my feelings nor will I attempt to describe them. I do not complain, but such is my anxiety that I since decided to visit the Island by Boat tomorrow so that I may meet the New York on its arrival and see Dr. Eiland,[7] as he will go directly to Marion. I can have no peace, in as much as I can not hear from you. Would I not hear from you by the New York, I will not say how or what my feelings will be! But surely I will truly be unhappy, and I would yield to despair. The occasion would be most reasonable. Do not suppose that I imagine that you have not written to me. No my Love, I could not suppose so, for I suppose that you were prostrate from some sickness. Any cause which may interpose to your happiness, your health or to my receipt of your letters.

If I am doomed long to endure my present situation, I will, I presume, become more calmed, if not more satisfied. This letter will reach Marion in 12 days, as I calculated from this time. I will look with some hope at the Island for your return by the New York. It is probable if you received all my letters. I will not be sanguine in my affections and not be disappointed much if you are not on board. Whether you are or not my Love, I will certainly attach <u>no censure</u> to you. It will be no fault of thine. Another reason I wish to go to the Island (and not the least) is that it may be possible Mother or sister may have had letters from you! This I have thought probable as I hear that some passengers came from Alabama by the Neptune! Notwithstanding thoughts of this either I am much pressed with business as the time when Congress is to meet draws nigh upon me. On the 24th inst I am called on to deliver a Masonic address to the Fraternity in the church. I have not consented to do it, but it is probable I will. If I should, it will not be published.

This evening at 5 oclock I have to render to poor Moreland's earthly remains the last sad tribute of my esteem for his goodness & valour and pity for his errors. Could my prayers and devout wishes secure him a happy immortality he would surely enjoy the kind favors of a benignant God. When I last saw him he could converse without much pain and left the scenes of earthly cares without one convulsive throe. True a soldier less exists in Texas!!!

I hope my Dearest that you will meet this letter ire it reaches its destination of Marion. Smith and his wife are to go to Galveston so I will be alone at home. I and the servants! How do you suppose I will make out with Negroes & Mexicans? I would be more happy if you were with me, I must confess. No matter what additional trouble you might bring with you. If it were even more debt I would stand it! But if it were Sarah Ann, so much the better. I will only have to increase my stack of provisions. I have not a tolerably smart one on hand. Bacon, etc was laid in on yesterday. If you can, do pray love come home, but I need not say this. I know you will!!!

Give my Love to all our kin & regards to friends. H.

[1]James Love.
[2]John A. Walton.
[3]This volume, Houston's "Private Executive Records," is in the Franklin Williams Collection, Sam Houston Regional Library and Research Center, Liberty, Texas.
[4]Isaac N. Moreland, Chief Justice of Harris County. He died June 9, 1842. For a biography see *Writings*, I, 463n.

[5]William R. Scott, Chief Justice of Brazoria County. See Houston to the Honorable Senate of Texas, December 16, 1837, *Writings,* II, 172.
[6]Houston had called a special session of Congress to meet in Houston City. See Proclamation, May 24, 1842, *Writings,* III, 58.
[7]Margaret's cousin, Oliver G. Eiland, was the son of Gincy Moffett and Asa Eiland. Madge W. Hearne Collection, San Antonio, Texas.

Parts of the following letter written to Houston by Margaret have been destroyed.

Marion, Perry County Alabama
June 3, 1842

My own loved Husband,

My mind has been in a state of torture for several days, because I could not write to you.... [torn] Your letter which I rec'd on saturday was handed to me just as a large party of my friends was assembled to dine with me at bro. Henry's and it made me cheerful during the whole day. My great friend Mrs. Gen King was present, and I read to her the part which interested me most. I need not tell you dearest, that I was most interested in the religious exercises of your mind. Oh, can I ever be thankful enough to my Heavenly Father for his mercies. Sometimes when I ask myself if your present impressions can be sent in answer to my own prayers, the bare possibility of such a thing is almost too much happiness for me. But you must remember that the work is not yet finished. Oh [edge of the paper is cut off] but "seek first the kingdom of Heaven" and the hand of God will direct you through all your difficulties.

Your permission to return home did not come one day too soon. I assure you my spirit pines to be with you, and in my present state of anxiety about you, I do not think that my health could be improved by a longer absence. To be candid my Love, I hardly think this climate agrees with me so well as that of Houston. Dearest how could you intimate such a thing as my staying until Nov! That was almost unkind. No it was not either, for your noble heart could never entertain an unkind thought, and I am sure you assigned it in gener[torn] understand[ing of] a wife's feelings. [torn] poems has said,

"Man's love is of himself
Tis woman's whole existence."

and indeed I believe there is as much truth [as] poetry in that sentiment. This Husband and especially the politician, has many things
to occupy his mind, totally unconnected with his wife, and these
may serve to amuse his attention during absence, but poor woman,
there is not one [beat] of her heart that does not speak of him! and
she turns with a sickened heart from all the pleasures around her if
he is not there. My relations and friends are violently opposed to
my returning before Oct., but I silence all opposition by telling them
what you say on that subject. Sarah Ann and Robert will accompany me, and we will try to be in New Orleans by the 22nd inst. We
expect to go by Aunt Lea's and spend a day or two with her and our
cousins. I have not yet been able to visit Aunt Eiland, but think I can
do so before we leave. Marion can not boast of its former health, for
it is almost a common [torn] the grave. They have the most malignant fevers I have ever known, and in fact, it seems that all healthy
parts of Ala have become sickly, but you need not be uneasy about
me, as we will leave before the sickliest season begins.

Rather than you should suppose that any thing [torn] would
prevent me from writing, I will tell you [the] true cause. I have been
ill, very ill. On last [torn] br. Henry and bro. Martin wrote to you but
[did not] mention my illness as they feared it would [cause] you a
great deal of anxiety, but I told them afterwards that I would rather
you should be [torn] on that account than ignorant of the true [rea-
son] of my not writing. I saw your letter of 44[1] pages [torn] last
saturday, and on monday evening, Young [torn] and brought me
another from you. Dearest [how] can I thank you for so much kindness? I [torn] therefore you must imagine all that I feel. Tuesday
Mrs. Fletcher and the Dr. gave me a dinner party, but I was too unwell to attend.
[Signature is missing]
Please have my piano brought up and tuned before I get home.

[1]Houston to Margaret, May 6, 1842.

Margaret became ill in Marion and sometime during her stay she was treated by Dr. Nathaniel Fletcher, a family friend. He wrote the following prescription which is preserved in the Franklin Weston Williams Collection at the Woodson Research Center, Rice University, in Houston, Texas.

Prescription for Mrs. Houston

I would advise Mrs. Houston to use Fowlers solution of arsnic [sic] as a tonic in doses of from six to ten drops, three time a day (morning, noon & night) for nine days together and then omit it for four or five days. If it is continued a greater length of time the system becomes so accustomed to it that it is of little efficiency. The Balsam of Toler and Tinct. of Assafoetida [sic] will at the same time be very beneficial in strengthening the nervous system.

When you apprehend an attack of the difficulty in breathing, I would advise you to smoke freely of dried Jamestown (stramonium) leaves, or tobacco—it aids expectoration, sooths [sic] the nervous system, and relaxes the pectoral and other muscles engaged in respiration—Should this not ward off an attack take Ipecac: in broken doses until vomiting is produced—after the stomach is cleansed take two tea spoonsful of Solution of Morphine, and repeat in tea spoonful doses every thirty or forty minutes until the pain subsides or great drowsiness is produced. In treating yours & similar cases, I have paid no attention to the <u>quantity</u> of medicine taken, but the <u>effects</u> produced. You on one occasion took more than an ounce in a few hours—I mention this to allay your fears, as no danger need be apprehended from the medicine so long as pain & watchfulness continue. I need not remind you how conducive it is to health for all the seentions [sic] to be kept well established; for a costive habit I would recommend the preperations [sic] of Rhubarb [and] the tincture of pills with castile soap.

The tincture of Gum Guiaccium (The dark tincture I left you) is by far the best remedy for supposed catamenia—commence a few days before the monthly time and take a tea spoonful morning, noon & night; continue it until it has the desired effect. Then stop. Aloe pills taken about this time are very efficacious.

And now Madam I must bid you adieu, but not until I express my deep regret that your visit among us should have been in such an unpropecious [sic] season. The most deleterious we possible could have for pulmenary [sic] affections. Since your arrival scarcely have we had three consecutive days without rain!

Soon may you reach a more genial clime, be restored to the arms of a fond husband, and to that health the loss of which is so much deplored by your friends and by none more than he who addresses you.

Nath'l M. Fletcher, M. D.

General Sam Houston
Houston, Texas

Marion Perry Co. Ala. June 14th 1842

Dearest Husband,

I had made all our arrangements to leave here on last saturday, so as to meet the boat of the 22nd at New Orleans, but when the day came, I was violently ill, and I am not yet sufficiently recovered to travel, for this is the first attempt I have made to sit up since a week ago. I know my husband will excuse my tremulous hand, especially as the mail will leave in a very few moments. Oh my Love, you can not imagine my impatience, and it would be folly for me to attempt a description of it. I am sure that it is injurious of my health, but I can not resist it. My friends can plan no amusements that will draw my mind one moment from you or reconcile me to the distance that lies between us. We rec'd letters by Dr. Eiland from sister A[ntoinette] and bro. Vernal and they stated that you were well. Thank Heaven for the blessed news. It relieves my heart of a painful weight, but still I am not reconciled. I would be with you again. Nothing short of that can make me happy. If my life is spared, no obstacle that I can overcome shall prevent me from leaving here soon enough to be in New Orleans on the 7th of July.

Oh my Love, shall I ever see you again! Can it be that there is such happiness in reserve for me! My heart often desponds, and a dark presentiment fills my soul—that I should never see you again! I can not bear it. My mind is confused and wild, and contains but one distinct image and that is my Husband's. I take little note of what is passing around me. My thoughts are far far away. I have visited Aunt Eiland since I wrote you last, and found the old lady in her usual seclusion, surrounded by books and papers, but the evening I passed with her, was as pleasant as any I have spent since I left you. Indeed you would be delighted with her conversation for genius speaks in every word. She is a great woman—but a very eccentric one. Aunt Lea has been expecting us for several weeks, but I have been unable to travel the greatest part of the time. I expect to go down so soon as I have sufficient strength. I have rec'd a letter from your particular friend Maj. Jesse Beene,[1] requesting me to spend the summer with his family at thier house near the Blount springs. They live in magnificent style, and if my health was good and you were with me it would be a delightful visit, but as it is, I am compelled to decline even a short visit and will write a polite letter to that effect. I could not visit both them and Aunt Lea, and you know I must see the latter if possible. I am told she is quite cheered at the idea of seeing me.

Maj. Townes[2] and Col. Star[3] spent last night with bro. Henry. They held a meeting, but I believe did nothing towards the cause. Bro. Martin went with them this morning to Selma. They have been expecting Gen. Pickens[4] here several weeks, but I believe that Gen. Edwin D. King is the most efficient man you could possible call upon. He is so interested in the cause that he would not hesitate one moment to thro[w] the bulk of his vast fortune upon the order and his influence throughout the state is known and moreover he has seen some service having fought bravely in two or more battles. Think of Love, will you not. Our dear [relations] are all well, and often speak of you with tender affection. Dearest I have written until the pen almost drops from my hand. Do write to Ma for me.

Farewell Love,
Thy Maggy

---

[1]Jesse Beene was an attorney and judge of Dallas county. For a biography see Owen, III, 124.
[2]S. A. Townes.
[3]Colonel James Starr. For information about the cause to which Margaret refers see Houston to General Pickens, May 1, 1842, *Writings,* IV, 92.
[4]General Andrew M. Pickens. For a biography see Owen, IV, 1359.

The following letter is torn and some of the words are missing.

City of Houston
25th June 1842

Dearest Love,

I can only say if possible I will be down before your arrival at the Island[1] there to embrace you. Congress has not yet organized, but I hope it will this evening. If it does, I will exert myself to leave here!

The Boat is ringing the Bell and I am told will be back before the New York arrives. All wish to see you at home, and I am miserably anxious. My message[2] is written. Those who have seen it say it [torn] I have ever [torn] My heart beats to embrace you, for oh my Love, your absence seems an age to me. I am almost distracted with solicitude for your arrival. I know you will not delay, but to me the wings of thought are sluggards in affection.

Oh my Love, I pray the Great God of our salvation to bless, and preserve you. My heart is thine only! and all thine Forever.

Thy devoted
Houston

Mrs. Houston
Love to Mother, Niece & Rob. No bad news.

H

[1]Galveston.
[2]Houston's message to Congress concerning the Vasquez invasion and the condition of the nation. For a copy of this message see *Writings*, III, 74–83.

Mobile, July 5th 1842

Dearest Husband,

We arrived here last night and have ascertained that the New York has left New Orleans on her last trip. I am almost frantic and maddened with disappointment. But what can I do! There is no prospect of any boat leaving before the Champion sets off from this place, but that will probably be detained 8 or 10 days. It seems like nonsense to write to you, when there is no possible conveyance for the letter, but at all costs I will send it by today's mail and perhaps some unforeseen chance may bear it to you. I have just finished a letter to go by the San Bernard which is now in port. She will leave this evening and Mrs. Stevens who called on me this morning says they will very probably fall in with some sail vessel by which it may be sent to you.

I am accompanied by Bro M, Robert and Sarah Ann. Bro. M has some idea of going all the way to Texas with us, but he has not decided yet.

The mail is starting and I must conclude.

Thy Maggy

Chapter VI

July 30, 1843–September 20, 1844

July 30, 1843: Sam Houston to Margaret Houston
August 3, 1843: Sam Houston to Margaret Houston
August 11, 1843: Margaret Houston to Sam Houston
September 1, 1843: Sam Houston to Margaret Houston
September 20, 1843: Sam Houston to Margaret Houston
October 6, 1843: Margaret Houston to Sam Houston
October 18, 1843: Margaret Houston to Sam Houston
January 23, 1844: Margaret Houston to Nancy Lea
April 19, 1844: Sam Houston to Nancy Lea
May 12, 1844: Margaret Houston to Sam Houston
May 18, 1844: Margaret Houston to Sam Houston
May 19, 1844: Sam Houston to Margaret Houston
[July, 1844]: Margaret Houston to Sam Houston
August 3, 1844: Margaret Houston to Sam Houston
August 7, 1844: Margaret Houston to Sam Houston
September 13, 1844: Sam Houston to Margaret Houston
September 20, 1844: Margaret Houston to Sam Houston

Margaret returned from Alabama in early July of 1842, and the couple made their home in Houston City until early November. At that time the capital was moved to Washington-on-the-Brazos for the seventh and eighth congresses. Because they were together, there were no letters between them until the summer of 1843. Any letters to other members of the family seem not to have survived. The following letters were written when Houston was on his way to a meeting with the Indians in east Texas. The first was written from Montgomery, Texas, where he had been invited to speak at a barbecue.

To Mrs. Margaret Lea Houston
Washington Texas
By Mr. I. B. from Captain Greens[1]

30th July 1843

Dearest,

Yesterday I arrived in time to speak at 1 o clock PM. The assembly was highly respectable, and I was kindly greeted. The matter went off with a pretty fair speech. This is a fine allotment of clever people. I came home with Captain Green, a wealthy farmer from Georgia, and a very clever gentleman. I had many invitations from the citizens to stay with them. All is right in this section.[2]

I did not find Green[3] of Houston at the Barbaque [sic] from some cause, and this will leave to you to order things, as you please with captain [John S.] Black about your going down. I will send by Mr. Shaw[4] to pay for the Waggon [sic] to Mr. Ford[5] and to get another seat put in if needful, and to have what money you may wish. I don't say need. Have enough! Call on Baker[6] if you go to Houston for all that is due, for Martha's[7] hire. Mr. [Thomas] Bagby may have some in his hands. You can get that also.

Let Mr. Shaw or Mr. Raymond[8] know any thing that you want. I spoke to Mr. Hatfield[9] to take my trunk of papers, and place it under his bed and Mrs. Hatfields[10] for safe keeping. Our house has too many doors in it for safety. Thin papers are precious and my trunk had best go with the paper trunk also. I told Mr. Hall,[11] & Mr. Mariners[12] to tie up my trunk with ropes for the safety of the papers.

Dearest, I will not pretend to say to you what my feelings were as the shades of evening were closing around me on yesterday. The hour when I have usually left my offices, and returned from the business of the day to meet you and inquire for Sam.[13] Indeed I felt as tho the earth was a desert, and I stood alone, in the midst of its waste. How painfully association presents to the mind and the heart the memory of departed or absent joys. I told you that Sam would visit my memory with you and only then this is true. Poor little Boy, I can see him with the minds eye of affection, cling to your bosom or impatiently struggling to command his meal, and or sighing on account that he had been badly treated by delay. The little scamp will have caused you scant repose ire we can meet again. I was right in saying that he should only be present when presented to me in your arms. He will be taken good care of and is too small or I should command a switch spanking to cause the healthy circulation of his blood.

The people expected you on yesterday on your way to the springs to stay until my return from the meeting and many expressed regret & disappointment at your absence. My Dearest, I do hope you will get on well, and without trouble until my return. If you go to Trinity write to me at Crockett, saying so, that I may get it on my return from the meeting, and know which way to shape my route home.

I wish you, my Love to hand my pipe & stem to Mr Shaw for Captain Green. It is a present from you to him, and must be forthcoming.

My Dearest, do in all things as you deem best. I have not had a harsh feeling, nor used a harsh expression since we parted. Do not suppose that it is my absence from you, but the press of official cares that take me from you.

My love to mother, Tose,[14] and squeeze and buss Sam for us.

Regards to friends
Ever thine dearest
Houston

Mrs. Maggy
Dearest, Mr. Shaw will attend to the waggon [sic] matter for you, and do as ordered, as he may think best for you about the additional seat etc. Also explain the enclosed orders.[15]

Thine
Houston

[1]J. E. Green. Identified in Beth and Emily Darman, compilers, *Taxpayers of the Re-*

public of Texas, (Grand Prairie, Texas: Published by the authors, 1988), 259.

[2]For Houston's acceptance to the invitation to speak at a barbecue in Montgomery see *Writings,* IV, 221–22.

[3]This probably refers to George Green, an associate of James Spillman. Identified in White, *They Also Served,* 55.

[4]James B. Shaw was comptroller for the Republic of Texas. For a biography see *Writings,* III, 197n.

[5]William G. Ford, *Writings,* IV, 222–23. Houston to James H. Raymond, July 30, 1843. It carries the endorsement: "Paid Wm G. Ford $180.00."

[6]William R. Baker was the former county clerk of Harris County. For a biography see *Handbook of Texas,* I, 101.

[7]Margaret's slave.

[8]James H. Raymond, Acting Treasurer, is identified in several drafts signed by Houston. See *Writings,* IV, 222–23.

[9]Major B. M. Hatfield, a local innkeeper in Washington-on-the-Brazos. Wallis and Hill, 41.

[10]Caroline Hatfield. Identified in Carpenter, IV, 2069.

[11]Houston is probably referring to John C. Hall, one of the founders of Washington-on-the-Brazos. Wallis, 11. (Not to be confused with John L. Hall of Crockett.)

[12]Charles Mariner. Identified in *Writings,* III, 436.

[13]Sam Houston, Jr., was born May 25, 1843.

[14]A nickname for Sarah Ann Royston.

[15]For a copy of this order to Raymond see *Writings,* II, 222. It authorizes the treasurer to pay Margaret $180.00, "the price of a waggon bought of Mr. Ford & any other amount of money which she may desire out of Salary fund." It also shows a payment of $34.00 to James Hurd.

Mrs. Margaret Lea Houston
Washington
Texas

Crockett Texas
3rd August 1843

My Love,

My trip has been quite expeditious. I arrived here on the 1st Instant. I say [sic] here at Mr. Halls,[1] two and a half miles from town, and on yesterday I rode into town, and spent a few hours, and returned. It is the same Mr. Hall at whose house we were so kindly entertained when we were last here.[2] My time passes quietly, and I only regret that I have been so long delayed from the Treaty. Tomorrow is to be the great day of meeting in Crockett.[3] If the day is fine, I presume there will be a vast concourse of the Sovereigns from various sections of the country. Genl [James Pinckney] Henderson has written to me, and says he will be here, and various other worthies from the East have promised to come also.[4] Great preparations are making to have great plenty at the Barbecue. Genl [George W.] Terrell and many others are to be in town to night, but I will not ride in, until morning. I will try and acquit myself so that you will hear a good report of me. The people here have but one fault to find with me, and that is I did not bring you, and the young Lion with me, and leave you here until I could return from the Treaty. I have promised to atone for this, by visits so soon as it may be in our power!

I have not suffered less in my life from travelling than from my present journey. I have not felt weary for one single moment nor fatigued. My appetite is good enough, yet I eat sparingly and plain food! I am pleased to witness the glow of happiness, which I see diffused over many faces at the prospects of peace and the manifestations of abundance which is every where seen. The cordiality with which I am received, and treated by all, that I meet seems equal to the change that has taken place in our political condition. Factionists and Traitors are either ridiculed or denounced by the great mass of people.

You will suppose that this is gratifying to me? It is so, but I can assure you, that I would truly exchange the expressions which may be offered to me for the pleasure which greeted me at home, when I returned care worn from my office, embraced you, and took a look at Sam or if you were not present inquired for you, and heard our dear Mother respond to my inquiry "they are well." I was right my Dear, in saying that I could not think of Sam without associating you with him. I can think of you, and not of him for a moment, tho' you are both very intimately blended in my thoughts, and inseparable in my affections. You may, if you chuse, make a quarrel with me on Sams account, but I can only submit to the penalty of the fault, but I can not admit that so small & homily [sic] a gentleman as Sam is, should rival his mother who has so long reigned supreme in my affections. It is so long since I have written to you, and of course written any love letters that I will not attempt to indulge in the tender strains of romantic fancy, but at the same time, I do confess that pure, and devoted affection for you is inseparable from my existence whether I may write 4 or 44 pages in this letter. It is true that I am relieved from the details of business in my office, which is some relief to me, but I would most cheerfully resume them, if I could only embrace you with them, or as a set off to them.

I suppose you have whipped Sam several times since I left, as you said you had done so before departure.[5] He has a much finer prospect if he is spared to [be] spoiled by your kindness, than to be corrected by your temper. I do seriously regret that I can not be there to worry him a little, as it wou'd cause a free circulation of his blood. Does he redden as usual in face, when his nursing is deferred for a moment? The Boy is rather impatient of delay, tho' I take comfort from the hope, that it indicated energy of character. And I do trust that his mothers care, and instructions will teach him to make his temper submissive to his reason! It is one of the great faults of early education that Parents are amused at the fits of temper which sprightly children are very apt to display. A look of disapprobation from a mother to infancy [sic] or an admonition in childhood, doubt-less wou'd often have an influence on the future character and des-tiny of the child. But dearest, I must not prate to you about matters in which I can not be cited as an instance. You will hear from me I know, for no being can more seriously deplore my infirmity in these matters than myself. I would much rather that I could leave to my off spring the benefit and my friends the pleasure of referring to my character as the model of every thing that is amiable, virtuous, & truly pious, without guilt, than that they should only have to say of my memory that "Your Father was the ablest of Generals, the wisest of Statesmen, and the most illustrious of mankind." However grati-fying the latter might be, in the enjoyment of health of hope and existence, I do feel conscious, that in the closing of lifes drama it can yield no pleasure in the anticipated presence of that Being who is infinite in all His attributes as the very Author of Eternity. Hence it is my Beloved, that I will endeavor to so act, thro' life as will conduce, most to the gratification of my relatives, and friends both in my ex-istence here and the hope of the joys of their society in a happy im-mortality.

Since we parted my dearest, I have meditated much and have had the good fortune not to indulge in any thing harsh, or violent in my feelings or expressions. It is true that my provocations have not been great and I hope that I am about to overcome every ebullition of temper and acquire a more becoming tone and gentle demeanour towards the whole human family. I often reflect upon your admonitions and feel deeply impressed with their justice & propriety. Sensible as I am, if they had not been both necessary and proper you would not have employed them. But Dearest, I hope soon again to meet you when we can talk over these matters, with a thousand others.

I have felt a deep and lively interest about your situation, and the family. If you go to Trinity, how matters are to be managed, and if you should not go, how our dear Mother is to get there. You must recollect of one thing, and act upon it. You can order what money you may think proper, either for your own use, or that of Mother, or our dear Niece Tose [Sarah Ann Royston]. If you do not use what ever you need, or that you might desire, you will distress me. I do assure you Tose has been long from home and may need many things. Mother has no income now, and may need some things and wish others for Tose or it may be that she wishes some for Antoinette, and if any, or all should be needful, you will please to see that it is attended to. All that you have to do, if you do not wish to extend your arrangements upon the Exchequers, will be to give an order to Mother on Major Cocke,[6] and it will be attended to. These are matters which I should have inquired into and arranged before I left home. I did say something to you on the subject I think, but made no definite arrangements. Now my Love, do you do what I ought to have done. If I played stingy, you ought not to do so! Since I have been here I have placed about ten thousand dollars in a train of collection. So you will see that I have not been Idle!

I intend to write to Dr [Anson] Jones[7] & I think Doctor Hill.[8] I write this letter in the expectation that it will find you at Washington. I will urge my way to the Treaty and return as soon as practicable. I find as much company here as I desire to go with me. It is thought that the Gentlemen from the East intend to go. Genl Rusk[9] as he went home was a "strong Houston man," and this will be gall and wormwood to Mayfield[10] & such wretches who will now wish to come over and mix with the faithful.

One thing we did not converse about and that was Colonel Morgan.[11] If you go to Houston, and he is there, he will wish to be very attentive. I need not say how you are to receive him, only you will of course be polite, and civil. As to Commodore Moore,[12] he is somewhat on a different footing. You can not of course act upon political ground and take part in my affairs, but you are anxious that he is "Dishonorably discharged" from service, and rests under the charges of Treason, Piracy, and murder. If he should wish to be presented to you, you will know how to treat the application. They have both failed in prostrating me,[13] and for Morgan, I entertain some kind feelings, but the other is base! The faulty, we do not always condemn, but the criminal deserve reprobation in proportion to their crimes.

You will write to me at this place and if I live to return, I will know by what route to go, so as to see you and the pledge. Write to me, and tell me if he is any prettier than he was. Your letter[14] I have not opened my dear, but I am anxious to do so. I have never yet violated a promise nor will I, that is concerned with your happiness, and all on that you require. You may have intended to tantalize my curiosity.

No matter, I will soon open it. I hope at the Treaty.[15] My intention is to start the day after the speech. If I can, I will write to you and let you know what sort of speech I may make.[16] I feel now that I would make a fair one if not very splendid, but I will dream of you & Sam tonight I hope and then I will make a fine one. It is sunset, and the distant hills remind me of more distant and far dearer objects. I am on a hill affording a view of more than twelve miles over the surrounding country. It is beautiful indeed! But a little while, and the silvery rays of the moon will succeed to the golden light of the departing sun. How very admonitory such scenes are of the vicissitudes of human life.

Dearest, the Indians have been down hunting within twenty five miles of this place, and are perfectly friendly. The people are all joyous at the prospects of the pending Treaty. I have seen Mr. Jno. J. Bunton here from Alabama, one of our departed brother Martin's greatest friends.[17] He is devoted to his memory, and was present in Mobile when Martin & Genl. Desha[18] had the difficulty. Mr. Hall, where I am, married a daughter of his.[19]

I pray you to give my best love to our Dear Mother & to Tose [Sarah Ann]. Hug Sam, Kiss him, and bite his ear a little bit for me. Salute our friends and make such arrangements about matters as you deem best. If you should not go to Trinity, write to me by every mail to this place—for I hope to be back in twenty two days, this far on my way home.

My Love I embrace you.
Thy devoted husband
Sam Houston

My Love, if you start to travel do not forget to inquire before you stop at any house, if the whoop, or Hooping cough is at the place. I find it very prevalent on the road and this is my reason for suggesting the matter.

I know your dread of the disease. If Sam does take it, do not be alarmed, it may not injure, or endanger his life. Put camphor on his neck. It will not be disagreeable.

Devotedly thine Ever
Houston

Maggy

[1]John L. Hall of Crockett.
[2]The Houstons visited East Texas shortly after their marriage in July, 1840. Friend, 98.
[3]For a report of the speech Houston made at this meeting see *Telegraph and Texas Register*, September 13, 1843.
[4]For further information see Houston to Anson Jones, August 3, 1843. *Writings*, III, 422–23.
[5]Houston had earlier recommended switching to improve the circulation. See Houston to Margaret, July 30, 1843.
[6]Major James Cocke of Galveston.
[7]See Houston to Jones, August 3, 1843, *Writings*, III, 422–23.
[8]Dr. George W. Hill, Secretary of the War and Navy.
[9]General Thomas Jefferson Rusk.
[10]James Mayfield was one of the most outspoken foes of Houston's stand on war with Mexico. He would later become counsel for Commodore Moore. Tom Henderson Wells, *Commodore Moore and the Texas Navy*, (Austin: University of Texas Press, 1960), 106, 169.
[11]Colonel James Morgan of Harris County.
[12]Commodore Edwin Moore.
[13]Both men had intefered with Houston's efforts to achieve an armistice with Mexico with the help of England's mediation. Houston had given the British consul his word that no attack against Mexico would be made while negotiations were in progress. Commodore Moore had been ordered to take the Texas ships to New Orleans for repair. Houston then appointed James Morgan as commissioner to proceed to New Orleans to inform Moore that his ships were to be sold and that he and his men were to return to Galveston. In the meantime Moore had received unauthorized financing from New Orleans capitalists for an expedition to Yucatan.

Morgan gave his approval to this act of disobedience. As a result Houston issued a proclamation charging Moore with piracy. Siegel, 194, 220–21. For Houston's comments on the events see Houston to Ashbel Smith, July 21, 1843, *Writings*, III, 418.

[14]No letter from Margaret during this time has been located.

[15]The peace treaty with the Indians was concluded at Bird's Fort on the Trinity River, September 9, 1843. *Writings*, III, 423.

[16]The *Telegraph and Texas Register* (September 13, 1843) reported that Houston "almost pledged himself to the people of Texas if they would give him a majority of the next Congress, that he would have peace between Texas and Mexico, and on a satisfactory basis." Friend, 111.

[17]Martin Lea had been killed in a duel with Napoleon Lockett on March 26, 1843. McFarland Collection, Peabody Library, Sam Houston State University. A death notice in the *Mobile Register and Journal* (November 22, 1843) reported, "Martin A. [Lea] murdered last March by Napoleon Lockett of Perry County. Trial in Marion." Mobile Genealogical Society, Inc., *Death Notices (Local and Foreign) 1840–1849*, (Mobile, Alabama: 1962), n.p.

[18]General Joseph Desha, a former congressman and governor of Kentucky, was married to a relative of William Bledsoe. John M. Gresham, compiler, *Biographical Cyclopedia of the Commonwealth of Kentucky*, (Chicago: John M. Gresham Company, 1896), 389. See also Lee, 329.

[19]Elizabeth Bunton Oatman Hall. For information about John Wheeler Bunton and his daughter see Kemp, 36–38.

Gen. Sam Houston
Crockett, Houston Co. Texas

Washington Aug. 11, 1843

Ever dear Husband,

Your letters were both joyfully received and with pleasure,[1] I now undertake to answer them. But if I should not write as long a one as you did from Crockett, you need not suppose that I have nothing to tell you, for indeed I have a great deal if you were with me, but perhaps it would not be so interesting on paper as I fondly hope it will be, if I should ever enjoy the happiness of <u>telling it to you</u>.

Mother and I expected to have been off for the Trinity before this, but it has been impossible for us to leave without violating your plan, which was for us to remain here until your return, unless Capt. [John S.] Black could come up for us. I wrote to the Capt. last week, requesting him to come for us, but two mails have passed since, and

I have recd [sic] no answer, except a confined and verbal message by Kane[2] that he was sick and could not come. I am pretty well satisfied that it is some trick of Kane's to take us down in his splendid vehicle, as he expressed great anxiety to do so, and seems quite disappointed because we will not consent to go in that way. It is certainly a great disappointment, but we submit to it with as much fortitude as possible. Mother and Tose have both had severe attacks of fever, but are now nearly recovered. Dr. Moore[3] attended to them, and at the same time the servants were all sick, so you may imagine the duties that devolved upon me. However, just as I was about to despair and think I could do no more, the time arrived for Mr. Herd[4] to move into the house, and since then, I have felt quite free, especially as we are all in pretty good health. I wish you could see our noble boy, as he is at this time. I can not describe him to you, but it does seem to me that God has entrusted us with an important charge, for he is surely a remarkable being! Every new object engages his attention, until he has examined it thoroughly, which generally takes him about ten minutes. At the first glance, he usually expresses his delight and astonishment by laughing and cooing, but this gradually subsides into a thoughtful silence, and look of seriousness and fixed attention, and he gazes upon the object with as much intenseness as Sir Isaac Newton could have watched the apple that led to so important a discovery. He is the wonder of every one that sees him. His health is excellent and he thrives and grows finely. He has had the thrush,[5] but I soon learned how to manage it, and he is now well of it.

Dearest I can not tell you how anxious I feel for your return. You will know the anxiety of mind I have heretofore incurred on your account when you were away from me. But then you were only my Husband, now you are the Father of my boy! Every look of his reminds me of you, but even his smiles are rather saddening than cheering to me, for you are not here to enjoy them with me! Ah do return soon to your wife and boy, for you are all the world to them! It is now about 12 o'clock at night. Sam has just waked, and is nursing on my left arm, so that writing is rather a clumsy business with me, but you know there is no getting off from him. I must have my letter mailed by day-break. I would have written today, but did not know until tonight that the mail would start so soon in the morning. I will write you again next week, and by that time I hope I shall be able to tell you where you will find us on your return. Dearest I must tell you goodbye, as I am so exhausted and not very well, having had a recent attack of asthma. Farewell

Thy devoted wife
M. L. Houston

[1]Houston to Margaret, July 30, 1843 and August 3, 1843.
[2]R. T. Kane. Identified in *Writings*, IV, 223. Kane operated a stage service from Houston to Washington. David G. McComb, *Houston the Bayou City*, (Austin: University of Texas Press, 1969), 30.
[3]Dr. Francis Moore, who was a member of the Congress at this time. For a biography see *Writings*, VIII, 125–26.
[4]This is possibly James Hurd (also spelled Heard) with whom Houston had some business dealing. Houston to James H. Raymond, July 30, 1843. *Writings*, IV, 222.
[5]A disease common in infants which results in ulcers in the mouth. Dorland, 1405.

Washington Texas
1st Sept 1843

Dearest,

By our friend Doct Hill[1] I send for you to come by the way [of] Galveston, or as you may please. My Love, you have no idea of the trouble since my return! No matter, You are not the less dear to me! Mr. Heard has acted badly, and Doct Hill will tell you all the news. If he should fail to do so, & as Kane will advertise [sic] you of every thing I send him along.

Now my Dearest, I do beseech you not to feel distress about any thing which has taken place or may do so while you are absent. Truly Mr. Heard has acted like <u>himself</u>, but will act well. I will see him, and must recover considerable damages.

We will my Dear, have to resume house keeping and therefore I send Kane to bring the Blue Waggon [sic] and Eliza[2] to Houston unless you should think otherwise! Doct says you can have Maria if you wish her! By the bye, the Doct, or the Madam[3] has a fine son. She is doing well! For my own part I wish to meet you at Houston, or Galveston as may be most agreeable to you or convenient to myself. On or about the 10th Inst. I intend to set out from this place for Houston. If you are not there, I will prosecute my journey until we meet. I hope you will not be deranged in any plans by this course for my conclusions have grown out of matters since my return. You will at once estimate my feelings and situation. I hope we will be much more comfortable than we could have been with them.

My Dear I wish you would think of Mrs. Holley,[4] at Hugh B. Johnson's, and if you can get her to keep house for you it would be well to do so. Or any one who will relieve you from the cares which would devolve upon you, while Master Sam claims your maternal care. He is ours, and with the blessing of Heaven, he must be cherished under a mother's eye!

I thought when I left him, that he was daily developing traits which bespoke some strange character. This may all be fancy, for parents will always think their progeny in possession of Genius. As for our boy, my dear, I hope those who live to see him in manhood will find that he is capable in the Department of life in which he may be thrown. I have seen in him much which I admire, and hope that some day it will yield fruit. I do not know what to write you, as Doct Hill can tell you all. I hope our Niece will treat him with great politeness. He has done me a kindness by going, so as to enable you to get to Galveston or as you may wish to Houston by water.

As to the aspect of Politicks [sic], it is better than I have anticipated and I hope I will have in the next Congress more friends than I have ever had. I send you various letters which may interest, or amuse you. Sister Eliza's [Eliza Houston Moore] and brother Will's [William Houston][5] will no doubt interest you much. Sister's is very gratifying to me, and so soon as I can see you, I will resolve on what answer to render her.

There is no news here, of any particular import. Hockley & Williams were here on my arrival, and in two days were dispatched for Matamoras.[6] I hope good will grow out of the Mission. You will see by Doct of Colonel Smith's letters what the king of the French say of us.[7] I have letters from the U. S. which are favourable to our affairs. This is Sunday, and I am annoyed by the reports of Heard & Lady. They show all the qualities which belong to such people. My Dear, I am satisfied that Mrs. Brown[8] was right in what she said. I miss many things (as I believe) but I cannot detect them. That Heard will perpetrate any meaness I am satisfied. What she may do, I will not conjecture as she is a lady! That we have fallen upon evil times, there can be no doubt.[9]

My Dearest, I reflect upon no one, for it could not be avoided. 'Tis done, and that is enough! Kane will tell you of the matter! Please give him a patient hearing of one half hour, and you can then learn all. He will tell you the fate of the poor <u>centre Table</u>. It made my heart bleed! I was sorry! It was the only relic of the first constitutional Presidency. No matter! 'Tis all for the best. Every injury was done to the Lot. Calf Lot & stable and the plank which I would not sell, has been destroyed or made away with. Once for all my Dear, Mr. Heard is any thing but an honest man. His Lady is all that she should be for such a husband. They are congenial spirits!!! They are not my dear a disgrace to religion, but they disgrace their profession. Kane will be happy to tell you all, as he says "we catholicks [sic] dont do so." He is a good deal nettled at the conduct of Mr. & Mrs. Heard! He thinks they have treated us badly. Kane says they are the worst example of Baptists, and ought to be excommunicated. This is as we expect in life! 'Tis the notion that people high in stations must submit to every indignity, or if the Vulgar assail them, they have every thing to gain, and nothing to lose!

My love, I again beseech you to feel no solicitude about our matters and do not I pray you to suppose for one moment, that I reflect upon you. 'Tis no such thing my Dearest! I am as you know, always in the belief that "the King can do no wrong." This is the maxim in English Law, and I have adopted it in Texas, whenever the Queen acts. For 'tis said my dear that you rule me. This is all well enough my dear, were you here.

I have two natures and you must be here to make me what I ought to be. I hope to meet you, and Sam with our dear Niece at Galveston or Houston.

Now my Love, on the subject of our dear Mother, can she be comfortable and happy on Trinity? If she can not, bring her with you for Heavens sake. There is not one fiber of my heart, that I will not truly have drawn for her sake. Bring her, if it will add to her comfort by all means.

My Love, I wish you and Niece to go to Galveston and I may meet you there, but if I should not I will meet you at Houston.

I will be proud to meet the whelp and his mother at Galveston! Tho' he is very homily [sic], I love him because he is your child!

My dear if I had the means I wou'd give a million to see you, and you first that you might show me Master Sam!

I can tell you but little about people here. I have only seen Mrs. Hatfield & Mrs. Norwood[10] of the Ladies. I have not seen any of the Miss Sims,[11] tho' I learned that they are all well.

In this vicinity the people are becoming more healthy. Since my return my sec'y has been confined to his bed with fever and ague.

My Dearest, if you think well of it, let Kane bring Eliza to Houston in the Buggy. You will wish her at home when you commence Housekeeping.

I had nearly forgotten to send you some cash. I must send all that I can spare, with the hope that it will answer your purposes. If it fails, you can borrow or go on credit. The reason why I concluded for you to return has been enforced by the state of the roads. They are very bad, and it has rained every day since my return.

You will think I wish to employ you for some time, as I sent you so many letters. Mr. [Washington D.] Miller has been in the office since my return. He sends his respects to you and Sam, and his "Love to Miss Royston." So you see sickness has improved Millers gallantry!

Doct Hill is ready, and Kane is off.

Do my Dearest embrace our mother, sister and Tose. Salute Bledsoe & Bro. if he has not gone to Alabama. Dearest! Do the best you can and so soon as I can, I will embrace you with great felicity.

Thine ever faithfully
Houston

[1]Dr. George Washington Hill, Secretary of War in 1843. *Writings,* III, 273–74n.
[2]Margaret's slave who served as her personal servant.
[3]Matilda Slaughter Hill. Identified in *Writings,* III, 274n.
[4]This is probably Mary Holley, who resided in Liberty County near Hugh B. Johnson. Identified in White, *1840 Census*, 103.
[5]Neither of these letters has been found.
[6]George W. Hockley and Samuel M. Williams were appointed commissioners to Mexico to work out the terms of an armistice with Mexico and to secure the release of the Mier prisoners. Friend, 86, and *Writings,* IV, 216–18, Houston to Hockley and Houston to Williams, July 14, 1843.
[7]For Houston's comments on Ashbel Smith's letters see *Writings* , IV, 224–26, Houston to Charles Elliot, October 5, 1843.
[8]Mrs. John D. Brown (Sarah Wade). Identified in *Handbook of Texas,* I , 223.
[9]The Heards were apparently looking after the Houstons' property while they were away.
[10]Mrs. Nathaniel Norwood (Margarite Adele Ewing). Identified in Best, 351.

[11]The Sims sisters were teachers who had transferred their school from Nacogdoches to Washington-on-the-Brazos. Hogan, 145. Sterne noted on December 12, 1842, that Ann Maria and Elizabeth Sims had "left here today" and that Martha would follow shortly. McDonald, 131.

Mrs Margaret L Houston
Washington Texas

Liberty
20th Sept 1843

Dearest Maggy,

Before sunset I reached here. The roads were horrible. I came the out-side road, and called for a few moments at Mr. Bowyers as well as Johnsons.[1] My carriage was about to break. I have had it repaired, and I hope it will stand to Washington. The 25th I hope will find me there. On tomorrow early, I wish to set out, but I am assured the roads are worse than what we found them in coming.

How our blessed mother ever made out to drive with the lines which she had I cannot imagine as well as the reins. They were short by two feet. The reins were not so fixed that the horses could be managed and really it was providential that she was not killed as well as our dear Niece. Thank God they are safe. I would write much, if I had anything which I could think wou'd interest you.

Tomorrow I hope to get to Adams[2] or to Dunmonds.[3] If the rains should last, I must contrive to have you taken to Houston by water from this place, if I have to come by the Island [Galveston] with a Boat from Houston. But we will see. If I can I will contrive you some arrow root and such things as you may need from Houston or the Island.

I do hope dearest, that you will enjoy yourself with your relatives, & that your health with theirs will be completely restored. That you will take care of the poor little scamp, I feel well assured. Poor fellow, I hope you will soon be able to resume his nursing of which I think he feels some anxiety, tho' he will not declare it, but give some significant intimations.

The Boat is expected here on tomorrow, and I hope Vernal will be able to get off with her, if he should conclude to go to Alabama. I feel a deep & abiding solicitude for Brother Royston, and will aid him to the full extent of my means if they can be of use to him, but it will be necessary for me to know his circumstances.[4] To expend my means without extricating him fully would be nonsense, and useless also. I will let him have what land he may need and where he may select, of my tract as I have Bledsoe and Vernal. If he can get off and come here is the great matter. If possible he should do so. Now we are all in the dark as to his real situation, and we can not act with advantage to him. Hence I have thought the necessity of Vernals speedy visit if at all.

I called to see Col & Mrs Hardin.[5] They are well, and made a thousand kind enquiries, as well as all that I have seen in relation to the family, and as you will suppose yourself & Master Sam in particular. Mrs Bowyers said she would, if possible be up to see you. She is a <u>Captain</u>, but I had not time to drive there today.

It is now late at night, and I must Conclude, as I hope to set out early. I stay to night at Lang's,[6] as he is sober, and I can pay him. It is not unpleasant. It would be wrong to spunge [sic] on a private family, with my retinue. Few as they are, in number, I have a pretty good <u>menagerie</u>, tho' [R. T.] Kane says he has lost his dog!! Poor Carlo! He has lost by losing Kane. Carlo was not the worst of dogs!!!

I will come for you as soon as I can. I will devise the ways and means, and beg that you will feel no solicitude on the subject if Heaven will kindly spare me. Kiss all for me, and hug poor little <u>Sam</u> close to your heart for me. Yes! and do it in his worst fit of temper for he is <u>then most be be pitied</u>! His infirmity is greatest.

Dearest Maggy Adieu
Thine Ever
Houston

Mrs. Houston

[1]Hugh Blair Johnson of Liberty.
[2]This was probably J. W. Adams of Montgomery County. Darman, 139.
[3]Joseph Dunman. Ibid, 129, and Miriam Partlow, *Liberty County and the Atascocito District*, (Austin: Pemberton Press, 1974), 101.
[4]Robert and Varilla Royston were experiencing financial difficulties.
[5]Cynthianna O'Brien and Franklin Hardin of Liberty. Identified in Daughters of the Republic of Texas, 349.
[6]Daniel J. Lang. Identified in Mullins, 96.

Gen. Sam Houston
Washington, Texas

Grand Cane Oct 6th 1843

My dear Husband,

Brother Vernal expects to leave for Galveston in the morning, and as I shall have so few opportunities of sending letters to any post office for you, I deem it a very fortunate thing. And now what shall I tell you? Our time has passed so smoothly along since you left that I hardly know what incident to begin with, but the unvaried scenes of our forest life at best, would not make a very vivid description on paper. But I know you would wish me to describe the budding beauties of our blooming boy, and describe the gradual developments of his genius. This I can not do. If I could, I would present you a most interesting volume, but if you could see him now, you would understand why I can not describe him. Indeed he is a wonderful boy! His health is excellent and his appetite very fine.

I recd [sic] your letter from Liberty[1] several days after it was written, but it was not the less welcome. I trembled for your journey home, but trust that it was performed without any serious accidents. My time has passed very pleasantly with my relations, and every day I grow more fond of quiet and retirement. When I leave these wild woods for the great world again, I shall remember with pleasure many a sweet hour of meditation.

Old Coleta[2] and his family have been camping near us several days. They have been a length of time at Pine island, but were compelled to leave there on account of the sickness that prevailed amongst them, and they are now returning to thier old homes. They are wretched looking objects. Haggard from sickness and suffering. Poor old Coleta is extremely anxious to see you, and I think he hopes to have his wrongs redressed when you come. He took Sam in his arms, and his dim eyes sparkled with delight. Oh how I wish that I could speak thier language! It pains my heart to know that there are human beings in our midst that know nothing of the Saviour. They are passing away, and soon the lone forests that they inhabit will know them no more! Oh that I could tell them of Jesus! Dearest Husband, have I wandered into a theme that touches no sympathetic chord in your bosom? Oh no I can not, I will not believe it, but let me now ask you of yourself! Dearest do you preserve invisible the good resolutions that you expressed to me just before our parting, or have they vanished like the "morning cloud" and "the early dew!"

Oh my husband! my husband! what language shall I employ to express the intense interest that I feel for the welfare of your soul! Time hurries on, and the cold grave will soon receive our lifeless forms! Then of what avail will be the excuses with which you now silence your conscience? If your soul is unprepared, will the nation that you have built up extend an arm to save you? No, the world itself shall flee before "the face of him that sitteth upon the throne!" Your excuse heretofore has been that you "had no time to think of these things." Are you quite sure of this? Are there no moments wasted in sleep and otherwise that might be spent in preparing for Eternity? Dearest this all important subject must not be neglected. Your soul shall live when the name of Texas will be lost amid the vast "wreck of matter" that shall take place at the final consummation of things. My husband, to tell you that religion could not lessen our present happiness would be an insult to your good sense, yet I can not but think how sweetly our lives would glide along in Christian union! Oh shall this fond wish of my heart ever be realized!

As to the time of my return, I wish you to consult your own convenience about [torn] Come for me whenever your business will allow you, but would it not be well for the stove to be taken up before I return? I think I would like to go through Galveston, if we can make it convenient. I hope Mrs Herd will take good care of our things. Beg her if you please, to move the piano, if she should scald my room, as the water will pass through the wall.

Present us affectionately to all our friends. Sis sends much love to you. Sarah also. Mother was over today. Her health is greatly improved. It is night, and our babe is sleeping. I will pray for you and lie down by his side.

Thy wife
M. L. Houston

[1]See Houston to Margaret, September 20, 1843.
[2](Also spelled Kalita) Chief of the Coushatta Indians. For an account of his helping settlers and rescuing a child during the runaway scrape see Partlow, 107.

Gen. Sam Houston
Washington, Texas

Liberty Oct 18th 1843

My dear Husband,

I have an opportunity of writing to you, and I avail myself of it, but I must confess it is with the hope that it will miss you, for I trust that long before it gets to Houston, Sam and I will be pressed to the dear bosom that I ought never to have left. It is the 10th day since I arrived in this dreary place. It is a terrible trial, yet I endeavor to submit to it with calmness and resignation. I do not feel, nor even despond a great deal, but try to nerve myself for very worst that can happen. I am staying at Judge Branch's,[1] and Sam and I are very comfortable and kindly treated. Judge B. says Jeff Wright's description of Sam was perfectly correct, and that he is the most extraordinary child he ever saw. Oh my Husband, do we deserve such a blessing? Would not Providence be perfectly just in punishing us for our sins by taking him from us? When I think of my own wasted hours, I look at my child and tremble! Alas, his infant smiles and prattle have wound themselves too closely around my heart. There seems some witchery about him, for he captivates every one that sees him.

It was truly a painful thing to part with my dear kindred, but I felt that I was going to my husband, and all other ties must yield to that. The fact of being so near them has made my detention in this place much more distressing. My dear relations are only a day's journey from me, and yet I can not see them! Sarah Ann is not with me. Her health is so bad that we thought it best for her not to come. I am getting my strength and complexions very fast, and I have some hopes that you will yet see me wear the hue of health. As for Master Sam, he is grown so much that you will hardly believe him the same. I think the climate of the Trinity agrees with us both very finely. The young gentleman makes himself perfectly at home where-ever he goes, and laughs in my face, when I look serious at the trials that assail me.

There is one more difficulty which I apprehend. That is, that the boat may be detained in the river, in consequence of which you may wait in Galveston or Houston for me, not knowing what has happened. I wrote to you by Mr Bledsoe as he went to the island, and told you all I could that would interest you. Dearest I hope we will meet soon. I am waiting impatiently for the boat or carriage.

Ever thy devoted wife
Margaret L. Houston

[1]Judge Edward T. Branch. For a biography see Jennet, 55–56.

As Houston's last administration drew to a close, Margaret wrote her mother a family letter. Houston added a postscript at the end.

Mrs. Nancy Lea
Grand Cane
Liberty County Texas

Washington Jan 23, 1844

Dearest Mother,

I was delighted to learn from Mr. R. last night the he would be able to send a letter to you immediately after his return home, for although I have little to tell you, yet it is a pleasure and a [blurred] which I prize immeasurably to assure my dear mother her sacred memory is as fondly cherished as ever. Just as I was often with her in my dreams, once more I was a joyous child, and leaning on her dear bosom! But suddenly a voice at my side aroused me, and I arose and remembered that I was myself a Mother!

Mr. Ros. gave me the first news that I have had of our dear relations in a great while, and oh how happy I was to learn that you were all well again. I wrote to you about two weeks ago, and I was so unwell at the time that I fear my letter has distrest you, if you read it, but I hardly think it likely that it has reached you. I am remarkable [sic] well. G. H. has had much trouble with honourable congress, but I hardly think we will suffer them to do the country a great deal of mischief.[1] He is pretty smart, and rather hard to catch a bother [sic]! If I should tell you how much his temper has improved, you would not believe me, so I would merely say that the change is astonishing. Indeed my dear Mother, I must think that it is the work of God and that his heart is under the influence of the Holy Spirit. His walk is certainly that of a pure Christian, and I think he is only [torn] livelier faith to claim promises that are held out to him. Oh that the Lord would remove the veil from his eyes and would make him to look upon the blessed Jesus as his friend and emancipator.

Judge Lockhart's two oldest sons[2] arrived a few weeks ago with their families. I have not seen them yet, but I have understood that they saw Cousin Columbus [Lea] [blurred] and also that they came down the river to visit with him and Bro Vernal. I have missed Tose very much since I came home, and I do realy long to [blurred] little things. And dear Sis, but [blurred] I about them! I shall be foolish if I do. Dear Ma, do not let them abuse me for not writing to them, for constant throngs of company, and health, will not allow me to write more than a letter now and then, and I think that would always be to you. I drew up to the table this morning intending to write you a very long letter, but I have been constantly interrupted by company, and Master Sam's requisitions, that I shall at last be compelled to finish it much sooner that I wish, as Mr. Ros. expects to start at 3 o'clock PM and it is now near 2. Tell Bro. Billy we have had some of his kinfolks to spend some time with us, Jno Scurry and lady, and realy seem delighted with her. She is a spirit lady, and a pleasant companion for me.

Ma, when you opened this letter and found who it was from, the first exclamation was, now we shall hear of nothing but Sam! and have I not punished you handsomely by saying nothing about him! I am strongly tempted to conclude just here, but I must tell you ma, that Sam is the greatest baby I ever saw, but I am greatly weakened by nursing him, and being up with him at night. Dr. Rowlet[3] whom I mentioned to you in my letter and Gen. H. are very anxious for me to wean him, but I can not do it unless you were with me. I expect we will visit Galveston in the spring, and I hope you will meet me there, and bring Tose with you by all means, and Sis too if possible. Present my love to them, and also to Bro. Billy [William Bledsoe]. Sam sends his love and respects to you all. I enclose a lock of his hair. Do make them write!

Thy daughter
M. L. Houston

I unite with my Dear Margaret with affectionate love to all the family. I have not time to write news, but will try to send papers occasionally.

Thy Devoted Son Truly
Sam Houston

Mother

[1]Congress had voted to return the capital to Austin. Lankevich, 50.
[2]William and Charles Lockhart, sons of Judge John Lockhart. Wallis and Hill, 336.
[3]Dr. Daniel Owen Rowlett practiced medicine in Fayette County. Identified in Daughters of the Republic of Texas, I, 82.

In the early spring the Houston family traveled to Houston City on their way to a meeting Sam had with the Comanche Indians. From there, Houston wrote to his mother-in-law, Nancy Lea.

Houston, Texas
19th Apr 1844

My Dear Mother,

As Mr Ellis[1] will leave tomorrow for Trinity,[2] I will not deny myself the pleasure of writing to you, as well as to gratify my Dear Margaret.

We did calculate when we left home to have been with you at fartherest by the 8th Inst, but when I came here I found that I was compelled to go to Galveston on important public business.[3] Then on my return, I had to send an Express to Washington.[4] By the time it returned, the rain fell in such quantities as to prevent our travelling. The waters are all very high and San Jacinto is said to be much higher than it was ever known before. We are compelled to wait for the floods to subside. We hope in the course of a few days to be able to set out and reach you. Margaret has now an attack of the asthma upon her, but I hope she will soon be entirely relieved. She has not suffered so much as she formally used to so. Yet she has suffered much—a good deal on Sam's account, for when he wills it, he must be attended to, or he will make a fuss and this she cant allow even at the expence [sic] of her own comfort. He too has rather a bad cold, or is taking the Hooping Cough.—it is prevalent in this city or at least in some parts of it.

We were very anxious that he shou'd reach you in good health, that you might judge of him as he was thro' the winter, and this spring. He is a clever child, and Margaret really thinks him handsome. He is truly good looking, but not pretty. We think him smart, of course, and as his Mother is popular people like to add to her happiness, and of course praise him very much. Many say that he resembles me, and others that he resembles you very much, and really I think he does resemble you quite as much as he does me. Some of his features are like my Fathers & his disposition will do for either Moffitt or a Houston. Every day his mother & myself fancy that he does some smart thing that he did not do yesterday!! He is quite as smart as any child that I have seen of his age. Of his size, he is very active & robust. You will have the pleasure soon, I hope of giving him some training, for he has never had but one trifling smack in his life, and that was yesterday for biting his mother when she was nursing him. He regarded it more as an insult than a matter of right on part of his mother. I have hope in his disposition and that is because he is cheerful and affectionate.

When I left home I expected to have returned, and gone to the Treaty which is now holding with the Comanchee [sic] Indians along the falls of Brasos[5] [sic]. As things now stand on the subject of annexation, as well as our relations to other countries, it is probably best that I should be at this point for the present. By the Neptune which is to arrive on to day, or it is confidently expected on tomorrow, I look for important information. By my next dispatches, I hope to be able to determine whether we are to be annexed to the U. States, or are to rely upon ourselves with the aid of friendly powers to be an Independent Nation at peace with Mexico.[6] If I live, I hope before my time of office expires, to be placed on some secure footing and leave the Government, as well as the peoples in the enjoyment of prosperity & happiness.

Margaret unites in all love to you and all the family. I do not particularize, but send it all together to divide as we are extremely anxious to embrace you all. Sam sends a thousand and one kisses to Grand ma. He hopes to be there soon and present them in person.

I have not mentioned that I had the pleasure to meet brother Vernal at the Island, as I suppose that you heard of the fact. We have seldom heard from you all and then only by chance since last fall, tho' we have frequently wrote and sometimes I have sent you papers containing messages and other Documents to let you know that I was not beaten down by the assembly of our Greatness. Their efforts did as much injury to the country as they did to me. Many of the members were well off for they were so base that they could not be injured by the loss of reputation. Indeed many of them were so utterly unworthy that it was dishonor to any cause or country that they should profess to serve it. They will meet their reward.

Truly your son
Sam Houston

Mrs Nancy Lea
Maggy thanks sister for her letter and its contents. Please tell Miss Tose that I will try and take a Beau. Doct [George W.] Hill was well last account, and sent plenty of love.

[1] Joseph Ellis, an agent to the Alabama and Coshatta Indians. *Writings,* V, 14.
[2] The Ellis family lived near the Leas and Bledsoes in the vicinity of Grand Cane. Reverend J. H. H. Ellis, *Sam Houston and Related Spiritual Forces,* (Houston: The Concord Press, 1945), 50.
[3] Houston met with Charles Elliot, charge d'affaires from Great Britain, to discuss terms proposed for future negotiations with Mexico and to check on the progress of the annexation agreement with the United States. *Writings,* IV, 301–303. Houston to Washington D. Miller, April 16, 1844.
[4] Ibid. Miller was writing Houston regularly to keep him informed of progress in Washington D. C.
[5] The falls were a crossing on the Brazos River and an Indian camping ground located a few miles south of the present city of Marlin. Ray Miller, *Ray Miller's Eyes of Texas Series: Fort Worth-Brazos Valley,* (Houston: Gulf Publishing Company, 1981), 106–107.
[6] U. S. Secretary of State had signed the treaty of annexation with Texas representatives Henderson and Van Zandt on April 12, 1844. Ten days later it was sent to the U. S. Senate with a message urging ratification. It would be rejected. Stanley Siegel, *A Political History of the Texas Republic, 1836–1845,* (Austin: University of Texas Press, 1956), 231–32.

Houston remained behind in Galveston. Margaret left on a trip to visit her family at Grand Cane. She sailed on a steamboat up the Trinity River and wrote the following description of the trip.

To Gen. Sam Houston
Galveston Texas
Care of Maj. James Cocke Collector at Galveston

Trinity River, Sabbath Night, May 12, 1844

My dear Husband,

We have anchored for the night and my mind is so thronged with the incidents of the last days, that I can not sleep. I feel like a wanderer in some enchanted palace. What may be the next scene in my varied life? For what hath God preserved me! Am I to be the happy instrument of bringing to him the wanderer whom I have cherished in my bosom or shall some new anguish fall upon my spirit for the love that hath perchance adored a mortal in his place, and that mortal, one who hath never yet truly repented of his sins and who yet stands exposed to his awful wrath! Oh my husband, all the transgressions of youth, the iniquity of riper years are before the blazing eye of God, and nothing but the blood of Jesus can wash them away! How long will you vainly dream that the Lord will convert you in his own good time without requiring any effort on your part. Awake! awake! Your convictions are even now passing away and purchance "the hot iron" is causing you heart searing that may render gloomy mists of fatalism and lead you into everlasting darkness!

13th 7 o'clock PM

We are now about 30 miles below Liberty. I supposed we would have been near there but, were several hours on ground yesterday. A melancholy incident happened on board last night. A stranger died unnoticed and entirely alone. I was interested in his case on yesterday and sent to ask him if he wished any medicine or nourishment. Finding that I could do nothing for him in that way, I requested Mr. Brasher[1] to come with him and ascertain something about his situation. He did so, and satisfied me by saying that his theory was that he was merely suffering from activity after an attack of fever. In the night I heard him calling most piteously and sent Eliza[2] so soon as I could raise her. Some one had just handed him a glass of water, for which he had no doubt been suffering for hours. This morning he was found cold and deep in the sleep from which the last love would awake him.

1. o'clock

We are now at Liberty. Tilly[3] and Mr. Brasher speak of taking a walk into the village and I will remain and employ the few minutes that we are still in writing to you. My health has been remarkably good so far and I trust that traveling may affect something for me. Sam is extremely playful and that is evidence enough of health. He held out his arms very readily to Eliza today to go and look for papa, but alas no papa is to be found. He has learned to take up Miss Tilly's hand very sentimentally and press it to his lips. I only gave him one kiss yesterday, and this morning when I told him to "kiss Miss Tilly's hand" he immediately took it up without his attention being directed to it and kissed it! He was very much astonished at the sight of a snake yesterday, a moccasin that was brought in alive by Mr. Pilot.[4] While it was held up by the throat, Sam looked on in silent amazement. I do not think he made more than one effort to obtain it. I suppose he soon learned from the countenances of those about him that it was not a very convenient thing to handle. Lest I should not have an opportunity of sending my letter to you I will leave it on the boat, and have another to add to it on its return if possible. The Capt. told me he will be in Galveston a week from the time of his departure. When will you come to us? Let it be soon I entreat you! Do not let the cares of state press too heavily upon you. Much of your time, dear husband, has already—I will not say gone to waste—for doubtless thousands have been made rich and comfortable by your public services, but in the eyes of God, what will this avail? Our Blessed Saviour hath assured us that on the last day the Lord will say unto the righteous, "Come blessed of my Father, and unto the wicked Depart ye cursed unto everlasting fire prepared for the devil and his angels!!" But unto none will he say, "It is true that on earth you did not seek my face but then your cares were so great that no time was left for repentance and godly sorrow, enter ye also into the abode of the blessed!" Dearest deceive not yourself. Weigh these words well.

It is now 10 minutes past 6 o'clock and we are about to go to Robinson's[5] where I suppose we will stay the night. In the hurry of departure, I may not have an opportunity of taking leave of you. Then Dearest of human beings, Farewell.

Thy devoted and confiding wife,
Margaret L. Houston

On outside:

We anchored last night 7 miles below Carson's and in a few minutes we expect to land. We are all very well. Come soon. Thy wife M. L. H.

[1]Margaret is probably referring to C. D. Brashear who lived at West Liberty (now called Dayton). Partlow, 205.
[2]Margaret's personal servant.
[3]Matilda Johnson.
[4]This may be Claude Nicholas Pillot, who lived 27 miles north of Houston on Willow Creek. Identified in Caroline Reeves Ericson, *Nacogdoches—Gateway to Texas: A Biographical Directory, 1773–1849*. (Nacogdoches: Ericson Books, 1991), 227.
[5]Robinson's Bluff, the plantation of James Robinson, was located 167 miles north of Galveston. Partlow, 66, 191.

Grand Cane May 18, 1844

My Beloved Husband,

I intended to have commenced a letter to you before, but the excitement of meeting two dear ones at home and the constant stir and bother that we have kept up have rendered it impossible. Besides, we have been very busy preparing Sarah Ann to go home. We landed safely at Robinsons about 4 O clock Tuesday[1] and conveyed the news to our family in sufficient time for them to get us home on the same day before night. We came up on horseback (the distance being about 9 miles) and I brought Sam almost the whole way on my lap as he seemed to expect that I would do so and you know Sam is not opposed to having his own way when it is perfectly convenient. The little scamp is thriving remarkably and enjoyes [sic] himself very finely running over the yard after the ducks and chickens. I almost forget the years of suffering that have past in the recollections of health and joy that the last few days have revived. The very topics that we have discussed seem to exercise a soothing influence upon me. And then the words of affection from loved ones far far away. Robert [Royston] brought me a great deal of news and many messages. Aunt [Margaret (Peggy) Moffitt] Lea writes that she has kissed Sam's lock of hair but she would rather kiss the dear boy himself. Cousin Columbus has established a new partnership "Lea and Houston attorneys at Law" (meaning the little boy[2] and Sam). I do hope Sam will ever plead very well, for he seems rather desposed to <u>command</u>. I have told you of the [blurred] tree below my chamber window, and of the roots there. I am told that Aunt Lea suffers no one to approach it, but treats it as a hallowed thing. Oh how sweet it is to be loved and remembered by one who was so dear to me! My husband will think that I am truly become a child. I am telling him so many little things that to him [are] unimportant and uninteresting. But as I [blurred] his generous heart for he has always [blurred] with me in joy or gloom in hopes and despondency that any ardour that ever stirred my heart hath met a responding throb from his.

I left a letter[3] on the boat for you and I suppose that you will get this and it at the same time. Look upon it and Dearest if the contents of the former should seem too young, Oh remember that they were dictated by true and devoted affection. By love that would not soothe its object into a false happiness by hiding its dangers about him. The picture there drawn may be harsh and forbidding but turn not away from him. Look upon it and seek the blood of Jesus to cleanse thy soul, else in the dying hour that picture shall arise before thee in fearful colours.

I shall soon be looking out for your welcome approach. Oh that you were with me dear, dear husband. I was afraid to be away not because I want confidence in you but I worry that you may die and we may never never meet again in this world nor the world to come. Oh can it be that such a thing is possible!

Mother has given Billy[4] to Sam and he is truly a wonderful gift for he is a healthier boy and one of the best negroes in the world. Would it not be a good plan to sell the carriage horses and bring Joshua with you to work on the farm? Billy can wait on us without any difficulty. I have concluded to hire Eliza to Mrs. Maffet[5] as she is so anxious to have her and will be bringing us something. I hope dearest you will try to economize a little. However I do not intend to lecture you. I think it probable I should go to Washington sometime during the summer, but if I do I shall go on horseback and leave Sam. I expect Tose and Bob[6] will start in this morning. Bob is in great haste to get back as he has a flourishing school in the canebrake.[7] Cousin Columbus sends news of the neighborhood. [blurred] have offered him three hundred dollars a year and all he can make over that. He teaches the different sciences and Greek and Latin, and is ever capable of conducting a fine school. Brother R[8] is entirely clear of debt and getting on better than he has ever done before. I wrote to Aunt Lea and told her that I thought we would go on to the Hermitage[9] next spring and make them a visit as we pass through Ala. Dear as soon as you have leisure wish you would write to her soon. It would be such a comfort to her.

19th Sabbath day. We have just dismissed our Sunday school. I am assigned with our project of [blurred] A good general of the children have learned to read and some have learned for the first time that there was a God.

Dearest I hope you will be willing to settle here. I should be so happy if you were with me. Mother has determined to keep Sam & Ann until the fall and then go home with her. I forget to tell you that Mother, Mr. Bledsoe, & Mr. Holliman had built a comfortable cabin on Ma's land. The family all send much love to you.

Ever thy own
M. L. Houston

[1]May 14, 1844.
[2]Wayne Emmet Lea, son of Columbus Lea, was born November 30, 1843. Gandrud, v. 182, 97.
[3]Margaret to Houston, May 12, 1845.
[4]A young family slave.
[5]Tilly's mother, Mrs. John Maffett of Galveston.
[6]Robert Royston, Sarah Ann's brother.
[7]The Canebrake is a region of river bottom lands in the valley of the Tom Bigbee River in Perry County, Alabama. Originally the land had been covered by a dense growth of cane. Owen, I, 199.
[8]Robertus Royston, the father of Robert and Sarah Ann.
[9]The Tennessee home of Andrew Jackson.

Mrs Margaret L Houston
at Maj. Bledsoe's
Liberty County
Texas
Mr. Lang

At Pruits[1]
Sunday 19th May 1844

Dearest,

It is impossible to conceive of my disappointment and regrets at finding myself unable to get over the Trinity. I have rode very hard and my nerves are so much affected that I can hardly write a legible hand or one that you can read I fear. I rode late last night as this morning flushed with hope that by this time of day (12 M) that I would be near you and the dear little Tiger, but it is not so. In a few moments I intend to start for Washington, as the court martial will meet there on tomorrow.[2] To night I expect to reach Mr Jones[3] on San Jacinto, and if possible tomorrow night to reach Mrs McCarley.[4] Could I have crossed the river, I intended to pass one night with you, and then proceed on and return so soon as possible.

Unless very important business should detain me, I will see you, my Love, very soon. I have engaged an express to send you a bundle, with it your medicine. The arsenic I did not get, but the nitric I found in a bundle sent to my room by Mr Lubbuck. I only spent one night in Houston, and was writing all the time that [I] was there. I ordered for you many trifles to be sent by the first Boat from Galveston. I ordered a Dozen Bottles of Selsers water, and you use it with great benefit. It is from Germany, but is the same of the Saratoga. Drink a Glass of it before each meal. It is fine. Our dear, dear little fellow may fancy it, and if he should get him to drink it.

If you desire soda, pour a glass pretty near full of the water. Then put in nearly a wine glass of claret, with a large Tea spoonful of Havana sugar, and it will be very pleasant. So soon as the sugar is put in after the claret let it be stirred soon, and drank.

I have ten thousand things to say to you my Dearest, for really, I thought that I always loved you, but now I think that I never loved you half so much as I have done since we parted. I wished to see you that I might tell you so with a thousand kisses. All last night I was dreaming of you, and Sam. I feel every day more sensible of my dependence upon you for my temperate happiness and joys arising more and dependent upon our relations.

You may be assured that I will be with you the first instant at my command. I am not, and therefore, I will not attempt to express my anxiety to see you, as well as mother and the family all. I hope Sarah Ann will not leave Texas until I can see her & Robert. As for Mother, I had no idea that she will go. If she does, I hope to see her first. In ten or twelve days I trust I will be with you. I could now cross the river in a skiff, but not with my horse. Today I offered six dollars to take us over with the horses, but I could not succeed. The express will cross in a skiff, & get the horse on the other side.

The Indians I expect will be in Washington by the time that I can get there.[5] Nothing over which I have control will keep me from my ever dear Margaret a moment longer than I can reach you. You need not think that I will give way to despondency. I will be too busy for that. Until last night, I have not slept one night since we parted.

I was invited to a Soiree on the first, on Tuesday after you left me, but would not attend because I supposed that you would prefer that I did not and moreover, I had not the least inclination. That day I had made a speech, and slam[med] my enemies. You would have been amused to see the wounded pigeons flutter. It was thought by my friends that I gained more by it than any speech which I made.

Captain Payn[6] accompanied me this far, and will return with me to Dunmans and go from there to Houston. I may come to see you by way of Swarthout, and if the river should be high, I can cross there when I could not on other places. I send a letter to Miss Tilly. It is sweet I expect. The Judge[7] sent it. Your friends were all well in Houston and I enclose a note from Mrs Reily[8] tho' I had not the happiness to see her, nor any Ladies, but those of the Capitol. I must ride and Oh my Dear fancy how I must feel. Hope the most ardent blasted, and to think that a very little distance seperates [sic] us and ensures me sorrow instead of the highest of earthly joys which I had so fondly anticipated.

Had I attempted to bring the carriage, I would have failed. Captain Payn desires his best compliments of yourself, Miss Sarah Ann, and all the Ladies, as well as the Gentlemen. He feels also much disappointment in not having the pleasure of seeing you and the other ladies. He sends 20 kisses and three lemons to Master Sam, or the kisses to Sam and the lemons to his mother.

Dearest, I can only say commend me affectionately to our dear mother, Sister, and the family.

I will see you so soon as I can, and I beseech you to be happy, not to[o] desponding. A thousand kisses and embraces to our dear Boy.

Yes, kiss the Ladies. I had forgotten Tilly and Sarah Ann when you and Sam had sole possession of my heart & head.

Thy ever devoted Husband
Houston

P. S. If mother or Sarah Ann should wish money let them have it that they may feel no embarrassment in or out of Texas.

Houston

[1]Several Pruit family members, including Jesse and Beasley, owned property on the Trinity River near Liberty. See Partlow, 199 and map on inside cover.

[2]Houston is referring to the trial of Commodore Moore on piracy charges.

[3]Houston may possibly be referring to John Jones, who is identified as owning property on the west side of the San Jacinto. Villamae Williams, ed., *Stephen F. Austin's Register of Families*, (Baltimore, Maryland: Genealogical Publishing Company, 1984), 132.

[4]The Texas Army had camped at the McCarley plantation prior to the Battle of San Jacinto. Zuber, 79–80, 242.

[5]Houston had invited the Waco Indians to come for a meeting. Houston to A-Cah-Quash, May 2, 1844, *Writings*, IV, 316–17 and Houston to Thomas G. Western , May 1, 1844, 311–13.

[6]This is probably Captain B. Owen Payne, Captain of the ordinance of the Texas Army. Identified in *Compiled Index to Elected and Appointed Officials of the Republic of Texas 1835–1846*, (Austin: State Archives Division, Texas State Library, 1981), 96.

[7]Judge Robert D. Johnson.

[8]Ellen Hart Reily.

Houston joined Margaret at Grand Cane on June 11, 1844, where he was seriously ill for over a month, probably with malaria. He returned to Washington-on-the-Brazos on July 27, 1844.[1] The following letter written by Margaret in Grand Cane to Houston is not dated, but it appears to have been written during the last week of July, 1844.

Through a letter from Mr. Withers to Mr. Bledsoe I received the joyful intelligence that you were safely commenced on your journey as far as the San Jacinto bottom, and that your health was much improved. Oh how kind and merciful is our Heavenly Father, thus to preserve you and grant you a return of health! I shall expect your return most anxiously. Indeed I can not be happy until I see you again.

My dearest, my mind retains some recollections that are exceedingly painful to me, and if it were in my power, I would obliterate them forever. This proud heart of Mine! It has caused it all. I alone am realy to blame. Yes, this foolish heart, with vain imagination and presumptuous conceit is ever distracting spiritual fears and it is not strange that my earthly happiness should suffer from it. Oh if I could only see you all would be right again! But you are far far away, and I must endure in silence my useless regrets. Heaven [torn] our future intercourse may be sweet as the past, which except for the recent interruption has been almost a continued interchange of fondness and affection. Our only clouds have arisen when my proud heart has claimed more than it is due, or trembled lest that had fallen short. Do you remember that in the heyday of our first acquaintance, I told you that my disposition was not perfect? What I then termed jealousy, I believe is pride, and I have since combated it in various forms, but I am firmly persuaded that it is my "besetting sin," and with the help of God I will strive to subdue it.

We have rec'd letters from Ala. and they are much disappointed and dissatisfied at Sarah Ann's not returning [torn] realy no one used any persuasions or exercised any authority except Mother. They write with great excitement and alarm, as they had heard that Sarah Ann was to be married. That is some excuse for them, but I assure you we do not relish the reprimand much.

I have received a very affectionate letter on yesterday from Tilly. She gave me an abundance of news, and big arms of flattery and foolery.

It is late at night and Mr. Bledsoe expects to start in the morning. Sam is now sleeping sweetly, but he has interrupted me several times since I commenced writing. The little fellow is in perfect health, and grows rapidly, but does not walk yet. I trust that with the blessing of Heaven, we may enjoy many happy hours with him.

Present me affectionately to our friends, and come soon to thy devoted wife.

M. L. Houston

P.S. The relations send love to you. I am truly distrest [sic] on Mother's account. Her health is failing rapidly through mental and bodily suffering, and without a speedy change, I fear the consequence. Heaven preserve her from all I forebode. My own health is fine, and the rest of the family well.

[1]Sue Flanagan, *Sam Houston's Texas,* (Austin: University of Texas, 1964), 75. See also Houston to W. B. Ochiltree, July 28, 1844. *Writings,* IV, 342–43.

Trinity River August 3rd, 1844

Dearest,

I wrote to you a few days ago and sent the letter to you by Mr. Bledsoe. I expect it will have reached you before you receive this, but as you may be detained in Washington, and trusting that a consideration of its home details and the little information I can give you will not be altogether uninteresting to you, I have commenced to begin a letter to you although I am far from feeling well. I have been suffering a day or two with the asthma brought on I think by taking quinine too freely to check the malaria with which I have been threatened.

I was delighted by Mr. Withers intelligence of you. I did expect <u>one little line from you</u> by the wait if it had been but one little line. Perhaps it was best that you did not write. The exertion might have fatigued you. Dr. Dismuke[1] also brought me news of you from Adams's.[2] I was truly happy to hear that your health and spirits were so much improved and that you enjoyed yourself so much with the friends who met you at Adams's but I do think that you ought to have slept more after so fatiguing a journey as on the day preceding.

You can not imagine how much Sam is grown and improved. He is beginning to step a little and I hope before you see him he will walk quite well. Mr. Worshem[3] has made him a beautiful whip and he pops it with such pomp as an up-country wagoner [sic] and he looks about very curiously when I talk to him about his pa. Oh my love, he is a sound bond of union between us. Heaven has blessed us in our child.

Sunday, 4th I am melancholy today, and very unwell. I wrote until late last night, in fact the pen almost dropped from my hand before I gave it up, but I was compelled to do so at last.

Mother's health has been wretched indeed but today she is better than for many days. Grief,[4] together with the infirmities of age and a violent cough is fast wearing her away and I fear that I shall soon be without a parent. Heaven grant that my fears may be groundless.

Do come back so soon as you can. Your wife and little one will cling to you with reverence, fondness and devotion.

I expect you have heard of Mr. Goodall's death. (Gen. Davis's son-in-law.)[5] He died of something like the jaundices.

Farewell, Thine devotedly,
M. L. Houston

P.S. Sarah Ann sends her love to you, and all wish to be included.

[1]Dr. A. W. Dismuke. Identified in Daughters of the Republic of Texas, 225.
[2]Probably the plantation of J. W. Adams in Montgomery County.
[3]Archer G. Worsham of Grand Cane. Identified in Ellis, 51.
[4]Nancy Lea was still grieving over the death of her oldest son, Martin Lea.
[5]Albert C. Goodall was married to Katherine Davis, the daughter of General James Davis. Madge W. Hearne Collection of Papers, San Antonio.

To General Sam Houston,
Huntsville, Texas,
Mr. Evans (forwarded)

Grand Cane, Trinity River, Aug 7, 1844

Dearest Husband,

Oh delighted I have been this evening by your kind letters.[1] Yes they have made me very happy, but oh, I have been saddened too for while my heart was cheered and refreshed by the language of affection, I was shocked and distrest [sic] by the mournful intelligence of Col. P's death. Oh my love, I do pray from my heart that the awful blow which has fallen upon his family may be sanctified to your good! Remember that "now is the accepted time" not tomorrow, not the next hour, but this moment. Oh seize it, as it speaks to eternity, and at once give your heart to God.

How true it is that "we all do fade as a leaf," that the hopes, joys, cares and anxieties of this life and the soul appear useless before the searching eye of its Creator with all its stains and "washed from its sins and made white in the blood of the Lamb of the Lamb." Oh how gloomy must be the death here of him who hath not love of God in his heart! The Saviour is not there to whisper "I am near thee, be thee not afraid!" Dark, dark may be "the valley of the shadow of death," for the Holy Spirit defuseth no light along his path-way, and the Father doth not bid him welcome!

Oh my husband, my husband, my heart is filled with awful fears on your account! Remember that the time spent in jesting and unprofitable conversation is made up of moments given you (each one worth more incalculably more than millions of worlds!) to prepare for eternity! Death is abroad in the land. Our friends are falling around us. Some even since we parted. Neglect not those solemn warnings.

Aug. 8th

I was only able to write one page to you last night. As usual after supper I was compelled to go through "the pomp and circumstance" of getting Master Sammy to sleep. Before I could commence, his first nap was finished and the same ceremony repeated. This time the night was far advanced and I lay down to rest with a sad heart, I must confess for you are far, far away.

We had preaching in our little church yesterday by Mr. Friend[2] the Methodist. He was in wretched health and almost worn out by travelling and preaching amongst people who do not even pay his passage across the river. We furnished him with medicine to relieve the suffering brought on by exposure for them. I gave him the medicine he required, and at the same time blessed the generous hand of my husband who had put in my power to perform the sacred duty of charity. And oh my Love, we must not forget from whom we receive all our things! I trust that he will ever bless us with the means sufficient to [torn] the wants of the poor and distrest that we may meet in [our] journey through life. But above all may we subdue the fears that had possession of our hearts!

I delivered your message to Mother, but it was hardly necessary for you were not gone very far from us before she was saying that you had borne your sufferings with more patience than she could have and enough to try the patience of anyone. But dearest we recollect that no chastisement is sent without some purpose, and our business is to find out that purpose and derive all the [blurred] that we can from our afflictions. Let us watch the development of His wise plan who careth for our souls and strive to find out "what he would have us to do."

I regret that you found it necessary to go west. Ma says "do not ride in the heat of the day" and I say "do nothing that may endanger your health." Sarah Ann has had another visit from Mr. Vanpredillis.³ He is a very fine looking, intelligent young man and highly polished I calculated. He is also said to be very wealthy and to live like a prince. But (there is no accounting for taste you know) her answer to his suit was so very evasive, but at the same time so polite that he called her a "perfect circle." I leave you to draw your own inferences. I must confess that I did expect to see her constancy waver a little, but I saw no signs of it. His family are catholics, but he agreed to turn protestant, heretic or any thing else she would say, but all to no purpose, and he went away this morning in great chagrin. So much for being a few days ahead in these matters.

Mr. Bledsoe started to Galveston almost two weeks ago on Mr. Holliman's boat. He is not yet returned and Antoinette is very anxious about him. I wrote to you by him but you have hardly received the letters. I also prepared one for Mr. Worshem to take to Houston,⁴ but Mr. Edmunds stopped for it as he came along, for which I am very glad though it does not contain much. You will learn this much that you are never absent from my thoughts. Oh my Love do hasten to me, for I am sad, very sad on your account. I have neglected to tell you that Mother's health is improving and my own is very good. Sam is as hardy as a pig and generally as dirty too for he has taken up his quarters in the yard and under the floor and there will be in spite of me. I must hasten to a close for Mr. E. will start very soon, but I will try to write a short letter to Miss Ann Grissum and send a note of thanks to Mr. [Washington D.] Miller.

Thine devotedly
Margaret L. Houston

[1] No letters for this period have been located.
[2] Presiding elder L. S. Friend of Liberty. Identified in Kemp, *Houston Post*, May 1, 1934.
[3] Albert Baldwin Vanpredillis was a wealthy merchant who lived three miles from Liberty. Identified in White, *1840 Census of Texas,* 105.
[4] Margaret to Houston, August 3, 1844.

Houston was on the way to East Texas to settle problems which had arisen in Shelbyville between two groups of vigilantes, the Moderators and the Regulators, both of whom were acting contrary to the constitution and the laws of the republic.[1] *He stopped at the plantation of James Davis and wrote Margaret to console her about an unidentified enemy who had previously slandered Margaret and her mother.*

Genl Davis'
13 Sept 1844

Dearest,

I will not forego the pleasure of writing you a line. We came here by night fall, and were very kindly rec'd by all. I think the coast would be clear for Bud, if he were to make an alliance in the region. I will mark his course. He seems somewhat smitten, or I am no judge.[2]

My Dear, I will tell you, tho' you wou'd hear of it from others, that I escaped the chills & fever, and talked until half past two this morning, and never closed my eyes since we parted in sleep. I rose before clear day. When I ceased talking and I rendered thanks of my Creator for his mercies, and offered prayers for a continuance of his goodness and blessings upon you and our dear Boy, my meditations rested upon you both, and while the recollections of you soothed & cheered me, it had the effect to vanish sleep from my pillows.

Dearest, I need [not] tell you how dearly, how devotedly, and how ardently I do love you, nor need I tell you how much I am attached to our dear little brat. Poor little fellow how my heart bled to see him torn from me by necessity. Tho' I was somewhat amused to see his resolution to resist the authority of his nurse when I called her to take him, he understood me & emphatically told her not to touch him. When I looked back and saw him leaning over her shoulder and looking at me, I was truly sorry that I had put him to such a test. But I can only say that on my part it was foolish fondness or a Fathers affections. I hope my Love it will not be long until we shall, under the care of a kind and merciful God, meet again, and enjoy Sams whims and anticks [sic] and again be happy. Take my advice my dear, as I gave it to you, and you will find the wisdom of my counsel. Do not think about the fruitless attempts of that poor despicable wretch to assail you and Mother.[3] They have failed here. The blow was aimed at me, and he knew that nothing which he could say of me would be regarded, and he thought that by his slanders of others, he cou'd inflict upon me an <u>incurable</u> wound. He has utterly failed, and punishment now awaits him. Don't tell Mother of the matter if you have not done so. It is two years since the creature told the lies, and there are not two houses in Nacogdoches that he dare enter so low has he sunk, and the report has never circulated, and I pledged myself never to mention the mans name who told me. If it were known he had told such a thing, the people of Nacogdoches would whip him out of the place. I have not yet told Bud [Vernal Lea], but I feel it my duty to do so, and if he takes my advice, it will all come out right! Don't doubt me.

Now dearest I pray you to be happy and rest assured that my heart beats for you, and you alone!

If our path is beset by enemies and snares are set for us, we have only to watch and pray, lest we enter into temptation. This I know you will do, and you may rest assured that I will look to Heaven for aid, to enable me to secure your peace here and your eternal happiness. Dearest I will write to you whenever I can, and all that I think will interest or amuse you.

My Love to our dear Mother, Howda to Virginia,[4] and to your dear, dear self all my best and devoted affections. Do be happy & cheerful, and don't let the past give you a moments pain nor ever bestow a thought upon it. No one would believe such a slander, if it had circulation, which it has not. You recollect Gen [Memucan] Hunt said some such witty thing once and was half scared to death about it. Don't regard such things, and I have thus dwelt upon this matter because I thought you were distressed much about the matter when we parted, and now I hoped if I was correct that you will think no more about the nonsense.

Give Sam a thousand kisses for me I pray you, and hug him as hard as he does you.

Thy ever devoted Husband
Sam Houston

I am better than I have been since I was attacked in the red lands. I began on yesterday to use Dr Randalls[5] tonic pills and that rice water is a great thing I think.

Houston

[1]Lankevich, 53, and Crockett, 199–200. See also Houston's "Open Letter to my Countrymen," August 15, 1844. *Writings*, IV, 361–62.
[2]Houston is referring to the fact that Vernal Lea was enamoured with the General's daughter, Katherine Davis Goodall. They would later marry. Hearne Collection, San Antonio.
[3]Houston may have been referring to Judge George Miles of Liberty. Identified in the *Compiled Index to Elected and Appointed Officials of the Republic of Texas 1835–1846*. See also Houston to Vernal Lea, October 14, 1845, in Chapter VII of this volume.
[4]Virginia Thorn was the nine-year-old ward of Vernal Lea.
[5]Dr. Leonard Randall of San Augustine. Identified in Carpenter, IV, 1712.

General Sam Houston
Washington Texas
By Col. Palmer[1] to Montgomery

Grand Cane September 20, 1844

Dearest Husband,

With the faint hope of having a letter conveyed to you I have commenced one, but I must confess it is more for the pleasure of writing to you than because I have any thing new or interesting to tell you. I have rec'd two precious letters from you and for which I thank you, but dearest my heart is agonized at your ill health and continued lameness.[2] I do not feel as if I could endure your absence. My heart is heavy with grief. My Love you bid me to be cheerful and happy. Alas the very words to my ear are like gay music in a sorrowing house! If I can be resigned when you are gone it is the highest degree of content that I aspire to. More than this I need not ask for I can not be happy or satisfied without you. I have not enjoyed one moment of health since you left me. Almost as soon as you were gone I took a terrible chill and fever and have had these every alternate day up to the present time. I have tried our usual remedy, opium, but it has failed and I am now taking arsenic which I sincerely hope will cure me. I perceive already that it is doing me good although I have used it but a day and a half.

But we will talk of something more agreeable. This morning for the first time I had the pleasure of receiving your letter to Santanna and I must say that I was highly pleased with it.[3] The sentiments are that of pure patrition and high-souled [blurred] and the language is just such as I would wish. I was a little concerned at your allusions to a Santa Fe traitor, but I suppose you would term that a <u>charmless presence</u>. Your retorts of his charge of perjury were very good. It is altogether a fine document.

Mr. Jo. Ellis has been down and brought me news of the barbecue. I am glad to hear the people there were so well pleased, particularly the ladies, for I am not jealous, and if I were I should not be as my dear old friend Mrs. Maxey[4] and I learned (but just by minute characterizing) that you were seen attentive to her sister Cary[5] [blurred].

I have not yet told you anything about our dear boy! His health is very fine, and he continues to grow rapidly. Poor fellow! he was sadly distrest when you sent him back, but I administered his usual cordial, and he was soon smiling through his tears, and his blue eyes looked up as joyously as every violet. Dear boy! I exclaimed to myself, you know not the magnitude of your affliction, and your Mother has cured your grief, but you can only soothe and can not cure hers. He still looks anxiously in the direction that you left, when we ask him "where his papa is?" I have very little trouble with him, except on rainy days, and then it is with great difficulty that I keep him within doors. He has learned to make a very good bow, and I think when you come home, you can soon teach him to make an elegant one.

I am anxiously expecting bro Vernal's return who will of course bring me news of you. Mr. Holliman, also I shall expect very soon. Heaven grant that they may bring me news of your improved health and hopes of a [blurred] reunion!

Our neighbor Mr. [blurred] has lost his wife and I am told he is dangerously ill himself. I am told that his house is a scene of suffering and poverty. I have not been able to visit them, but I have sent them a little aid. It is almost 4 o clock PM and I am taking a hard chill, so good-by for the present.

Saturday 21st I suffered intensely last night with my chill and fever, and today I am nervous and feeble. I wish you were with me dearest, kindest, and truest of earthly friends. My soul seems sick and weary within me, and I have no pleasure in my life. When will you return? Oh when will you cheer this heavy heart again? I trust that My Heavenly Father will not suffer me to relapse into despondency. But if he should, I dare not complain, for I deserve his surest chastisements. Oh how often have I backslid and forgotten his tender mercies! God hath recalled me again, like a wandering sheep, and received me into the Heavenly fold. Sometime I long to cast off "this earthly tabernacle," this tiresome body, and "depart and be with Christ," but oh when I think of the husband and child that would be left in this dangerous world, I cling to earth, for thier dear selves! Oh my husband! would to God I could lift your thoughts and affections with mine to that Heavenly country where all our sufferings and sorrows shall be forgotten, or remembered as the incidents of an adventurous journey, and there bye embrace our joys around the throne of God! Perchance our very trials on earth shall be celebrated in our future song of triumph. Let us "strive to enter in at the strait [sic] gate."

I have written to Mr Huckins[6] since you left, and requested him to subscribe my name to some Babtist [sic] paper, and if he thought it best to pay the subscription in advance, to call on Maj Cocke[7] for the money. I knew that my dear Husband would not deny me any thing that could contribute so much to my happiness. Moreover, if my demands of this character should grow exorbitant, such as books, papers, and benevolent funds, there are many useless expenditures that I can throw off, in order to meet them. But of this we will speak more fully here after, if the Lord should will our reunion. The family are all well except myself. Col. Palmer has promised to forward this from Montgomery, and I shall hope to hear from you occasionally until you return.

Thine truly and devotedly
M. L. Houston[8]

[1]Martin Palmer, also spelled Parmer.

[2]Only one letter, September 13, 1844, has been located. Margaret is referring to Houston's ankle wound received at the Battle of San Jacinto.

[3]For a copy of this letter see Houston to Santa Anna, July 29, 1844, *Writings*, IV, 346–49.

[4]Mrs. Maxey was the daughter of James Davis.

[5]Caroline Davis, daughter of General James Davis, and sister of Mrs. Maxey.

[6]Reverend James Huckins in Houston.

[7]Major James Cocke of Galveston. Identified in *Writings*, III, 70.

[8]The letter written from Liberty on September 28, 1844, containing Houston's reply to this letter can be found in *Writings*, IV, 373–74. In it he mentions his upcoming trip to the Falls of the Brazos and his regrets that he will not be able to attend the Treaty with the Indians farther north. He also tells of the election of Anson Jones to the presidency, his efforts to obtain an antelope skin for Sam, and his pleasure that Margaret was pleased with his letter to Santa Anna on July 29, 1844. This would be his last letter to Margaret written while he was President of the Republic.

Chapter VII

January 24, 1845–November 10, 1845

In the latter part of 1844 Houston purchased a farm about fourteen miles west of the town of Huntsville. He named it Raven Hill and began to build a home there and planned to retire to country life. The following letters were written as he traveled to see his new property.

To Mrs. M. L. Houston
Grand Cane
Liberty County
Texas

Genl Davis'[1]
Friday 24th Jany 1845

My Dearest,

Last night and this morning I was ill with sore throat and cold. I am much better. The Judge[2] was ill when I came or rather had been so. To day he is well. In a few minutes we intend to set out.

Before I left home I was pressed and oppressed by many causes. On reflection I have concluded to assure you, as I think it was cause of some apprehention [sic] that you need be under no anxiety for my intention is not to drink any thing during by absence, at any time. But you may rest assured that under no circumstances will I indulge in taking one drop in Washington County. Now my Dearest, I wish you to be happy! You may be satisfied that I will act in such manner, as will promote your happiness as well as my own!

Joshua[3] will come up with Vernal and I wish him to bring some ten or fifteen Fig cuttings from Mr. Cherrys.[4] I have nine pretty ones with me. Do make my friend Vernal bring my dogs up with him. They will follow after they cross the River or when they get as far as Mr. Ellis'.[5]

Now dearest, I can tell you that I will return at the earliest moment possible to embrace you and that I will not be happy until I can again see you. I will be lonely, but I will be busy. I will do all in my power to get forward with my business.

You need have no care about General Hamilton.[6] If any thing is done I will manage it proper and have no fighting. I have begged Mrs. Davis[7] to let Miss Carey[8] remain with you until my return. I hope she will comply.

Commend me to all the family and embrace our dear, dear Boy. I will write by every chance on my way.

I can hear of impostors. Do be on your guard, as there will be many in sheeps clothing. We must be on our guard against such. Our cousin Judge sends his love to you & the family. He has not bought land nor will he until he sees Raven Hill. Rely upon my dear everything to make you happy. I embrace you with my whole heart.

Thy ever devoted Husband
Sam Houston

[1]General Davis's Polk County plantation was about four miles from Raven Hill. Ellis, 50.
[2]Judge John T. Jones. For a biography see Zella Armstrong, *Notable Southern Families*, v. III, (Baltimore, Genealogical Publishing Company, Inc., 1971), 187, and Byron and Barbara Sistler, *David County, Tennessee Marriages*, (Nashville: Byron Sistler & Associates, 1985), 122. See also Houston to Margaret, January 27, 1845.
[3]Houston's slave.
[4]William and Aaron Cherry lived near Ellis and Vernal Lea in Liberty County on the west bank of the Trinity. *An Abstract of the Original Titles of Record in the General Land Office*, 103.
[5]The Ellis plantation home, named Pleasant Lawn by Houston, was located about thirty miles north of Liberty on the east side of the Trinity River. Here lived Benjamin Ellis and his family, including his brother, Joseph. Ellis, 49–50.
[6]James Hamilton. On September 12, 1844, Hamilton had written U. S. Secretary of State John Calhoun that he would go to Texas in November and that he "could carry the country in the direction we desire against Houston. . . . my friends will be in power and he will be out of power on the 1st Dec. and we will carry matters with a rush." Friend, 143–44.
[7]Mrs. James Davis (Ann Eliza Hill). Identified in *Handbook of Texas*, III, 230.
[8]Caroline Davis, the daughter of James and Ann Eliza Davis.

Grand Cane Texas
To Mrs. M. L. Houston
Grand Cane
Liberty County, Texas

Raven Hill, 27th Jany, 1845

My Very dear Wife,
    In writing to you I have many doubts as to your getting the letter. I am so far out of the way of business people and travelling world

that there is but little chance of letter sending. No matter I will write. After leaving Gen'l Davis I came on very well and at Col. Williamson[1] I related to my shrubbery plants. For instance, strawberries rasberry [sic] bushes, quinces, plums, plenty of figs. They are all set out, as today was rainy and favorable.

Yesterday was the Sabbath and I would not violate it by worldly employment. M was preaching at Squire Palmer's[2] and after that was over I read the Book which you sent to Mr. [Washington D.] Miller. Today I went much over our place, and when I came to look over it, I found as I had been told that it had two fine salt licks. To appearances they were the best I have ever seen and I have no doubt but what salt can be made to any extent and the water easily obtained.

After riding over the land Judge Jones set out for home and I fear got miserably wet. He would go tonight to Col. Woods.[3] He was pleased with the land in this section but he selected no place. I had half a notion to let him have my lower half of the tract, but would not without your advice and consent. He wanted Bruin[4] more than any one I ever saw but I told him that he really was yours and that I had promised not to part with him or he should have had him. So you see my dear how faithful I am in small matters. Now I loved the Judge and Cousin Caro[5] [and] would have greeted him almost as a relation but all would not do. Bruin could not go.

I have bargained to have a good lot and some fence enclosed around a neat Garden inside of it to be paled in pretty neat style. It will be 220 ft. one way and 200 the other. It will be so that rabbits can not get into it and I am sure that you will think it tasty. I was about contracting for a house on [blurred]. I will do it. (postponed) A wife I must have, not a kitchen. I calculate every penny that I contract for and really feel penurious when I think of you and Sam! I have thought more about him this time, since I left home than on any former occasion but even thus, and I do not think of him nor speak of the young man as often as I do of his dear, dear Mother. He is stout and healthy and is not an object of constant sympathy and suffering. Thus my dearest it is easy to account for your being always present with me. I think of you in my heart every hour.

Last night I was quite ill and since I left Gen'l Davis I have been hoarse and at times could not speak. To day although I was much in the rain I feel much better tonight. Tomorrow if spared I hope to set out for Washington, and will hope and try to attend to my business and return in the least time possible. You may rely upon this matter as one of trusts. I am using all means to get on with all my business and to be rid of them to go to the states or be at home leaving the whole matter to my dear wife. I learn the people are all well above so you can say to Bud [Vernal Lea] and tomorrow I hope to make the fair one such a bow as she is not used to greet. Do not let any one make Sam bow but his dear Mama. If they do it will spoil him. If I could I would return from here and consult you as I have learned what a house would cost with a beginning. It would be $840.00 and this is more than I wish to lay out until I conversed with you on the subject. I have seen my horse here and he is doing well. I hope when I have turned my attention to my own business that I will be enabled to make something and that I can take care of what I do make.

28th I have made a minute calculation of the cost of House Kitchen, and farm of 60 acres of open land in the case. With farming utensils, cooking matters and all that will be necessary for farming complete accurate terms will cost on the most accurate terms will cost [sic] $1,200. This may astonish you but when we come to look at the whole requirements we must conclude that it can not be done for less.

The House would be two storys [sic] high—passage 12 feet. Each room to be 20 by 24 feet. Galleries the whole length of the building 12 feet wide. The length of the House will be 62 feet. The Galleries will be neatly bannistered or paled. A neat kitchen with pealed logs. They would engage to have the House ready to take possession of by the last of October so that if we conclude to have the improvement made when we confer, it will enable us to visit the U. States.

Do not my dearest have any uneasiness about this or other matters, for you may be assured that I will use every exertion in my power to arrange my matters to the best advantage. You will need to hear that Judge Jones intends to settle nearby and if he does not buy Col Wood's farm I am to try and purchase one adjacent to our place. The overseer was not here, and he became so anxious to see Caro and the boys that he could not stay any longer. I fear that he has suffered much by the awful rain of last evening. It is now nine o'clock AM and I intend to set out in a few minutes and will pass by Stubblefield's.[6] The roads may be so bad that I may not attempt to bring the furniture and in that event I will arrive much earlier than

I anticipated when we parted.

I must conclude with expression of my great anxiety to embrace you and the young barbarian. I find that I can only be happy or at rest where you are. There my time is happiness. Absent, endurance is the only quality which I exercise. You need not fancy that I am writing you or trying to write a "love letter." I am in a matter of FACT mood and can only assure you of my <u>perfect devotion to you and Sam</u>. Present regards to all the family.

Thy ever devoted Husband,
Houston

[1]Robert McAlpin Williamson.
[2]Houston is referring to either Martin Palmer or his son, Thomas, both of whom lived near Raven Hill. For biographies see *Handbook of Texas*, II, 340.
[3]George T. Wood, who settled on the Trinity near the present town of Pt. Blank. For a biography see *Handbook of Texas*, II, 929.
[4]Houston's mule Bruin was one of his favorite means of transportation.
[5]Sarah Caroline McEwen, daughter of Houston's cousin Robert McEwen, was married to Judge John T. Jones of Helena, Arkansas on August 12, 1839. Sistler, 122.
[6]John Stubblefield owned property in Polk County near Vernal Lea. Identified in Polk County Bicentennial Committee and the Polk County Historical Commission, *A Pictorial History of Polk County, Texas (1846–1910)*, (n.p.: Polk Historical Commission, 1976), 40, and Carpenter, III, 1556.

On February 28, 1845, Houston was in Liberty. He wrote to Margaret who was visiting her family at Grand Cane, mentioning that he had attended church and signed a temperance pledge along with many others and that "If all keep their vow it will be a good thing for society."

He speaks of pending court cases and comments: "I do not know what I will do with all the cases offered to me. I feel disposed to stay at home and attend to my family, and for years to come there will not be much pleasure in the practice of law. There will not be comforts such as should be desirable nor would all the fees which I might get recompense me for the loss of your society & Sam." Because so much of the letter is faded and illegible, it is not fully transcribed here.

To Mrs. M. L. Houston
Grand Cane
Texas
Mr. B. F. Reynolds

Mr. Ellis'
11th March, 1845

Dearest,

I came here well enough and hear that I can pass Drews Creek in a small boat. So I hope I will meet with no obstructions on the way. I came with Mr. Reynolds and found Col. Palmer here. We intend to start in a few minutes anyway to get to Captain Roan's[1] by sunset. Gen. Davis has gone ahead no doubt. Several more will be at Roan's tonight. From here to Mr. Ratcliff's,[2] the dining place, it is about fifty-five miles. Unless it rains tomorrow I intend to go on. If it does rain I may decline going on as I do not deem it of matter sufficient to expose myself.

I have no notion of engaging Mr. [B. F.] Reynolds as an amanuensis. That is with us only. I will hurry back as I am informed the river is yet rising, and I wish to go either up or down by the first Boat that we can board. About this time [George] Hockley, I think will be at the Island[3] from Corpus Christi and I should like to see him. There is Hockley, Sam Williams, and [Thomas] McKinney, that I have been a friend of and I am well satisfied that they would now be gratified at my ruin or disgrace. Williams and McKinney I am anxious to settle with as they must owe me more than $500.00. My ac'nt can not be $500.00 and I let them have two Drafts, one on Elisha Roberts and the other on Pete Sublett, each for $500.00 and interest now on them for years!

My dear, if our kind Creator does spare me, I will try and attend to the affairs of this world, and a better one in such manner as a rational being should do—as one who owes something to this world in the way of duty to those whom I am related to and everything to a kind and mighty merciful God.

Salute all, hug Sam and kiss him for me. I will try to return as soon as possible.

Thy devoted Husband, Sam Houston

[1]W. J. Roan, who founded the community of Roans Prairie. For a biography see *Handbook of Texas,* II, 481.

[2]Probably William V. Ratcliffe, listed as a resident of Henderson County in Mullins, 139.

[3]Hockley resided in Galveston. A breech in the friendship had occurred in 1842. Hockley resigned as Secretary of War when Houston publicly denounced the efficiency of the volunteer troops as a reason for being against the war bill. Wisehart, 408, 411.

To Mrs. M. L. Houston,
Grand Cane
Trinity, Texas
Mr. Holliman

Mr Ellis'
26th March 1845

My Dearest Wife,

I told you that I would write whenever I could. So my love, I write if for no other reason than to tell you that I had the gratification of a tedious, tho' not long chat with my friend Fitz Green.[1] Mr Holliman[2] too was along, and pretty clever in company. I arrived at 1 oclk PM, and found Palmer with the oxen near here. They are now on good pasture, where they are to stay until tomorrow, and then proceed to Raven Hill. To day I have been sad and I think depressed. I regret much that I have to leave you and Sam, and that we could not all go to Raven Hill. Tho' somewhat perplexed to day, I had time to reflect, and then run my reflections. We feel depressed at the apprehension of temporal evils, which may or may not happen, and are careless about the eternal displeasure of God, which is inevitable, tho' to that, all suffering and misfortune is in comparison nothing and less than nothing! To this subject and its consequences, I will endeavor to conform my earnest attention, and will do so because I hope that in fitting time, the Almighty will deign to hear me, of his gracious mercy!

I know well our fallen, or lost estate, by the wise dispensation of an almighty Creator and a beneficent God, and whether we have ourselves incurred the guilt or it is by the fall of our first Parents, is not the care of mortals. Can we by the attonement [sic] of Christ Jesus, be redeemed from our lost estate? I am satisfied that we can, and thro' His mediation, I hope the Father will grant in answer to prayer such portion of His Grace as will be sufficient for the salvation of those who seek Him in Sincerity & truth! We have the promise that if we "seek, we shall find." This is an important question!! How shall we seek? The proper frame of mind surely must come by the Spirit of God working, or operating thro' Grace. I could write much, but I know I am ignorant on these all important and Eternal Subjects.

I am fearful my <u>dearest</u>, that I am hindered by something not more commendable than <u>self sufficiency</u>. It is not pride, nor is it for the want of rational conviction of Gospel Truths. All that I can say is that I have not been born again or that I have not enjoyed a new condition of heart. Yet I hope, and pray that God will in due season enlighten my mind, and teach me the sovereign efficacy of Christ Jesus' death and the fulness [sic] of Salvation.

My Dearest, I pray God that we and all those whom we are in duty bound to pray for, may receive his blessings [and] mercies with grateful hearts and submit to his will and Providence as such poor dependent creatures should whose breath is in their nostrils.

My Love, you may rely upon my writing whenever I can, and if I live I will return at the first moment in my power.

My Love to all, and hug Sam for me. I suppose the poor little fellow will miss me much unless his waggon [sic] may engross his thoughts.

I am thy truly devoted Husband
Sam Houston

P.S. I hope you can make out my meaning, tho the impressions are confused, as I wrote in great haste.

Thine,
Houston

[1]Fitz Green resided in Liberty. White, *1840 Census of Texas*, 102.
[2]A neighbor of Vernal Lea's.

Mrs. M. L. Houston
Grand Cane
Texas
By Mr. Chambers

28 March 1845

Dearest Wife,

This morning I came here by way of [torn] Swarthout[1] and last night Genl Davis was [torn] and myself stayed with Col Williamson. They [torn] very glad to see us and made enquiries for yourself, Ladies and Sam. We came by Captain Maxey's[2] & found all well. The son from Alabama who had brought the news of annexation (after a fashion). I will get Mr. Chambers[3] whom we met to take a [blurred]. I think you will see that our visit to the U. S. is anticipated. I send by Mr. Chambers your dress [faded] Our matters have [blurred] on well. Billy[4] is mending and nearly well. Maria[5] has been papoosing for some time. She [torn]. Vincy[6] is doing well and her children. The house, kitchen, and garden nearly so. Tomorrow I expect before day to be up, and by sun rise at our place, and from there proceed to Huntsville. I may go to Washington or Houston or both. I will try and let you hear from me. I am wanted at Wash. no doubt at this juncture! I may or may not go. In the event of commissioners being appointed to treat with others from the U. States, doubtless I may be called upon for that purpose, and if it should be the case, you may rest assured I will refuse the station.[7] I would not for any office or post loose [sic] the opportunity of a visit with you to our relations in the U. States, and the duty if well [torn] will not be full of thanks. I am well out of the scrape. Be assured, my Love, that nothing short of our mutual interest will (within my control) detain me from you one moment.

I am most sincerely anxious to see and embrace you and Sam again. You are my earthly goods, and so it is that I can not be happy away from you! I am not courting, my dearest, but "speak the words of truth and soberness." All the little shrubs that I set out are doing well, and not one has died. The hearts ease blossomed and the rose has bloomed also since they were set out. I hope this is a good omen. The Bois 'd Arc [sic] and figs are all flourishing. The strawberries have borne, and are bearing. I must tell you my Love, that the Negroes are very anxious to get to our house. Jose,[8] Mr. Parmer[9] says is one of the best hands he has ever seen and works finely & well.

I sincerely hope my Love that you are happy and cheerful. You have the comfort and solace of Religion, and the Grace of [torn], and this I hope and believe wou'd be sufficient for you in every situation. [torn] your spirit in every trial of life. 'Tis midnight and I will in prayer [torn]. My Love to all, and embrace our dear boy. Watch with double vigilance. Virginia[10] is a fearful child. If you can, by any safe road you might send the cotton. Send of which you spoke to Mr. Palmer. I promised to bear Mr Marneys expenses, and give him seven dollars. I will leave a paper if the Hogs have been bought by Hugh.[11] They have not come by yet. Excuse this confused letter.

Thy ever devoted and truly affectionate Husband
Sam Houston

[1]Swarthout was located on the Trinity River about 221 miles upstream from Galveston. For a description of the town see Bob Bowman, *The 35 Best Ghost Towns in East Texas*, (Lufkin: Best of East Texas Publications, 1988), 85–88.
[2]Maxey was the son-in-law of James Davis.
[3]This is probably William Martin Chambers of Liberty County. For a biography see *Handbook of Texas*, III, 159.
[4]A Lea family slave.
[5]Maria was a servant of the Lea family.
[6]A Houston slave.
[7]Houston is referring to negotiations concerning an annexation treaty.
[8]Maria's husband, a field hand and servant of the Lea family.
[9]Houston is probably referring to Thomas, who was assisting Margaret in managing Raven Hill. The name was also spelled Palmer.
[10]Virginia Thorn, the ward of Vernal Lea.
[11]Houston is probably referring to Hugh B. Johnson, his friend from Liberty.

Mrs. M. L. Houston
Grand Cane
Trinity Texas

Montgomery, Texas
1st Apr., 1845

My very dear Love,
    I am home safe. My trip was quite pleasant and my reflection

rational after writing to you from Raven Hill.[1] I saw the place the next morning. It looked changed and improved. It will be beautiful. I have found much excitement on the subject of annexation, but have foreborn the expression of any opinion. All wish to know how I look upon or in what fashion of thought I entertain about the matter and my reply is "I do not know what action has taken place or what may be necessary to be done. There fore I can give no satisfactory opinion in the case." I send for your approval some letters which may shed some light on the state of affairs.[2]

Judge Ochiltree[3] has just come and from him I have enough to show me that things will be done right by the President. He is pretty smart!!![4] I have much business affairs to do at this court and I think my dear that I will be able to secure at least one thousand dollars in fees. This is private my Love and you are my only confidante in these matters. I will be at no expense during court and even that is something these hard times! Now my love, I assure you that even the prospects here will not compensate for my anxiety to see you and our young Barbarian. You are both present to me day and night. I feel in fine health and the uncertainty of my getting off from court and my detention from you bear much upon my heart.

I may go to Washington[5] if I find it to our mutual interest or I may return from court directly home. It will adjourn on the 11th inst. if not sooner. If I do return it will be with intention to try and git [sic] you and Master Sam to Houston so that I can attend to business and have more of your society until we can set out for the U. S.[6]

Mr. Ben Ellis has come back without a wife and is not married! This is all as it should be! I send you by Mr. Beal a pair of shoes which I hope will fit if they should not suit you. I like them for muddy weather. I have but little time to write. My Love, do not feel, as our friend Miller did if you should hear any false reports. I have passed the Temptor at Huntsville and met it here and do not feel that I will be off my guard. I feel a new impulse to exertion. In part as a sign from my increased affection for yourself, and Sam as well as my improving health. I must weigh some several pounds more than I did when we parted. I am needed in the court room and must close. If I had only time I could write 44 pages!!! I ought to fear that I may plague you by writing so often and so much. Ben Ellis will bring you many letters. I am told our friend Payne[7] writes much. You must read his letters.

Beware of "Virginia."[8] There is no telling what the little <u>monster</u> may do. Embrace for me our dear Boy. Salute all our friends, and kiss the Ladies for me. Let Cap take care of the oxen. I paid Palmer $150.00 for the house, and $30 for other improvements.[9] In all, one hundred and eighty dollars. I yet owe fifty for the Garden but I am not out of cash but did not chuse [sic] to pay it yet as the work is not quite done!

Tho' distant my Love, I embrace you with the most pure and devoted affection.

I may be able to see you on the 13th (if spared by a kind and merciful Providence). If not by that time I will write to you, and if any opportunities occur in the meantime I will always write.

Thy devoted Husband
Sam Houston

I send you silk, my Love. I hope it will suit you. I owe Palmer nothing but good wishes!

[1]Houston to Margaret, March 28, 1845.
[2]It is unclear to what letters Houston refers.
[3]Judge William B. Ochiltree. For a biography see *Writings*, IV, 343n, and Thrall, 595–96.
[4]President Anson Jones was being silent on the subject of annexation. Lankevitch, 56.
[5]Washington-on-the-Brazos.
[6]The Houstons were planning a trip to Nashville to visit Andrew Jackson.
[7]Owen B. Payne.
[8]Virginia Thorn. For information about the problems Margaret was experiencing with Virginia see Roberts, 145, 149.
[9]Houston is referring to improvements made at Raven Hill.

Mrs Houston
Grand Cane Trinity
Col. Palmer

Montgomery Texas
4th Apl 1845

My Dear Wife,

Colonel Palmer will leave to day, for Trinity, and by him I will send this letter. Nothing new has occurred since I last wrote you. To day is friday, and on tomorrow or Sunday, I may ride over to Washington[-on-the-Brazos]. They are anxious to see me, and if I do go, I will try, and bring for you such articles of your clothing as I think you will need.[1] I am sure you will think that I am "courting again," and by my frequent writing. It must apprehend some opposition, or rivalry. This is not the case exactly, but nevertheless, I will see you so soon as I can. To day it may be that I will trade my mare for a horse, that will bear me nobly [sic], and I can make rapid marches homeward. You need not be uneasy my dear, I am not to give booty, but get it, if I can. I intend to pass but one day in Washington if I should go there, as I intend. Should I be so happy as to get home again, or to see you, and Sam, my stay with you unless I can git [sic] you to Houston, will be short.

You may say to Sam, that Papa has a <u>hatchet</u> for him, and that he must be a good boy, and must have his head combed when Papa gets home. I apprehend that I may not be home until the 16th or 17th Inst as the waters are high, and will compel me to go out of my way to reach Grand Cane!

To day I am, and will be busy in court. May a Kind and Beneficent God preserve you and our dear boy, and make you happy. Salute all, and hug the Boy. I embrace you with the purest affection.

Thy devoted Husband
Sam Houston

Mrs Houston

P.S. I took a moment from business to write this hasty note.

Houston

Mrs Houston

[1]All of the Houstons' belongings had not been moved from their previous home in Washington.

Washington
10th May 1845

My Love,

The stage is just starting, and will wait a moment for me to say, "How are you my love" as well as to ask for our dear Boys welfare. My trip here was thro' awful roads. They were about as bad as they could be. On tomorrow I hope to reach Tiger Point[1] & return direct to Houston. Staying on Monday night at our relations Captain McDades,[2] so that by Wednesday I hope in the evening to meet you and Sam happy and in fine health.

I will write you no politics. Let them be!! I am happy that we are to be absent and removed from impending scenes, where I can be so without ruinancy. You will concur with me, when you hear all from me.

I will be quiet, and still, and what I do say, shall be measured and not inconsistent with the past nor insensitive to the future.

I have seen no one but Mrs Norwood of the ladies. I saw her as I came to the Presidents office, where I am writing. Mrs N. made many kind inquiries for you and regretted that you did not come up.

I can only tell you that every person who sees me asks for you and Sam particularly.

Embrace Sam. Commend me to our friends. Salute the ladies. This letter is an apology for not writing more.

Thy ever devoted
Houston

Mrs Houston

[1]A settlement six miles southwest of Brenham. *Handbook of Texas*, III, 1009.
[2]James W. McDade, a lawyer in Washington County. It is unclear how he was kin to the Houstons. Ray, 159.

In late May, 1845, the Houstons left Texas for a trip to the United States to visit Andrew Jackson. They arrived at the Hermitage a few hours after Jackson had died. Houston and Margaret remained in Tennessee for an extended visit. They later traveled to Alabama to visit Margaret's family. Margaret remained in Alabama while Houston traveled home to Texas, making several speeches along the way and writing to Margaret at every stop.

Mrs. Margaret L. Houston
Marion Alabama
by Doctor Shivers[1]

Greensboro
17th Sept 1845

My Dearest Margaret,

Until after my speech to day I was miserable. During the time I was speaking or the latter part of it, I saw Dr. Shivers, and tho' you had been almost constantly present and I engaged in thinking of you, and our dear boy, since we parted, the moment that I saw him my anxiety to hear all, became intense, and painful. So soon as I came from the stand, and heard that you were well, Oh! I was "so appee," that I could have spoken and discoursed most eloquently of love, and joy, and gratitude! I made a fair speech, & perhaps the best, taking it all in all, which I have made in the States.

I came in good time last evening, and was met, greeted and welcomed by the committee and received, and escorted by uniformed Cavalry, and artillery. I said only a few civil things until to day. You will hear all.

My intention was not to attend the party last evening, but as they did not dance I consented to walk into the room and be introduced to the bridal pair. So soon as this was known Miss Aurulia Blasingame[2] sent me word that she wished me to escort her into the room as her protector. This I did—all on your dear account!! We walked into the room, and thrice rounded, when I surrendered her to a younger Beau! The party was quite agreeable to many, as they sat up long after I retired as I learned. To day I got Miss A. to bear the present which my dear niece gave, and then we squared accounts!!! At dinner I saw her, and Miss Goree, and said that Sam Houston Moore[3] was to be disposed of. They both laid claim, but I referred them to you, for your decision of the matter! and I said that you would prefer Miss Goree, on the ground that you would not want Houston coqueted by any one. You may make choice for him of either, so far as you can, but don't let him be tortured. You know the family cant stand it. To day in my speech I made up for my omission to mention the Ladies in Marion.[4] To day I said civil, sensible, and elegant things of, and about them! Oh! how I did tickle them.

I am on the eve of setting out this evening, again on my journey.

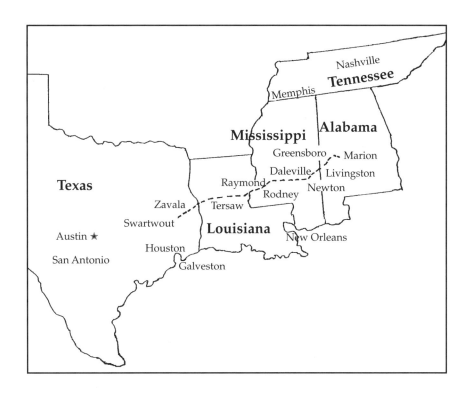

Houston's travels September 16, 1845 to October 14, 1845

All things seem to go well!

You must, my Dearest, give my love to Brother, Sister, Nieces, and all! Advise as you think prudent in relation to our dear niece Elizabeth.[5] I will be satisfied with whatever you do, or say in this matter!!! When you do see Mother and all our Kindred in the Canebrake,[6] at Eilands, render my love.

My dear embrace our dear boy, and impress upon his dear face, Kisses, numberless!

My Love, I can only say, that you are the spring of my joys, and the object of my hopes. In short you are the companion of my heart, and the only star that sheds a light upon my affections. How painful it is to be seperated from you. Unworthy as I am, I will beseech Heaven on your behalf! Doubt me not!!!

Thy devoted Husband
Sam Houston

Mrs M. L. Houston

[1]Dr. Orlando L. Shivers. For a biography see Owen, IV, 1549–50.
[2]The daughter of William E. and Eliza Townes Blasingame. Identified in Owen, III, 163.
[3]Houston's nephew, the son of Eliza Houston and S. A. Moore.
[4]Houston had been invited by a committee in Marion to speak on his opinion concerning the annexation of Texas to the U. S. He accepted and spoke on "Annexation and our relations with Mexico." For the newspaper article concerning this speech (*Alabama State Review,* September 17, 1845) see *Writings,* VI , 14–15n.
[5]Elizabeth (Betty) Moore, the daughter of Eliza Houston and S. A. Moore.
[6]This name refers to the family plantation of Gincy (Virginia) Moffitte Eiland as well as to the region in Perry County, Alabama.

Mrs. M. L. Houston
Care of the Postmaster, Marion Alabama

Livingston
18th Sept, 1845

My Dear Maggy,

At night fall I reached this place. Today we travelled about 35 miles. It was warm oppressively. Last night I was most hospitably entertained by Dr. Withers[1] who married a Miss Withers,[2] sister to

Mrs. Gov. Clay.[3] She is quite an agreeable lady. There was a Miss Withers and a Miss Sawyer there, but I was too sleepy to make myself at all amiable or interesting! The Doctor and Lady are anxious for you to visit them! I did not tell you of the inquiries and regrets expressed about you at Greensboro. There were several. I wish you could have been there and here in health. You would have been very agreeably entertained and pleased with the pageant or show!

I inquired for your friends Mrs. Lipscomb,[4] Mrs. Bragg,[5] and Mrs. Tate.[6] So you see how well I remember your instructions. Neither was there. Here I found our Cousins in comfort, and glad to see me. They regret much that you can not come also. They live in pretty style and I judge they are wealthy. The house which M. C. Houston[7] lives [in] cost upwards of $5000.00 and the yard displays a corresponding taste with the House. They are well off too in the way of daughters—only seven and all quite pretty. I tell them come to Texas and marry off the gals. They have had one son at Princeton, I suppose promising. I wish you could see them, as they much desire you should do so. I saw a pretty Piano, but did not ask for "a tune."

I intend to write my next letter to Marion and after that to Woodville, as I suppose you will go to the Cane Brake soon. I am doing wrong to write so often at the start. Tomorrow I hope to reach Daleville in Miss. Tell Maj. Townes[8] that I will write to him so soon as it may be in my power!

I will only add my love to all, and embraces and kisses to Sam! Dear, write to me at Houston soon and often as you please. Pay postage to New Orleans. I will try and "persecute" you with letters until we meet.

Thy ever devoted Husband,
Houston

P.S. I left a Bridle and Martingale besides the one for Miss Betty.[9] Let it be handed over to Young Royston!!! My little filly is a fine Buggy animal and improves daily. We will have to travel rapidly and I found a Buggy a wonderful relief, and hope it will hold out well. The roads are dusty as we progress and water is scarce for horses. The wells here barely support the people with what is left by the country people who get water in Town and haul it to their houses.

Thine Ever, Houston

[1]Dr. John Withers. For a biography see Owen, IV, 1793.
[2]Susana Claiborne Withers, Owen, II, 342–43.
[3]Mrs. Clement Cameron Clay. Ibid.
[4]Probably Mrs. Abner Lipscomb.
[5]This may be Martha Crook (Mrs. Newport) Bragg. Identified in Owen, II, 203.
[6]This may possibly be Mrs. Charles Tait. Brewer, 43.
[7]Matthew C. Houston. For more information about this Houston cousin see R. D. Spratt, *History of Livingston, Alabama*, (Published privately, 1926), 25. Available in the Clayton Library, Houston, Texas.
[8]Major Samuel Townes of Marion, Alabama.
[9]Elizabeth Moore.

Mrs. M. L. Houston
Woodville Perry County Alabama
mail

Rodney
26th Sept 1845

My Dearest,

This evening at dusk I came to this place, we are all well. We had the luck to be joined by a Ruling Elder of the Methodist Church. He is a Mister Gould,[1] from "old Blount County," and has been stationed on the Red river. He is a clever gentleman, & has been in North Alabama. He saw a fine looking young lady. He was not introduced to her, but said he sought an introduction, but she left before he obtained one. He said that she was at [the] table with a number of Ladies, and that she from her modesty and fine appearance, attracted his notice above all the rest. So you have the story! Tomorrow we intend to set out early and hope to see Raven Hill in six days travel. At this time travelling is very fine, and we make from 30 to 38 miles each day. I feel no fatigue, but travel on as tho' you were at home, which would certainly render me much more happy, than I will be when alone. I do not say this to make you <u>hurry by any means</u> or induce you to hurry home!!! I wish you to come when it will be consistent with your health, and convenience. You will be <u>provoked</u> at my <u>patience</u>. It is not patience, nor the absence of great anxiety to see you my dear, for I assure you that I do not think an hour has passed, when waking, that you, and Sam have not been present to me, and the most intense solicitude felt for you!

I will write again if I can before I reach home, and from home.

I hope my dear, that you attend to your correspondence. To Mrs Gaines,[2] Mrs Reily,[3] Our Cousins, and Sisters. If you could, I wish you would write to Mrs Dr Shelby.[4]

It is late at night, and I must close. I have yet to read my chapter! as I do every night, but then it was impossible!

Give my love to all our dear Kindred, and for yourself my Dearest, receive my whole heart & divide it with our dear Boy. Do hug and kiss him soundly.

Thine truly, and Ever
Houston

[1]This was probably Reverend William Gould. Gandrud, 494.
[2]This may be either Mrs. James (Susana) Gaines or Mrs. Edmund (Mahala) Gaines. Identified in Marion Day Mullins, *First Census of Texas 1829–1836,* Number 22, (Washington D. C.: Special Publication of the National Genealogical Society, 1959), 32.
[3]Ellen Hart Reily.
[4]This was probably Mrs. John Shelby of Nashville.

Mrs. Margaret L. Houston
Woodville
Perry County Alabama
Mail

Teusard 30 miles
From Rodney 28th Sept 1845

My dearest,

I wrote to you from Rodney,[1] and on yesterday, we reached this place. To day is Sunday, and we rested. There was preaching near here, and I went to hear the sermon. It was quite a clever sermon by a young Methodist Preacher. Our travelling companion did not preach, but made a beautiful prayer, in conclusion of the service. To day has been rainy, and to night, it continues. I fear tomorrow will be unpleasant to travel, as we have yet ten miles to travel in the low lands, and the worst part of our journey. We hope to reach court by the third day, if we have no bad luck. Yesterday Sam's Sally O'Flannegan[2] was taken lame, but seems better to day. I hope her lameness will not cause any detention.

We travel quietly, and harmonize well on our journey. I have not shewn [sic] the least impatience, or bad temper on the route. Yesterday, as I was leaving Rodney, I was waited upon by the citizens, and addressed by a Mr Wilcox,[3] in a very neat and appropriate address. I responded in a few remarks of thanks for the unexpected courtesy, to a stranger, and we parted all in good humour [sic]. I met there some men who had been with me at the "Horseshoe" and one who played the drum, at the time that I enlisted![4] I never had experienced so much feeling, and generous enthusiasm in my life, as what was evinced in Mississippi when I afforded an opportunity for its display. I bear it modestly, and I have not shaved since I left Greensboro, for which I apologize by saying that "I will not shave until I meet my dear wife again."

My health and looks have both improved since my journey commenced. I am fattening, and have only complained of my little toe, on my wounded foot. From some cause I took a rising on it, and for several days, I could not wear my shoe. It rose, and on yesterday I opened it, and to day (or to night) it is mended and seems nearly well again.

My thoughts are constantly with you, and sometimes I fancy myself willing to tell Sam "Tiger tales," as long as he would be willing to listen to them if I could only see you, and the dear lad once more!

I know you do not my dear, wish me to write love letters, but it is as much as I can do, to keep from courting you again. To tell you how truly, how devotedly I do love you, wou'd be superfluous to facts, which are borne to you every mail. I learn my Love, that the epidemic has commenced in New Orleans with much fury! This will I fear render it proper for you to detain longer in Alabama than I had hoped would be needful. I pray you my Love not to adventure to Mobile, Orleans, or Galveston, until you can do so in perfect safety. I will not trust myself at Houston, or Galveston until I can go in safety. You may be assured my dear that I will use every prudence, as to my health, and all that will conduce to it.

I yet regret my dear, that it was not in my power, to have seen more of our Aunt Eiland, and again visited the Canebrake. You must represent my regrets to all and express my regards. Our dear Cousin Betty[5] has reason to be glad of my departure without ceremony, in as much as I sat up so late at night with cousin Columbus. You may tell her, that if she and Columbus will come to see us in Texas, that I will make <u>him</u> behave <u>better</u> than <u>I</u> did at her house!!!

I would like to know how our dear niece Elizabeth [Moore] is moving on, and to know how her curls become her. The entire control of matters was left with you, and I have no doubt but what all will be right. You must bring one of your Nieces with you, and you have money which will I hope enable you to alleviate any objects, which could arise on that score! Whoever of the kin may return with you must take especial care of the baggage, and see that no <u>loss</u> is sustained. You can write if you wish to Cousin Caroline Jones to have your trunk sent to the care of Thos. B. Eastland New Orleans. This tho' may be left until you reach home! I hear no important news from Texas. There will be no war[6]—that has always been my opinion, and I think you so heard me express myself!

Since we parted, my urgency has been great to reach Texas on account of my business, so as to have it pretty well arranged by the time you come, that I may be enabled to stay at home the winter out.

You may be assured that I (if spared) will pursue the course which I think will best conduce to our mutual happiness and interest.

I trust my Dearest, that you will pass your time happily, and enjoy your health with Sam. But I know that you can not be happy unless Sam is well. Bless the little fellow. I hope he will be grown and thrifly [sic] when he returns to his native land. I really do wish our <u>reannexation</u> may take place so soon as it will be prudent for you to return.

Render my affectionate regards to all. If any <u>extraordinary</u> occasion required it, give an uncles benediction to our dear Niece! On all occasions, render my assurance of sincere wishes for the happiness and prosperity of our dear kindred.

Do dear attend to your correspondence!

Most truly, & affectionately, thy ever devoted Husband
Sam Houston

To
Mrs. M. L. Houston
Woodville Ala.

P.S. My hand writing improves very much, and I suppose it is because I write so much to you.

Adieu

Houston

[1]See Houston to Margaret, September 26, 1845.

[2]A horse Houston had bought for Sam Jr.

[3]G. H. Wilcox, of Rodney, Mississippi. Identified in Gwen Platt, et. al., *Mississippi Southern District Index to United States Censes of 1840*, (Santa Anna, California: GAM Publishers, 1970), 58.

[4]Army recruiters attracted attention upon entering a town by beating on a drum. Silver dollars were then placed on the drum. Young men entered the military ser-vice by taking a coin from the drumhead. Houston enlisted in the War of 1812 on March 24, 1813. James, 29.

[5]Elizabeth Parker Lea, wife of Margaret's cousin, Columbus Lea. Identified in Gandrud, v. 182, 97.

[6]Houston is referring to a Mexican invasion.

Gen. Sam Houston
Houston
Harris Co.
Texas

Canebrake, Sept 30, 1845

My own Love,

Your truly heart cheering letters came in from Greensborough
and Livingston[1] and I hope this will meet you on your arrival in
Texas. Our circumstances are generally as you left them except that
our dear niece Elizabeth has changed her mind with regard to the
marriage then in contemplation.[2] She seemed melancholy for several days and at length confessed to me that she feared her feelings
were not sufficiently interested to insure her happiness in the con-
nection and that she had sincerely agreed to think of the matter because she saw that it was a desirable thing in the family. My dear
husband will no doubt imagine how I acted in the matter. I presented the same course that I would have taken with a daughter
and she has seemed perfectly happy ever since the termination of it.
There are no hard feelings in the family. On the contrary, I have no
doubt that Aunt Lea[3] will feel as I at this result for I am convinced

that it is her determination that Cousin Waine shall never marry.[4] Betty is vindicated by several members of this family from Mother down as a piece of perfection. I have never seen any one more admired and I do not think she has now ever a sad feeling.

I have prefaced my letter with Betty because I knew you would be anxious about her. She and Sam are both dearer to me since you left us than they were before and I sometimes feel that I could take them into my heart because they look so much like you. Our dear boy is more interesting than you ever saw him and speaks in a very practiced style of his father. We left Marion on the day from your departure and expect to return home next Friday.

The Baptists have held a protracted meeting in the neighborhood during our visit and we heard some fine preaching, but the people seemed as cool as the snow on [blurred]. It seems as if this God of this world had so blessed the hearts of this cotton raising region that it is impossible for them to enter the kingdom of Heaven!!! Oh that the Lord would reveal them the awful criminality of this worship of mercers.

I have promised my self the pleasure of seeing our friend Mr. Crawford[5] (to whom you are in some degree [blurred] for a sustaining wife and I for the best of husbands) at the meeting. But he was just convening a new session of his school and I supposed by that circumstance was detained. He is living as well in his present situation there. I have no hope of persuading on him to go to Texas, but I am told that Mr. Clements,[6] an old acquaintance of ours and a very learned man and devoted minister of the gospel is anxious to see me on the subject of his removal to Texas. He has a small family, only a wife and one child, and I think he would suit us very well. But of course, we would not wish him to go out at this time as it would be necessary to make some preparation for his reception.

Oh my dear husband, since your departure I have felt a deeper concern for your immortal interest! When you are with me I am so happy that I fear my earthly devotion gets the better of me and it is only in a [blurred] and solitude of feeling, that never leaves my heart when you are away, that I can look upon things as they really are. Occasionally there is a sweet whispering within my heart that perhaps you are already justified and hope that the Lord will soon reveal himself to you. Oh, my husband, lay hold with instant hands upon that dear hope which is set forth in the gospel as an anchor to the soul, both sure and steadfast. Remember the words of our Saviour, "The kingdom of Heaven suffereth violence and the violent take it by force." Approach the throne of God with deep humility, but with as much energy as if you were storming a castle, and determine never to give up the struggle, never to leave your Saviour's feet until he shall bless you. When you can bring yourself to the resolution, he will suddenly appear to you, and the light of Heaven will break in upon your soul. This is the plan laid down by the great Saviour of souls, and it is the only way to seek him. Oh my husband, magnify the Lord with me, and let us call his name together.

I rec'd a letter a few days ago from cousin Caroline Jones at Nashville. She says Mrs. McEwen[7] wishes to know if you read Judge Jones' letter on the subject of his Texas land. I replied that you did and I was sure of it, but I have since feared that I might have been mistaken. Do if you can write to tell me the subject. All sent thier love to you.

Thine most devotedly
Maggy

[in the margin] Dearest after I finished my letter Sam did a thing which was so smart that I must tell you of it. He took up a letter and said, "Ma let me read" and began as follows. "Mine pa, I is dood boy and be very happy to see you." When all present burst into such a [blurred] of laughter they [blurred]

[1]Houston to Margaret, September 12 and September 18, 1845.
[2]Margaret's cousin Waine Lea, son of Peggy and Green Lea and brother of Columbus Lea, had proposed to Elizabeth Moore.
[3]Peggy Moffitt Lea.
[4]Waine [sometimes spelled Wayne] Lea would indeed later marry Sarah Ann Talbert on September 24, 1846. Flora D. England, *Alabama Notes*, IV, (Baltimore: Genealogical Publishing, 1978), 28.
[5]The Reverend Peter Crawford presided at the Houstons' marriage.
[6]Margaret may possibly be referring to the Reverend Andrew E. Clemmons, a preacher in Jackson County who later went to Texas. The names Clemmons and Clements were sometimes confused. For a biography of the Reverend Clemmons see John Henry Brown, ed., *The Encyclopedia of the New West*, (Marshall, Texas: The United States Biographical Publishing Company, 1881), 500–501.
[7]Mrs. Robert McEwen (Henrietta Kennedy), the wife of Houston's cousin and mother of Caroline Jones. Identified in Armstrong, III, 187.

Gen. Sam Houston
Houston,
Harris Co.
Texas

Marion, Oct. 8th, 1845

My beloved husband,

Ere this, I trust you have rec'd two letters[1] from me, and though my stock of information is not much increased since I last wrote to you, and a very few days have past since that time, yet I know you will be glad to hear that your dear boy and devoted wife are still living and well. We left the cane brake on last Saturday 4 days ago. Only Mother, Sam and I came up. Our dear niece Betty preferred remaining with the girls as Lucy Ann[2] was going to school and they were so unwilling to give her up. I have never seen a greater devotion than thiers to each other. There must be some congeniality in the blood! If we remain here many days we will send down for her and one of Martin's girls.

Soon after our arrival here, I read your letter from Newton[3] in Miss. Oh, it was a sweet letter indeed! The very night before it came bro. Henry signed a solemn temperance pledge drawn up by Mr. Dustie. I read to him the portion of your letter on that subject and he seemed much affected by it. At that very time a hunting expedition was on foot and he was to be of the party, but he did not go, and perhaps your advice entered him. May Heaven bless you for it!

And here, my love, I must tell you how sorely I have been grieved since you left me. You know bro. H's unhappy situation when you left. I knew it too and might have foreseen the consequence, but I shut my eyes to it. On last Saturday the case was brought into the church. Mr. Dustie, the pastor did all in his power to retain him, pleaded his liberality to the church, his general excellence of character and told them they were doing wrong. But the Locket influence[4] was there even in that holy place and prevailed. They required him to give them a pledge of future abstinence which they knew he would not do and on his rcfusal they expelled him. But thanks to my Heavenly Father, it has been satisfied to his good. It seemed a sudden check upon him, and from that day he has been a "different man."

My brother is himself again. Oh my love, will you not unite with me in thanking the Author of all our happiness for this blessing.

Since I read your last, I have not been so impatient to set off home, as you inform me it will be several weeks before you can be at home with me. I think we will leave during the first week in Nov. Bro. Henry read a letter from Maj. Hopkins[5] from a few days ago containing a request from Mrs. Peck of Greensborrough that she might join our company to Texas. She is a sister in law of Judge Ochiltree's[6] and is going out for some of his children. I expect we will find her an agreeable companion on our trip, as she is a lady of firm standing, and I think quite interesting.

Thursday 9th.

I have a piece of news for you Love. Margaret King (the Gen'l's[7] daughter) told Lucy Ann yesterday that Col. Homes had staid [sic] at her father's Thurs night before and told them that he was with you the first evening you spent in my company so that Col. Henry Homes is not dead. He told them moreover, so M. says, that he was terribly smitten with me at that time, but I think she had the wrong end of the story, and that Col. H. meant to say that Gen. Houston was smitten as I have heard something of that before and the former was quite new to me.

Monday 13th

Since I laid my letter aside, the weather has become intensely cold and if there was the slightest hope of meeting you in Galveston I would set off in a few days, but as it is, I think we will not leave before the 1st week in Nov. I expect on next Thursday to go to Aunt [Gincy Moffitt] Eiland's and I will ascertain whether Cousin Ovid[8] will go with us or not. If he does not I must make some other arrangements.

I heard an eloquent sermon from Mr. Hamilton[9] of Mobile on yesterday morning and another at night. His sermon in the morning was from the 18th of Ezekial first clause of the 4th verse. At night from the 7th ch, of Revelations, 18th verse. His eloquence surpassed any thing I have ever heard. He seemed inspiration itself. He is in bad health and has lost much of his former pomp and self-complacency but is far more interesting on that account.

Today I have a great many calls to return. I will then tell you goodbye, and close my letter. At night: I did not make my calls, as I designed, but postponed them until tomorrow. Oh how I long to see you! Our dear little prattler is more interesting than you ever saw him. His ideas and language would astonish you. We have many sweet conversations about dear papa far away, and he is truly a great comfort to me.

Dearest if the time I have named for leaving Ala. be sooner than you would wish to be in Galveston I hope it will cause you no inconvenience for you know I can either wait in Galveston until it would suit your business to come or I could go up the Trinity with Mother, but of course I would be much delighted to meet you on my arrival. I hope however to hear from you next when you will probably be there. On Saturday I rec'd a letter from Judge Hutchinson[10] containing an account of your visit to Jackson and to Raymond. It is of course highly gratifying to me to hear that my busy husband receives all honors due to him. However, Love, Dinna forget her who loves you far more than words can tell.

Thy devoted wife,
Maggy

[on outside of envelope] I am rejoiced, Love, to hear that you read your bible regularly. Oh, continue that sacred employment and perchance your eyes may soon be opened and you enabled to behold wondrous things out of his law!!!!!!

[1]Only one previous letter from Margaret for this time period has been located.
[2]Lucy Ann Lea, the oldest daughter of Henry Lea.
[3]This letter has not been located.
[4]The Lea and Locket families were not on good terms. Napoleon Locket had killed Martin Lea in a duel.
[5]This is probably Major F. M. Hopkins, an instructor at the Military Institute. Identified in England, 49.
[6]Judge Ochiltree was married to Novaline, the former Mrs. Thomas Peck. Gandrud, 52.
[7]General Edwin King.
[8]Ovid Eiland, Gincy's son.
[9]Owen (III, 733, 735–36), lists two preachers in Mobile at this time by the name of Hamilton: Jefferson Hamilton, a methodist minister, and William Thomas Hamilton, a Presbyterian minister. It is unclear to which one Margaret refers.
[10]Anderson Hutchinson, a former judge of the Republic of Texas, was now a lawyer in Rodney, Mississippi. For a biography see *Writings*, III, 524n.

Houston returned to Texas in October of 1845. He wrote the following letter to Vernal Lea.

Swarthout
14th Oct 1845

My Dear Vernal,

I returned on friday [sic] last after a fatiguing trip. I left Marion on the 17th of last month, and travelled more or less every day except Sundays.

I left all well in Alabama. At Zavala I learned for the first [time] that our brother Bledsoe was no more.[1] I wrote from thence to Alabama. Since my return, I have heard that our <u>dear</u> Sister Antoinette is inconsolable in her bereavement. I do most truly condole with her in her grief and sorrow. I can only recommend that solace which is found in the Sacred Volume. There we are taught resignation to the will of our Divine Master & Saviour Jesus Christ! It must be a source of the consolation to her that our brother departed in the assurance of Eternal Happiness, and the hope of a righteous reward. It gave me unfeigned pleasure to know or learn that he departed with a full assurance of Salvation. Let us all strive for such an assurance thro' the merits of Jesus Christs atonement.

I would ordinarily go down and see you all, but particularly Sister, at this time if it were possible but it is not in my power to do so.

I find myself in a bad condition in my affairs. Poor Morris[2] had done but little and all that he has done has been to my injury. I have not seen him as he is at camp meeting. I will be compelled to go for my furniture and get that home if possible.[3] I have corn and every thing to get, so as to enable me to live. I must go on the first of next month, so as to meet Margaret & Master Sam etc between that and the 10th at Galveston. I started with one of my nieces[4] to bring to Texas, but will not be surprised if she & Cousin Wayne were to marry. He spoke to me on the subject, and I refered [sic] it to her and her Aunt [Margaret].

The relations are all much gratified at your marriage & prospects![5] They were delighted to hear of you & of their relations in

Texas. I think one of our Royston nieces will come with Margaret & her Grand Ma. Which I do not know. Henry (brother) or Robt Royston, I think will come with the Ladies. Sam is not quite capable of undertaking the task. Write to me at Houston. Margaret, and all the relations, sent a thousand regards to your family, Sister and our departed brother.

All Sister's Marion relations are well. I saw Dr Evans[6] yesterday and all his family are well. He is doing well.

I left Troup[7] with him in the best order that I ever saw him. I brought him for you supposing that you wanted him. I came in a Buggy, and drove a three year old filly. Troup was rode by a young man (rather small). I rode down this morning from Col Williamson's[8] that I might write to you.

You must render my sincere love to my Dear Sisters. I have no news. My health, thank God, is fine. Faithfully thy brother. Tell Sister Antoinette to write to me at Houston

Sam Houston

Maj V. V. Lea
P.S. Don't be vexed about Judge Miles.[9] Let it rest.

Thine
Houston

Mum! Private
Write to me where Mrs. Hollimans[10] Brother Grace[11] lives in Alabama, or the wife of her deceased Brother.

Houston

---

[1]William Bledsoe had died. It is believed that he is buried in the Hardin Cemetery near Liberty, but no marker exists for him. He was a relative of the Hardin family. Partlow, 222.

[2]Houston may be referring to William Morris, a neighbor in the Raven Hill area. Identified in White, *Citizens of Texas, 1840,* v. I, 131.

[3]Houston is referring to moving his personal belongings from Washington-on-the-Brazos to Raven Hill.

[4]Elizabeth Moore.

[5]At some point, Vernal had married a young lady named Mary, who would die a few months later on November 7, 1845. Hearne collection of Family Papers. See also Margaret Houston to Almira Woods, June 14, 1846, in the Alva Woods Collection (MSS816) in the manuscript collection of the Rhode Island Historical Society Library, Providence, Rhode Island.

[6]Dr. William F. Evans of Polk County. For a biography see Nixon, 477.

[7]Houston's horse.

[8]Colonel Robert M. Williamson.

Marion
Oct. 20th, 1845

My dear husband,

On yesterday I read your letters from Raymond[1] and Terseaud.[2] They were truly acceptable, but alas our pleasures are never unmingled with pain. At the same time, came the news of Mr. Bledsoe's death. We are all deeply distrest [sic]. I can scarcely hold my pen, but oh my dear, I must write and influence you to fly to my dear sister and comfort her in her desolation. I need not ask this for I know you will go to her if you can. Oh how my heart is agonized for her!! If it is indeed true you will anticipate my wishes with regard to her—that is that she should be with us.

I think it would be best for you to meet us in Galveston, and we will go by way of Grand Cane and take her home with us. If the yellow fever is in New Orleans, I do not think we will leave Ala. before the last week in Nov. I returned yesterday evening from a visit to Aunt Eiland. She seemed very much cheered by it and I had quite a pleasant visit. I have never seen any one more gratified by a present than she was at yours. She sends many kind messages which I reserve for our meeting. Young [Lea Royston] came up on Saturday and left yesterday. He says Betty and the girls are enjoying themselves very finely. They attended several weddings and parties and seem very happy. He says also that cousin Wayne has made another offer of his hand to our dear niece Betty, but she again declined it, and I am not at all disposed to quarrel with her about it. I certainly would have been gratified if she had fancied him, for I knew his excellent qualities, but I left her to the free exercise of her judgment and discretion, and she has undoubtedly declined wisely if she could not love him.

I was delighted to hear of the pleasant company with which you were travelling and I hope dearest, you were satisfied by the conversation of the Elder. Oh how deeply, how intensely I feel for your eternal welfare! Why do you hesitate? Believe in the Lord Jesus Christ and you shall be saved!!! This is all that is required of you. So soon as you can say with all your heart—

There Lord I give myself away
'Tis all that I can do!

the struggle will be over, and the voice which calmed Gennesaret's stormy waves will soothe the troubles of your heart. Oh that the Lord would enlighten your darkness.

We have had a great deal of rain lately, and the roads are exceptionally bad. So soon as they can be travelled we expect to go to the canebrake. I neglected to mention that our sad intelligence was merely a paragraph in a Mobile paper. We know not how to evaluate the truth of it, yet it seems strange that we have no letters concerning it. Mother is sometimes almost frantic, and I am deeply grieved. I long for the time of our departure to come, but I will try to be patient. Sam is just recovering from the chicken pox and is doing very well. I think it is highly probable that the affliction has [blurred] to his health.

My dear, I must remind you again of Maj. [Samuel] Towns. I feel much interest for his family, and if any thing can be done for him with Mr. Polk,[3] I wish you would write to him again. At all counts, write. He has perhaps forgotten Maj. T's application. I think it probable that one of Cousin Ovid's sons (the eldest) will go with us, but it is not yet decided.

Bro. Henry has some idea of taking his family to Sumpter county, to a little farm which he has there, until he can settle up his business here and go to Texas. I wish you could see him. He is perfectly temperate, and you would love him a thousand [times] more than you ever did. Truly the Lord doth mingle blessings with our sorrows.

It is late at night dearest and the mail closes at 10 tomorrow. Do you see this mark?[4] Well, I will tell you how it happened. After finishing my first two pages this evening, I carelessly left my letter on the table with the pen and ink beside it and on returning who should I find in my seat but Master Sam, my pen in hand with all the dignity of an arch-bishop!

Farewell dearest Love,
Thy devoted wife,
M. L. Houston

P. S. Your watch-seal is found. I will endeavor to write to so many as possible of the friends whom you mentioned but I think dearest you were taxing me pretty surely. I was as much pleased as you could possibly have been at your accounts of Isabella.[5] Oh how I wish I could see our dear sister Eliza [Moore]!

[1]This letter has not been located.
[2]Houston to Margaret, September 28, 1845.
[3]President James K. Polk.
[4]A line is drawn across the center of the page here.
[5]Isabella Moore, the daughter of Eliza Houston and S. A. Moore.

Houston traveled to Galveston in the hopes of meeting Margaret. From here he wrote to William Palmer who was helping take care of affairs at Raven Hill. The whereabouts of the original letter is unknown. A copy is in the Sam Houston vertical file at the DRT Library, San Antonio Texas.

To Wm Palmer, Mgr
Palmers P. Office
Montgomery City, Texas

Galveston, 7th Nov. 1845

My Friend Palmer,

I came by way of Washington and Houston to this place in the hope of meeting Mrs. H. & Sam. They have not yet come but I hope they will be here by tomorrow's Boat. I rec'd three letters, and it is not certain that they will come until the first of December, but I truly hope they may. I think my Niece will come also, and Mrs. Lea certainly.

When at Washington I packed my furniture and it will be sent in your care soon. You will please to put the Piano, and Trunks, and the Boxes with Papers and Books in the room next [to] the Garden, and the others in the other room. You will please tell Maria to sleep in that room and say to her that I did not see Hosea but sent him word. I only stayed a little while in Houston.

Be pleased to do the best you can in forwarding my matters and taking care of them. I have been truly industrious and will not relax while I am able to work, or until I get thro' my business. I will send you a Newspaper.

If I live I want a good crop next year. Don't allow the Boys to let my horses or mares to die off. I had sent to me from New York the finest Dog you ever saw. Half Mastiff and dog of the Alps. I hope to take him safe home. I will be at home the first moment in my power, and not to leave if I can avoid it.

You will please to give to Mrs Palmer[1] and family my regards, and to Thomas[2] & his family. Say to the Negroes if you please, that I expect them to do faithfully, and obey you while I am absent. I will take them some clothes when I come up. The man who lived with you formerly, but whose name I can not recollect, I think I will want to hire this year. You may say so if you please. I have no news.

Truly Yr Friend,
Sam Houston

[1]Cornelia Emaline Allen Palmer. Identified in Daughters of the Republic of Texas, 215.

[2]Thomas and William Palmer were brothers.

Galveston Texas
10th Nov 1845

Ever Dearest Margaret,

On the 6th Inst I came to this place, hoping to meet you, when the New York should arrive, but she came without you. I did not much expect you, so that my hopes were mainly disappointed and not my expectations. I never heard any word of you, or from you, until I went on board the Steam Boat at Houston to come down, and then I had the pleasure to receive your three letters of the 30th—the 8th & 20th of October—In the last I was sorry to learn that you would not perhaps leave until the last week of this month.

Think dear of the painful anxiety which I must endure until your arrival, with your company. Master Sam, for instance, just to give him one dear squeeze, next to his dear, dear Mother, would be the hight [sic] of earthly bliss. Oh my Love, you cannot have the least idea of my feelings.—The void of heart cannot be filled by all the means which philosophy, and resignation can muster to my aid. Because you could not be present, and the hope that it might exercise some charm upon your coming, I have declined two dinners, the one at Washington,[1] and the other at Houston.[2] Here I agreed for many reasons to accept one. When I consented, I hoped you might arrive in time to be present at the speech, and be gratified, as it would be in Galveston where I have been so often, and so much reviled. Moreover, there was a committee, and one of some 15 or 20 to wait upon me (I think). I learn that there are not less than 150 subscribers to the dinner. I have been told that I am to speak in the Presbyterian church, where I made my temperance speech last May. Speaking of Temperance My dear, I think you may give me full credit for in truth I have not drank even cider since we parted, nor will I ever forget myself, so far as to drink any thing which can intoxicate any one. But my dear I am now <u>intoxicated</u> and have been for some time past. You will, I hope excuse me for my intemperance? It is no less than the intoxication of <u>love</u>, and you are the dear object!!! This, I know you will excuse, but I will not ask you to do so, until we meet, and that I hope will be soon. Some matters would engage my attention, but I declare to you, that my affection for you is so ardent that it engrosses my thoughts. Sam, the dear little fellow is often present with you and I, and seems to say, "Ma, what are you [and] mine pa talkin bout." And "Ma stop and let me talk!" As well as "Ma stop, and sing so, like me." Dear, don't be jealous of Sam or think the dear lad is about to rival you in my affections. He if he did not love his dear Ma so much might be jealous of rivalry, for certainly tho' I love him much, he is not his Fathers Better Half!!! When you come home Love, I will discourse upon this subject. Until then I will look with painful anxiety for your coming!

I have heard lately from Sister [Antoinette], & Buds [Vernal's] family. They are all well, and our dear Sister is gradually recovering from the shock which her feelings have sustained. At first she was inconsolable, and almost heart broken.[3] The situation of my affairs was such that I could not go to see her! I wou'd have done so, [if] it had been in my power, and after Boxing our furniture and coming to Houston, I would have then gone to see her, if I had not hopes to meet you here on the 7th Inst, tho' I requested you not to start until the 1st or 7th. But as there was no sickness in Mobile or New Orleans this season, I hoped that you might start sooner, and I wished to be here when you wou'd arrive. Mrs. Price,[4] & Mrs. Cocke[5] desire you to go and stay with them. I am now at Mrs. Maffitt's[6] and intend to stay until you come, unless I should learn that you should not be here for some time to come. Tho' of your speedy return to Texas I will not doubt, as it would add to my unhappiness which is now too great almost to bear. Tilley Johnson is "looking out" as I learn day, and night.[7] The judge is constantly on guard! It is interesting in family affairs. There are several slanders in this place upon Ladies, and one of them has left the city for the U States. I do not know the merits, or demerits of the parties. The people here treat me more kindly than they have ever done before, and that in the face of all my enemies. When the Dinner was set on foot, an attempt was made to get one up for Lamar, but it was "no go." So some of the Gentry left the place. My Dearest I only wish that you were here, for I have many things to say to you, which I would say to no one on earth beside—<u>One is, I love you more than all created beings</u>. This I can say in truth to you, and you only, and you tell me never to use insincerity or to be uncandid—Therefore, I am compelled to speak out! It is now midnight, and I could write until day, only that I must rise early to take this letter to the Boat as it will sail at 9 AM tomorrow. I will so arrange matters, that if you are not in Orleans, or if you are yet in Alabama, that you may get my letters.

I send you a slip from the Telegraph of Houston[8] containing a letter of mine, in reply to an invitation to Dine at Washington. You will see that I have put the subject of annexation pretty much to rest! Burnet claims it since then in a letter of to day, but I found an old letter that I suggested it previous to the Battle of San Jacinto.[9] I am you know lucky in some things. The party here has dwindled to nothing, almost. You may if you are in Orleans, be called on by a Mr. Kent, an Editor from Kentucky. He has been much with me since I came down, and put up at Mrs. Maffitts. Two new Books have made their appearance in these waters. One is Tom Jeff Green's Book,[10] and one is from the pen of the <u>elegant</u> Mrs. Storms, alias "Corin Montgomery."[11] The first (I have read neither, nor do you) I have heard pronounced a "lousy" production and very low. The other came in a "norther" and it is said was froze to death. They are both gone to a long sleep. They will never awake! I saw a letter to day from Washington City on the subject of the Books, and it states that they are now forgotten or only remember'd with disgust.

What a deplorable want of taste. Only think of fine thoughts and pretty chaste language not admired? Oh, degenerate age!! You may rest assured my Dearest, that I have [not] felt one single pain, or regret at these publications! They could not do me a greater service than what they have done, and I have been told that my enemies in Washington City, from Texas have lost cast at the "White House." So much for so much! I would go over to meet you at New Orleans, if I were sure that I could do so in spite of economy, but I might by chance miss you on the way. There are two Boats expected every day. The Galveston and the Telegraph which is to run from Mobile to this Port. I presume you will take the first safe Boat, and I would be uneasy to sail, least I might by chance be in Orleans, while you would be here! You may measure my solicitude by your own. Poor little Sam knows none of our cares, though no doubt he has little cares, of which we know nothing! My Love, my heart swells with hopes that I will soon clasp you, and our dear Boy to my devoted heart.

I look for Mother, and one of your nieces with Elizabeth [Moore]. I have a kiss for each one of the company, and a thousand for your dear self! I will ask no questions of you, but I am really curious to know how Betty, & cousin Wayne, settled their matters. You did right in the matter, and so did Betty, tho' I would have been delighted if she had loved, and married him! He is worthy of her if she could love him! She acted nobly, not to take fortune into the estimate of happiness! It is a mark of wisdom, and piety, in one so young.

Dearest, I will weary you no longer with my prosing epistle. Tho' I could scribble much longer. Mrs. Maffitt and all send their regards to you. William[12] is sitting up with me!

My Love to all, and pinch Sam for me until he asks the reason.

Thy devoted & faithful Husband
Sam Houston

[1]For Houston's letter declining the Washington invitation, see *Writings,* IV, 425–28.
[2]For Houston's letter declining the Houston City invitation see *Writings,* IV, 429.
[3]Houston is referring to the death of Antoinette's husband William.
[4]This may be Elizabeth Morgan (Mrs. James) Price.
[5]Mrs. James Cocke.
[6]Mrs. John Newland Maffitt.
[7]Matilda Maffit (Mrs. Robert D.) Johnson was expecting a baby.

[8]*Telegraph and Texas Register*, November 5, 1845. See also *Writings*, IV, 428.

[9]It is unclear to which letter Houston refers.

[10]*Journal of the Texian Expedition Against Mier* by Thomas Jefferson Green was reprinted in Austin in 1935 by Steck Company.

[11]Jane McManus Storms (who wrote under the pen name of Corine Montgomery), *Texas and Her Presidents: with a glance at her climate and agricultural capabilities*, (New York: E. Winchester, New World Press, 1845). This was a pamphlet of 122 pages which sold for twenty-five cents in 1845. It may be seen on microfilm at University of Texas, Arlington and Austin. Historian Linda Hudson to Madge Roberts, September 28, 1993.

[12]This is probably William Maffit, the brother of Tilly and Henrietta Maffit.

Margaret returned to Texas shortly after receiving this letter. On December 29, 1845, the Congress of the United States approved the constitution of the State of Texas which had been submitted several months earlier. The formal transition ceremony to end the government of the Republic of Texas would take place February 19, 1846.

Bibliography

Manuscript Collections:

Hearne, Madge W. Collection of family papers in the possession of Madge Thornall Roberts, San Antonio, Texas.

Houston Family Correspondence. Texas State Archives, Austin, Texas.

Houston, Margaret. Papers. Barker History Center, University of Texas, Austin, Texas.

Houston, Sam. Papers. Barker History Center, University of Texas, Austin, Texas.

Houston, Sam. Papers. Catholic Archives of Texas, Austin, Texas.

Houston, Sam. Vertical File, Daughters of the Republic of Texas Library, The Alamo, San Antonio, Texas.

Irion Collection of Original Documents. Archives Division, Sam Houston State University, Huntsville, Texas.

McFarland, Mrs. I. B. (Mae Wynne). Collection of Papers. Peabody Library, Sam Houston State University, Huntsville, Texas.

Roberts, Madge Thornall. Collection of Papers, San Antonio, Texas.

Taylor, Charlotte Darby. Collection of Houston materials, Houston, Texas.

Williams, Franklin. Collection of Houston Letters. Sam Houston Memorial Museum, Huntsville, Texas.

Williams, Franklin Weston. Collection of Sam Houston materials. Woodson Research Center, Rice University, Houston, Texas.

Woods, Alva. Papers (Mss 816). Manuscript collection of the Rhode Island Historical Society Library, Providence, Rhode Island.

Books, Articles, and Miscellaneous:

An Abstract of the Original Titles of Record in the General Land Office.

Austin: Pemberton Press, 1964.

Armstrong, Zella. *Notable Southern Families.* III. Baltimore: Genealogical Publishing Company, 1971.

Bass, Feris, Jr., and B. R. Brunson. *Fragile Empires: The Texas Correspondence of Samuel Swartout and James Morgan, 1836–1856.* Austin: Shoal Creek Publishers, 1978.

Best, Hugh. *Debrett's Texas Peerage.* New York: Coward-McCann, 1983.

Biographical Encyclopedia of Kentucky of the Dead and Living Men of the 19th Century. Cincinnati, Ohio: J. M. Armstrong & Company, 1878.

Blake, R. B. "Transcripts of Documents from Records of the District Court of Nacogdoches County Concerning Individuals Who Participated in the Texas Revolution 1836." Barker History Center, n. d.

Bowman, Bob. *The 35 Best Ghost Towns in East Texas.* Lufkin, Texas: Best of East Texas Publications, 1988.

Bracken, Dorothy Kendall and Maurine Wharton Redway. *Early Texas Homes.* Dallas: SMU Press, 1956.

Brewer, Willis. *Alabama: Her History, Resources, War Record and Public Men From 1540 to 1872.* Spartanburg, South Carolina: Reprint Company Publishers, 1975.

Brooks, Elizabeth. *Prominent Women of Texas.* Akron, Ohio: The Werner Co., 1896.

Brown, John Henry, ed. *The Encyclopedia of the New West.* Marshall, Texas: The United States Biographical Publishing Company, 1881.

_____. *Indian Wars and Pioneers of Texas.* Austin: L. E. Daniell Publishers, 1880.

Carpenter, V. K., transcriber. *1850 Census of Texas.* 4 vols. Huntsville, Arkansas: Century Enterprises, 1969.

Carroll, B. H., ed. *Standard History of Houston.* Knoxville, Tennessee: H. W. Crew & Company, 1912.

Chabot, Frederick C. *With the Makers of San Antonio.* San Antonio: Privately Published by Artes Graficas, 1937.

Compiled Index to Elected and Appointed Officials of the Republic of Texas 1835–1846. Austin: State Archives Division, Texas State Library, 1981.

Crockett, G. L. *Two Centuries in East Texas.* Dallas: Southwest Press, 1932.

Crook, Cornelia English. *Henry Castro: A Study of Early Colonization in Texas.* San Antonio: St. Mary's University Press, 1988.

Darman, Beth and Emily Darman, compilers. *Taxpayers of the Republic of Texas.* Grand Prarie, TX: Published by the authors, 1988.

Daughters of the Republic of Texas, Miss Ima Hogg Chapter. *Ancestral Biographies.* Houston: Printed Privately, 1992.

Daughters of the Republic of Texas. *Founders and Patriots of Texas: The Lineages of the Members of the Daughters of the Republic of Texas.* Published privately, v. I, 1963; v. II, 1974; and v. III, 1985.

Dictionary of Alabama Biographies. Spartanburgh, South Carolina: Reprint Press, 1978.

Dixon, Sam Houston and Louis Wiltz Kemp. *Heroes of San Jacinto.* Houston: The Anson Jones Press, 1932.

Dorland, W. A. Newman, ed. *The American Illustrated Medical Dictionary.* Philadelphia: W. B. Saunders Company, 1937.

Doughty, Robin W. *At Home in Texas.* College Station: Texas A&M University Press, 1987.

Ellis, J. H. H. *Sam Houston and Related Spiritual Forces.* Houston: The Concord Press, 1945.

England, Flora D. *Alabama Notes.* Baltimore: Genealogical Publishing Co, Inc. 1978.

Ericson, Caroline Reeves. *Nacogdoches—Gateway to Texas: A Biographical Directory, 1773–1849.* Nacogdoches: Ericson Books, 1991.

Ericson, Joe E., comp. *Judges of the Republic of Texas 1836–46: A Biographical Directory.* Dallas: Taylor Publishing, 1980.

Federal Census of Alabama, 1840. Mobile County. Microfilm. San Antonio Genealogical Library, San Antonio, Texas.

Flanagan, Sue. *Sam Houston's Texas.* Austin: University of Texas Press, 1964.

Ford, John Salmon "Rip." *Rip Ford's Texas.* Austin: University of Texas Press, 1963.

Freund, Max, ed. *Gustav Dresel's Houston Journal.* Austin: University of Texas Press, 1954.

Friend, Llerena. *Sam Houston: The Great Designer.* Austin: University of Texas Press, 1954.

Gambrell, Herbert. *Anson Jones: The Last President of Texas.* Austin: University of Texas Press, 1964.

Gandrud, Pauline Jones, comp. *Alabama Records.* Easley, South Carolina: Southern Historical Press, 1958.

_____. *Marriage, Death and Legal Notices from Early Alabama Newspapers 1819–1893.* Easley, South Carolina: Southern Historical Press,

1981.

The Goodspeed Biographical and Historical Memoirs of East Arkansas. Chicago: Goodspeed Publishing Company, 1890.

Graham, Philip. *The Life and Poems of Mirabeau Bonaparte Lamar.* Chapel Hill: University of North Carolina Press, 1938.

Grammer, Norma Rutledge, comp. *Marriage Records of Early Texas, 1824–1846.* Fort Worth: Fort Worth Genealogical Society, 1971.

Gresham, John M. *Biographical Cyclopedia of the Commonwealth of Kentucky.* Chicago: John M. Gresham Company, 1898.

Gulick, Charles Adams and Winnie Allen, editors. *The Papers of Mirabeau B. Lamar.* Austin: Von Boeckman Jones, 1922–1926.

Hale, John A. *Religion, A Factor in Building Texas.* San Antonio: Naylor, 1940.

Haly, James. *Texas—An Album of History.* Garden City, New York: Doubleday, 1985.

Hardy, Demont H. and Ingham S. Roberts, eds. *Historical Review of Southeast Texas.* Chicago: Lewis Publishing Company, 1910.

Harris, Mrs. Dilrue. "Reminiscences." *Southwestern Historical Quarterly* 7 (January 1904): 214–22.

Hatch, Jane M. *The American Book of Days.* New York: H. W. Wilson Company, 1978.

Hatcher, Mattie Austin. *Letters of an Early American Traveller: Mary Austin Holley, Her Life and Her Works, 1784–1846.* Dallas: Southwest Press, 1933.

Haynes, Emma. "A History of Polk County," 1937. Bound manuscript in the DRT Library, San Antonio, Texas.

Henderson, Mary Virginia. "Minor Empresario Contracts for Colonization of Texas—1825–1834." *Southwestern Historical Quarterly* 31(April, 1928): 295–324.

Henricks, Pearl. "Flavor of City Sam Houston Knew in Early 40's Gleaned from Dim Pages of Pioneer Newspapers." *Houston Chronicle*, January 24, 1937.

Hogan, William Ransom. "Pamelia Mann, Texas Frontierswoman." *Southwest Review* 20 (Summer 1935): 360–70.

_____. *The Texas Republic: A Social and Economic History.* Austin: University of Texas Press, 1969.

Hollon, W. Eugene and Ruth Lapham Butler, eds. *William Bollaert's Texas.* Norman: University of Oklahoma Press, 1956.

Hopewell, Clifford. *Sam Houston: Man of Destiny.* Austin: Eakin Press,

1987.

Houghton, Dorothy Knox, et. al. *Houston's Forgotten Heritage*. Houston: Rice University Press, 1991.

Houston, Sam. *The Writings of Sam Houston*. Edited by Amelia W. Williams and Eugene C. Barker. 8 vols. Austin: University of Texas Press, 1938–43.

Hunt, Lenoir. *My Master*. Dallas: Manfried, Van Nort & Company, 1940.

Institute of Texan Cultures. *Texas and the American Revolution*. San Antonio: University of Texas at San Antonio, 1975.

James, Marquis. *The Raven*. New York: Blue Ribbon Books, 1929.

Jenkins, John Holmes III, ed. *Recollections of Early Texas: The Memoirs of John Holland Jenkins*. Austin: University of Texas Press, 1958.

Jennet, E. L. *Biographical Directory of the Texan Conventions and Congressses, 1832–1845*. n.p., 1941.

Johnston, Marguerite. *Houston: The Unknown City 1836–1946*. College Station: Texas A&M University Press, 1991.

Kartaltepe, Altan. *Early Alabama Marriages*. San Antonio, Texas: Family Adventures, 1991.

Kemp, Louis W. "Glimpses of Texas History" columns from 1910s to 1930s in the *Post Dispatch* (Houston). The Sons of the Republic of Texas compiled many of these in 1993 and gave them away for a patriotic project.

_____. *The Signers of the Texas Declaration of Independence*. Houston: The Anson Jones Press, 1944.

Lankevich, George, ed. *The Presidents of the Republic of Texas*. Dobbs Ferry, New York: Oceana Publications, 1979.

Lee, Rebecca Smith. *Mary Austin Holley, A Biography*. Austin: University of Texas Press, 1962.

Lubbock, Francis R. *Six Decades in Texas, or Memoirs of Francis Richard Lubbock, Governor of Texas in War-Time, 1861–63, A Personal Experience in Business, War, and Politics*. C. W. Raines, ed. Austin: B. C. Jones & Company, 1900.

Lucas, Silas Emmett, ed. *Obituaries from Early Tennessee Newspapers 1794–1851*. Easley, South Carolina: Southern Historical Press, 1978.

McAshan, Marie Phelps. *On the Corner of Main and Texas: A Houston Legacy*. Houston: Hutchins House, 1985.

McComb, David G. *Houston, the Bayou City*. Austin: University of

Texas Press, 1969.

McDonald, Archie P., ed. *Hurrah for Texas! The Diary of Adolphus Sterne, 1838–1851*. Waco: The Texian Press, 1969.

Matthews, Harlan J. *Centennial Story of Texas Baptists*. Dallas: Baptist General Convention of Texas, 1936.

Miller, Ray. *Ray Miller's Eyes of Texas Series: Fort Worth-Brazos Valley*. Houston: Gulf Publishing Company, 1981.

Mobile County Genealogical Society. *Death Notices (Local and Foreign) 1840–1849*. Mobile, Alabama: Mobile Genealogical Society, 1962.

Montgomery, Robin. *The History of Montgomery County*. Austin/New York: Jenkins Publishing Company/The Pemberton Press, 1974.

Morris, Mrs. Harry Joseph, ed. *Citizens of the Republic of Texas*. Dallas: Texas State Genealogical Society, 1978.

Muir, Andrew Forest, ed. *Texas in 1837*. Austin: University of Texas Press, 1958.

Mullins, Marion Day. *First Census of Texas 1829–1836*. Washington, D.C.: Special Publication of the National Genealogical Society, Number 22, 1959.

Murray, Lois Smith. *Baylor at Independence*. Waco, Texas: Baylor University Press, 1972.

Nance, Joseph Milton. *After San Jacinto: The Texas-Mexican Frontier, 1836–1841*. Austin: University of Texas Press, 1963.

_____. *Attack and Counter-Attack: The Texas-Mexican Frontier, 1842*. Austin: University of Texas Press, 1964.

Nevin, David and eds. *The Texans*. New York: Time-Life Books, 1975.

Nixon, Pat Ireland. *The Medical Story of Early Texas, 1528–1853*. San Antonio: Mollie Bennett Lupe Memorial Fund, 1946.

Owen, Thomas McAdory. *History of Alabama and Dictionary of Alabama Biography*. 4 vols. Chicago: S. J. Clarke Publishing Company, 1921.

Partlow, Miriam. *Liberty County and the Atascocito District*. Austin: Pemberton Press, 1974.

Pauls, Katherine. *Gannie*. Privately printed, n.d.

Phares, Ross. *The Governors of Texas*. Gretna, Louisiana: The Pelican Publishing Company, 1976.

Pickrell, Annie Doom. *Pioneer Women of Texas*. Austin: The Steck Company, 1929.

Platt, Gwen, et. al. *Mississippi Southern District Index to United States*

Census of 1840. Santa Anna, California: GAM Publishers, 1970.

Polk County Bicentennial Committee and the Polk County Historical Commission. *A Pictorial History of Polk County 1846–1910.* Bi-Centennial Committee, Polk Historical Commission, 1976.

Pool, William C. *A Historical Atlas of Texas.* Austin: The Encino Press, 1975.

Prather, Patricia Smith and Jane Clements Monday. *From Slave to Statesman: The Legacy of Joshua Houston, Servant to Sam Houston.* Denton: University of North Texas Press, 1993.

Ray, Worth S. *Austin Colony Pioneers.* Austin: Pemberton Press, 1970.

Red, George Plunkett. *The Medicine Man in Texas.* Houston: Standard Printing & Lithographing, 1930.

Richardson, T. C. *East Texas: Its History and Its Makers.* New York: Lewis Historical Publishing, 1940.

Riley, B. F. *History of the Baptists of Alabama from the Time of Their First Occupation 1808–91.* Birmingham, Alabama: Roberts & Son, 1891.

Roberts, Madge Thornall. *Star of Destiny: The Private Life of Sam and Margaret Houston.* Denton: University of North Texas Press, 1993.

Schmitz, Joseph William. *Texas Statecraft 1836–1845.* San Antonio: Naylor, 1941.

_____. *Thus They Lived: Social Life in the Republic.* San Antonio: Naylor, 1935.

Seale, William. *Sam Houston's Wife.* Norman: University of Oklahoma Press, 1970.

Sibley, Marilyn McAdams. *The Port of Houston: A History.* Austin: University of Texas Press, 1968.

Siegel, Stanley. *A Political History of the Texas Republic, 1836–1845.* Austin: University of Texas Press, 1956.

Silverthorne, Elizabeth. *Ashbel Smith of Texas.* College Station: Texas A&M University Press, 1982.

Sistler, Byron and Barbara. *David County, Tennessee Marriages.* Nashville: Byron Sistler & Associates, 1985.

Spaw, Patsy McDonald. *The Texas Senate: Republic to Civil War.* v. 1. College Station: Texas A&M Press, 1990.

Spratt, R. D. *History of Livingston, Alabama.* Published Privately, 1926.

Sulzby, James T., Jr. *Historic Alabama Hotels and Resorts.* Montgomery: University of Alabama Press, 1960.

Swenson, Helen Smothers. *8800 Texas Marriages, 1823–1850.* St. Louis: Frances Terry Ingmire, 1981.

Taylor, Paul O. "Progress Dooms City Landmark to Wreckers." *Houston Post*, October 3, 1937, Section I, p. 16.

Thompson, Karen R., ed. *Defenders of the Republic of Texas: Texas Army Muster Rolls, Receipt Rolls and Other Rolls, 1836–1841*. v. 1. Austin: Laurel House Press, 1989.

Thrall, Homer S. *A Pictorial History of Texas, from the Earliest Visits of European Adventurers, to A. D. 1879*. St. Louis: N. D. Thompson and Company, 1879.

Townes, Samuel A. "History of Marion and Sketches of Life 1844." Reprinted in the *Alabama Historical Quarterly* 14 (1952): 171–229.

Turner, Martha Anne. *Texas Epic: An American Story*. Wichita Falls, Texas: Nortex Press, 1974.

Wallis, Johnnie Lockhart and Laurance Hill. *Sixty Years on the Brazos*. Austin: Texian Press, 1967.

Webb, Walter Prescott, et. al. *The Handbook of Texas*. 3 vol. Austin: The Texas State Historical Association, 1952.

Wells, Tom Henderson. *Commodore Moore and the Texas Navy*. Austin: University of Texas Press, 1960.

White, Edna McDaniel and Blanche Findley Toole. *Sabine County Historical Sketches and Genealogical Records*. Beaumont: La Belle Printing Company, 1972.

White, Gifford, ed. *1830 Citizens of Texas*. Austin: Eakin Press, 1983.

_____. *1840 Census of the Republic of Texas*. Austin: Pemberton Press, 1966.

_____. *1840 Citizens of Texas*. St Louis: Ingmire Publications, v. 1 (Land Grants), 1983; v. 2 (Tax Rolls), 1984; v. 3 (Land Grants), 1986.

_____. *First Settlers of Galveston County, Texas* . Nacogdoches, Texas: Ericson Books, 1985.

_____. *They Also Served: Texas Service Records from Headright Certificates*. Nacogdoches, Texas: Ericson Books, 1991.

Williams, Alfred M. *Sam Houston and the War of Independence in Texas*. Boston: Houghton, Mifflin Company, 1893.

Williams, Villamae, ed. *Stephen F. Austin's Register of Families*. Baltimore: The Genealogical Publishing Company, 1984.

Wisehart, M. K. *Sam Houston: American Giant*. Washington: Robert B. Luce, 1962.

Zuber, William Physick. *My Eighty Years in Texas*. Austin: University of Texas Press, 1971.

Newspapers:

Alabama State Review (Montgomery, Alabama)
Austin City Gazette (Austin, Texas)
Courier (Crockett, Texas)
Daily Bulletin (Austin, Texas)
Herald (Marion, Alabama)
Houston Chronicle (Houston, Texas)
Houston Post (Houston, Texas)
Post Dispatch (Houston, Texas)
Telegraph and Texas Register (Houston, Texas)
Texas Sentinel (Austin, Texas)

Maps:

An Early Map of Chambers County. n. d. in the San Antonio Genea-
    logical Society Library.
Morris, Dana, compiler and drafter. A Map of Washington on the
    Brazos. LaGrange, Texas, 1974.

Appendix

Robert Houston m. Margaret (some accounts say "Mary")
Davidson
  I. John Houston m. Ann Logan
    A. John "Jack" Houston*
      1. Mary Houston* m. Lt. Gardiner*
      2. James B. "Buck" Houston*
  II. Samuel Houston m. Elizabeth Paxton* (see notes below)
    A. Paxton Houston (died young)
    B. Robert Houston (never married)
    C. James Houston m. Patience Bills
    D. John Houston
    E. Sam Houston* m. (1)Eliza Allen,* (2) Margaret Lea*
      1. Sam Houston, Jr.* m. Lucy Anderson
      2. Nancy Elizabeth Houston* m. Joseph C. Styles Morrow*
      3. Margaret Lea Houston* m. Weston Lafayette Williams
      4. Mary William Houston* m. J. Sims Morrow
      5. Antoinette Power Houston* m. William Bringhurst
      6. Andrew Jackson Houston* m. (1) Carrie Glenn Purnell
          (2) Elizabeth Hart Good
      7. William Rogers Houston*
      8. Temple Lea Houston* m. Laura Cross
    F. William Houston* m. Mary Ball*
      1. Sallie Houston*
      2. Mary Houston*
      3. William Houston*
      4. Claude Houston*
      5. Eugene Houston*
    G. Isabella Houston
    H. Mary Houston* m. (1) Matthew Wallace* (2) William
        Wallace* (nephew of Matthew)
    I. Eliza Houston* m. Samuel Moore*
      1. Phoebe Jane Moore* m. N. A. Penland*
      2. Houston Moore*
      3. Isabella Moore* m. Col. William Taylor
      4. Elizabeth "Bettie" Moore*
      5. Mary Moore* m. John Lehr*
      6. William Louis Moore*

III. Bettie Houston m. John McClung
IV. Margaret Houston m. James Hopkins
V. Ester Houston m. James McKee
VI. Mary Houston m. John Letcher
  A. William Houston Letcher m. Elizabeth Davidson
    1. John Letcher* m. Mary Susan Holt
      (He was governor of Virginia, 1860-1864.)
  B. Sallie Letcher m. Robert Hamilton.
    1. Narcissa Bertonia Hamilton*

John Houston, brother of Robert Houston, m. Sarah Todd
  I. James Houston
  II. John Houston IV
  III. Rev. Samuel Houston
  IV. William Houston
  V. Robert Houston
  VI. Matthew Houston
  VII. Alice Houston m. William Stephenson
  VIII. Margaret Houston m. Alexander McEwen
    A. John McEwen
    B. Ebenezer McEwen
    C. Alexander McEwen
    D. Robert Houston McEwen* m. Henrietta Kennedy*
      Their daughter Caroline* m. Judge John T. Jones*
    E. Sarah McEwen
  IX. Ester Houston

notes:
a. Hannah Paxton (sister of Elizabeth Paxton Houston) m. James Caruthers. Their grandson was Robert Caruthers.*
b. Joseph Paxton (brother of Elizabeth Paxton Houston and Hannah Paxton Caruthers) m. Margaret Barclay. Their third daughter Hannah Paxton* m. Major David Edmondson.*
*Starred names are mentioned in either this or future volumes of the personal correspondence.

George Lea m. Lucy Talbert
  I. Frankey Lea m. Asa Atkins
  II. Sallie Lea m. a Mr. Black
  III. Rhoda Lea m. William Miles
  IV. Ranson Lea m. Mrs. Mckinzie
  V. Eunice Lea m. Mr. Deane
  VI. Temple Lea* m. Nancy Moffett*
    A. Martin Lea* m. Opphia Kennon*
      1. Robertus Lea
      2. Williams Jones
      3. Henry Clinton Lea
    B. Varilla Lea* m. Robertus Royston*
      1. Young Lea Royston*
      2. Robert "Rob" Royston*
      3. Sarah Ann "Tose" Royston* m. Thomas Power* (brother
        of Charles, who married Antoinette)
      4. Serena "Seen" Royston* m. Mr. Patton
      5. Neantha Royston* m. (1) Mr. Bordman (2) Mr. Sample
      6. Martin Royston*
    C. Henry Clinton Lea* m. Serena Root*
      1. Lucy Ann Lea* m. Dr. John H. Langhorne
      2. Sumpter Lea* m. Susan Isadore Hill
      3. Martin Armstrong Lea*
      4. Henry C. Lea m. Bettie Mosely
      5. Martha Jacqueline Lea m. James Allen Harwood
      6. Mary Willis Lea m. Beverly Franklin Harwood
    D. Vernal Lea* m. (1) Mary (2) Catherine Davis Goodall*
      1. Temple Lea*
      2. Maggie Houston Lea
      3. Marie Lea
      4. James Vernal Lea
    E. Margaret Lea* m. Sam Houston*
    F. Antoinette Lea* m. (1) William Bledsoe* (2) Charles
        Power* (3) W. H. Robert
      1. Thomas Power*
      2. Margaret Houston Power*
      3. Lillie Power

VII. Judy (died young)

VIII. Letty Lea m. M. I. Bittings

IX. Green Lea m. Margaret Moffett* ("Aunt Lea," sister of Nancy)

    A. Columbus Lea* m. Mary Parker*

        1. Wayne E. Lea*

        2. Margaret Lea

        3. Knox Lea*

    B. Wayne Lea m. Sarah Ann Talbert

note:

Mary Talbert (twin sister of Lucy Talbert Lea and aunt of Temple Lea) m. William Miles. Their daughter Polly m. Capt. Timothy Rogers. William Rogers* was the son of Polly and Timothy Rogers. The seventh child of Margaret and Sam Houston was named William Rogers Houston in honor of this cousin.

Children of Henry and Margaret Moffett
I. Nancy Moffett* m. Temple Lea*
II. Gabriel A. Moffett
III. Virginia (Gincy) Moffett* (Aunt Eiland) m. Asa Eiland
   A. Ovid Eiland* m. Henrietta Ford*
      1. Wayne Emmet Eiland*
   B. Dr. Oliver G. Eiland*
IV. Margaret Moffett * m Green Lea (brother of Temple Lea)

*Some names of more distant relatives not appearing in the correspon-
dence were omitted from the chart. For more information on the Houston, Paxton, Lea and Moffett families see these works:*

Armstrong, Zella. *Notable Southern Families.* v. 3. Baltimore: Genea-
logical Publishing Company, 1971.
Houston, Samuel Rutherford. *Brief Biographical Accounts of Many
Members of the Houston Family.* Cincinatti: Elm Street Printing
Company, 1882.
Paxton, W. M. *The Paxtons.* Platte City, Missouri: Landmark Print-
ing, 1903.
Roberts, Madge Thornall. *Star of Destiny: The Private Life of Sam and
Margaret Houston.* Denton: University of North Texas Press,
1993.
Rose, Ben L. *Report of Research on the Lea Family in Virginia & North
Carolina Before 1800.* Richmond, Virginia: Printing Services,
1984.
_____ and Margaret M. Marty. "The Lea Ancestry of Margaret Lea,
Wife of Gen. Sam Houston." Addendum #2 to *Report on the Lea
Family in Virginia & North Carolina Before 1899.* Typescript,
1987.

[1] The name is also spelled Moffett and Moffitt.

Index

7, 19, 63, 81, 102, 103, 105, 113, 115, 119, 157, 175–76, 217, 231, 233, 242, 246, 272, 283, 314, 350, 352, 356

Bledsoe, William, 2, 4, 5, 7, 13, 18, 19, 20, 25, 26, 28, 32, 33, 38, 60n, 63, 68, 81, 84, 86, 101, 105, 113, 119, 141, 176, 187, 233, 244, 246, 248, 293, 297, 298, 306, 310, 311, 314, 350, 351n, 352

Blount Springs, Alabama, 3, 273

Bonnell, George, 72, 73n

Borden, Gail, 144, 152n, 243, 247n

Bowyer, James, 99, 100n, 292

Bowyer, Mrs., 293

Bradshaw farm, 17, 18n

Bragg, Martha Crook (Mrs. Newport), 339, 340n

Branch, Edward T., 296, 297n

Brannum, W. T., 83, 84n, 93

Brashear (Brasher), C. D., 302, 304n

Brigham, Asa, 132, 133n

Briscoe, Andrew, 130, 131n

Briscoe, Mary Jane Harris, 131n

Brower, John, 258, 259n

Brown, Pamelia Mann (Mrs. T. K.), 38, 39n, 221, 236n

Brown, Sarah Wade (Mrs. John D.), 289, 291n

Bruin (mule), 210, 324, 326n

Bullock, Richard, 72n, 98

Bullock's Hotel (Austin), 72n

Bunton, John J., 284

Burleson, Edward, 106, 135, 136n, 217n

Burnet, David G., 45, 46n, 76, 78, 80n, 85, 86, 106, 126n, 195, 357

Burnett, Matthew, 37, 38n

Burnley, Albert Triplett, 206, 208n

Butler, Anthony, 31

Butler, Mrs., 178, 182–83, 192, 211

Cahaba (Cahawba), Alabama, 3, 4n, 239, 240n

Canales, Antonio, 42

Cannan, William Travis, 11, 12n

Carey, Seth, 201, 202–203, 205n

Carr, William. *See* Kerr, William

Cartwright brothers, 18, 20n

Case, Joel Titus, 46, 47n

Castro, Henry, 200, 201n, 203, 211

Cedar Bayou, Texas, 161n

Cedar Point, Texas, 10, 38, 52, 69, 70, 89, 98, 106, 116, 118, 119, 141, 146, 149, 161, 170, 173, 228, 247

Centralists, 42

Chalmers, John C., 85, 87n, 206, 207n

Chambers, Thomas Jefferson, 330, 331n

Chambers, William Martin, 330, 331n

Cherokee Bill, 39, 40, 41n

Cherry, Aaron, 322, 323n

Cherry, William, 322, 323n

Christy, Katherine Krieder Baker (Mrs. William), 103, 105n, 215, 216n, 219

Christy, William, 103, 105n, 233

Cincinatti, Texas, 17, 19

Hamilton, James, 200, 201, 203, 205n, 206–207, 208–10, 322, 323n
Hamilton, Jefferson, 349n
Hamilton, Mr., 348
Hamilton, William Thomas, 349n
Hamphill, John, 136
Hardin, Cynthianna O'Brien (Mrs. Franklin), 293
Hardin family, 351n
Hardin, Franklin, 256, 258n, 293
Harris, John R., 152n
Harris, Louis Birdsall, 168, 182
Harris, Mr., 143
Harris, William P., 152n
Harrisburg, Texas, 69, 130, 164, 167, 188, 221
Harrison, George W., 64, 65n
Hart, William, 171, 172n, 182
Hatfield, B. M., 278, 280n
Hatfield, Caroline, 278, 280n, 291
Hawkins, Mrs. Robert, 101
Hawkins, Robert, 101, 102n, 103
Henderson, Frances Cox (Mrs. J. P.), 7
Henderson, James Pinckney, 7, 7n, 34, 107, 129, 206, 236n, 281, 301n
Herburt, Walter, 72, 73n
Hermitage, 335
Highsmith, Samuel, 123, 124n
Hill, George W., 80n, 283, 285n, 288, 291n, 301
Hill, Harry, 232
Hill, Matilda Slaughter (Mrs. George W.), 288, 291n
Hockley, George W., 44, 49, 58, 78, 123, 136, 144, 148, 152n, 162, 174, 186, 216, 249, 264, 289, 291n, 327, 328n
Holley, Mary, 289, 291n
Holliman, Howell H., 306, 314, 318, 328, 329n
Holliman, Mrs. Howell, 351, 352n
Homes, Henry, 348, 349
Hopkins, F. M., 348, 349n
Horton, Albert C., 127, 128n, 132
Horton, Eliza Holiday (Mrs. A. C.), 122, 123n, 127, 128n
Hosea (field hand), 330, 331n, 354
Houston, Margaret Moffette Lea, books 89; courtship, 2, 4, 59; domestic matters, 129; dreams, 159–60, 199; financial matters, 130, 239, 306; health, 13, 22, 23n, 65, 99, 101, 106, 114–115, 120, 129, 136, 140, 143, 163, 171, 173, 212, 218, 223, 241, 242, 270–72, 288, 297, 299–300, 303, 307, 311, 312, 318, 319; in Canebrake (Alabama), 344; in Galveston, 11–13, 27–31, 39–96, 98–105; in Grand Cane, 294–95, 304–306, 309–15, 317–20, 322–35; in Houston, 37–38, 112–212, 299–301; in Liberty, 296–97, 307–309; in Marion (Alabama), 2–5, 8–9, 216–73, 336–40, 347–59; in Mobile (Alabama), 274–75; in Washington-on-the-Brazos, 13–23, 32–34, 278–95, 297–98; in

Woodville (Alabama), 340–44; marriage, 10; on politics, 98, 157–58; on religion, 118, 159, 178, 183, 199, 269, 294–95, 298, 302, 303, 305, 310, 313–14, 319, 345–46, 352–53; on Temperance, 347; on Trinity River, 302–304; poetry, 60, 104, 121, 136

Houston, Matthew C., 339, 340n

Houston, Sam, at Cedar Point, 106–107; at Raven Hill, 323–26; courtship, 59; dreams, 132, 261, 308; elections, 5, 20n, 106; financial matters, 160, 170, 187, 193, 225, 229, 247, 259, 283, 291, 293, 325, 327, 333; health, 13, 138, 140, 142, 143, 144, 145–46, 148, 162, 169, 173, 221, 222, 223, 229, 243–44, 246, 250, 251, 281, 307, 309, 317, 324–25, 342; in Austin, 6, 39–96, 112, 120–212; in Crockett, 13, 280–91; in Galveston, 302306, 354–59; in Greensboro (Alabama), 336–38; in Houston, 11–12, 216–75, 299–301, 344–49; in Huntsville, 312–15, 332; in Liberty, 292–93, 326; in Livingston (Alabama), 338–40; in Montgomery (Texas), 112–117, 278–79, 333–34; in Nacogdoches, 21–25, 98–105; in Polk County, 322–23; in Rodney (Mississippi), 340–4; in San Augustine, 15–18, 25–34; in Swarthout, 330, 350–52; in Washington-on-the-Brazos, 294–97, 317–20, 325, 334–35, 334; inaugurations, 134–36; marriage to Margaret, 10; nominations, 104–105; on children, 279, 281–82, 289, 316; on Indians, 155; on marriage, 166, 230–31, 267; on Mexico, 53, 63, 86, 106, 133, 155, 180–81, 195–96, 216, 227, 251, 262, 343; on religion, 146, 150, 165–66, 173, 175, 190, 221–22, 232, 245, 252–53, 327, 328–29, 350; on Temperance and drinking, 113, 117, 120, 135, 145, 147, 205, 322, 332, 356; on Texas politics, 74, 75, 77, 90, 92–93, 95, 96, 125, 126, 127, 133, 137, 139–40, 144, 146, 147, 151, 155, 166, 177, 181, 184–85, 191, 192, 195, 197, 201–204, 208, 216, 224, 226, 227–28, 234–35, 246, 248–49, 260–62, 281, 283–84, 289, 330, 332, 358; on Texas Revolution, 54, 63, 185; on Trinity River, 307–309; personal conduct, 134–36; poetry, 154, 158; real estate matters, 173, 225, 226, 228, 232, 244–45, 252, 255, 290, 322, 324, 325, 332, 333, 354; speeches, 140, 145, 149, 155, 268, 278, 280, 284, 285n, 308, 336, 356; uniform, 85–86; use of tobacco, 149

Houston, Sam, Jr. (son of Margaret and Sam), 278, 279, 280n, 281–82, 285, 287–88, 289, 290, 292, 293, 294, 298,

Locket, Mr., 8
Lockett, Napoleon, 286n
Lockhart, Charles, 298, 299n
Lockhart, John, 299n
Lockhart, William, 298, 299n
Love, James, 206, 207, 208n, 214, 215n, 230
Loveland, Ann, 8, 9n
Lubbock, Adele Baron (Mrs. Francis), 131, 195, 198n
Lubbock, Anna, 165
Lubbock, Francis R., 118, 119n, 129, 130, 131, 138, 141, 144, 192, 194, 195, 198
Lubbock, Thomas, 220, 236n
Lynch, James, 187, 189n

MacCarley, Mrs., 307, 309n
McDade, James W., 335
McDonald, Alexander, 231, 238n, 258
McEwen, Henrietta Kennedy (Mrs. Robert), 346
McEwen, Robert, 326n
McEwen, Sarah Caroline. See Jones, Sarah Caroline McEwen
McGehee, General, 225
McKinney, Thomas F., 76, 80n, 98, 102, 327
McKinstry, Ann C., 64, 65n
Maffet, Anne Carnic (Mrs. John Newland), 46, 47, 48n, 244, 247n, 305, 306n, 357, 358n,
Maffett, Caroline Matilda (Tillie), 40, 48n, 55, 70, 244, 247n
Maffett, Henrietta, 48n, 70, 244, 247n

Maffitt, William, 358, 359n
Mann, Pamelia. See Brown, Pamelia Mann.
Maria (servant), 19, 20n, 80, 86, 288, 330, 354
Mariners, Charles, 278, 280n
Marion, Alabama, 2, 5, 8, 99, 239
Marney, Mr., 331
Martha (slave), 100, 214, 216, 235, 278
Maryland (boat), 88
Matagorda, Texas, 127
Maxey, Mr., 330, 331n
Maxey, Mrs., 318, 320n
Mayfield, James, 43, 44n, 71, 165, 167n, 283, 285n
Mayfield, Mrs., 151
Mayfield, Robert, 172, 185
medical practices, 13, 20, 271–72, 317, 318
Megginson, Sarah Hill (Mrs. George D.), 218, 219n
Meggenson, Joseph C., 92, 93n
Menefee, William, 80n
Miles, George, 316, 317n, 351, 352n
Miller, Eliza Ann, 8, 9n
Miller, Washington D., 89, 138, 140, 141, 154, 163, 230, 245, 250, 262, 263, 291, 314, 324
Mills, Nancy Ann, 143, 152n, 177n
Milton, John, 222, 237n, 230
Mobile, Alabama, 2, 50, 60, 94
Moderators, 315
Montgomery, Corine. See Jane McManus Storms
Montgomery, Texas, 176, 187

Moore, Alexander, 43n, 52, 54, 55
Moore, Edwin, 152n, 283, 285n
Moore, Francis, 287, 288n
Moore, Francis, Jr., 67, 68n, 88, 103, 172
Moore, Eliza Houston, 17n, 231, 246, 289, 338n, 354
Moore, Elizabeth (Betty), 338, 339, 340n, 343, 344, 345, 346n, 350, 351n, 352, 358
Moore, Isabella, 122, 123n, 354
Moore, John W., 27, 29n, 211, 212n
Moore, Samuel A., 231, 238n, 338n
Moore, Samuel Houston, 336, 338n
Morehouse, Edwin, 182
Moreland, Isaac N., 37, 38n, 81, 83n, 264, 268
Morgan's Point, Texas, 226, 237n
Morgan, James, 54n, 119n, 200, 201n, 237n, 244, 247n, 251, 252, 283, 285n
Morgan, Ophelia Morgan, 200, 201n
Morris, John D., 148, 152n
Morris, Mr., 350
Morris, Richard, 257, 258n
Morris, William, 351n
Murray, Nancy, 143n

Nacogdoches, Texas, 15, 21, 23, 98, 149, 316
Nashville, Tennessee, 242
Neely, James, 86
Neighbors, Robert Simpson, 60, 61n, 194
Neill (Nail), James C., 131, 170
Neptune (boat), 101, 122, 217, 240n, 250, 267, 268, 300
New Orleans, Louisiana, 42, 214–15, 352
New York (boat), 42, 214, 226, 232, 233, 235, 248n 274
Newton, Mississippi, 347
Nichols, Ebenezer B., 255, 258n
Niles, Joseph W. J., 115, 117n
Norwood, Margarite Adele Ewing (Mrs. Nathaniel), 178, 179n, 291, 335
Norwood, Mr., 259

Ochiltree, Novaline Peck, 349n
Ochiltree, William C., 332, 333n, 348, 349n

Packenham, Richard, 196, 198n
Page, Mrs., 221
Palmer (Parmer), Cornelia Emaline Allen, 355
Palmer (Parmer), Martin, 317, 319, 320n, 324, 326n, 327, 333–34
Palmer, Mr., 328, 331, 333
Palmer (Parmer), Thomas, 324, 326n, 330, 331, 355
Palmer (Parmer), William, 354
Parsons, Enoch, 3, 4n
Payne, B. Owen, 308, 309n
Peck, Mrs., 348, 349n
Penicar (Penneger), James, 218, 219n
Penland, Phoebe Jane Moore, 16, 17n
Perry County, Alabama, 2, 232